Taking Liberties

The Tree of LIBERTY, - with, the Devil tempting John Bull.

Taking Liberties

The struggle for Britain's freedoms and rights

by Mike Ashley

First published 2008 by
The British Library
96 Euston Road
London NW1 2DB

ISBN 078 0 7123 5071 6 (hardback)
ISBN 978 0 7123 5029 7 (paperback)

British Library Cataloguing in Publication Data
A CIP Record for this book is available from The British Library

Designed by Esterson Associates
Printed in England by The Beacon Press

Published on the occasion of the exhibition
"Taking Liberties: The struggle for Britain's freedoms and rights"
at The British Library, 31 October 2008 – 1 March 2009.

Acknowledgements
The author is grateful to the following for their help and advice:
Ian Cooke, Peter Berresford Ellis, William Frame, Rhidian Griffiths, Pippa Hayward, Arnold Hunt, Dennis Lien, Andrew Martin, Simon Morgan, Joanna Newman, Sally Nicholls, Heather Norman-Soderlind, Andrew Prescott, Matthew Shaw.
In particular, my thanks to David Way.

Photographic acknowledgements
Cliché Atelier photographique des Archives Nationales 29, 83; The Art Archive/Eileen Tweedy 120; The Art Archive/Gianni Dagli Orti 50–51; Ken Walsh/The Bridgeman Art Library 32; Private Collection/ The Bridgeman Art Library 121; Getty Images 1, 20, 68, 72, 73, 91, 92, 95, 108, 109, 110, 118, 119, 123, 124, 125, 128, 129, 131, 132, 136, 137; Historic Scotland 30; Mary Evans Picture Library 70, 87; Mirrorpix 129; NMeM Daily Herald Archive/Science & Society Picture Library 130; Courtesy of the Palace of Westminster Collection 84; United Nations Photo Library 95.

Half-title image
Unemployed and hunger marchers converge in Hyde Park in November 1932.

Frontispiece image
The Tree of Liberty by James Gillray, 1798.
The tree withers under a repressive government but the serpent (the Whig leader Charles Fox) tempts John Bull with the apple of reform.
British Museum, 1868.0808/6739

Double page spread details
Page 6: Detail from The Domesday Book (see page 21)
Page 10: Detail from an engraving of the execution of Charles I (see page 41)
Page 134: Children on the steps of the Charles Thompson Poor Children's Mission, Birkenhead, in 1905. National Archives, Copy 1/481
Page 138: Detail from the Kennington Common meeting (see page 104)

Contents

Herveus de Wiltune ...

Osuuard tenuit T.R.E. Tra. e. i. car. Ibi st. iii. bord. 7 tant. pa. 7 pasture quu cuenit. i. hide. Valet. xxx. solid.

Herueus ten. i. hid. 7 dimid. hanc tenuit Eduin T.R.E. Tra. e. i. car. Ibi st. iiii. ac pasture. Valuit 7 val. xxx. sol. H. e in Istkora.

Ricard Sturmid ten. i. hid. 7 una v. tre. 7 dim. in Lowis. Tra. e. iii. car. Lora. In dnio. e una car. 7 iiii. servi 7 iii. uitti 7 iiii. coscez cu. ii. car. Ibi. iiii. ac pa. 7 Silua. i. leu. lg. 7 iii. qrc lat. Valuit xxx. sol. m. lx.

Id. R. ten Boberge. 7 Witts de eo. Aluric tenuit T.R.E. 7 geldb p. ii. hid. 7 dim. Tra. e. ii. car. q ibi st cu. i. seruo. 7 i. uitto 7 iiii. coscez. Ibi. ii. arpenz pa. 7 Silua. iiii. qrc lg. 7 ii. qrc lat. Solid.

Id. ten in Grastone. i. hid. Valet. xx. solid. Valet. xxx. solid.

Id ten in Haredone. i. hid. 7 dimid. 7 Robt de eo. Aluric tenuit T.R.E. Tra. e. i. car. q ibi. e in dnio. Valet. x. solid.

Id ten in Saldeborne. i. hid. 7 iii. v. tre. Orduuold tenuit T.R.E. 7 p tanto geldb. Tra. e. iii. car. In dnio st. ii. car. 7 uii. serui. 7 iii. uitti 7 iii. coscez cu. i. car. Ibi. iii. arpenz pa. 7 Silua. iii. qrc lg. 7 ii. qrc lat.

Robert f. Radulf ten in Grastone. i. hid. 7 ii. v. tre 7 dim. Valet. xl. solid. Ulmar tenuit T.R.E. Tra. e. ii. car. q ibi st in dnio. cu. i. seruo. 7 v. coscez. 7 ii. arpenz silue. Valet. xxx. solid.

Radulfus de Halvile ten in Grastone. iii. hid. 7 dimid. 7 supa. v. tre. Aluuin 7 Aluuold 7 Leuuin 7 Celestan tenuer T.R.E. de eo. Tra. e. iiii. car. 7 dimid. In dnio st. iii. car. 7 iii. serui. 7 iiii. coscez cu. i. car. 7 dimid. Ibi pastura. ii. qrc lg. 7 dimid. qrc lat. Valet. vii. lib.

Id. R. ten in Mertone. i. hid. Duo taini tenuer T.R.E. Tra. e. i. car. q ibi. e in dnio cu. ii. seruis. 7 ii. coscez. Ibi. ii. arpenz pa. 7 ii. ac pa.

Id. R. ten in Burbed. ii. hid. 7 una v. tre. Aluric tenuit T.R.E. Tra. e. ii. car. q ibi st cu. i. seruo. 7 ii. uitt 7 i. bord. Silua. iii. qrc lg. 7 ii. qrc lat. Valet. xxx. solid. Fuit. Val. xl. sol.

In Wivela habet. iiii. hid. Turold 7 Aluuin tenet T.R.E. 7 p tanto geldb. Tra. e. iii. car. 7 nil pecunie. Ibi molin redd. xvi. solid. 7 iiii. uitti 7 iiii. coscez. Silua. ii. qrc lg. 7 tntd lat. Valet. xxx. solid.

Turbert ten in Mertone. i. hid. Leuuin tenuit T.R.E. 7 p tanto geldb. Tra. e. i. car. Ibi st. ii. coscez 7 vi. ac pa. 7 x. ac pasture. Valuit 7 val. xl. solid.

Croc ten Lodewrde. Tres taini tenuer T.R.E. 7 geldb p. iii. hid. Tra. e. i. car. 7 dimid. De ea ten Croc. iii. v. tre. 7 un milefet. ii. hid. Ibi. e. i. car. 7 ii. bord. 7 un uitt. 7 pastura. ii. qrc lg. 7 una qrc lat. Valuit. xx. solid. modo. l. solid. Eduuard uicecom ten una v. tre. q pun

Herveus ten Rotefelde. Herald com tenuit T.R.E. 7 geldb p. ii. hid. Tra. e. i. car. q ibi. e in dnio. 7 v. bord. Ibi. viii. ac pa. 7 pastura. ii. qrc lg. 7 una qrc lat. Valuit. xxx. sol. modo. xl. sol. his. iii. hid.

Teibald 7 Hunfrid ten Wiseshille. Robt f. Wimarc tenuit 7 geldb p. v. hid. Tra. e. v. car. In dnio st. ii. car. 7 ii. serui. 7 vi. bord. Ibi. l. ac pa. 7 lx. ac pasture. Valuit. xx. solid. modo. xl. sol.

Anschitil ten Butremere. Goduin tenuit T.R.E. 7 geldb pro dimid. v. tre. Tra. e. ii. bou. Valet. xl. denar.

Johs hostiar ten Eltone. Godric 7 Bollo tenuer T.R.E. 7 geldb p. v. hid. Tra. e. iiii. car. In dnio st. ii. car. 7 ii. serui. 7 iiii. uitti 7 ii. cotar cu dimid. car. Ibi. viii. ac pa. 7 pastura. iii. qrc lg. 7 ii. qrc lat. De hac tra ten Turstan. i. hid. 7 Fraunin. i. hid. Ibi. e. un bord. 7 i. cotar cu dimid. car. 7 ii. ac pa. pastura. iiii. qrc lg. 7 ii. qrc lat. Tot ualet. c. sol.

Ide ten dimid. hid. in Bereford. Aluric tenuit T.R.E. Tra. e. i. car. Ibi. e un bord cu. i. seruo. 7 iiii. ac pa. Valuit 7 ualet. x. solid.

Witts Scudet ten Wesberie. Vluuard tenuit T.R.E. 7 geldb p. iiii. hid. 7 dimid. Tra. e. vii. car. In dnio st. iii. car. 7 iiii. se. iii. 7 xx. bord cu. iii. car. Ibi. xx. ac pa. 7 iii. ac silue. 7 ii. molini redd. xxv. solid. Valuit 7 ualet. viii. lib.

Goisfrid ten Draicote. Edric tenuit T.R.E. 7 geldb p. v. hid. Tra. e v. car. In dnio st. ii. car. 7 iiii. serui. 7 vii. uitti 7 x. coscez cu. iii. car. Ibi molin redd. v. solid. 7 xl. ac pa. pastura. ii. qrc lg. 7 una qrc lat. Silua. iiii. qrc lg. 7 ii. qrc lat. 7 un burgens redd. xii. den. Valet. c. solid.

Witts f. Ansculf ten Lortone. Stanni tenuit T.R.E. 7 geldb p. vii. hid. 7 dimid. Tra. e. v. car. In dnio st. ii. car. 7 v. uitti 7 v. bord. 7 v. coscez cu. iii. car. Ibi molin redd. v. solid. 7 xl. ac pa. 7 x. ac silue. 7 pastura ii. qrc lg. 7 ii. lat. Valuit 7 ual. c. solid.

... secdm testimoniu tainor. Valent. xx. solid. ... dedit ad Wive eo Gislebert.

Wibert ten Eliue. H fuit de tra Vlueue bedellui. 7 geldb p. v. hid. 7 una v. tre. Tra. e. iii. car. In dnio st. ii. car. 7 ii. uitti 7 v. bord. 7 i. coscez cu. i. car. In Crichelade una dom redd ... Ibi. xl. ii. ac pa. 7 dimid. 7 qrc xx. 7 iiii. ac pasture. 7 xx iiii. ac silue. Valuit. xx. solid. modo. iii. lib. 7 x. solid.

Odinus Camerari ten Suindone. Torbert tenuit T.R.E. 7 geldb p. xii. hid. Tra. e. vi. car. In dnio st. ii. car. 7 ii. serui 7 vi. uitti 7 viii. bord cu. iii. car. Ibi molin redd. iiii. solid. 7 xx. ac pa. 7 xx. ac pasture. Valuit. lx. solid. modo. c. solid.

De hac tra ten Milo crispin. ii. hid. 7 ibi ht. i. car. Odin eis calumniat.

Turstin Camerari ten Eliue. Aluuin tenuit T.R.E. 7 geldb p. iii. hid. Tra. e. i. car. 7 dimid. In dnio. e. i. car. cu. i. seruo. 7 iiii. coscez. Ibi molin redd. v. solid. 7 xii. ac pa. 7 viii. ac pasture. Valet. l. sol.

Albericus Camerarius ten Smalebroc. Mainard tenuit T.R.E. 7 geldb p. ii. hid. Tra. e. iii. car. In dnio. e. i. car. 7 un uitt 7 xvi. bord cu. ii. car. Ibi. vi. ac pa. 7 xv. ac silue. Valuit. xxx. sol. m. xl. sol.

Albericus Camerarius ten Deuret. Duo taini tenuer T.R.E. 7 geldb p. i. hida. Tra. e. i. car. Ibi st. viii. coscez cu. i. car. 7 molin redd. iii. solid. 7 una ac pa. pastura. iiii. qrc lg. 7 ii. qrc lat. Silua. i. lg. 7 una qrc lat. Valuit. xl. solid. Modo. xxx. sol.

Gunduinus Granetarius ten Wesicliue. Aluui tenuit T.R.E. 7 geldb. i. hid. Tra. e. i. car. q ibi. e in dnio cu. i. seruo 7 i. coscet. Ibi. ii. ac pa. 7 pastura. iii. qrc lg. 7 una qrc lat. Silua. i. qrc 7 altera lat. Valuit. xx. solid. modo. xxx v. solid.

Warinus arbalistarius ten Celeworde. Edric tenuit T.R.E. 7 geldb p. i. hid. Tra. e. ii. car. In dnio. e. i. car. cu. iiii. bord. Ibi. viii. ac pa. 7 x. ac silue. Valuit 7 ual. xl. solid.

Croc ten dimid. hid. in Stoche. Tra. e dimid. car. Valet. x. sol.

Witts Corniole ten Wichelford. Aluuius tenuit T.R.E. 7 geldb p. ii. hid. Tra. e. ii. car. Ibi st. iii. uitti 7 ii. bord cu. i. car. 7 molin redd. xv. solid. Ibi. viii. ac pa. Valuit 7 ual. xl. solid.

Eduuard ten una v. tre in Aluuardberie. Bode tenuit T.R.E. Valet. xl. denar.

In Dorecestre tẽpore Regis Edwardi. erant clxxii. dom̃. Hę p omi seruitio regis se defendeb̃ 7 geldab̃ p x. hid. Scilicet ad opus huscarliũ unã markã argti. exceptis ↄsuetudinib; que ptin̄ ad firmã noctis. Ibi erant ii. monetarii. q̄sq; eo4 reddeb̃ regi unã markã argti 7 xx. solid. quando moneta uertebatur. Modo st ibi qt xx 7 viii. dom̃. 7 c. penit̄ destructę a tẽpore hugonis uicecomit̄ usq; nunc.

In Brideport T.R.E. erant. c.xx. domus. 7 ad omẽ seruitiũ regis defendeb̃ se 7 geldab̃ p v. hid. Scilicet ad opus huscarliũ regis dimid. mark argti. exceptis consuetudinib; que ptin̄ ad firmã uni noctis. Ibi erat un̄ monetari9 reddt regi i. mark argti 7 xx. sol qdo moneta uertebat. Modo st ibi. c. dom̃. 7 xx. sunt ita destitute. qd q̄ in eis manẽt geld soluere n̄ ualẽt.

In Warham T.R.E. erant. c.xl.iii. dom̃. in dnio regis. Hęc uilla ad omẽ seruitiũ regis se defdb 7 geldab p x. hid. Scilicet i. mark argti huscarlis regis. exceptis ↄsuetudinib; que ptin ad firmã uni noctis. Ibi erant ii. monetarii. quisq; reddt i. mark argti regi 7 xx. solid qdo moneta uertebatur. Modo st ibi lxx. dom̃. 7 lxxiii. st penit̄ destructę a tpr Hugonis uicecom. De parte S Wandregisili st ibi. xl. v. dom̃ stantes 7 xvii. uastę. De parte alio4 baron st ibi. xx. dom̃ stantes 7 lx. st destructę.

In Burgo Sceptesberie T.R.E. erant. c. 7 iiii. dom̃. in dnio regis. Hęc uilla ad omẽ seruitiũ regis se defdb 7 geldab p xx. hid. Scilicet ii. mark argti huscarl regis. Ibi erant iii. monetarii quisq; reddeb i. mark argenti 7 xx. solid qdo moneta uertebatur. Modo st ibi. lxvi. dom̃. 7 xxxviii. dom̃ st destructę a tpr hugonis uicecomitis usq; nc. In parte abbatissę erant T.R.E. dom̃. cl iii. Modo st ibi. c.xi. dom̃. 7 xlii. sunt omino destructę. Ibi ht abbissa. cl. 7 un burgs. 7 xx. mans uacuas. 7 i. hortu. Reddt lx v. solid.

HIC ANNOTANT TENENTES TRAS IN DORSETE.

I. Rex Willelmus.
II. Eps Sarisberiensis.
III. Monachi Scireburn.
IIII. Eps Baiocensis.
V. Eps Constantiensis.
VI. Eps Lisiacensis.
VII. Eps Lundoniensis.
VIII. Abbatia Glastingber.
IX. Abbatia Wintoniens.
X. Abbatia Creneburnens.
XI. Abbatia de Cernel.
XII. Abbatia de Middetune.
XIII. Abbatia de Abedesberie.
XIIII. Abbatia de Hortune.
XV. Abbatia de Adelingi.
XVI. Abbatia de Tauestoch.
XVII. Abbatia de Cadomis.
XVIII. Abbatia S Wandregisili.
XIX. Abbatissa de Sceftesberie.
XX. Abbatissa de Wiltune.
XXI. Abbatissa de Cadom.
XXII. Abbatissa de Monast uillar.
XXIII. Canonici Constantienses.
XXIIII. Reinbald pbr 7 alii clerici.
XXV. Comes Alanus.
XXVI. Comes Moritoniensis.
XXVII. Comes Hugo.
XXVIII. Rogerius de Belmont.
XXIX. Rogerius de Curcelle.
XXX. Robertus filius Girold.
XXXI. Eduuard de Sarisberie.
XXXII. Ernulfus de Hesding.
XXXIII. Turstinus filius Rolf.
XXXIIII. Willelmus de Ou.
XXXV. Witts de Faleise.
XXXVI. Witts de Moiun.
XXXVII. Witts de Braiose.
XXXVIII. Witts de Scohies.
XXXIX. Walscin de Dowai.
XL. Walerān uenator.
XLI. Walterius de Clauile.
XLII. Balduin de Execestre.
XLIII. Berenger Gifard.
XLIIII. Osbernus Gifard.
XLV. Maci de Moretanie.
XLVI. Rogerius Arundel.
XLVII. Serlo de Burci.
XLVIII. Aiulf9 uicecomes.
XLIX. Hunfrid9 camerarius.
L. Hugo de Porth.
LI. Hugo de S Quintino.
LII. Hugo de Boscherbti. LIII. Hugo de Iuri 7 alii franc. LIIII. Vxor hugonis f. Grip. LV. Iseldis. LVI. Godmund 7 alii taini. LVII. Witts belet 7 alii seruient regis. LVIII. Comitissa Boloniens.

TERRA REGIS.

Rex tenet insulã quę uocat Porland. Eduuard9 rex tenuit in uita sua. Ibi ht rex. iii. car in dnio. 7 v. seruos. Ibi sunt uitti 7 c. bord. cũ xiiii. car. hnt. xxiii. car. Ibi. viii. ac pti. Pastura. viii. q̃c lg. 7 viii. lat. Hoc m cu sibi ptinẽtib, reddt lxv. lib albas.

Rex ten Bridetone 7 Bere 7 Colesberie 7 Sepetone 7 Bratepolle 7 Cidihoc. Hę tenuit Rex E. in dnio. Nescit quot hidę st ibi. nec geldb T.R.E. Tra. e. l.v. car. In dnio st. viii. car. 7 xx. serui. 7 xl i. uitti 7 xxx. bord. 7 vii. coliba. 7 lxxiii. cotarii. Int oms hnt. xxvii. car. Ibi. viii. molini reddt. iii. lib 7 xxxv. denar. 7 c.xi. ac pti. Pastura. iii. leu lg. 7 dimid lat. Silua. ii. leu lg. 7 una leu lat. Hoc m cu suis appendic 7 ↄsuetudinib, reddt firmã uni noctis. Boscus de Hauocumbe ptin ad Bridetone. ita qd T.R.E. duę partes ei erant in firma regis. tcia u pars 7 tcia quercus erat Eduini comitis. que m ptin ad Frantone m S Stefani cadomensis.

Rex ten Winborne 7 Scapeuuic 7 Chirce 7 Opewinburne. Rex E. tenuit in dnio. Nescitur qt hidę st ibi. qa n reddid geld T.R.E. Tra. e. xl v. car. In dnio st. v. car. 7 xv. serui. 7 lxii. uitti 7 lxviii. bord. 7 vii. cotar hnt. xxii. car. Ibi. viii. molini reddt. c. x. solid. 7 cl. ac pti. Pastura. vi. leu lg. 7 iii. leu lat. Silua. v. leu lg. 7 una leu lat. Hoc m cu append suis reddt firmã unius noctis.

Rex ten Dorecestre 7 Fortitone 7 Sutone 7 Gelingeha 7 Frome. Rex E. tenuit. Nescit qt hidę sint ibi. qa n geldb T.R.E. Tra. e. l vi. car. In dnio st. vii. car. 7 xx. serui 7 xii. coliberti 7 c xiii. uitti 7 qt xx. 7 x. bord. hntes. xl ix. car. Ibi. xii. molini reddt. vi. lib. 7 v. solid. 7 c lx. ac pti. Pastura. ii. leu lg. 7 una leu lat. Silua. iii. leu lg. 7 una leu lat. Hoc m cu appendic suis reddt firmã unius noctis.

Rex ten Pinpre 7 Cerletone. Rex E. tenuit in dnio. Nescit qt hidę sint ibi. qa n geldb T.R.E. Tra. e. xx. car. In dnio st. iii. car. 7 vi. serui. 7 i. colibt. 7 xxiiii. uitti 7 lxviii. bord. cu. xiii. car. Ibi. ii. molini reddt. xl. sol 7 vi. den. 7 qt xx. 7 xiii. ac pti. Pastura. ii. leu lg. 7 ii. leu lat. Silua. i. leu lg. 7 dimid leu lat. Hoc m cu append suis reddt dimid firmã unius noctis.

Rex ten Wintrode 7 Luluorde 7 Wintreborne 7 Chenoltone. Rex E. tenuit in dnio. Nescit qt hidę sint ibi. qa n geldb T.R.E. Tra. e. xxiiii. car. In dnio st. iii. car. 7 iii. serui. 7 xxx. uitti 7 xxx. bord cu i. cotar. hntes. xvi. car. Ibi. iii. molini reddt. l. solid. 7 qt xx. ac pti. Pastura. iii. leu lg. 7 tantd lat. Silua. tntd in lg 7 lat. Hoc m cu append suis 7 ↄsuetudinib, reddt dim firmã uni noctis.

~~Ista maner que secunt tenuit Heraldus comes T.R.E.~~

Rex ten Acford. T.R.E. geldb p v. hid. Tra. e. vi. car. De ea st in dnio. iii. hidę 7 ibi. ii. car. cu i. seruo. 7 vi. uitti 7 iii. bord cu. ii. car. Ibi. ii. molini reddt xx. sol 7 xl. ac pti 7 ii. q̃ent pasturę. Silua. iii. q̃c lg. 7 una q̃c 7 dim lat. Valuit 7 ual. x. lib.

Rex ten Piretone. T.R.E. geldb p dim hida. Tra. e. xv. car. In dnio st. iii. car. 7 xii. serui. 7 xiiii. uitti 7 xxx. cotar. cu. x. car. Ibi. ii. molini reddt xxxii. sol. 7 c xxvi. ac pti. Pastura. i. leu 7 dim lg. 7 una lat. Silua. ii. q̃c lg. 7 tntd lat. Huic m ptin. i. hida 7 dimid in Porbi. 7 in Mapertone dimid hida. Tra. e. i. car 7 dimid. Huic etiã m Piretone adiacet tcius denar de tota sira Dorsete. Reddt cu omib, appendic. lxxiii. lib.

Rex ten Celberie. T.R.E. geldb p v. hid. Tra. e. iii. car 7 dimid. De ea st in dnio. iii. hidę 7 dim. 7 ibi. i. car. 7 iii. serui. 7 v. uitti 7 iii. bord cu. i. car 7 dimid. Ibi silua. ii. q̃ent lg. 7 una lat. Valuit 7 ual. xx. lib.

Introduction

Have you ever had to stare authority in the face and declare, "I know my rights"? The chances are we've all said that at some time or another when up against a bastion of bureaucracy, struggling for fairness and justice.

The inhabitants of these islands have been doing that for hundreds of years. At the time of the Peasants' Revolt in 1381, the vast majority of the population had very few rights, but deep down they believed they had some, drawing upon a vague memory of Magna Carta and Domesday Book. Over the centuries, brave individuals, from Wat Tyler to John Wilkes to Emmeline Pankhurst, have stood up to the might of authority to fight for their rights. Not all were successful, and many suffered imprisonment, transportation or death, but most left their mark.

John Wilkes championed the free press, calling it "the firmest bulwark of the liberties of this country". (Engraving by William Hogarth, 1763.)
British Museum, Cc,2.206

It is their story that we explore in this book. It charts how our rights and freedoms were won, the individuals who fought for them, the key events and the important documents that enshrine our rights in law. It does this through a series of sections. The first covers the initial struggle to stake out the basic principles in a society where the king was the law. The second looks at how the growth of Parliament had to balance the rights of those who govern against those of the governed – and that means not only individuals, but the constituent "nations" of the United Kingdom. Other sections cover our various civil, democratic and human rights, including the freedom to worship, freedom of the press, the right to vote and our rights to health and wellbeing.

On this journey we also encounter some basic paradoxes. We may say "I know my rights", but do we? Where do we turn to in order to verify them? Unlike the USA, France or India, Britain does not have one unifying document that serves as a constitution. The Human Rights Act did not exist in Britain before 1998. Our constitutional system has built up over time and exists in a series of documents which include Magna Carta, the 1689 Bill of Rights, the Treaty of Union, and a plethora of Acts of Parliament. Britain came close to creating a constitution in 1653 with the Instrument of Government, compiled during the Protectorate under Oliver Cromwell. But when the monarchy was restored in 1660, all Acts of Parliament passed during the Republic were declared illegal, and our one written constitution was cast aside. The question is often raised: should we have a formal written constitution or, does our unwritten one benefit from being flexible and organic, able to adapt to changing demands and pressures?

This raises another paradox. In a country so closely associated with rights and liberty, the power and vigilance of the state over the lives of individuals is arguably greater than ever. Surveillance cameras, a DNA database, stop-and-search powers and talk of Identity Cards, are seen as threats to personal liberty, although they are presented as necessary for our safety and national security. One of the basic functions of government is to protect its subjects, but fulfilling that role may at times seem oppressive. The United Kingdom has been called a "nanny state", accused of taking

A Freeborn Englishman by George Cruikshank, 1819. This image was used by several artists to show the impact of repressive legislation in the years during and after the Wars with France.
British Museum, 1865,1111.2136

that protection too far. But where do you draw the line? Soon after the French Revolution, and even before the War with France began in 1793, the British government introduced many repressive measures to curb the possibility of revolution in Britain. That may seem to be a government protecting its own interests, but it can equally be argued to be a government doing its duty to the majority of its subjects. So the struggle for our political rights has always been one of balance between liberty and security.

The government of Great Britain – and before that, of England – is often seen as strong, controlling, even aggressive. The kings of England, whilst still trying to recover their lands in France, also sought to subjugate the remainder of the British Isles. When the once independent countries of Wales, Ireland and Scotland were incorporated as part of Great Britain and subsequently the United Kingdom of Great Britain and Northern Ireland, they were ruled by a strong centralist Parliament in London.

That strength enabled the growth of the British Empire, and Britain's beliefs in freedom and liberty went with it – arguably another paradox. Magna Carta, in which the barons made King John recognise their rights, and which he soon had annulled, refused to die. It was resurrected and reasserted in the reigns of subsequent kings and reinterpreted as part of English common law by Sir Edward Coke and Sir William Blackstone. Through them, its principles made its way into later documents, such as the Petition of Right, and through that into the American Bill of Rights.

The concept of "liberty" became peculiarly British. When the American colonists declared their independence from Britain they recognised a legacy of British liberty. The American Revolutionary Patrick Henry said in 1788: *We are descended from a people whose government was founded on liberty; our glorious forefathers of Great Britain made liberty the foundation of everything. That country is become a great, mighty, and splendid nation; not because their government is strong and energetic, but, sir, because liberty is its direct end and foundation.*

Yet one might ask how much we really value our rights. Do we take advantage of the freedoms past generations have fought for? How often do we vote in general or local elections? How much do we appreciate the freedom of the press? Or do we only demand our rights if we believe our privacy has been infringed, or complain about hospital waiting lists rather than appreciate the benefits of the welfare state? They are questions worth pondering when reading this book.

It is illustrated with many of the key documents and other images to show the scale and intensity of the battle for individual rights and freedoms. Many have been provided by the British Library, the British Museum, the National Libraries of Scotland and of Wales, The National Archives and the Parliamentary Archives as part of the exhibition held at the British Library from October 2008 to March 2009.

They reveal the rich story of the people of these islands who fought for and defended our rights.

ANCKET HAV
F
E
A

C
D

The Roots of Liberty

The majority of our rights have only been granted in the last century or two, but some – such as the right not to be cast into prison without the chance of a fair trial – go back, at least for the English, 800 years to Magna Carta, the document which would later prove so fundamental to our basic rights. The jury system was also taking shape around that time. The Domesday Book had established a grand reckoning of who owned what, and would have its own benefits in later disputes over rights. The common law, meaning common across the land, was documented so that all were tried equally – at least for those free to benefit. Freedom was a scarce commodity in those days, especially for the serfs, some of whom were barely above slave level. Yet even they would eventually make their voices heard.

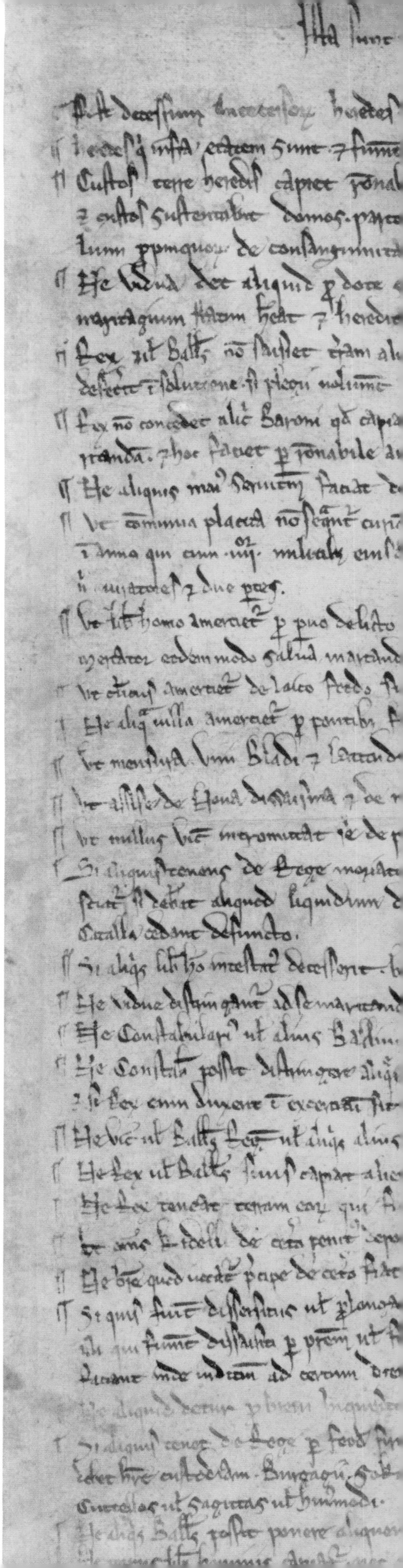

The Articles of the Barons. This document, originally agreed at Runnymede in 1215, was the basis for Magna Carta.
BL, Add. MS 4838

...q[ue] barones petunt et dominus Rex concedit.

...s habebunt hereditatem suam per antiquum relevium exprimendum in carta.

... cum ad etatem pervenerint, habebunt hereditatem suam sine relevio et fine.

... consuetudines et servitia sine destructione et vasto hominum et rerum suarum; et si custos terre fecerit destructionem et vastum, amittat custodiam...

... stagna, molendina, et cetera ad terram illam pertinentia de exitibus terre eiusdem; et ut heredes ita maritentur ne disparagentur et per consil...

...tagio post decessum mariti sui, et maneat in domo sua per xl dies post mortem ipsius, et infra terminum illum assignetur ei dos...

...o dum catalla debitoris sufficiant, nec plegii debitoris distringantur dum capitalis debitor sufficiat ad solutionem; si vero capitalis debitor...

... debitoris donec debitum illud persolvatur plene, nisi capitalis debitor monstrare poterit se esse inde quietum erga plegios.

... de liberis hominibus suis nisi ad corpus suum redimendum, et ad faciendum primogenitum filium suum militem, et ad primogenitam filiam suam semel ma...

...tis quam inde debetur.

... sed assignentur in aliquo certo loco; et ut recognitiones capiantur in eisdem comitatibus in hunc modum: ut rex mittat duos justiciarios per quatuor vices...

...us electis per comitatum capiant assisas de nova dissaisina, morte antecessoris, et ultima presentatione, nec aliquis ob hoc sit summonitus...

...m delicti, et pro magno delicto secundum magnitudinem delicti, salvo contenemento suo; villanus etiam eodem modo amercietur salvo waynagio suo; et...

...mentum proborum hominum de visneto.

...dum aliorum predictorum, et non secundum beneficium ecclesiasticum.

... riparias nisi ubi de iure antiquitus esse solebant.

...rum et rerum aliarum emendetur; et ita de ponderibus.

...is abbrevientur; et similiter de aliis assisis.

...coronam pertinentibus sine coronatoribus; et ut comitatus et hundredi sint ad antiquas firmas absque nullo incremento, exceptis dominicis maneriis re...

...re ut alii ballivo regis seisire et imbreviare catallum ipsius per visum legalium hominum, ita tamen quod nichil inde amoveatur donec ple...

... Regi; et tunc debitum Regis persolvatur; residuum vero relinquatur executoribus ad faciendum testamentum defuncti; et si nichil Regi debetur, omn...

...num proximorum parentum suorum et amicorum et per visum ecclesie distribuantur.

...re sine marito vivere, ita tamen quod securitatem facient quod non maritabunt se sine assensu regis, si de rege teneant, vel dominorum suorum de quibus tenent.

...talla, nisi statim denarios inde reddat, nisi respectum habere possit de voluntate venditoris.

...andum denarios pro custodia castri, si voluerit facere custodiam illam in persona sua, vel per alium probum hominem si ipse eam facere non possit per rationabilem cau...

...stodia secundum quantitatem temporis.

...t equos et carettas alicuius liberi hominis pro cariagio faciendo, nisi ex voluntate ipsius.

... ad castra vel ad alia agenda sua nisi per voluntatem ipsius cuius boscus ille fuerit.

...t de felonia convicti nisi per unum annum et unum diem, sed tunc reddatur domino feodi.

...misia et de Medewaye et per totam Angliam.

...tenemento unde liber homo amittat curiam suam.

... sine iudicio de terris, libertatibus, et iure suo, statim ei restituatur; et si contentio super hoc orta fuerit, tunc inde disponatur per iudicium xxv baronum; et ut...

...ctum habeant sine dilatione per iudicium parium suorum in curia Regis; et si Rex debeat habere terminum aliorum cruce signatorum, tunc archiepiscopus et episcopi...

...remota.

...t membris, sed libere concedatur sine pretio, et non negetur.

...enuerit per burgagium, et de alio per servitium militare, dominus Rex non habebit custodiam militum de feodo alterius occasione burgagii vel sokagii, nec...

...firme; et quod liber homo non amittat militiam suam occasione parvarum serjantiarum, sicut de illis qui tenent aliquod tenementum reddendo inde...

... simplici loquela sua sine testibus fidelibus.

... dissaisiatur, nec utlagetur, nec exuletur ... [illegible]

Magna Carta

The starting point for the story of our rights and freedoms is undoubtedly Magna Carta, the Great Charter agreed by King John in 1215. Even though John soon had the Charter annulled by the Pope, its purpose and power continued, eventually gaining an iconic status as a basis for liberty throughout the world.

Sir Edward Coke.
BL, 508.g.5.(2.)

Opposite:
Seal of King John.
BL, Add. MS 4838

In May 1628, the noted jurist Sir Edward Coke, stood in the House of Commons to defend his Petition of Right which he had proposed a few days earlier to enshrine the rights of the people of the realm. His speech touched on the royal prerogative which the king, Charles I, was exercising without restraint. He stated:

I know that prerogative is part of the law, but "Sovereign Power" is no parliamentary word. In my opinion it weakens Magna Charta, and all the statutes; for they are absolute, without any saving of "Sovereign Power"; and should we now add it, we shall weaken the foundation of law, and then the building must needs fall. Take we heed what we yield unto: Magna Charta is such a fellow, that he will have no "Sovereign".

This stated the Rule of Law and, thanks to Coke and those who followed, Magna Carta became its foundation stone, establishing the fundamental liberties of all those governed by the laws of England. Yet it had not started out that way. King John, who had agreed the original Charter, had little regard for any rights his barons might claim. That is how our rights and freedoms have been won, as it is only when they are under threat that we seek to identify them.

Magna Carta had come about in that way. John, struggling to regain his lands in Normandy, set ever more demanding taxes upon his barons. Those who defaulted were punished severely. In January 1215 a deputation of barons met with John, seeking assurances. John prevaricated and soon the barons rebelled. When the barons captured London, John was forced to negotiate and the two sides met at Runnymede, near Windsor, in June 1215. The result of the negotiations was written down as the Articles of the Barons and it was this document, sealed in the presence of John, which was converted by the King's clerks into the formal royal grant known as Magna Carta.

Much of the document dealt with recent grievances regarding the ownership of land, the regulation of the justice system, and feudal taxes. It established the principle that no taxes could be demanded without the "general consent of the realm", meaning the leading barons and churchmen. It re-established privileges which had been lost and allowed certain sureties. For instance, it linked fines to the severity of the offence so as not to threaten an individual's livelihood. It also confirmed that a widow could not be forced to remarry.

Amongst its many clauses, all of which applied only to free men, meaning those not indentured to their lord, were two of lasting significance.

- No Freeman shall be taken or imprisoned, or be disseised [dispossessed] of his Freehold, or Liberties, or free Customs, or be outlawed, or exiled, or any other wise destroyed; nor will We not pass upon him, nor condem him, but by lawful judgment of his Peers, or by the Law of the Land.
- We will sell to no man, we will not deny or defer to any man either Justice or Right.

These gave all free men the right to justice and a fair trial. It was the first appearance of the principle of *habeas corpus*, namely that no one could be imprisoned unlawfully.

Magna Carta allowed the barons a right of redress if the King did not comply. Not surprisingly, John ignored the charter, and had it annulled by the Pope. Within months he was at war again with his barons. He died a year later, but Magna Carta did not die with him. A slightly revised version was issued in the name of his young son, Henry III, in November 1216 and again the following year. Upon reaching eighteen in 1225, Henry reissued it in a shortened version and that version was enshrined in English law in 1297 by Edward I. By then Magna Carta was taking on its status as the source of English liberty.

Magna Carta beyond England

A part of Magna Carta originally applied to Wales, as it specified: "English law shall apply to holdings of land in England, Welsh law to those in Wales, and the law of the Marches to those in the Marches." This was dropped in the 1297 version. However, Magna Carta never applied in Scotland, and the writ of *habeas corpus*, which was standardised in England under the Habeas Corpus Act of 1679, has no meaning in Scotland. The Scottish Criminal Procedure Act in 1701 made similar provision for "wrongous imprisonment" and undue delay in trials. Ireland had its own Habeas Corpus Act in 1782.

Magna Carta.
It is not certain how many copies of Magna Carta were originally issued, although it is likely a copy was sent to each of the forty shires. Only thirteen copies were specifically noted in royal archives and only four of these survive, two in Lincoln and Salisbury cathedrals and two at the British Library, one of which was badly damaged by fire in 1731.
BL, Cotton Augustus MS II.106

The Rule of Law

When King John set his seal on Magna Carta, he was conceding that he was not above the law. Everyone's rights and liberties are dependent upon the law and will only be honoured if the laws are kept. For that reason it was important to establish a proper system of laws and a way to administer them.

Nottingham's Town Charter. Issued in 1154, it included a clause that if a serf escaped from his lord and lived for a year and a day in Nottingham, he was allowed his freedom.

Nottinghamshire Archives, CA4151

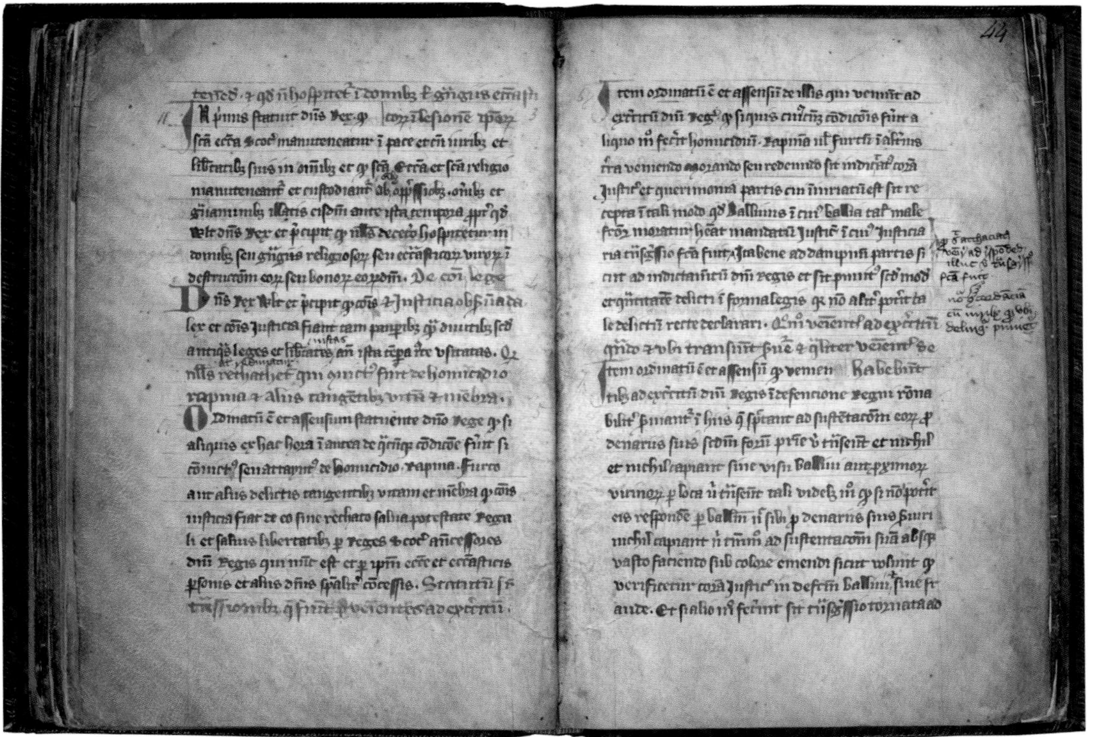

The Ayr Manuscript dates to the reign of Robert Bruce in the early fourteenth century, and incorporates some of the earliest surviving Scottish laws.
National Archives of Scotland, PA5/2

To medieval minds, the King was the law. He was both lawgiver and protector of his people. This was a standard belief throughout Europe and the nations of Britain. The coronation oath of the Saxon king Edgar, for instance, in 973 was: *First that the church of God and the whole Christian people shall have true peace at all time by our judgment; second, that I will forbid extortion and all kinds of wrong-doing to all orders of men; third, that I will enjoin equity and mercy in all judgments.*

Henry I's coronation included not just a basic oath but an extensive charter of liberties, some of which were drawn upon for Magna Carta. Although the oath has evolved, even today Queen Elizabeth II still swore to uphold law and justice.

When William of Normandy conquered Saxon England and established himself as king in 1066, he needed to understand the laws of the land. He sent justices throughout England to record local legal practices and from this developed a basic set of "custom and practice" which became regarded as common law. This continued to develop, particularly under Henry II and Richard I in the last half of the twelfth century.

So that justice could be dispensed equally, in 1166, following the Assize of Clarendon, Henry II introduced a body of judges who travelled the country holding "petty assizes". From 1176 these circuit judges also heard disputes about dispossession of land. A sworn jury of twelve was asked about the ownership of the land and their responses decided the case. This was the start of a verdict by jury that would develop into a trial jury after 1220, when Trial by Ordeal was banned. It was not yet the trial jury as we know it, and few benefited from it, as it excluded women and the poor.

The English legal system was adopted, to some degree, by Scotland during the thirteenth century, but it evolved separately with its own laws. Wales, which had its own laws dating back to the 940s, had English laws imposed for all criminal cases from 1277.

The Norman and Plantagenet kings also issued charters to various boroughs which granted them certain rights and privileges. London's charter, for example, issued in around 1133, allowed that all London men and their goods "are to be exempt from and free of toll, passage, lastage, and all other customs, throughout all England and the seaports".

The Charter of the Forest, issued with the revised Magna Carta by Henry III in 1217, granted free men access to the forest for such rights as *pannage* (pasture for their pigs) and *estover* (collecting firewood). The death penalty was removed for anyone stealing venison, though they were still subject to fines or imprisonment. Special Verderers' Courts were set up within the forests to enforce the laws and these still exist today in the New Forest and the Forest of Dean.

One of Henry II's major problems was in resolving the rift between church and state law. The freedom of the church had long been recognised and the church had developed its own canon law. At times this was at variance to secular law, which Henry naturally believed should have sovereignty. Henry called a council at Clarendon in 1164 to resolve this. It resulted in the Constitutions of Clarendon, to which Thomas Becket, the Archbishop of Canterbury, objected. Henry believed that unordained clerks should be tried under secular law, even after they had been tried in an ecclesiastical court, where sentences were usually more lenient. Becket called this "double jeopardy": being tried for the same crime twice. Henry would not concede, but a decade later, remorseful after the murder of Becket, he capitulated, and revoked the ruling. The principle of double jeopardy remained in England and Wales until amended by the Criminal Justice Act in 2003, but still applies in Scotland.

Henry II and Thomas Becket in debate. Depicted in the *Chronicle of England* by Peter de Langtoft, written between 1307 and 1327.
BL, Royal MS 20 A. II, f.7v

Domesday Book

Despite the importance of Magna Carta, its true significance did not emerge until the seventeenth century. For the majority of English people, who were lowly serfs bonded to their master, Magna Carta meant little, but they believed another document might help them, namely the Domesday Book.

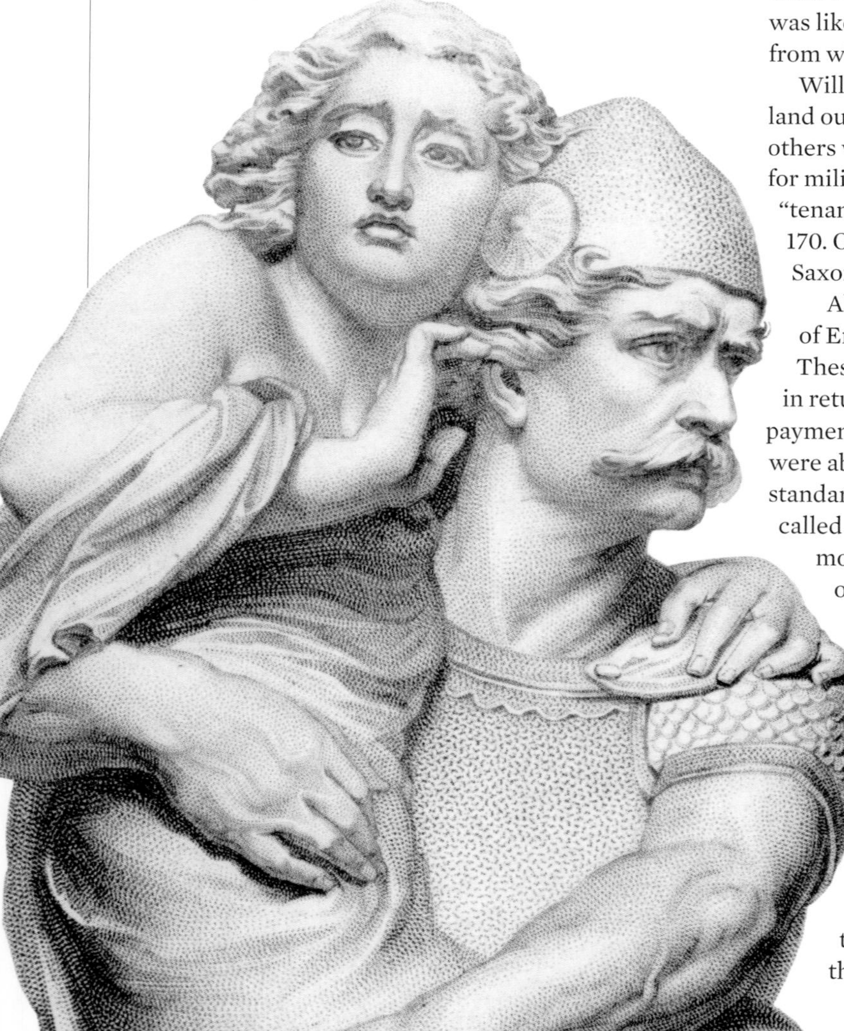

Hereward the Wake sustained the English resistance against the Normans in the Lincolnshire Fens and forests until 1073. He passed into legend as the last stand of English liberty against Norman oppression. (Illustrated by H. C. Selous from *Hereward the Wake* by Charles Kingsley.)

William the Conqueror may have respected the law, and even granted London all its former rights and liberties, but he expected loyalty in return. Any rebellion was dealt with savagely. The most notorious was the "harrying of the north" during 1069-70, when much of the land was laid to waste. An estimated 150,000 people perished. Elsewhere rebels held out, notably Hereward the Wake, but even his resistance faded. By 1073 William's conquest of England was complete. He even pushed into South Wales in the 1080s.

The cost of this was severe and one reason for the great survey of 1086 was to assess the value and ownership of land. The survey was thorough. The *Anglo-Saxon Chronicle* recorded that "not even one ox, nor one cow, nor one pig ... escaped notice". The record became known as the Domesday Book. *Dome*, or 'doom', was the Old English word for judgement, and the survey was likened to a Day of Reckoning from which there was no appeal.

William had parcelled most of the land out amongst his barons and others who had given help in return for military service. These were the "tenants in chief", numbering about 170. Only 8% of land remained in Saxon hands.

About 80% of the population of England were serfs or villeins. These held land from their lord in return for service and feudal payments. Over time, some villeins were able to live to a reasonable standard, but the lower class of serf, called bordars or cottars, were little more than slaves. Less than 10% of the population was free. This compares to over 50% in Wales by 1300, whilst in Scotland serfdom had all but vanished by 1400. It was the English peasants, dominated by their overlords, who were oppressed, falling under what was later called the "Norman Yoke". Although they had recourse to the law, they were seen as the property of their lord, and courts would not interfere between the lord and his men.

So the serfs themselves looked for loopholes. They discovered that if the land upon which they toiled was recorded in Domesday Book as having been in royal ownership – known as "ancient demesne" – this granted them special privileges. For example, the villein could petition the royal court rather than the manorial court if he had complaints about changes in work or rents, and they believed this also gave them a right to apply to be a free man. Any such privileges had changed over time and often the peasants' understanding was misguided, but this did not stop them pursuing what they believed were their rights, driven by an overriding belief in the King as their protector. Peasants colluded to help finance the cost of obtaining authenticated extracts from Domesday Book to state their case and occasionally they won. The belief spread, culminating in what was the equivalent of a peasants' strike in 1377 across parts of southern England. This was different to the uprising of 1381, and was just as quickly quelled, but it was a sign that the peasants felt strongly about their rights and, like the barons, expected the King to uphold them by the rule of law.

Domesday Book today

The Domesday Book was consulted in court as recently as 1960. A resident of Bosham in Sussex went to court arguing that the Domesday Book record gave Bosham special status as a former royal demesne, and thus anyone born there did not have to pay the harbour tolls. The judge disagreed.

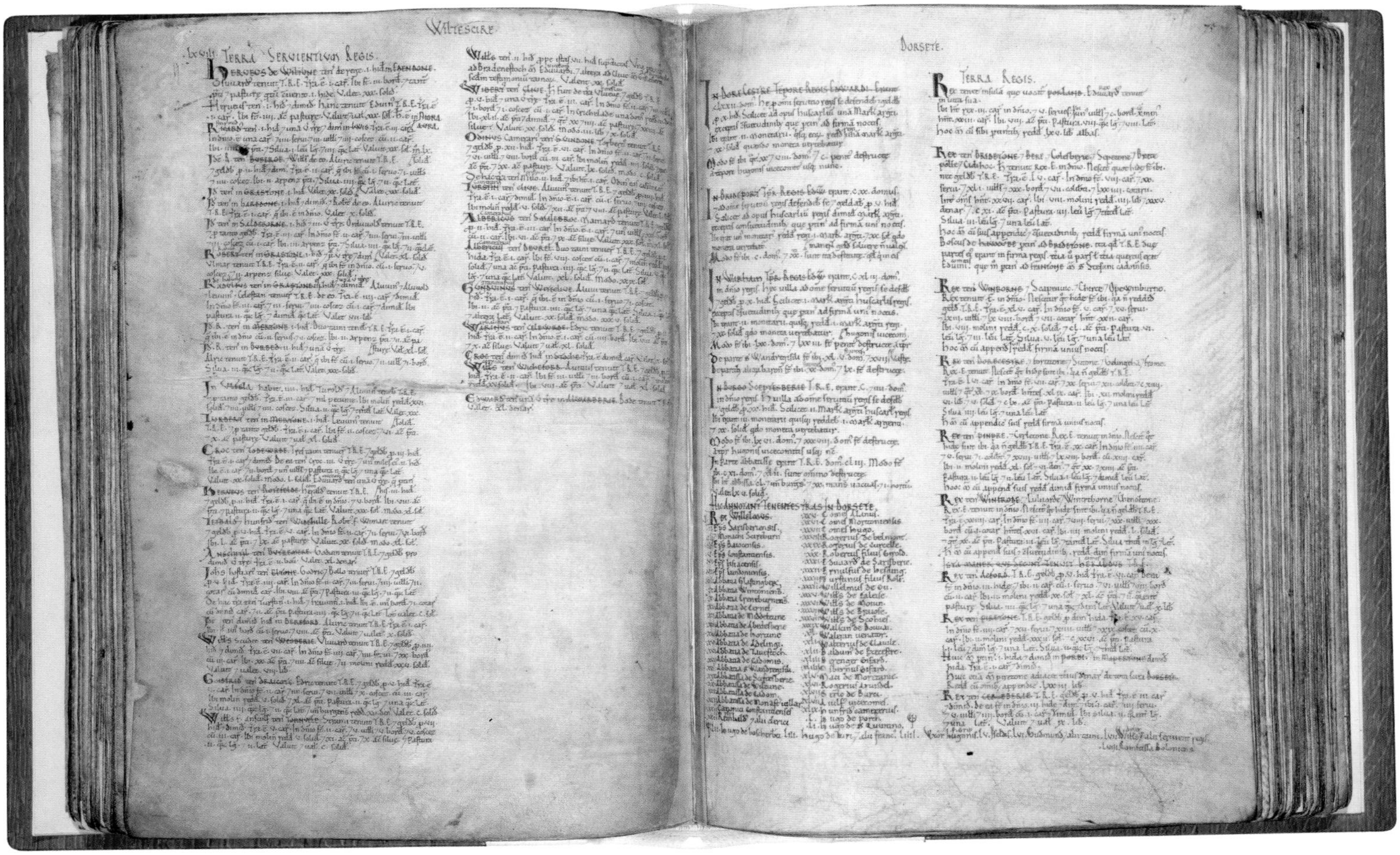

The Domesday Book is really two books: Great Domesday (above) and Little Domesday (below). For the survey England was divided into seven circuits and considerable detail was acquired on all land, its owners and occupiers. By the time William died in 1087 the unedited data for the eastern circuit (Norfolk, Suffolk and Essex) filled 475 pages. This became Little Domesday. The remaining information was summarised in Great Domesday, which filled only 413 pages.

National Archives, E31/2/1 f.75
National Archives, E31/1/3

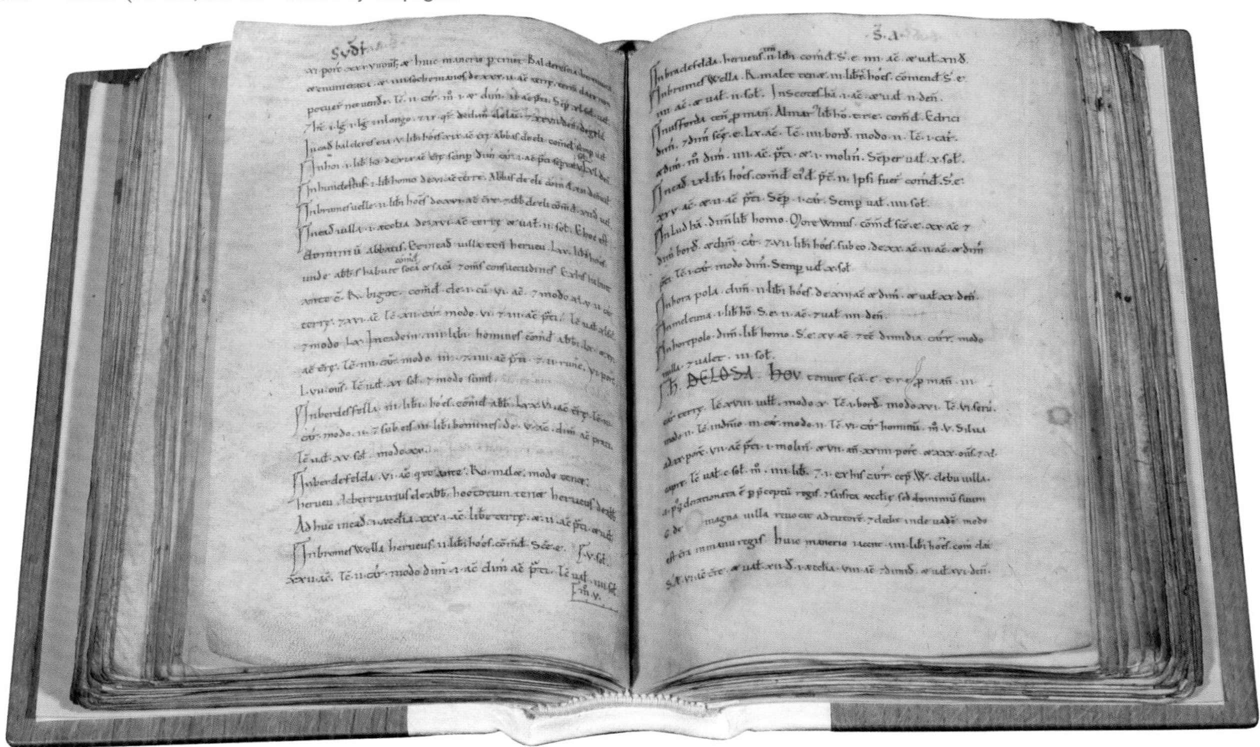

The Voice of the People

600 years ago the peasants found that they too had a voice which could be used against oppression and inequality. They rose in revolt and, although it had little effect at the time, it was something the nobility did not easily forget.

Death from famine as depicted by Jean de Wavrin in *Chroniques d'Angleterre*, *c.*1470–80.
BL, Royal MS 15 E.IV f.187

In the twelfth and thirteenth centuries life for the peasants became increasingly difficult. In 1235, the Statute of Merton allowed lords of the manor to "enclose" (set apart for their own use, rather than fence in) any land they deemed surplus to the needs of those working the land. As a result the access to common pasturage was restricted.

A series of wet winters and summers between 1314 and 1317 led to widespread famine. Perhaps as much as 20% of the population died from disease and malnutrition. Yet the serfs, in bond to their lords, still had to work the land and pay their dues. In the summer of 1348, the Great Plague, or Black Death, reached Britain and over the next fifteen months wiped out up to 40% of the population. Lesser plagues struck in 1361, 1368 and 1375.

With fewer men to work the fields the peasants worked harder and demanded better wages, some profiting considerably. The cost of food increased. An Ordinance of Labourers was introduced in 1349, reinforced by subsequent statutes, to control prices and fix wages at the pre-plague level.

Another factor was Edward III's ongoing conflict with France, now called the Hundred Years' War. Edward was determined to recover lands now lost but the conflict was going badly with French attacks along the south coast. To finance the war, further taxes were imposed, of which the most notorious was the poll tax ("poll" for "head"). This was a fixed rate per person, regardless of status. It started in 1377 at fourpence for

Poll Tax riots, 1990
There were echoes of the Peasants' Revolt six centuries later when the Poll Tax riots erupted in March 1990 against the proposed Community Charge. Once again the voice of the ordinary person was heard.

The death of Wat Tyler depicted in *Chroniques de France et d'Angleterre* by Jean Froissart, published *c.*1460–80.
BL, Royal MS 18 E. I, f.175

everyone aged over fourteen but neither this, nor a second levy in 1379, raised sufficient money. In 1380 a savage rate was set at one shilling (twelve pence) on everyone over fifteen. Since a serf seldom earned more than twenty shillings a year, it was a significant imposition on top of other taxes, and many evaded the tax. The scene was set for the rebellion of 1381, known as the Peasants' Revolt.

Tax collectors were told to take any measures necessary. During May and June 1381 they met with violent opposition. Fighting broke out in several eastern counties, notably Essex and Kent. The Kentish rebels, under the leadership of Wat Tyler, gathered at Blackheath and presented a petition to the 14-year-old Richard II, who was at Greenwich. It named officials whose corrupt policies the peasants believed were ruining the country, including the King's uncle (John of Gaunt), the Archbishop of Canterbury and the Lord Treasurer. The meeting was unsuccessful. The rebels continued to London, joining forces with those from Essex. They emptied several prisons and burned down John of Gaunt's palace at the Savoy. Richard II met the rebels at Mile End to hear their demands, which included the end of villeinage. The King agreed and asked the rebels to disperse.

Meanwhile, others attacked the Tower of London, executing the Archbishop and Treasurer amongst others. The King met the rebels again, at Smithfield. Wat Tyler presented further demands, asking for an end to serfdom, the break up of church lands, and that all men should be free and serve no lord save the King. During the confrontation there was a scuffle in which Tyler was stabbed. The King took control, despite his youth, claiming he was now their leader, and had them escorted out of London.

Despite his promises, the King never did enact the demands. Most of the leaders of the rebellion were tracked down and executed. Yet they did not wholly fail. This was the first time the "power of the people" had shown itself, and the nobility were concerned it could happen again. No more poll taxes were levied and the lords had to give in to wage demands. Serfdom was in its final stages.

Robin Hood

Little wonder that the stories of Robin Hood became popular at this time. He first appears in the poem *Piers Plowman*, written in the 1370s by William Langland. It relates a peasant's dream of a corrupt society and the need for strong Christian values. Plowman's dream became part of the egalitarian preachings of the renegade priest, John Ball, who was a figurehead in the Peasant's Revolt.

National Liberties

In the years leading up to the Civil War, John Pym, who led the House of Commons, argued that Parliament was one of the country's three fundamental liberties. Just how much Parliament has demonstrated this through the centuries is a matter of debate, but the growth of Parliament is closely allied to our rights. It is the story of the governed versus those who govern, each side determined to protect its privileges. It has led to various attempts to create a constitution or a Bill of Rights. It is also the story of how the Parliament of England grew into the Parliament of the United Kingdom, with the consequent loss of independence of Wales, Ireland and Scotland. Those "nations" put up a powerful defence of their national identity and their own right to freedom.

Detail from the *Exemplification of the Act of Union*, completed in March 1707, the final document that sealed the union between England and Scotland.
National Archives of Scotland, SP13/10

nna Dei gratia Magn

Franciae et Hiberniae Regina Fidei Defensor etc Omnibus ad quos presentes litere pervenerint
Breve nostrum de Certiorando e Cur Cancellar nostre nuper emanan Dilecto et fideli nostro Mathew J
nostrorum direct unarum quodam Retorno sive Indorsamento in Dorso eiusdem Brevis indorsato
retornatum et in filaciis ibidem de Recordo residen in hec verba Anna Dei gra Angl Scot Fran
sibi Mathew Johnson Ar Clerico Parliamentor suor salutem Volentes certis de Causis certiorari
ento nostro apud Westm fact et ordinat intitulat An Act for an Union of the two Kingdoms of England and S
edit cum omnibus illud tangentibus Nobis in Cancellar nram sub Sigillo tuo distincte et aperte sine dilatione mittatis
tuno Regni nri quinto Wrighte Executio huius Bris patet in quadam Schedula huic Bri annexa prout interius
mentor Inspeximus etiam Schedulam prementionatam continentem tenorem Actus predict eidemque Brev
et Sigillat in Cancellar nram predictam sic retornat et in filaciis ibidem de Recordo quoque residen in hec verba
master decimo quarto die Junii Anno Domini Millesimo Septingentesimo Quinto Annoque Regni Serenissim
ibernie Regine Fidei Defensor etc Quarto Communi omnium Dnor tam Spiritualium quam Temporal et Communitatis Co
Sancitum Inactitatum et Stabilitum fuit hoc sequens Statutum viz An Act for an Union of the Tw
Gracious Sovereigne Whereas Articles of Union were agreed on the Twenty second day of July in
issioners nominated on behalfe of the Kingdom of England under your Majesties Great Seal of England bearing date at W
suance of an Act of Parliament made in England in the third year of your Majesties Reign and the Commissioners nominat
Majesties Great Seal of Scotland bearing date the Twenty seventh day of February in the fourth year of your Majesties Re
ssion of the present Parliament of Scotland to treat of and concerning an Union of the said Kingdoms And Where
d at Edinburgh the Sixteenth day of January in the fifth year of your Majesties Reign wherein tis mentioned th
rticles of Union of the Two Kingdoms had agreed to and approved of the said Articles of Union with some Additions
e and Consent of the Estates of Parliament for Establishing the Protestant Religion and Presbyterian Church Governme
he same Session of Parliament an Act Intituled Act for securing of the Protestant Religion and Presbiterian Churc
ated to be inserted in any Act ratifying the Treaty and expressly declared to be a fundamental and Essential Conditi
ing The Tenor of which Articles as Ratified and Approved of with Additions and Explanations by the said Act of Parlia
e Two Kingdoms of England and Scotland shall upon the first day of May which shall be in the year One
er be United into one Kingdom by the Name of Great Britain And that the Ensigns Armorial of the s
shall appoint and the Crosses of Saint George and Saint Andrew be conjoyned in such mann
in all Flaggs Banners Standards and Ensigns both at Sea and Land Article 2. That the Successi
e of Great Britain and of the Dominions thereto belonging after her most Sacred Majesty and in default o
nne to the most Excellent Princess Sophia Electoress and Dutchess Dowager of Hanover and the H
on the Crown of England is setled by an Act of Parliament made in England in the Twelfth year of the R
Intituled An Act for the further Limitation of the Crown and better securing the Rights and Liberties of the Subj
ng Papists shall be excluded from and for ever incapable to Inherit Possess or Enjoy the Imperial Crown of Gre
t or any part thereof And in every such Case the Crown and Government shall from time to time descend to and
t as should have Inherited and Enjoyed the same in case such Papist or Person Marrying a Papist was nat
t of the Crown of England made by another Act of Parliament in England in the first year of the Reign of their

The First Parliaments

In 1865 the radical MP John Bright described England as "the Mother of Parliaments". His comment may be true insofar as the English Parliament has served as a model for many around the world, but it was not the only, or the first, Parliament in the isles of Britain.

The death of Simon de Montfort at the Battle of Evesham as shown in the *Chronica Roffense*, compiled in the early fourteenth century.
BL, Cotton MS Nero D ii, f. 177

The word Parliament comes from the French and means to talk or discuss, the same as "parlay". It was first used in England in 1236 but it was only a new name for the King's Court, the *Curia Regis*. The French had their own *parlement*, also developed from the King's court, but this developed in a different direction, with a growth in local *parlements* or councils. For centuries kings had consulted a selective body of lords and bishops over policy. The Saxon kings had their *witan* ("wise men") who had the added authority that they confirmed the successor king. The Scots had their *colloquium* ("discussion"), and the Vikings had their *þing* or *thing* ("assembly"), a local council of free men. The word is remembered in the placenames Dingwall in Scotland, Thingwall on the Wirral Peninsula and as the name of the Parliament of the Isle of Man, the Tynwald. This has met continuously since 979 and is one of the oldest Parliaments in the World.

Parliament met at the behest of the King, summoned occasionally when he needed advice. Under Magna Carta the King had to summon his council before levying any new taxes. John's son, Henry III, chose to ignore this and the barons called him to order in 1258 under the Provisions of Oxford. Like his father, Henry agreed to the Provisions and then obtained the Pope's approval to ignore them.

A forgotten Parliament
Cornwall's Stannary Parliament dates from at least the 8th century and probably earlier. It had jurisdiction over the tin mines and related towns. Amongst powers granted in 1508 was the right of veto over the Parliament at Westminster. The last Stannary Parliament officially met in 1753 but was never formally dissolved. Since 1974 the Parliament has been revived by local activists claiming its old right for Cornwall.

On more than one occasion he and his barons almost came to blows before matters were calmed.

One of the most powerful barons was the Earl of Leicester, Simon de Montfort, who had married Henry's sister. Like Henry, Simon was hot-headed and stubborn. The barons called upon Simon to head their campaign. Despite trying to find a peaceful settlement, confrontation spiralled into civil war. At the Battle of Lewes in May 1264, de Montfort was victorious and suddenly found himself running the country, through the King.

De Montfort called a Parliament in order to agree a constitution. Wanting to do things properly, he not only summoned the usual barons and knights of the shires but also called for two elected representatives from each of the major boroughs and cities. Although burgesses had been present at a couple of earlier Parliaments, this was the first time they were elected by

The King and his Parliament depicted in *Modus Tenendi Parliamentum*. Believed to date from the 1320s, this text set down in detail the process for summoning and running Parliament and gave emphasis to the role of the Commons. In 1322 during the reign of Edward II, his court favourites, the Despensers, who virtually ran the kingdom, proclaimed that for a decision of Parliament to become law "the commonality of the realm had to be involved". This became a permanent arrangement from 1327 and by 1341 the Commons met separately from the Lords.
BL, Cotton MS Nero D. VI, f.72

the freemen of the borough.

It would be good to say de Montfort's Parliament achieved much, but it was taken up trying to resolve the problems of the previous few years. De Montfort's determination to do things his way turned many barons against him and allegiances shifted not to Henry III but his son, the fiery 26-year-old Prince Edward. Edward and de Montfort clashed at Evesham in August 1265 where de Montfort was killed and his body hacked to pieces.

Edward succeeded his father in November 1272, the start of a reign that would be one of the most momentous in Britain. Like his great-grandfather, Henry II, Edward undertook a major programme of legal reform. He learned from the conflict between his father and the barons and used Parliament not only for raising taxes – its primary role – but for keeping an eye on his barons. Starting with the Statute of Westminster in 1275, Edward undertook a series of reforms culminating in the "Model" Parliament of 1295. In addition to two knights from each shire, there were two burgesses elected by each borough and two citizens from each city: in total 49 lords and 292 commoners. The Scottish Parliament first involved commoners, representatives from the royal burghs, in 1326.

When summoning the Archbishop of Canterbury to the Parliament of 1295, Edward I used an old phrase from Roman law, "What touches all, should be agreed by all." This has since become a keystone of democracy though Edward seldom followed it. Of his 52 Parliaments only thirteen had representatives from the shires and boroughs.

The Subjugation of Wales

Wales was the first of the "nations" of Britain to succumb to the power of the warrior king, Edward I, and to lose its independence. But Welsh nationalism did not fade and its power would be felt again under Owain Glyn Dŵr, who fought to regain Welsh independence and pride.

Dating from around the year 1483, this depicts Owain's revolt and defeat as one image. The comet inspired Owain's followers and encouraged the uprising, but Owain was defeated by the Earl of Warwick in 1404. The picture comes from the *Beauchamp Pageants*, the Earl of Warwick's book of triumphs.
BL, Cotton MS Julius E. IV, art. 6, f.3v

William the Conqueror established a buffer zone between Wales and England, the Welsh Marches, controlled by the powerful Marcher Lords. They had almost complete authority to do as they wished, with their own laws. Wales was composed of a number of small kingdoms, of variable power. Llywelyn the Great gained sufficient authority to rule all of Wales from 1210 to 1240, but only by acknowledging the English king as his overlord.

After Llywelyn's death, power in Wales crumbled. His grandsons, Llywelyn and Dafydd, were the last independent rulers of Wales and their rebellion against Edward failed. In March 1284, the Statute of Rhuddlan brought Wales under English control.

Most of the Welsh princes were dispossessed and their lands passed to English barons. In 1301, Edward made his eldest son Prince of Wales and the title has remained with the heir to the English throne ever since. The old laws of Hywel Dda, which had been part of Welsh justice since the 940s, were retained for cases dealing with land, but otherwise English law prevailed. English clerks took over most of the administration of Wales and English became the language of business. Edward established a ring of castles around Wales which still remain as evidence to the power of English domination.

Despite this there were regular rebellions of which the most significant was in 1400. It arose almost by chance from a land dispute between Owain Glyn Dŵr and his English neighbour who managed to have Glyn Dŵr falsely charged with treason. Glyn Dŵr, then in his forties, found himself on the run and gathered about him a growing army of supporters. Despite punitive attacks by Henry IV, Glyn Dŵr had a series of successes and won over to his cause Edmund Mortimer, brother of the Earl of March, the most powerful landowner in Wales, and Henry Percy, the Earl of Northumberland. It was rumoured that they planned to overthrow Henry IV and split England and Wales between them.

Henry IV issued a series of severe Penal Laws against the Welsh (and any Englishman married to a Welsh woman), forbidding them meeting together, bearing arms, living in fortified towns or holding public office. Most Welsh were effectively outlawed.

Glyn Dŵr gained the support of the French. He grew sufficiently confident to summon Parliaments at Machynlleth and Harlech. However, at the height of his success his authority waned and he lost the support of Percy and Mortimer. In March 1406 Glyn Dŵr appealed to the French king for additional forces against the "barbarous Saxons, who usurped to themselves the land of Wales". His request, known as the Pennal Letter, set out his plan for Welsh greatness. Alas, the request went unanswered. With dwindling support and with Henry IV regaining territory, Glyn Dŵr's grand scheme crumbled. Yet he held out against the English and eluded them to the end of his days. He was last heard of in 1415 and probably died soon after. He has remained a symbol of Welsh national feeling ever since.

The Penal Laws remained in place and eventually became redundant following the Act of 1536, which was effectively an Act of Union, and which was imposed on Wales. It abolished the Welsh legal system and banned the Welsh language in courts of law, but it did otherwise grant a degree of equality between the Welsh and the English and allowed the Welsh to be represented in the English Parliament for the first time.

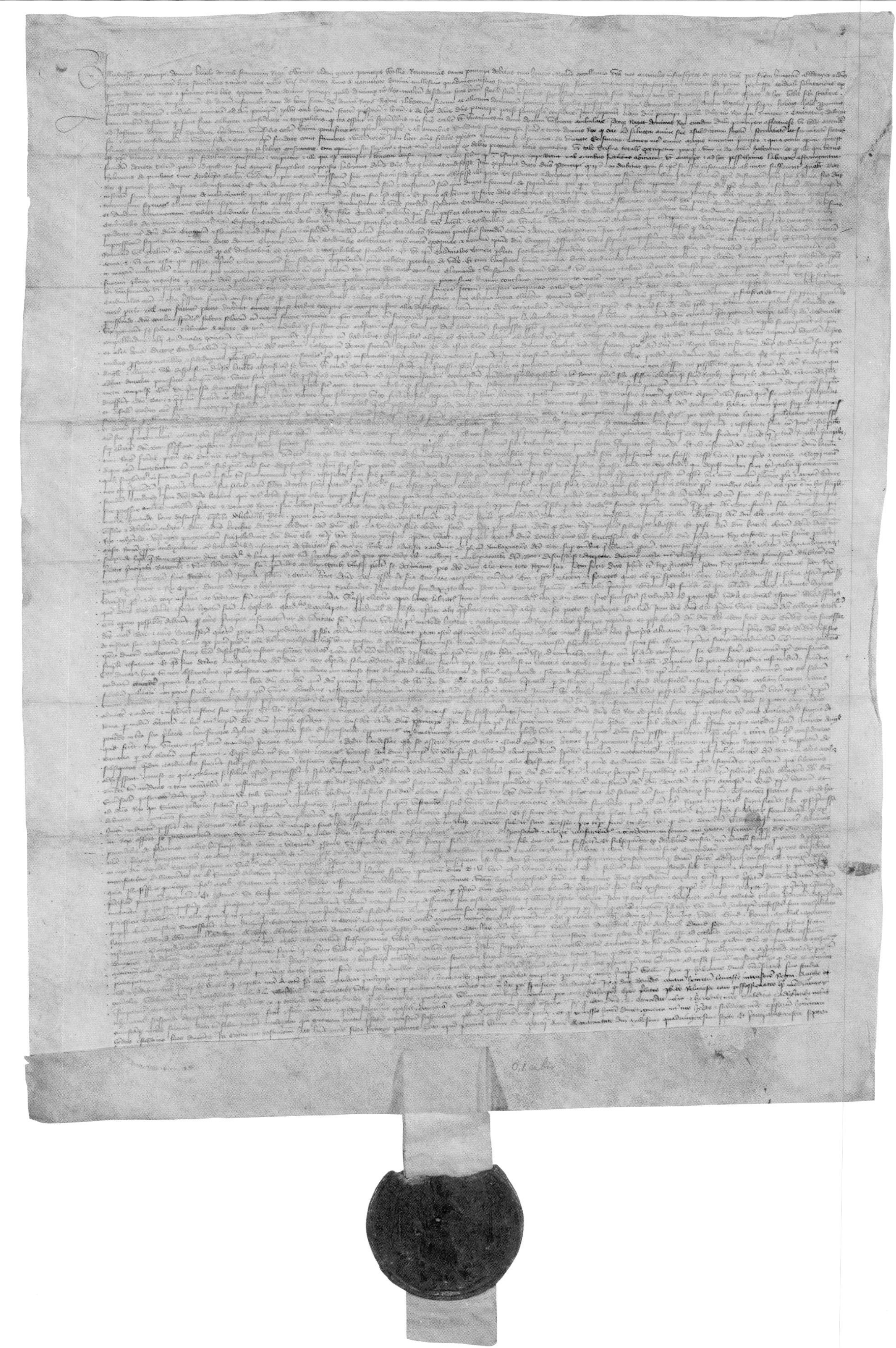

The Pennal Letter. Glyn Dŵr proposed to re-establish St. David's as a major archbishopric with authority over not only the three Welsh bishoprics but also five English ones. He also proposed the creation of two universities to enhance Welsh learning and reputation.

Archives nationales, Paris. J/516, A, 29

The Declaration of Arbroath

Scotland retained its independence for far longer than Wales, although in the early fourteenth century it nearly fell to the schemes of Edward I. The Scots fought back under not one, but two national heroes, and produced a defiant statement of national liberty, arguably even more rousing than the Magna Carta.

The Stone of Destiny. This block of sandstone is the ceremonial stone upon which the kings of Scotland were inaugurated from at least Kenneth MacAlpin in 843. The Stone was returned to Scotland in 1996 and is kept at Edinburgh Castle.

Opposite: *The Declaration of Arbroath.* Its authorship is usually attributed to Bernard de Linton, the Chancellor of Scotland, but it was more likely composed by the up-and-coming canon of Dunkeld, Alexander de Kininmund for the Abbot of Arbroath. It bears the seals of eight earls and 45 barons.

National Archives of Scotland, SP13/7

Robert Bruce from the statue in the gatehouse of Edinburgh Castle.

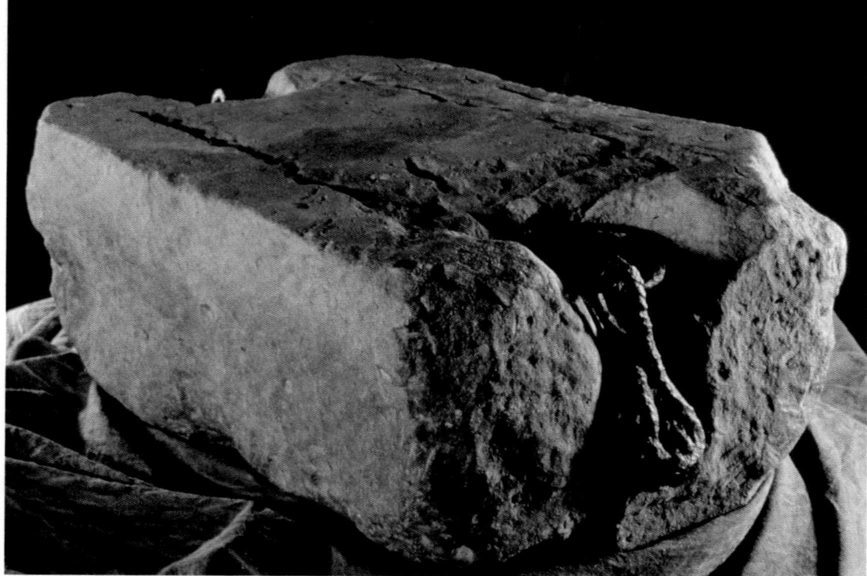

In 1290 when Margaret, the young heir to the Scottish throne, died aged only seven, with no natural successor, the Scots turned to Edward I to arbitrate in the hope of avoiding civil war. From the dozen contenders, Edward chose John Balliol, whom he knew would be subservient. In fact Balliol was so much under Edward's control that he found his position untenable and in 1296 rebelled. He was soundly defeated by Edward who marched into the heart of Scotland and seized the symbol of Scottish nationality, the Stone of Destiny, at Scone. Edward had it incorporated within the Coronation Throne in Westminster.

The Scots fought back, the most famous rebel being William Wallace. He trounced the English at Stirling in 1297 and was declared Guardian of Scotland. He was severely defeated the following year at Falkirk but evaded capture until 1305, when he was hanged, disembowelled, beheaded and quartered.

Robert Bruce witnessed Wallace's death. He was of Norman ancestry and had sworn fealty to Edward I but when he supported Wallace's revolt, Edward laid waste to Robert's lands. They made their peace and Robert became one of the Regents of Scotland. However, in February 1306, while Edward planned to take over the governance of Scotland, Robert was wondering how to defeat him. He tried to collaborate with his nearest rival to the throne, John Comyn, but unable to agree, Robert ended up killing Comyn during a heated argument.

Robert had to act quickly for fear of arrest and on impulse had himself crowned king of Scotland. It was a high-risk tactic, knowing what had happened to Wallace. At first Robert's luck failed. He was defeated several times and sought refuge, during which period was born the famous story of Robert hiding in a cave and watching a spider trying to build its web. He came back with renewed success.

Edward I marched against him but died before reaching Scotland. His son Edward II was a weak king who, for a while, abandoned Scotland until Robert had captured all but two English castles, Berwick and Stirling. In 1314 Edward II brought his army to Stirling and was defeated at Bannockburn, one of the Scots' greatest victories. The fighting was not over but eventually, in 1328, the Treaty of Northampton recognised Scottish independence.

In 1320 Robert Bruce had sent an embassy to Rome bearing the Declaration of Arbroath and requesting the Pope to recognise Scottish sovereignty. Originally in Latin, it is one of the most rousing documents ever written in support of a nation's freedom. It details the ancient history of the Scots and lists the oppressions of the English. At the heart of the document is the following defiant, stirring and justly famous section:

...for, as long as but a hundred of us remain alive, never will we on any conditions be brought under English rule. It is in truth not for glory, nor riches, nor honours that we are fighting, but for freedom – for that alone, which no honest man gives up but with life itself.

The Pope took eight years, but in 1328 recognised Robert as King of Scotland. The nation remained independent for another 379 years.

The Irish Remonstrance

Part of the inspiration for the Declaration of Arbroath may have come from the Remonstrance sent by the Irish Chiefs to the Pope at Avignon in 1317. This told the Pope in no uncertain terms what their views were of the English.

Opposite:
The Remonstrance of the Irish Chiefs as incorporated in the *Schotichronicon,* compiled in the 1380s.
BL, Harley MS 712 ff.210v-211r

In 1166 Dermot MacMurrough, the dispossessed King of Leinster, sought the help of Henry II to recover his lands. Henry granted Dermot the aid of his barons and in 1169 the main contingent of Norman forces landed in Ireland. They were so successful that they were soon acquiring territory of their own. In May 1171 Dermot died and Richard de Clare, the earl of Pembroke, who had married Dermot's daughter, claimed the kingship of Leinster. Alarmed that his barons might establish a separate Norman kingdom, Henry arrived there with his army in October 1171, under the pretext of reviewing the Irish church, which the Pope believed was in disarray. Henry's triumph was swift. With few exceptions, the kings and nobles submitted to him, though it was not until the Treaty of Windsor in 1175 that this included the Irish High King Ruaidrí. So began England's involvement with Ireland.

The Pope was pleased with Henry II's review of the Irish church and granted him the Lordship of Ireland. In 1254 Henry III passed the Lordship to his son, Prince Edward, under a charter that specifically stated that Ireland should not be separated from the English crown. In 1297 an Irish Parliament was established in Dublin along the lines of Edward's English Parliament, though its members included only Anglo-Irish and no native Irish at all.

During these years, the Norman lords fought the Irish and each other for possession of land, the in-fighting often coming close to civil war. The native Irish took advantage of this where they could, but made only minor gains. In 1315, they sought the aid of Robert Bruce, flush from his success at Bannockburn. Robert, envisaging a united Celtic front across Scotland and Ireland, sent his brother Edward Bruce to help the Irish against the English. Edward was inaugurated as High King in June 1315.

The Irish chieftains, under Domnal O'Neill, wanted to override the original Papal Bull which had granted the English the lordship of Ireland. In 1317 they sent the Pope a long document, known as the "Remonstrance of the Irish Chiefs", providing full details. Their views on the English were evident from the opening words: "Lest the sharp-toothed and viperous calumny of the English and their untrue representations should to any degree excite your mind against us..." They continued, in words similar to those later used in the Declaration of Arbroath:

Let no one wonder then that we are striving to save our lives and defending as we can the rights of our law and liberty against cruel tyrants and usurpers.

Dublin Castle.
King John established the castle at Dublin in 1204 on the site of an old Viking fortress, although it was not completed until 1230. The castle also served as the local Parliament from 1297; the original Parliament Great Hall burned down in 1684. The Royal Tower shown here is the last remaining original Norman tower from 1226.

The Pope did not recognise the claim. Soon afterwards Edward Bruce died in battle against the English, his army destroyed.

In the succeeding years the English who had settled in Ireland began to assimilate with the local Irish and became regarded as the "Old English". When Edward III's son, the Earl of Ulster, came to Ireland in 1361, he was horrified to find how degenerate the Anglo-Irish had become. The Statutes of Kilkenny were issued in 1366 to ensure that the English remained distinct from the Irish. They forbade marriage between the English and the native Irish as well as trade. They also forbade the English to speak Irish, take Irish names, or use the ancient Irish Brehon Law.

The main effect was to foster even more hatred of the English. To all intents the Old English in Ireland allied themselves with the native Irish whilst those who remained pure to their Anglo-Norman heritage found themselves increasingly isolated in the area around Dublin, which became known as the Pale. Although the so-called Irish Parliament nominally had authority over all Ireland, it was in practice limited to the Pale, and its authority was increasingly diminished by the powerful Anglo-Irish lords. Eventually in 1494 Sir Edward Poynting, Henry VII's Viceroy in Ireland, passed an Act which placed the Irish Parliament directly under the authority of the English Parliament. In 1542 the Crown of Ireland Act made Henry VIII King of Ireland as well as King of England. The Act still applies to Northern Ireland to this day.

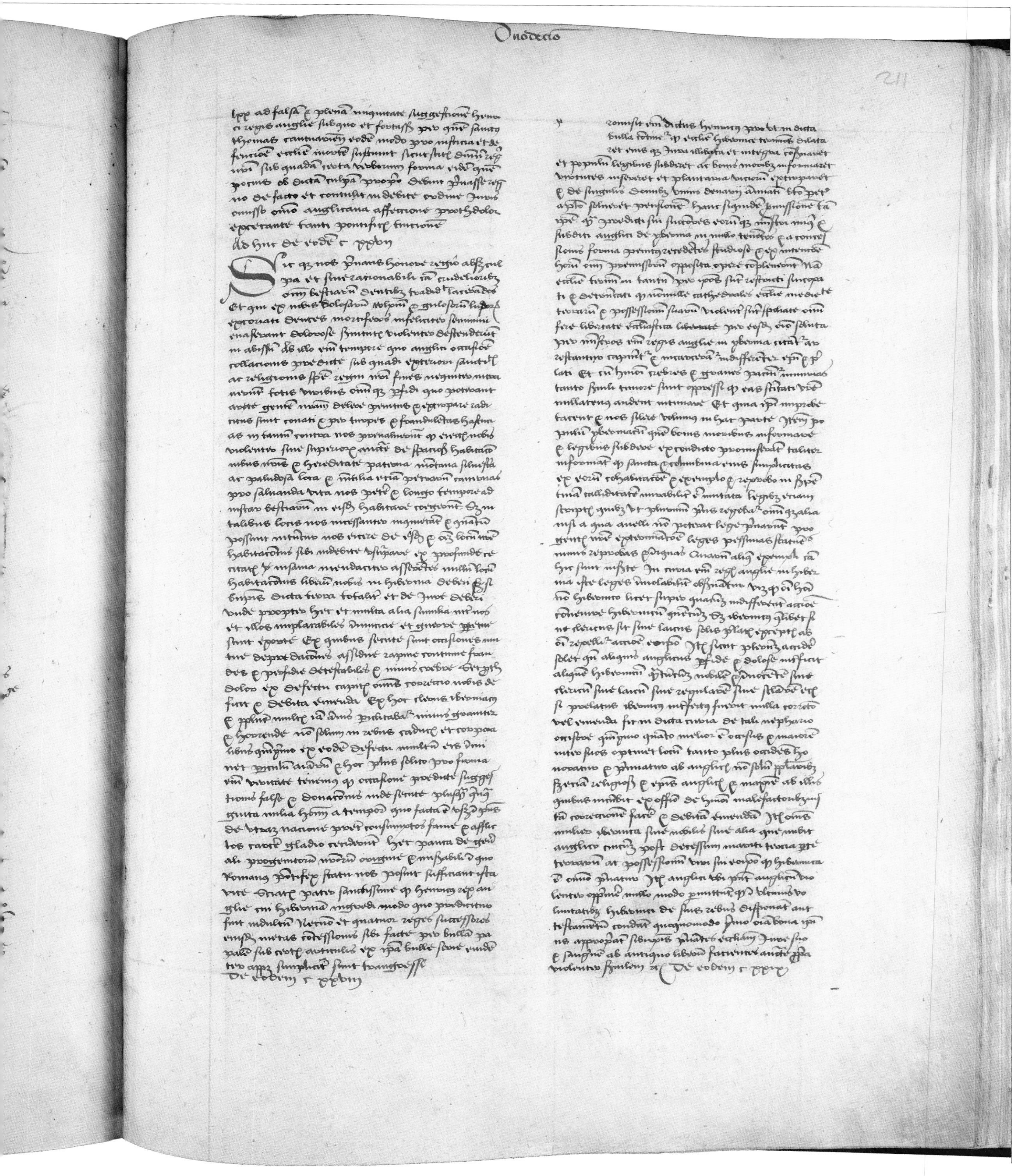

The Petition of Right

Scotland and England would eventually share one King when James VI of Scotland also became James I of England and Ireland in 1603. This began the Stuart dynasty in England which, within a lifetime, would lead all three countries into civil war and witness the end of the monarchy.

The Basilikon Doron, which is Greek for "royal gift", was written by James VI as a treatise on kingship and includes his views on the Divine Right of Kings.
BL, G.4993

When James VI succeeded Queen Elizabeth as James I of England and Ireland, he favoured a closer political union, a true United Kingdom, but although he styled himself King of Great Britain, there was no merger of the countries or Parliaments.

James was initially uncomfortable with the power of the English Parliament, especially the House of Commons, which he was unable to command as freely as Scotland's. He believed that kings ruled by Divine Right, with their authority direct from God. He included this view in a guidebook on kingship, the *Basilikon Doron,* which he presented to his son, the future Charles I, who was thus indoctrinated with the view from childhood. It made Charles intractable, and set him on a collision course with the English and Scottish Parliaments.

Charles would have happily ruled without Parliament but had to summon it occasionally in order to levy taxes to finance his military exploits. Charles had tried to collect taxes directly and his commissioners imprisoned without trial those who failed to pay, thus flouting *habeas corpus*. When, in 1628, Charles was compelled to call Parliament he was presented with the Petition of Right. It was written by the jurist Sir Edward Coke, champion of the common law, who had renewed the significance of Magna Carta. Coke knew that the King would reject any attempt at a new Bill of Rights, so he presented Charles with a statement of the existing law, virtually a new Magna Carta, cleverly worded to redefine basic freedoms. Coke

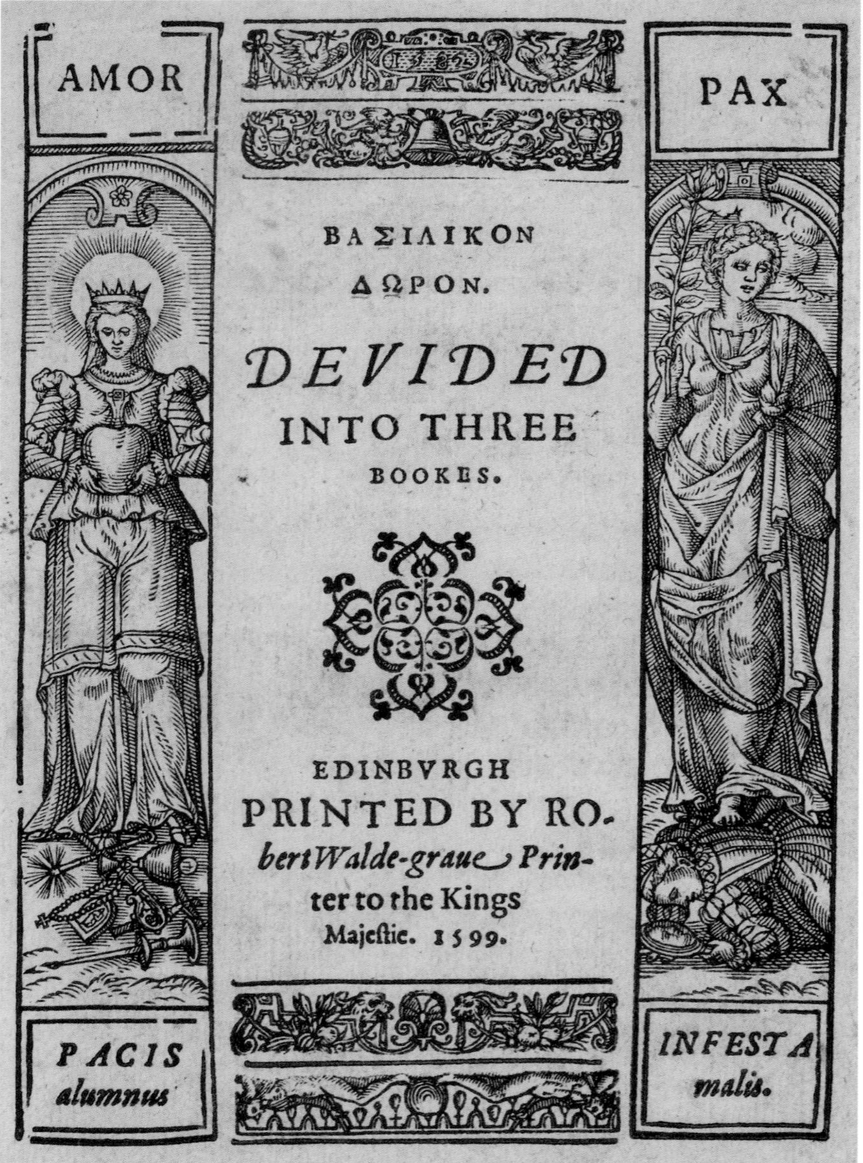
ΒΑΣΙΛΙΚΟΝ ΔΩΡΟΝ.

DEVIDED INTO THREE BOOKES.

EDINBVRGH PRINTED BY ROBERT Walde-graue Printer to the Kings Majestie. 1599.

summarised Parliamentary and individual freedom as follows: *... that no man hereafter be compelled to make or yield any gift, loan, benevolence, tax, or such like charge, without common consent by Act of parliament; and that none be called to make answer, or take such oath, or to give attendance, or be confined, or otherwise molested or disquieted*

King James hoped for a formal treaty of union between England and Scotland and had a draft prepared. He also commissioned the Earl of Nottingham to prepare various designs for a Flag of the United Kingdom of England and Scotland.

National Library of Scotland, MS 2517, f.67v

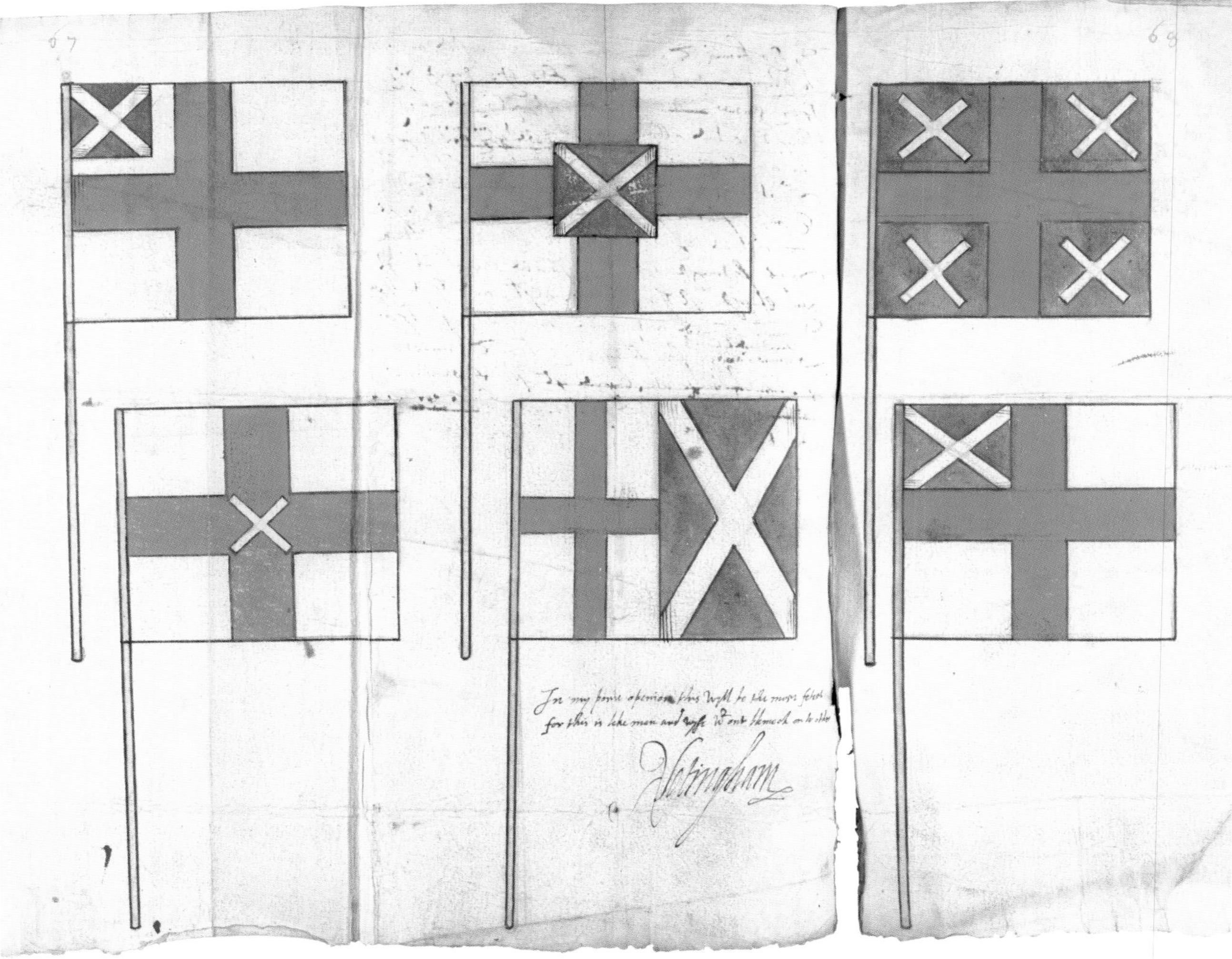

concerning the same or for refusal thereof; and that no freeman, in any such manner as is before mentioned, be imprisoned or detained...

Charles accepted the Petition, but it rankled him. After he dismissed Parliament he refused to call another for eleven years. He tried to raise taxes by other means, but once he fell into conflict with Scotland over his religious reforms, the Bishops' Wars, he ran out of money and had to reconvene Parliament in April 1640. The Commons used it as an opportunity to berate the King with their complaints. One of the main protagonists was John Pym, who would soon become the leader of Parliament. A staunch Puritan he championed Parliamentary freedom. In addressing the King he identified three great liberties: religion, justice and the privilege of Parliament, calling Parliament "the fountain of law, the great council of the kingdom, the highest court ... to prevent evils to come ... and remove evils present".

Charles dismissed Parliament after three weeks but, in dire need of funds and his war with Scotland failing, he summoned Parliament again in November 1640. This time Parliament passed a law stating that it could not be dissolved without its own approval.

The Wars of the Three Kingdoms

As the Civil War progressed, Charles hoped to gather support from the Catholics in Ireland. For the last century, and especially during the reigns of Elizabeth and James I, settlers, mostly Protestant, had been granted land in Ireland confiscated from the Catholic owners. In 1641, various disaffected landowners rebelled, forming the Irish Catholic Federation. They sought to negotiate with Charles I hoping that, with their support, he would treat the Catholics favourably in the event of his victory. The conflict in Ireland, together with the English Civil War with Parliamentarian support from the Scots, has led historians to call them the Wars of the Three Kingdoms. Their battle would lead to savage retribution by the English.

Charles had to listen to their grievances again, presented this time in a long document called the Grand Remonstrance, prepared by Pym. This was perhaps too radical for some Parliamentarians whose sympathies shifted to the King. Charles tried to ignore the document but in the end promised to consider it. His true designs were clear, though, when Charles tried to arrest Pym and four other Members in January 1642 on grounds of treason, sending soldiers into the House of Commons. He failed and soon after Parliament passed its own Militia Bill without Royal Assent, effectively taking control of the land forces. The momentum was gathering towards Civil War.

When Charles I raised his standard in the market town of Wellington in September 1642 he declared, somewhat belatedly, that he would "uphold the Protestant Religion, the Laws of England, and the Liberty of Parliament".

The Petition of Right. Produced by Sir Edward Coke in 1628, this was virtually a new Magna Carta as it restated the basic principles of rights and privileges which Charles I had been ignoring.

Parliamentary Archives, HL/PO/PU/1/1627/3c1n2

Soit droit fait come est desire.

Kings most Excellent Maiestie

rall, and Comons in Parliament assembled. That whereas it is declared and enacted by a Statute made in the tyme
Tallage, or Ayde should be layde, or levyed by the King or his heires in this Realme, without the good will and assent of the
this Realme . And by authority of Parliament houlden in the five and twentith yeare of the raigne
pelled to make any Loanes to the King against his will, because such loanes were against reason and the franchise
ny charge, or imposition called a Benevolence, nor by such like charge . By which the Statutes before mentioned, and
ey should not be compelled to contribute to any Tax, Tallage, Ayde or other like charge not sett by comon consent
verall Counties with instructions haue issued. By meanes whereof your people haue been in divers places assembled, and required
haue had an oath administred unto them not warrantable by the Lawes or Statutes of this Realme, and haue
ouncell, and in other places, and others of them haue been therefore imprisoned, confined and sundry other wayes
in severall Counties by Lord Lieftenants, deputie Lieftenants, Comissioners for Musters, Justices of Peace and
and free customes of the Realme . And where also by the Statute called the Greate Charter of the liberties
isseised of his freehould or liberties, or his free customes, or be outlawed, or exiled or in any manner destroyed
and Twentith yeare of the raigne of King Edward the third, It was declared and enacted by authority of
his land, or tenements, nor taken nor imprisoned nor disherited, nor putt to death without being brought
other the good Lawes and Statutes of yo Realme to that end provided, divers of your Subiects haue of late been
fore yo Justices by yo Maiesties writts of *Habeas corpus* there to undergoe and receive as the Court should
but that they were deteyned by yo Maiesties speciall comaund signified by the Lords of yo Privy Councell, and
y might make answer according to the Lawe . And whereas of late greate Companyes of Souldiers and
their wills haue been compelled to receive them into their howses, and there to suffer them to soiourne against the
And whereas also by authority of Parliament, in the five and twentith yeare of the raigne of King Edward
he forme of the Great Charter and the Lawe of the land . And by the said Greate Charter and other the Lawes and
this yo Realme, either by the customes of the same Realme, or by Acts of Parliament . And whereas no offender
awes and Statuts of this your Realme . Neverthelesse of late tyme divers Comissions under yo Maiesties Greate
d with power and authority to proceede within the land according to the Justice of Martiall Lawe against such
Robbery, felony, mutiny, or other outrage or misdemeanor whatsoever, and by such summary course and order as is
ndemnation of such offenders, and them to cause to be executed and putt to death according to the Lawe Martiall
ath when, and where if by the Lawes and Statuts of the land they had deserved death, by the same Lawes and
grevious offenders by colloꝛ thereof, clayming an exemption haue escaped the punishments due to them by the
haue unjustly refused, or forborne to proceede against such offenders according to the same Lawes and Statuts, upon
omissions as aforesaid . Which Comissions, and all other of like nature are wholly and directly contrary to the said

man hereafter be compelled to make or yeild any guifte loane benevolence, tax or such like charge without comon consent
wer or take such oath, or to give attendance, or be confined, or otherwise molested, or disquieted concerning the same, or
beforementioned be imprisoned or deteyned . And that yo Maiestie would be pleased to remove the said Souldiers and
tyme . And that the aforesaid Comissions for proceeding by Martiall Lawe may be revoked and annulled . And that
on, or persons whatsoever to be executed as aforesaid, least by colloꝛ of them any of yo Maiesties subiects be destroyed

s theire rights and liberties according to the Lawes and Statuts of this Realme . And that yo Maiestie would alsoe
e to the preiudice of your people in any of the premisses shall not be drawne hereafter into consequence or example
ther comfort and safety of yo people to declare yo Royall will and pleasure That in the things aforesaid all yo officers
his Realme, as they tender the honor of yo Maiestie and the prosperity of this Kingdome

Agreement of the People

The struggle against the King saw the need for a peace agreement that might serve as a constitution. Various factions put forward their proposals, including the Levellers, who produced a remarkably modern approach to liberty: the Agreement of the People.

Opposite:
The Agreement of the People. This is the second version presented to Parliament in January 1649.
BL, Egerton MS 1048, f.91

The Solemn League and Covenant agreed between the English and Scottish Parliaments in September 1643 brought the Scottish army into the English Civil War and shifted the overall balance. Previously, Charles's Royalist forces had the upper hand with further promise of support from the Irish Catholic Confederation, which was fighting Parliamentarian forces in Ireland. However, at the battles of Naseby and Langport in June and July 1645, with the emergence of the Parliamentarian New Model Army under Thomas Fairfax and Oliver Cromwell, the Royalists suffered major losses. Charles I's surrender in May 1646 concluded the first phase of the Civil War, though he rejected all proposals intended to bring a peace. However, he did reach a secret agreement with the Scots regarding Presbyterianism in England, which incensed the English Parliament.

There was also growing unrest between Parliament and the New Model Army, many of whom were still awaiting payment. It was important to reach a constitutional agreement with the King. The Council of the Army, under Henry Ireton, put forward a draft document, the "Heads of Proposals", based largely on old constitutional principles. A more radical proposal, the "Agreement of the People", came from extremists in the army, known as the Agitators, and their political allies, the Levellers. A debate about both documents was held during the autumn of 1647 at Putney, where the New Model Army was based, chaired by Oliver Cromwell. The discussion found itself focussing on who should have the vote. Ireton and his Proposals had gone for householder suffrage, whilst the Levellers were after a wider franchise including small traders and craftsmen. During the debate there was a lengthy exchange between Ireton and Leveller supporter Colonel Thomas Rainsborough who went so far as to say: *I think that the poorest he that is in England hath a life to live as the greatest he; and therefore truly, Sir, I think it's clear that every man that is to live under a Government ought first by his own consent to put himself under that Government.*

When Parliament discussed the "Agreement of the People" it dismissed it as "destructive to the being of Parliaments, and to the fundamental government of the kingdom." The original Agreement had been written in haste and not all Levellers agreed with it. It was twice revised, the final version completed by the leaders of the

The True Levellers

In 1649 the True Levellers, or Diggers, began the first communist movement. They believed that true liberty meant land was free to everyone. They moved onto enclosed land in Surrey to grow vegetables. At this time food was in short supply and expensive. The landowner had them ejected and similar groups across the country found landowners and Parliament unsympathetic. The movement was over within two years.

Irish atrocities

In the Irish Confederate War of 1641-52, over 600,000 people were killed – almost half the population of Ireland and mainly Catholics. Amongst the atrocities was Cromwell's massacre of the Royalist garrison at Drogheda in September 1649. Few of the 3,100 survived. Some took refuge in a Church which was burned down and all who fled were killed. Cromwell declared that his actions had been "... by the assistance of God, to hold forth and maintain the lustre and glory of English liberty in a nation where we have an undoubted right to it."

An Agreement of the people of England and the places therewith incorporated, for a secure and present peace, upon grounds of common right, freedome and safetie.

Having by our late labours and hazards made it appeare to the world att how high a rate wee value our just freedome, And God having soe farre owned our cause as to deliver the Enemies thereof into our hands, Wee doe now hold our selves bound in mutuall dutie to each other to take the best care wee can for the future to avoide both the danger of returning into a slavish condition, and the chargeable remedy of another warre. for as it cannot bee imagined, That soe many of our Countrymen would have opposed us in this quarrell, if they had understood their owne good, Soe may wee hopefully promise to our selves that when our common right and liberties shall bee cleared their endeavours will bee disappointed that seeke to make themselves our Masters. Since therefore our former oppressions, and not yett ended troubles have bin occasioned, either by want of frequent Nationall meetings in Councell, or by the undue or unequall constitution thereof, or by rendring those meetings ineffectuall, Wee are fullie agreed and resolved (God willing) to provide, That hereafter our Representatives bee neither left to an uncertaintie for time nor bee unequallie constituted, nor made uselesse to the ends for which they are intended.

In order whereunto wee declare and agree.

1 **That** to prevent the manie inconveniencies apparentlie arising from the long continuance of the same persons in supreame authoritie, This present parliament end and dissolve uppon or before the last day of Aprill, in the yeare of our Lord, One Thousand, Six hundred and fourtie nine.

2 **That** the people of England being att this day verie unequallie distributed, by Counties, Citties, and Burroughes, for the Election of their Representatives bee indifferentlie proportioned. And to this end, That the Representative of the whole Nation shall consist of fower Hundred persons, or not above, And in each Countie and the places thereto subjoyned, there shall bee chosen to make upp the said Representative att all times, the severall numbers hereunder mentioned, (vizt)

In

The Countie of Kent, with the Burroughes, Townes, and parishes therein, Except such as are hereunder particularlie named	Ten.	10.
The Cittie of Canterburie with the suburbs adjoyning and liberties thereof	Two.	2.
The Cittie of Rochester with the parishes of Chatham and Stroude	One	1.
The Cinque ports in Kent and Sussex, viz. Dover, Rumney, Hyde, Sandwich, Hastings, Rye and Winchelsey	three	3.
The Countie of Sussex with the Burroughes, Townes, and parishes therein (Except Chichester)	Eight.	8.
The Cittie of Chichester with the suburbs and liberties thereof	One.	1.
The Countie of Southampton with the Burroughes, Townes, and parishes therein, (Except such as are hereunder named)	Eight.	8.
The Cittie of Winchester	One	1.
The Countie of the Towne of Southampton	One	1.
The Countie of Dorset with the Burroughes, Townes, and parishes therein (Except Dorchester)	Seaven.	7.
The Towne of Dorchester	One	1.
The Countie of Devon with the Burroughes, Townes, and parishes therein (Except such as are hereunder particularlie named)	Twelve	12.
The Cittie of Exceter	Two	2.
The Towne of Plimouth	Two	2.
The Towne of Barnstaple	One	1.
The Countie of Cornewall with the Burroughes, Townes, and parishes therein	Eight.	8.
The Countie of Somersett with the Burroughes, Townes, and parishes therein, (Except such as are hereunder particularlie named)	Eight.	8.
The Cittie of Bristoll	Three	3.
The Towne of Taunton Deane	One	1.
The Countie of Wilts with the Burroughes, Townes, and parishes therein (Except Salisbury)	Seaven	7.
The Cittie of Salisbury	One	1.
The Countie of Berkes with the Burroughes, Townes and parishes therein (Except Reading)	Five	5.
The Towne of Reading	One	1.
The Countie of Surrey with the Burroughes, Townes, and parishes therein (Except Southwarke)	Five	5.
The Burrough of Southwarke	Two	2.
The Countie of Midd. with the Burroughes, Townes, and parishes therein (Except such as are hereunder named)	fower.	4.
The Cittie of London	Eight.	8.
The Cittie of Westminster, and the Duchy	Two.	2.
The Countie of Hertford with the Burroughes, Townes, and parishes therein	Sixe.	6.
The Countie of Buckingham with the Burroughes, Townes, and parishes therein	Sixe	6.
The Countie of Oxon with the Burroughes, Townes, and parishes therein (Except such as are hereunder named)	fower	4.
The Cittie of Oxon	Two.	2.
The Universitie of Oxon	Two.	2.
The Countie of Gloucester with the Burroughes, Townes, and parishes therein (Except Gloucester)	Seaven	7.
The Cittie of Gloucester	Two	2.
The Countie of Hereford with the Burroughes, Townes, and parishes therein (Except Hereford)	fower	4.
The Cittie of Hereford	Two.	2.
The Countie of Worcester with the Burroughes, Townes, and parishes therein (Except Worcester)	fower	4.
The Cittie of Worcester	Two.	2
The Countie of Warwick with the Burroughes, Townes, and parishes therein (Except Coventry)	ffive	5.
The Cittie of Coventry	Two.	2
The Countie of Northampton with the Burroughes, Townes, and parishes therein (Except Northampton)	ffive	5.
The Towne of Northampton	One.	1
The Countie of Bedford with the Burroughes, Townes and parishes therein	ffower	4.
The County of Carnarvan with the Burroughs and parishes therein	Two	2.
The County of Denbigh with the Burroughs and parishes therein	Two	2.
The County of fflint with the Burroughs and parishes therein	One	1.
The County of Monmouth with the Burroughs and parishes therein	ffower	4.

The Countie of Cambridge with the Burroughes, Townes, and parishes therein (except such as are hereunder particularlie named)	ffower	4
The Universitie of Cambridge	Two	2
The Towne of Cambridge	Two.	2
The Countie of Essex, with the Burroughes, Townes, and parishes therein (Except Colchester)	Eleven	11.
The Towne of Colchester	Two	2
The Countie of Suffolk with the Burroughes, Townes, and parishes therein (Except such as are hereunder named)	Ten	10
The Towne of Ipswich	Two	2
The Towne of St Edmunds Bury	One	1.
The Countie of Norfolke with the Burroughes, Townes, and parishes therein (Except such as are hereunder named)	Nine	9.
The Cittie of Norwich	Three	3.
The Towne of Lynne	One	1.
The Towne of Yarmouth	One	1.
The Countie of Lincolne with the Burroughes, Townes and parishes therein (Except such as are hereunder named)	Eleven	11
The Cittie and Countie of the Cittie of Lincolne	One	1.
The Towne of Boston	One	1
The Countie of Rutland with the Burroughes, Townes, and parishes therein	One	1.
The Countie of Huntington with the Burroughs Townes and parishes therein	Three	3.
The Countie of Leicester with the Burroughs Townes and parishes therein (Except Leicester	ffive	5
The Towne of Leicester	One	1
The Countie of Nottingham with the Burroughs Townes and parishes therein (Except Nottingham)	ffower	4
The Towne of Nottingham	One	1
The Countie of Derby with the Burroughs Townes and parishes therein (Except Derby)	ffive	5
The Towne of Derby	One	1
The Countie of Stafford with the Cittie of Litchfeild the Burroughs Townes and parishes therein	Sixe	6
The Countie of Salop with the Burroughs Townes and parishes therein (Except Shrewsbury	Six	6
The Towne of Shrewsbury	One	1
The Countie of Chester with the Burroughs Townes and parishes therein (Except Chester)	ffive	5
The Cittie of Chester	One	1
The County of Lancaster with the Burroughs Townes and parishes therein (Except Manchester)	Six.	6
The Towne of Manchester	One	1
The Countie of Yorke with the Burroughs Townes and parishes therein (Except such as are hereunder named	ffifteene	15
The Citty and County of the Cittie of Yorke	Three	3
The Towne and Countie of Kingston uppon Hull	One	1
The Towne and parish of Leeds	One	1
The Countie Palataine of Durham with the Burroughs Townes and parishes therein (Except Durham and Gateside	Three	3
The Cittie of Durham	One	1
The Countie of Northumberland with the Burroughs Townes and parishes therein (Except such as are hereunder named)	Three	3
The Towne and Countie of Newcastle uppon Tyne with Gateside	Two	2
The Towne of Barwick	One	1
The County of Cumberland with the Burroughs Townes and parishes therein	Three	3
The County of Westmorland with the Burroughs Townes and parishes therein	Two	2
The Isle of Anglsey with the parishes therein	Two	2
The Countie of Brecknock with the Burroughs Townes and parishes therein	Three	3
The Countie of Cardigan with the Burroughs and parishes therein	Three	3
The Countie of Caermarthen with the Burroughs and parishes therein	Three	3
The Countie of Glamorgan with the Burroughs, and parishes therein	ffower	4
The Countie of Merioneth with the Burroughs and parishes therein	Two	2
The Countie of Mountgomery with the Burroughs and parishes therein	Three	3
The Countie of Radnor with the Burroughs and parishes therein	Two	2
The Countie of Pembrooke with the Burroughs and parishes therein	ffower	4.

Provided, That the first or second Representative may (if they see cause) assigne the remainder of the fower Hundred Representors (not hereby assigned) or soe many of them as they shall see cause for unto such Counties as shall appeare in the present distribution to have lesse then there due proportion. Provided also that where any Cittie or Burrough to which one Representor or more is assigned shalbe found in a due proportion not Competent alone to elect a Representor, or the number of Representors assigned thereto, it is left to future Representatives to assigne such a number of parishes or villages neare adjoyning to such Cittie or Burrough to be joyned therewith in the Elections as may make the same proportionable.

3 **That** the people doe of course choose themselves a Representative once in two yeares and shall meet for that purpose uppon the first Thursday in every second May by eleven of Clock in the Morning and the Representatives soe chosen to meete uppon the second Thursday in June following at the usuall place in Westminster or such other place as by the foregoing Representative or the Councell of State in the intervall shall bee from time to time appointed and published to the people at the least twenty dayes before the time of Election And to Continue their session there or else where untill the second Thursday in December following unlesse they shall adjourne or dissolve themselves sooner But not to Continue longer. The Election of the first Representative to be one the first Thursday in May 1649 And that all future Elections to be according to the rules prescribed for the same purpose in this Agreement, vizt.

1 **That** the electors in every Division shall be natives or Denizons of England not persons receiving Almes, but such as are assessed ordinarilie towards the releife of the poore not servants to and receiving wages from any particular person and in all Elections (Except for the Universities) they shall bee men of one and twentie yeares old, or uppwards and Housekeepers dwelling within the division for which the Election is provided. That untill the end of seaven yeares next ensuing the time heerin lymitted for the end of this present parliament noe person shall be admitted to or have any hand or voyce in such Elections who hath adhered unto or assisted the King against the Parliament in any the late warres or insurrections or who shall make or joyne in or abett any forcible opposition against this Agreement.

2 That such persons and such onlie [illegible] who have not voluntarilie assisted the Parliament against the King [illegible] the fourth of June [illegible] or abetted the Treasonable engagement in London in the yeare [illegible] or engaged themselves for a Cessation of Armes [illegible] uppon the propositions [illegible] of May 1648 or who have joyned [illegible]

[illegible]

4 That one Hundred and fiftie Members at least bee alwayes present in each sitting of the Representative [illegible]

That each Representative shall within twentie dayes after their first meeting appoint [illegible]

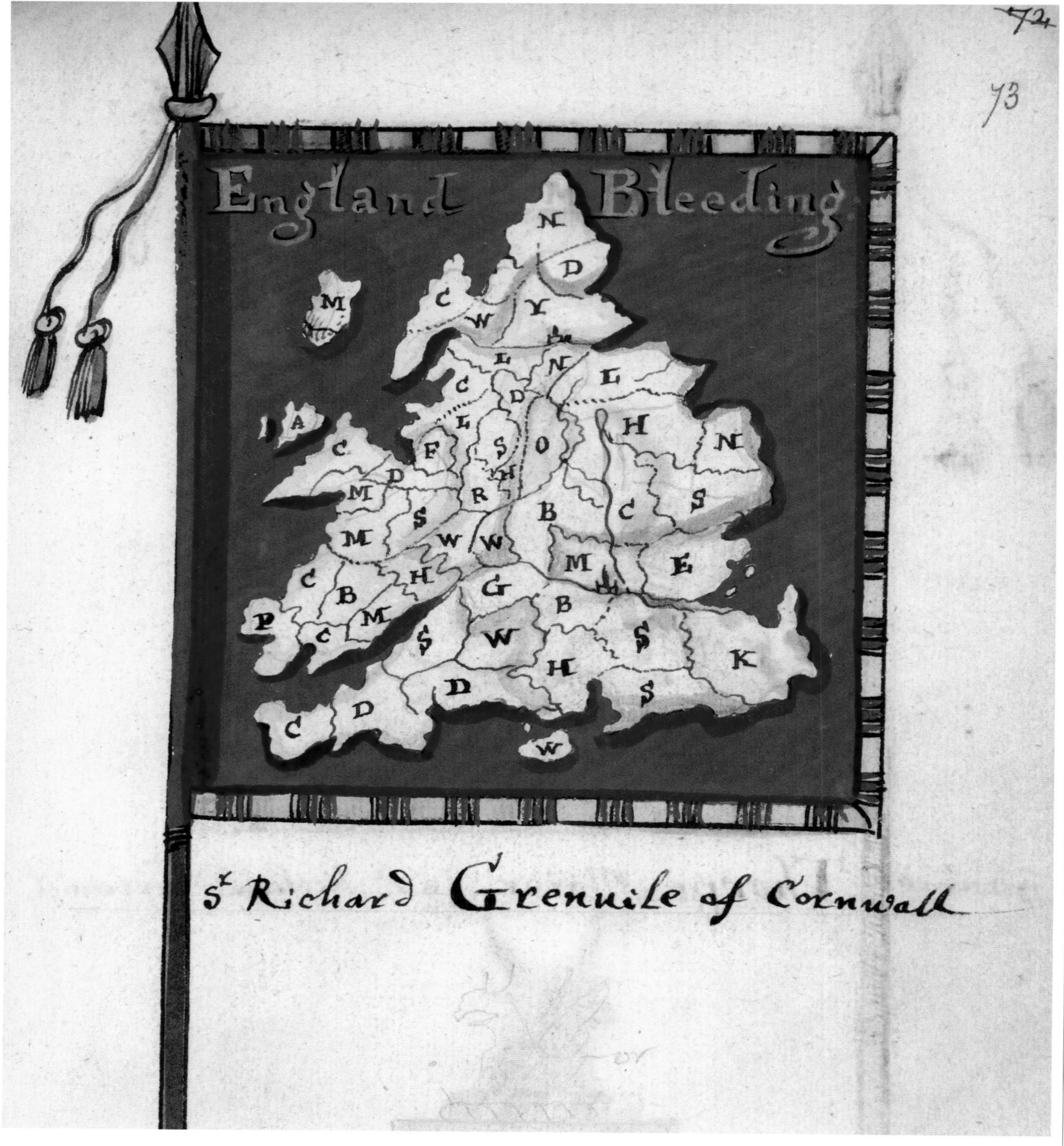

The cornet, or cavalry banner, of Sir Richard Grenville when he served briefly in the Parliamentary army. The motto "England Bleeding" denotes his views towards the war. He took the first opportunity to switch to the Royalists in 1644 and spent much of the War defending Cornwall.
BL, Add. MS 5247, f.73r

Levellers – John Lilburne, William Walwyn, Thomas Prince and Richard Overton – while they were imprisoned in the Tower of London charged with treason and inciting mutiny.

Fundamental to the Agreement was what the Levellers called native or natural rights:

- freedom of worship
- freedom from compulsory conscription
- all men should be treated as equal under the law
- all laws should be good and not detrimental to the well-being of individuals.

In addition, they advocated the following political rights:

- suffrage for all men aged 21 and over, except servants, beggars or Royalists
- annual Parliamentary elections, and Members serve only one term
- no one to be punished for refusing to testify against themselves (i.e. the right to remain silent)
- all those on trial have the right to call witnesses in their defence
- trials to be in front of twelve sworn men of the neighbourhood, freely chosen
- no hindrance to free trade
- no one to be imprisoned for debt
- death penalty abolished except for murder.

When the Agreement was discussed by Parliament in January 1649, it was set aside because of the trial of the King and was not discussed again. Except for annual Parliaments, all would be achieved– but not for some 300 years.

Death of a King

In 1649 Parliament achieved the unthinkable when it tried and executed the ruling monarch, establishing a complete break with the past.

German engraving of the execution of Charles I.
The executioner wore a mask and was not identified, although tradition states that it was an Irish soldier, James Gunning, as no Englishman would undertake the task.
BL, Crach.1.Tab.4.c.1(18)

The Civil War reached the end of its next phase with the trial and execution of the King in January 1649. The charges against Charles were noted in a special Act of Parliament, namely that he "had a wicked design totally to subvert the ancient and fundamental laws and liberties of this nation", and that he had "levied and maintained a civil war in the land..." The latter was the equivalent of treason, though the basis for it was weak.

The decision that the King would have to be executed and the monarchy abolished had come to Cromwell once he realised the gulf between King and Parliament could never be bridged. There was not much support for it in Parliament, which had to be purged of royalist sympathisers, to leave a core (known as the Rump Parliament) of 80 MPs. The House of Lords refused to acknowledge the process and the House of Commons took the unprecedented step of excluding the Lords and acting on its own. It was this reduced Rump Parliament that voted through the ordinance agreeing the King's trial. The reduced Parliament was, in effect, a High Court of Justice. The King refused to acknowledge the court or the charges and did not testify on his own behalf. The trial and its legal basis corrupted the very freedoms and liberties over which the Civil War had been fought.

His execution was on a cold and solemn day and the assembled crowd groaned as the axe severed his head. Charles had borne his final moments with great dignity, claiming he was a "martyr of the people". The execution not only severed his head from his body, but severed the link with the old-style of feudal and all-powerful monarch. Although the monarchy would be restored eleven years later, and although there had to be another revolution in 1688, to the country the King was no longer unassailable. No matter how illegally it was achieved, Parliament had asserted its own right.

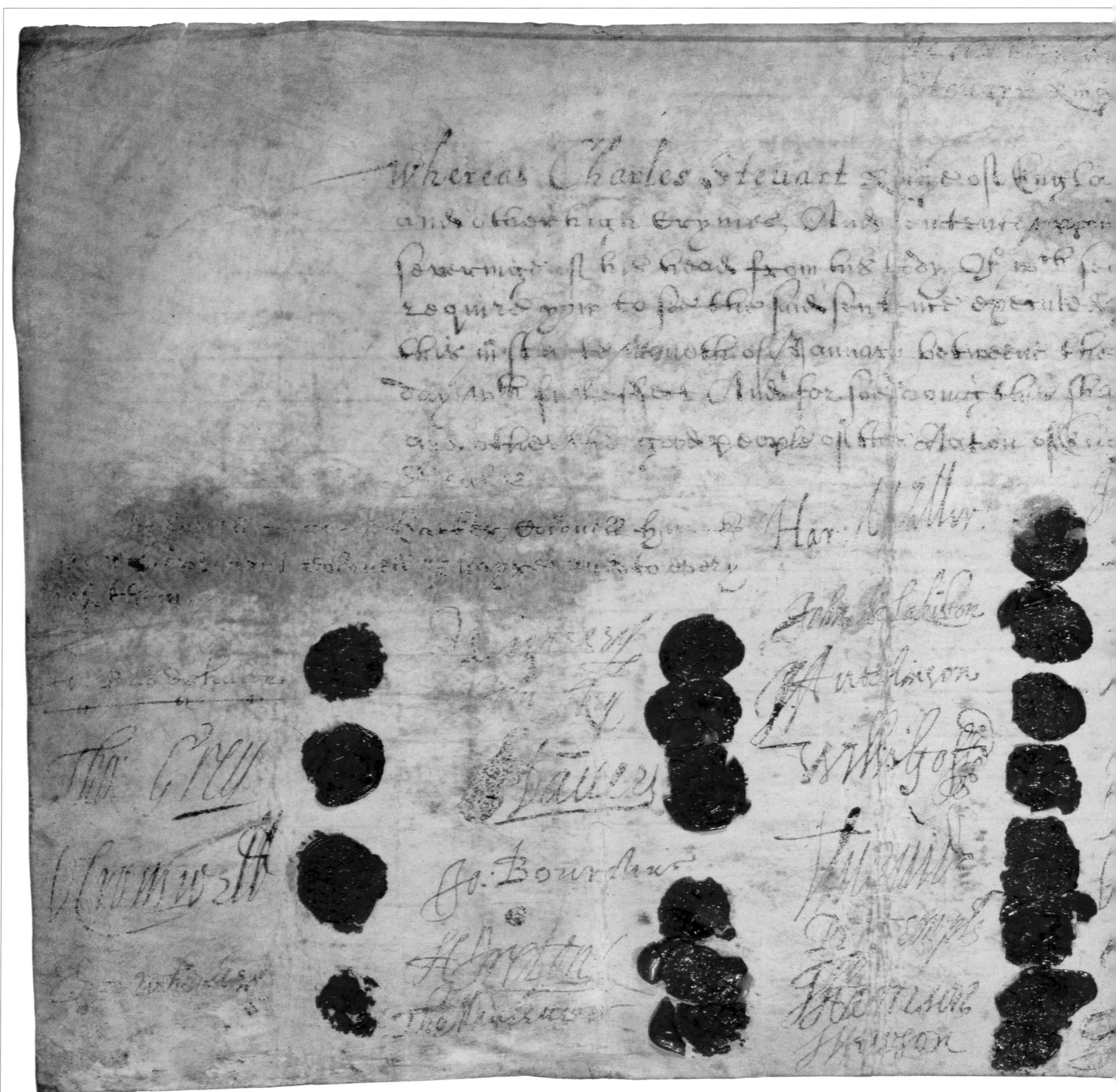

Charles I's Death Warrant. Some 59 individuals signed the death warrant, but after the Restoration of the Monarchy in 1660 only 38 were still alive. A few had fled the country, but of the others nine were executed and fifteen were imprisoned. Only one, Richard Ingoldsby, was pardoned and allowed to keep his lands. He claimed Cromwell had seized his hand and forced him to sign.
Parliamentary Archives, HL/PO/JO/10/297A

A British Constitution?

Under Oliver Cromwell the country was governed for the first time under a formal Constitution, the Instrument of Government, although its days were not to last. This was also when theatres were closed, Christmas was banned and the country was monitored for any ungodly behaviour.

From 1649 Parliament governed England as a Commonwealth, but Cromwell was dissatisfied with how little was being achieved. In December 1653 he established a Protectorate with himself as Lord Protector. A Council of State was created and a written constitution produced, called the Instrument of Government. This was partly derived from the "Heads of Proposals" and other documents discussed in the Putney Debates, but included new material.

For the first time it united England, Wales, Scotland and Ireland under a single system of government. It detailed the roles, responsibilities and limitations of the Lord Protector, his Council of State (with 21 non-elected members) and Parliament (with 460 elected members representing all four constituent "nations").

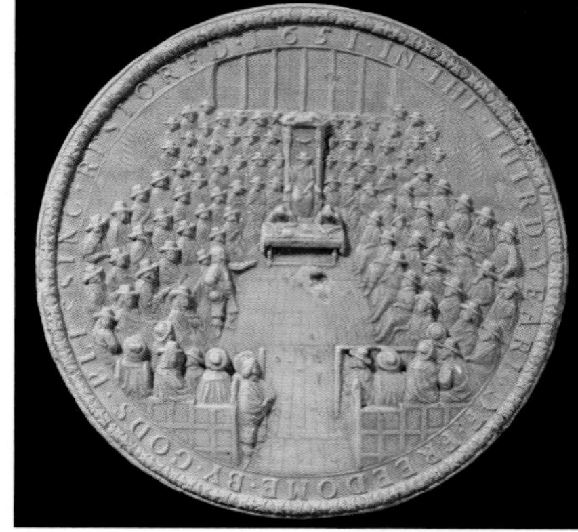

An impression of the Second Commonwealth Seal showing the interior of the House of Commons during session. Originally produced in 1651.
BL, Add. MS Ch. 34941

It extended the vote to all individuals whose estate was valued at £200 or more, provided they were not Catholics or Anglicans, had not fought for the Royalists or supported the Irish Rebellion. With the same exceptions, anyone of good character over the age of 21 was eligible for being elected to Parliament, which would run for three years.

It allowed for a regular standing army of 30,000 men, with scope for a larger army if security demanded. It also allowed for a permanent navy, though its size was not stipulated.

It recognised a degree of religious tolerance, provided such did not disturb the peace, though again this did not extend to Catholics or Anglicans.

One phrase in the Instrument of Government has come to typify Puritan rule, namely that such freedoms did not extend to those who "hold forth and practice licentiousness". To the Puritans, the nation's liberty and prosperity depended on good, clean living. As early as 1642, the Puritan Parliament had instigated a series of restrictions aimed at purifying people's mind and soul. These included closing theatres, brothels, gaming-houses and unlicensed ale-houses, banning such celebrations as May Day and Christmas, and all sports involving animals. Sunday was to be strictly observed as a Holy Day, with other days set aside for relaxation and fasting. Under the Protectorate, the country was monitored to put a stop to "all profaneness and ungodliness". People could be fined or imprisoned for drunkenness, swearing or sexual promiscuity.

The Instrument of Government was superseded by the "Humble

Be it Declared and Enacted by this present Parliament and by the Authoritie of the same That the People of England and of all the Dominions and Territoryes thereunto belonging are and shall be and are hereby Constituted made established and confirmed to be a Commonwealth and Free State And shall from henceforth be Governed as a Commonwealth and Free State by the Supreame Authoritie of this Nation the Representatives of the People in Parliament and by such as they shall appoint and constitute as Officers and Ministers under them for the good of the People and that without any King or House of Lords.

It took only a few words of this Act of 19 May 1649 to change England from a kingdom to a "Commonwealth and Free State".
National Archives, C204/9

v. Scobell, p. 451.

111 115

The Lord Protectors Oath.

I doe in the Presence and by the name of God Almighty promise and sweare That to the vttermost of my Power I will vphold and mainteyne the true Reformed Protestant Christian Religion in the purity thereof as it is conteyned in the holy Scriptures of the old and New Testament to the vttermost of my Power and Vnderstanding and encourage the Profession and Professors of the same; And that to the vtmost of my Power, I will endeavour as Cheife Magistrate of these three Nations the maintenance and preservacon of the Peace and Safetie and of the iust rights and priviledges of the People thereof, And shall in all things according to my best Knowledge and Power governe the People of these Nations according to Law.

His Highnes Oliuer Cromwell Lord Protector of the Comonwealth of England Scotland & Ireland & of the Dominions & Territoryes therevnto belonging tooke the Oath abouewritten on the xxvj th day of June 1657 in Westminster hall, where the same was administred vnto Him by the Speaker of the Parliament in ye presence of the Parliament, his Highnes Councill, diuerse Earls & noble persons, the Officers of State, the Judges, the Mayor & Aldermen of the City of London & a great multitude of the Nobility, Officers of the Army Gentry and People: besides seuerall Ambassadors of forraigne Princes & States.

The oath taken by Oliver Cromwell as Lord Protector, in Westminster Hall on 26 June 1657.
BL, Egerton MS 1048, f.115

This medal depicts Oliver Cromwell before the battlefield at Dunbar. It was given to all who fought at Dunbar in September 1650 where Cromwell's army had a major victory at the start of his campaign against Scotland.
British Museum, CMG3, E.M.309

Petition" in May 1657, replacing a document of military origin with one drawn up and formally approved by Parliament. This introduced a second chamber, the "Upper House" of between 40 and 70 members selected by the Lord Protector but approved by Parliament. It also proposed that the Lord Protector be made King, but Cromwell refused.

The Protectorate did not last. When Cromwell died in September 1658 his son, Richard, despite his competence, never received the full support of the military and soon other factions weakened his position. The military took over, but others demanded the recall of the original Members of Parliament, dismissed in 1653. This re-established a Royalist majority. Following elections, the government accepted the terms of Charles II and the monarchy was restored in May 1660. The Scots had already crowned Charles as their King in 1650, which had led to retribution by Cromwell. Charles II was treated as having succeeded upon his father's death so that all Acts passed since 1649 were null and void.

The United Kingdom

England, Scotland and Ireland had been united under the Protectorate, but, with the Restoration of the monarchy, the former system was re-established. With a single King it was likely that over time the individual nations would be drawn together under one Parliament, but it still took another 140 years.

Die Martis 12° Februarii 1688
The Declaration of the Lords Spirituall and Temporall and Commons Assembled at Westm[r]
Whereas the late King James the second by the assistance of diverse evill Councellors Judges and Ministers imployed by him did endeavour to subvert and extirpate the Protestant Religion and the Lawes and Liberties of this Kingdome.
By assumeing and exerciseing a Power of dispencing with and suspending of Lawes and the execution of Lawes without consent of Parliament.
By committing and prosecuteing diverse worthy Prelates for humbly petitioning to be excused from concurring to the said assumed Power
By issueing and causing to be executed a commission under the Great Seale for erecting a Court called the Court of Comissioners for Ecclesiasticall causes.
By levying money for and to the use of the Crowne by pretence of Prerogative for other time and in other manner then the same was granted by Parliament.
By raiseing and keeping a standing Army within this Kingdome in time of Peace without consent of Parliament and quartering Souldiers contrary to Law.
By causeing severall good subjects being Protestants to be disarmed at [illegible]
By violateing the [illegible] Members to serve in Parliament
~~By causeing [illegible] and prosecuted in the [illegible] for matters and causes [illegible] ament and by diverse other [illegible] illegall courses.~~ By Prosecutions [illegible] of Kings Bench for matters and causes cognizable only in Parliament and by diverse other arbitrary and illegall courses.

The Declaration of Rights was approved by Parliament on 12 February 1689. It was formally enacted on 16 December 1689 as the Bill of Rights.

Parliamentary Archives, HL/PO/JO/10/1/403D

Although Charles II was Anglican, he married a Catholic, and his brother, the future James II, was openly Catholic. Parliament tried to pass an Exclusion Bill to stop Catholics inheriting the throne, but Charles II barred it. James II used his prerogative to issue a Declaration of Indulgence, restoring all rights to Catholics. With the birth of a Catholic heir in June 1688, a group of English statesmen and other dignitaries, the "Immortal Seven", sent a secret invitation offering the throne to William of Orange, who had married James's daughter, Mary. When William landed in England, James fled to France, and then Ireland where he remained King until defeated at the Battle of the Boyne in July 1690.

In England, a provisional Parliament issued a Declaration of Rights in February 1689 condemning the actions of James II as "contrary to the known laws and statutes and freedom of this realm". The Declaration was read to William and Mary and their acceptance effectively sealed a contract between the English people and the King. The Declaration was ratified by a formal Parliament in December 1689 as the Bill of Rights. The Scottish Parliament approved it as the Claim of Right.

The Bill of Rights limited the royal prerogative and established the supremacy of Parliament. Most of the rights covered had been raised before, notably under the Petition of Rights, but not all had been enshrined in law. These included:

- the King could not suspend or create laws without the consent of Parliament
- the King could not raise taxes by royal prerogative or without the

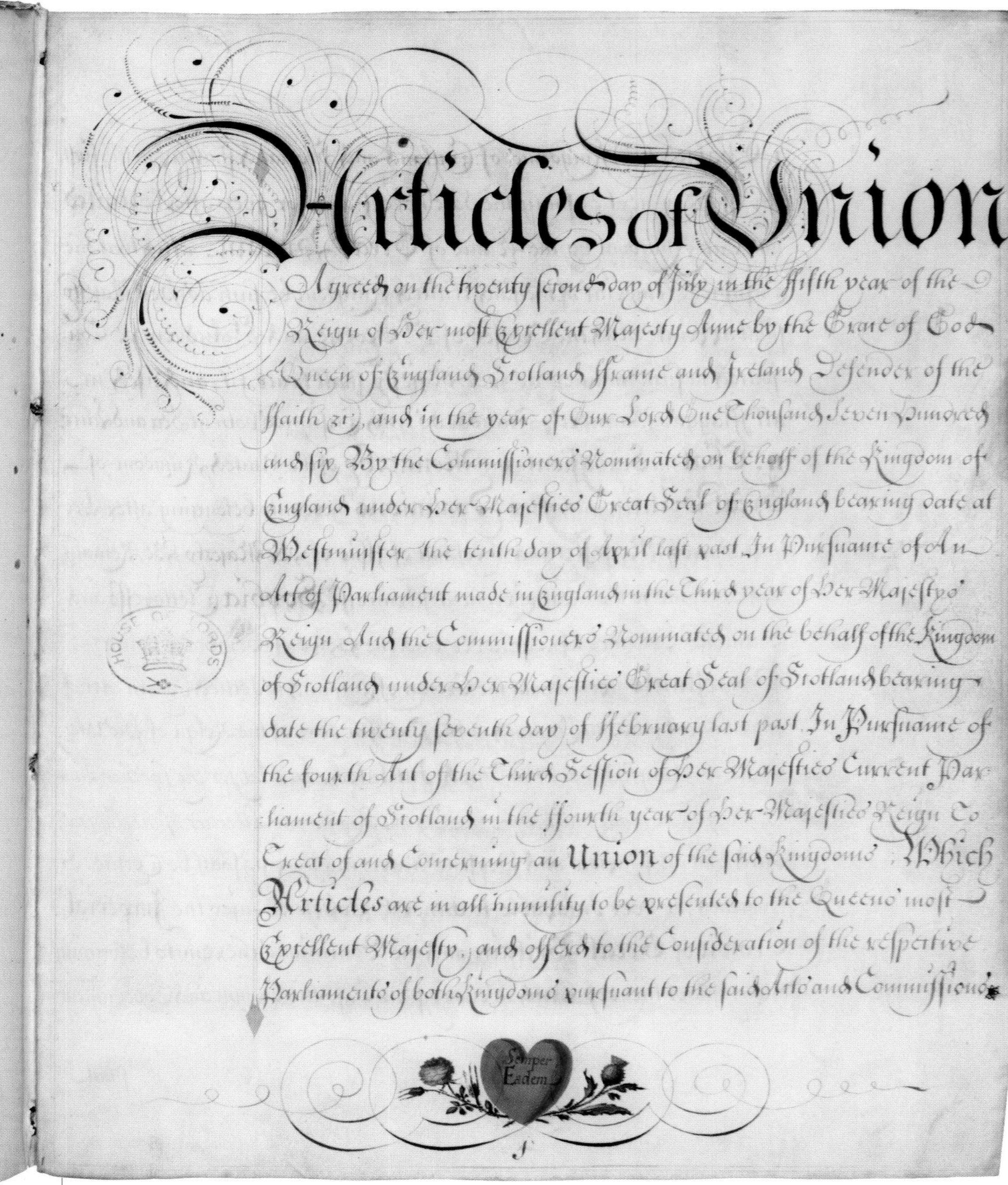

Articles of Union

Agreed on the twenty second day of July in the Fifth year of the Reign of Her most Excellent Majesty Anne by the Grace of God Queen of England Scotland France and Ireland Defender of the Faith &c. and in the year of Our Lord One Thousand Seven Hundred and six By the Commissioners Nominated on behalf of the Kingdom of England under Her Majesties Great Seal of England bearing date at Westminster the tenth day of April last past In Pursuance of an Act of Parliament made in England in the Third year of Her Majestys Reign And the Commissioners Nominated on the behalf of the Kingdom of Scotland under Her Majesties Great Seal of Scotland bearing date the twenty seventh day of February last past In Pursuance of the fourth Act of the Third Session of Her Majesties Current Parliament of Scotland in the fourth year of Her Majesties Reign To Treat of and Concerning an Union of the said Kingdoms Which Articles are in all humility to be presented to the Queens most Excellent Majesty and offered to the Consideration of the respective Parliaments of both Kingdoms pursuant to the said Acts and Commissions

Semper Eadem

The Articles of Union were the result of lengthy negotiations, and were finally agreed on 22 July 1706. They took months to be approved by the Scottish Parliament but passed quickly through the English Parliament and became the Act of Union in May 1707.

Parliamentary Archives, HL/PO/JO/10/6/106/2307

consent of Parliament

- the King could not raise a standing army in peace time without the consent of Parliament
- the people could petition the king without being prosecuted
- Parliaments should be held frequently.

The Bill dealt mostly with constitutional matters, but it did include a few civil rights, which only applied to Protestants. Two were of particular significance:

- Freedom of speech and debates or proceedings in Parliament ought not to be questioned in any court or place out of Parliament. This is a crucial Parliamentary privilege first raised by Thomas More and agreed by Henry VIII in 1523.
- Protestants may have arms for their defence suitable to their conditions and as allowed by law. This was the basis of the "right to bear arms" in the American constitution.

A Triennial Act in 1694 set the maximum life of each Parliament at three years (this was changed to seven years in 1716 and five years in 1911). It also ensured that monarchs could not dissolve Parliament at their whim.

Queen Mary died childless in 1694 and by 1700 it was likely that her sister, Anne, would have no surviving children. The 1701 Act of Settlement restated that there would be no Catholic succession, and specified that the Crown passed to the heirs of James I's Protestant grand-daughter Sophia, Electress of Hanover, which is how George I became King in 1714.

Unfortunately, the English had not consulted the Scots about this, causing a rift with the Scottish Parliament. William III had developed good relations with the Scots and made plans to unite the two countries, but after William's death in 1702, the Scots refused to pass the Act of Settlement. Their Parliament introduced Bills to allow them to choose their own monarch. The English feared they might choose a Catholic. James II had died in September 1701 and his son, the "Old Pretender", was in exile in France and was recognised by the French king as James III of England and Ireland and James VIII of Scotland.

It took five years of difficult negotiations with Scotland before the Articles of Union were agreed in July 1706 and came into force on 1 May 1707. It united England, Wales and Scotland as the Kingdom of Great Britain under one Parliament at Westminster.

Ireland retained its Parliament, though it was subordinate to Westminster. The Irish rebellion of 1798, so soon after the French revolution, galvanised the British government into securing their "back door". A further Act of Union came into effect on 1 January 1801, creating the United Kingdom of Great Britain and Ireland. From that date the entire kingdom was controlled from Westminster. A new Act changed the name to the United Kingdom of Great Britain and Northern Ireland in 1927. Southern Ireland had declared its independence in 1919 and in 1922 became the Irish Free State (renamed Eire in 1937 and formally the Republic of Ireland in 1949). Northern Ireland had its own Parliament from 1922 to 1972. In 1999 devolution re-established the Scottish Parliament and created the National Assembly for Wales. The Northern Ireland Assembly was restored in May 2007.

Freedom of Worship and Conscience

Within all of us is a feeling of what is right or wrong, whether based on religious, ethical or moral principles. Each of us is entitled to our own opinions and belief systems, and we should be able to express those views provided they do no harm to others. Those who have the courage of their convictions have faced persecution, from the earliest religious martyrs to the conscientious objectors of the two World Wars. In the Middle Ages it was very dangerous to express views at variance to those of the Church or State and many lost their lives as a result. The arrival of the printing press created a means whereby the minority could influence the majority. It became the enemy of the repressive state and was fiercely controlled, which is why the "freedom of the press" is so valued today.

Detail from *The Booke of the Common Prayer*, 1549.
BL, G.12100

THE

booke of the common
prayer and admi-
nistracion of
the
Sacramentes, and other
rites and ceremonies of
the Churche: after the
vse of the Churche
of England.

LONDINI IN OFFICINA
Edouardi Whitchurche.

Expulsion or Sanctuary?

Over the last two thousand years these islands have been both a refuge for those escaping from religious persecution and a place of suffering for those whose religion did not conform. Many refugees brought with them new ideas which led to prosperity.

The first to suffer significant religious persecution in England were Jews. They had settled in England after the Norman Conquest under the direct protection of the King. When the Pope condemned usury by Christians, the Jews became the money-lenders. This, in itself, did not lead to resentment, but with the onset of the Crusades, especially during the reign of Richard I, feelings ran high. Richard issued a Charter to protect Jews, but many Jewish communities were massacred, most notoriously in York in 1190 and Canterbury in 1264.

A series of laws issued by Edward I deprived most Jews of their livelihood. From 1269 they could no longer own land and children could not inherit money. From 1275 they could not charge interest on loans, and they had to wear yellow badges as identification. In 1290 Edward I became the first European monarch to banish Jews. Under the Edict of Expulsion all Jews had to leave England or face execution. None openly returned until 1656.

Not only religious groups but racial minorities were persecuted. In 1530, Henry VIII decreed that all "Egyptians" (gypsies) should be expelled from England. Under Queen Mary, they had to settle in one place or risk execution. Under Elizabeth, nine of them were executed in York in 1596, simply because they had not been born in England.

At the other extreme, England became a sanctuary for Protestant refugees during the Reformation. The French who converted to Protestantism became known as Huguenots. As a number were amongst the aristocracy, they became a significant political force. The clash between the Huguenots and the

The first British martyr

According to tradition, the first martyr in Britain was Alban, after whom St Albans is named. He lived during one of the periodical persecutions of the Christians by the Romans, probably in the early or mid-third century. The story goes that Alban gave shelter to a Christian, substituting himself in the Christian's place, and was executed.

The St Bartholomew's Day Massacre, 1572, as depicted by the Huguenot artist François Dubois, who was believed to have been an eyewitness.
Musée des Beaux Arts, Lausanne

The persecution of the Jews as depicted in the 14th-century document the *Chronica Roffense*.
BL, Cotton MS Nero D. II, f.183v

Seeking security
John Houblon, a grandson of one of the earliest wave of Flemish refugees, was the first Governor of the Bank of England in 1694. It was on the site of his house in Threadneedle Street, an area for Huguenot refuge, that the original of the Bank was built in 1734. Houblon's face is on the back of some £50 notes.
British Museum, 1902, 1011.6699

French Catholic elite came to a head in Paris in August 1572 following the marriage of the Catholic King's sister to the Protestant Henry of Navarre. Many Huguenots came to Paris to celebrate the wedding and Catholic supporters (possibly encouraged by the King's mother, Catherine de Medici) slaughtered thousands of them in what became called the St. Bartholomew's Day massacre. Some of those who escaped sent word to Queen Elizabeth in England who sent a small fleet of ships in a valiant attempt to rescue them.

Refugees also flooded into England from Flanders, then part of the Spanish empire. Over the next century, especially during the late 1600s, perhaps as many as 50,000 Huguenots fled to England and another 10,000 to Ireland. The Huguenots and Flemings brought their crafts with them, such as lace, silk, weaving and hat-making. It was thanks to the Flemish Huguenots that it was possible to drain the Fens and gain new farmland. England and the Huguenots both prospered as a result.

The Right to Read the Bible

During the Middle Ages the Catholic Church held a rigid control over the Bible and would not allow it to be translated from Latin into other languages. The first English-language Bible was therefore a story of great sacrifice.

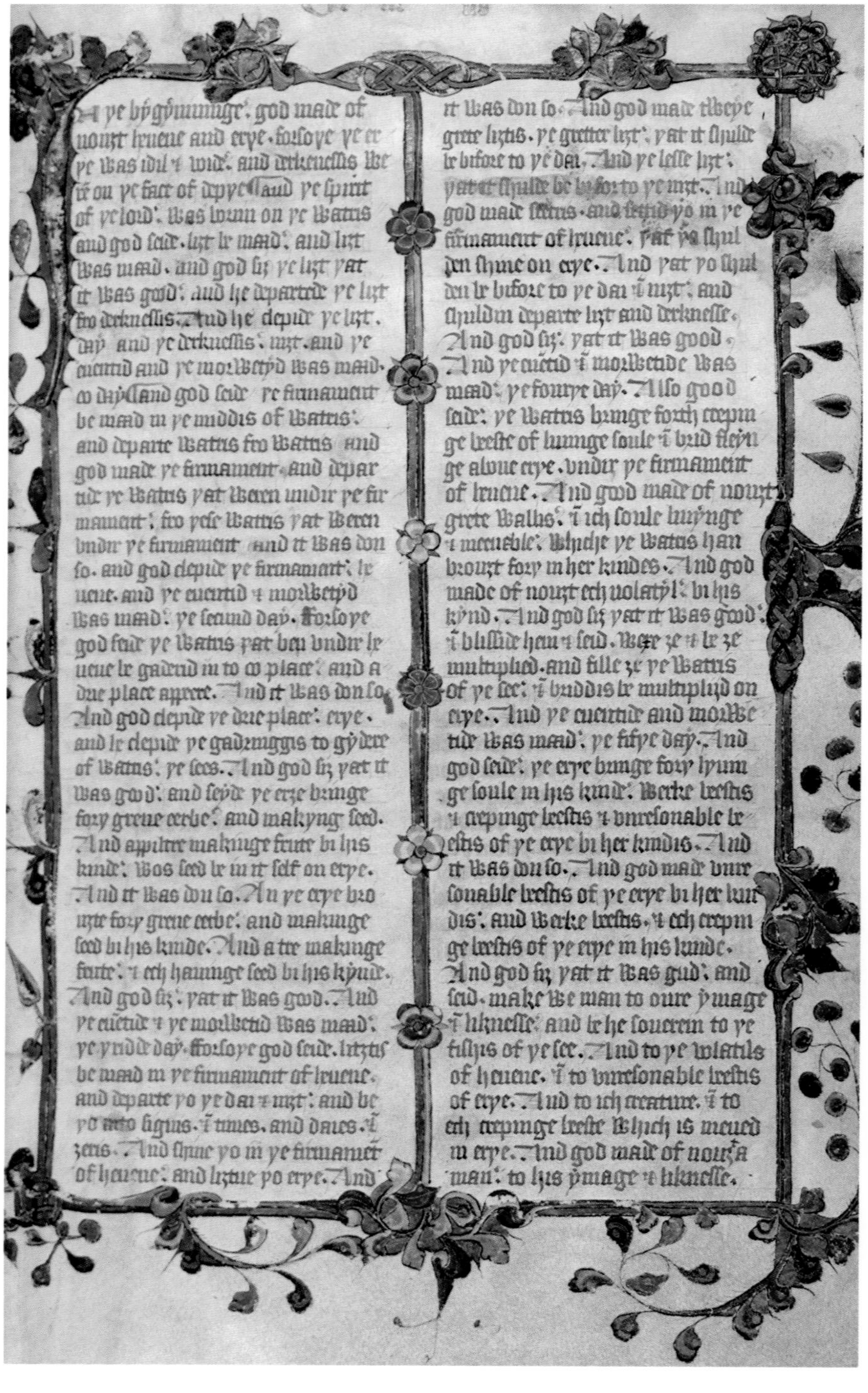

John Wyclif completed his translation of the New Testament in around 1380. He was assisted on the Old Testament by Nicholas de Hereford and others. Their work, a verbatim translation from Latin, was completed by 1384. The Church condemned the translation as inaccurate and opinionated, but as the first full version in English it proved very popular. About 30 copies survive.
BL, Arundel MS 104, vol.1, f.11

In the Middle Ages, holding any view contrary to the teachings of the Catholic Church could be seen as heresy – the word comes from the Greek for "to choose". Although both Roger Bacon and William of Ockham were warned by the Pope about their writings, the first major threat in England came in 1376 from the Oxford theologian, John Wyclif. He argued that the Church should not have wealth or possessions and that the Pope had no right to claim sovereignty over kings. He denied transubstantiation, believing in the spiritual rather than physical Eucharist. Maintaining that all authority derived from the scriptures, he worked on an English translation of the Bible, so that everyone could have direct access.

Wyclif's work encouraged the Lollards, whose preachings found much popular support in the social unrest of the late fourteenth century. In 1401, on the advice of the Archbishop of Canterbury, Henry IV introduced a law, *De haeretico comburendo* ("Regarding the Burning of Heretics"), which outlawed the translation of the Bible and made heresy a capital crime, punishable by burning at the stake. The first martyr was William Sawtre, a priest in London who preached Wyclif's teachings, and who perished at the stake in February 1401.

Although Wyclif had died in 1384, he did not escape Papal retribution. In 1415 he was declared a heretic, his bones were exhumed and burned along with his books, and the ashes cast into the River

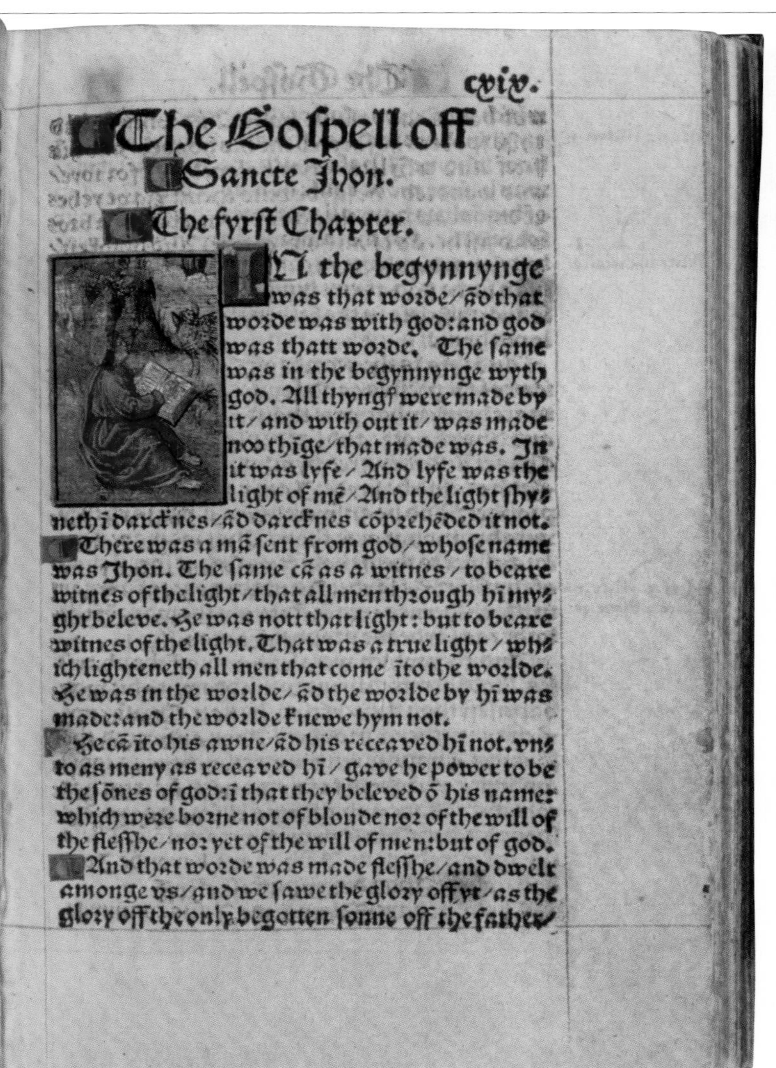

cxiv.

The Gospell off
Sancte Jhon.
The fyrst Chapter.

In the begynnynge was that worde/ ād that worde was with god: and god was thatt worde. The same was in the begynnynge wyth god. All thyngf were made by it/ and with out it/ was made noo thīge/ that made was. In it was lyfe/ And lyfe was the light of mē/ And the light shyneth ī darcknes/ ād darcknes cōprehēded it not. There was a mā sent from god/ whose name was Jhon. The same cā as a witnes/ to beare witnes of the light/ that all men through hī myght beleve. He was nott that light: but to beare witnes of the light. That was a true light/ which lighteneth all men that come ītō the worlde. He was in the worlde/ ād the worlde by hī was made: and the worlde knewe hym not. He cā ītō his awne/ ād his receaved hī not. vnto as meny as receaved hī/ gave he power to be the sōnes of god: ī that they beleved ō his name: which were borne not of bloude nor of the will of the flesshe/ nor yet of the will of men: but of god. And that worde was made flesshe/ and dwelt amonge vs/ and we sawe the glory off yt/ as the glory off the only begotten sonne off the father/

The Byble in Englyshe, that is to saye the content of all the holy scrypture, bothe of ye olde and newe testament, truly translated after the veryte of the Hebrue and Greke textes, by ye dylygent studye of dyuerse excellent learned men, expert in theforsayde tonges.

Prynted by Rychard Grafton & Edward Whitchurch.

Cum priuilegio ad imprimendum solum.

1539.

Above left:
William Tyndale's translation was the first English Bible to be printed. He worked directly from the Greek and Hebrew texts. Although Tyndale died for his views, much of his translation survived into both Henry VIII's Great Bible and King James's Authorised Bible in 1611.
BL, C.23.a.5

Above right:
The Great Bible. The first authorised English Bible, translated by Myles Coverdale who had worked with Tyndale. The large woodcut border depicts Henry VIII, Archbishop Cranmer and Thomas Cromwell distributing Bibles.
BL, C.18, d.1

Swift at Lutterworth. By then the Lollard movement was in decline and it would be a hundred years before further attempts were made for an English Bible.

The preachings of Martin Luther, challenging the authority of the Pope, lit the flames of Protestantism across Europe in the 1520s. In 1521, the Pope condemned Luther's writings and ordered that they be burned. Henry VIII, who had an extensive theological education, opposed Luther's views in *Defence of the Seven Sacraments* for which the Pope conferred on Henry the title "Defender of the Faith". There were public burnings of Luther's books in London in May 1521 and again in 1524 and 1526.

Despite the ban on translating the Bible, William Tyndale published his English version of the New Testament in Germany in 1526. Copies were burned but some still found there way to Britain, smuggled in by Richard Bayfield, a former Benedictine monk who had converted to Protestantism. He was burned at the stake in November 1531. Tyndale continued with his translation of the Old Testament, but was betrayed and captured in the Netherlands. After sixteen months in prison, he was burned at the stake in October 1536. His last words were reportedly, "Lord! Open the King of England's eyes."

Henry VIII had been waiting since 1526 for the Pope to annul his marriage to Katherine of Aragon, and when this did not happen he initiated a series of measures that culminated in the Act of Supremacy, agreed by Parliament on 3 November 1534. It established Henry as head of the Church of England and no longer answerable to the Pope.

As a consequence he needed an English Bible and in 1539 he gave approval to a translation, which became known as the "Great Bible", completed in 1540. Henry VIII decreed that it should be available to everyone in every church in England. Tyndale had died four years too soon.

Other translations

Although the Welsh language was no longer used in official documents, a Welsh translation of the Great Bible was achieved by William Morgan and published in 1588. A Gaelic version of the New Testament was published in Ireland in 1603, but the Old Testament did not appear until 1685. Both were adapted for Scottish Highlanders in 1690, with more suitable translations in 1767 (New) and 1801 (Old). A complete Manx translation appeared in 1772 but although parts of the Bible were translated into Cornish during the eighteenth century, it was not until 2004 that the New Testament was completed.

The English Reformation

When Henry VIII became Head of the Church of England in 1534 it meant a change to all church practices in England. Any who did not accept Henry as the Head but still looked to the Pope were guilty of treason.

Many refused to accept the split with Rome or the validity of Henry's divorce. Both the Bishop of Rochester John Fisher and the former Lord Chancellor Thomas More were amongst those who rejected the Oath of Supremacy, and were executed in 1535.

It was not just churchmen who opposed the split. There was unrest across the country. An uprising in Lincolnshire in October 1536 was soon suppressed but it was immediately followed by another in York, called the Pilgrimage of Grace, where Catholic worship was restored.

Dissolution of the monasteries

The Act of Supremacy allowed Henry control over the English monasteries which he believed were too rich and powerful. Between 1536 and 1540 all monastic houses were closed down and their lands sold. The official reason was because they were guilty of "manifest sin, vicious, carnal and abominable living". The last to go was Waltham Abbey on 10 April 1540.

There were many factors that influenced these uprisings but at their core was the fear that the churches would be dismantled resulting in, their leader Robert Aske declared, "the destruction of the whole religion in England". Henry promised their complaints would be considered, but when they weren't, further uprisings broke out in north-west England. The leaders were executed for treason, along with the abbots of Jervaulx and Fountains abbeys.

More riots erupted when *The Book of Common Prayer* was introduced in 1549, when Edward VI was King. The Act of Uniformity, which made this book compulsory, laid down the punishment for not using it. If found guilty a third time it meant life imprisonment, with all possessions

The Act of Supremacy, enacted in November 1534, established Henry VIII as Head of the Church of England and no longer answerable to the Pope.

National Archives, C.65/143 m 5 nos 8 & 9

Queen Mary and her husband Philip issued this Proclamation in June 1555, listing various works they denounced as heretical including the works of Martin Luther, William Tyndale, Thomas Cranmer and *The Book of Common Prayer*.

Far right: *The Booke of the Common Prayer*, 1549. This dictated a standard service in English across the country, and led to riots and unrest.

By the kyng and the Quene.

Whereas by the Statute made in the seconde yeare of kynge Henry the fourth, concernyng the repressing of heresies, ther is ordeyned and prouided a great punishment, not onely for the aucthors, makers, and wryters of bokes, conteynynge wycked doctryne, and erronious and hereticall opinions, contrary to the catholyque fayth, and determination of the holy churche, and lykewise for theyr fautours and supporters, but also for suche as shall haue or kepe any such bokes, or wrytinges, and not make deliuerie of them to the Ordinarie of the dioces or his ministers within a certayne tyme limited in the sayde Statute, as by the sayd Statute more at lardge it doth appeare. Which act or statute being by auctoritie of parliament of late reuiued, was also openly proclamed, to thintent the subiectes of the Realme vpon such proclamation should the rather eschue the daunger and penaltye of the sayd Statute, and as yet neuerthelesse, in most partes of the realme, the same is neglected, and lytle regarded.

The kyng and quene, our soueraygne Lord and Lady therfore, most entierly, and earnestly tendering th e preseruation, and saulfty, aswel of the soules, as of the bodyes, landes, & substaunce of al theyr good and louyng subiectes, and others, and myndyng to roote out, and extinguysh al false doctrine and heresies, and other occasions of scismes, diuisions, and sectes that come by the same heresyes and false doctryne, straytly charge, and commaunde, that no person or persons, of what estate, degree, or condicion soeuer he or they be, from henceforth presume to brynge or conueye, or cause to be brought or conueyed into this realme, any bookes, wrytynges, or workes, hereafter mencioned: that is to saye, any boke or bokes, writtinges, or workes, made or set forth by, or in the name of Martyn Luther, or any boke or bokes wrytynges, or workes, made or sette forth by, or in the name of Oecolampadius, Swinglius John Caluyne, Pomerane, John Alasco, Bullynger, Bucer, Melancthon, Barnardinus Ochinus, Erasmus Sarcerius, Peter Martyr, Hughe Latymer, Robert Barnes, otherwyse called freere Barnes. John Bale, otherwyse called freer Bale, Justus Jonas, John Hoper, Myles Couerdale, Wyllyam Tyndale, Thomas Cranmer late Archebyshop of Cãterburye, Wyllyam Turner, Theodore Basyll, otherwyse called Thomas Beacon, John Fryth, Roy, and the boke commonly called Halles Cronycles, or anye of them, in the latyne tongue, Duche tongue, Englyshe tongue, Italyan tongue, or Frenche tongue, or any other lyke boke, paper, wrytynge, or worke, made, prynted, or set forth, by any other person or persons, conteynynge false doctryne, contrarye, and agaynste the catholique faythe, and the doctryne of the catholyque Churche.

And also that no person or persons, presume to wryte, prynt, vtter, sell, reade, or kepe or cause to be wrytten, prynted, vttered rede, or kept any of the sayde bookes, papers, workes or wrytynges, or any booke, or bookes wrytten or prynted in the Latyne or Englyshe tounge, concernyng the common seruyce and mynystration, set forth in englyshe, to be vsed in the churches, of this realme, in the tyme of Kynge Edwarde ye sixt, commonly called the communion booke, or bookes, of common seruyce and orderyng of ministers, otherwyse called the booke set forth by aucthoritie of parliament, for common prayer and admynystratiõ of the Sacramentes, to be vsed in the mother toungue, within the churche of Englande, but shall wythin the space of fiftene dayes nexte after the publication of this proclamation, bryng, or deliuer, or cause the sayd bookes wrytinges, and workes, and euerye of them remayning in their custodies and keping, to be brought and delivered to thordinarye of the dioces, where such bookes, workes, or wrytinges, be or remayne, or to his Chauncelloure or Commyssaryes, wythout fraude collour or deceyppte, at the sayde Ordinaryes will, and disposition, to be burnte, or otherwyse to be vsed or ordered by the sayd Ordinaryes, as by the Canons and spirituall lawes, it is in that case lymytted and appoynted, vpon payne yt euery offendour contrary to this proclamation, shal incurre the daunger and penalties conteyned in the sayd Statute, and as they wyll auoyde their maiesties high indignation and displeasure, and further aunswere at their vttermost periles. And their maiesties by thys proclamation, geueth full power and aucthoritie to all Bisshoppes and Ordinaries, & all Justices of peace Maiors, Sheriffes, Baylyffes of cities, and townes corporate, and other hedde officers within this realme and the dominions therof, and expresselie commaundeth and willeth the same, and euery of them, that they and euery of them within their seueral lymytes and iurisdictions, shal in the defaulte and necligence of the sayde subiectes, after the sayd fiftene dayes expyred, enquire and search out the sayd bookes, wrytinges, and workes and for this purpose entre into the house or houses, closettes, and secretes places of euerye person of whatsoeuer degre, being negligent in this behalfe, and suspected to kepe any such booke, writing, or workes, contrary to this proclamation. And that the sayd Justices Maiors, Sheriffes, Bayliffes, and other head officers aboue specified, and euery of them within their sayd lymytes and iurisdictions, fyndyng any of the sayd subiects negligent and faultie in this behalfe, shall commytte euery such offendour to warde, there to remayne wythoute bayle or maynepryse, tyll the same offendour or offendours haue receaued such punyshmẽt as the sayd statute doth lymytte and appoynte in this behalfe. Geuen vnder our Signes Manuell, at our honour of Hampton courte, the. xiii. day of June, the first & second yeares of our reygnes.

God saue the Kynge and the Queene

Excusum Londini in aedibus Iohannis Cawodi

Typographi Regiae Maiestatis.

Anno. M.D.LV.

confiscated. There was countrywide resentment to the changes. People raised on the traditional service feared this threatened their very souls, and those of their children, because of changes to baptism. In June 1549 thousands from Cornwall and Devon marched in protest to Exeter. An army was sent to quell the rioters and it ended in a bloodbath with over 5,500 protestors killed. Despite this, a second version of the Prayer Book, issued in 1552, moved even further from the traditional service.

With the death of Edward VI in 1553, his half-sister Queen Mary came to the throne. She was a staunch Catholic and restored what she could of the old Order. She threw out *The Book of Common Prayer* and the Great Bible. With England back under the Church of Rome the Papal legate declared in November 1554 that all heretics must be burned. So began Mary's reign of terror that earned her the name, "Bloody Mary".

Over the next four years nearly 300 victims would perish in the flames until the Protestant faith was restored under Queen Elizabeth. They included Thomas Cranmer who, as Archbishop of Canterbury, had been the individual chiefly responsible for organising the English Reformation and producing the key documents. He survived the reigns of Henry VIII and Edward VI but fell foul of Queen Mary. He was burned at the stake as a heretic on 21 March 1556.

The National Covenant

The Scottish Reformation happened over twenty years after the English, but it came with a rush and a deep conviction from the populace. Although they did not know it, their zeal would light one of the fuses that helped ignite Civil War.

Mary, Queen of Scots was only a week old when her father died in 1542 and she became Queen. Her mother Marie de Guise, who governed Scotland on her behalf from 1554 to 1560, was both Catholic and French. The Scottish Protestants linked their religious freedom with their national identity. In December 1557 a group calling themselves the Lords of the Congregation signed a declaration to establish a Protestant faith. The growing crisis was defused when Marie de Guise died in 1560 and a "Reformation" Parliament was formed.

Two months later this Parliament passed a series of Acts renouncing the authority of the Pope. It endorsed the "Confession of Faith", written mostly by John Knox, which laid down the Protestant doctrine. Mary, Queen of Scots, rejected it but it became law after her abdication in 1567. Knox also wrote the *Book of Discipline*, detailing the church service.

The English and Scottish reformist churches existed separately even after the union of the crowns under James VI/I in 1603. Attempts by him and his son, Charles I, to unite the two churches met with considerable opposition, as the Scottish church had taken the Reformation more deeply to heart than the English. What's more, two movements had emerged, the Presbyterian, which favoured a church governed by elected elders, and the Episcopalian, which favoured a more orthodox structure, governed by bishops.

The first Scottish martyr

The first Scot to be executed for heresy was Patrick Hamilton, a great-grandson of the Scottish King, James II. Although he fled to Europe to escape persecution from preaching Lutheran doctrine, he returned to Scotland to face the inevitable.
In February 1528, aged only 24, he was burned at the stake outside St. Andrew's University. His fate did much to attract interest in his beliefs.

St. Giles' Cathedral in Edinburgh has a plaque to Janet Geddes who, tradition says, threw a stool at the Dean in July 1637 when he tried to use *The Book of Common Prayer*. The plaque says she "struck the first blow in the great struggle for freedom of conscience which after a conflict of half a century ended in the establishment of civil and religious liberty". This contemporary woodcut shows the riot that ensued.
BL, G.4099

Though born in Scotland, Charles I had shown little interest in his northern kingdom, and it was eight years after his English coronation before he travelled north to be crowned in Scotland. He had already imposed several unpopular measures. The situation was further aggravated when, in 1637, he tried to replace Knox's *Book of Discipline* with a new *Book of Canons* and impose a modified *Book of Common Prayer* without consultation with the Scottish Parliament. The Scots would have none of it and rioting broke out.

In March 1638, Alexander Henderson and Archibald Johnston prepared a document based on the original "Confession of Faith", which became known as the National Covenant. This was intended as a Covenant between the Scots and God and not with the King. It was "signed" by over 300,000 people – almost every adult male in Scotland, except the Highlands – making it the first wide-scale vote taken throughout the populace. The Covenant laid down the rights of the Scottish people to govern themselves without interference from the King and to their freedom of Presbyterian worship.

Charles I rejected it and relations spiralled into the conflict known as the Bishops' Wars. Charles was out of his depth. With no support from the English Parliament, he had to negotiate an ignominious treaty with the Scots. This later led to an alliance between the English and Scottish Parliaments, with the Solemn League and Covenant agreed in September 1643, as a joint pact in the Civil War that had started in England the previous year.

Unfortunately, after the Restoration Charles II fought back against those he believed had betrayed his father. Several of the original Covenanters, including Archibald Johnston, were executed. The Covenant was made illegal. An uprising of Covenanters in November 1666 was savagely put down. Matters simmered for over ten years before the final clashes, culminating in the notorious "killing time" of 1682-5, overseen by the future James VII. Remaining Covenanters were killed if they failed to renounce the Covenant and swear an oath of allegiance to the King. Some were shot simply for stuttering over the words. The last to be hanged and beheaded publicly was James Renwick, aged 26, in February 1688.

Scottish National Covenant. Introduced in 1638, this laid down the rights of the Scottish people.

National Library of Scotland, Adv Ms.20.6.15

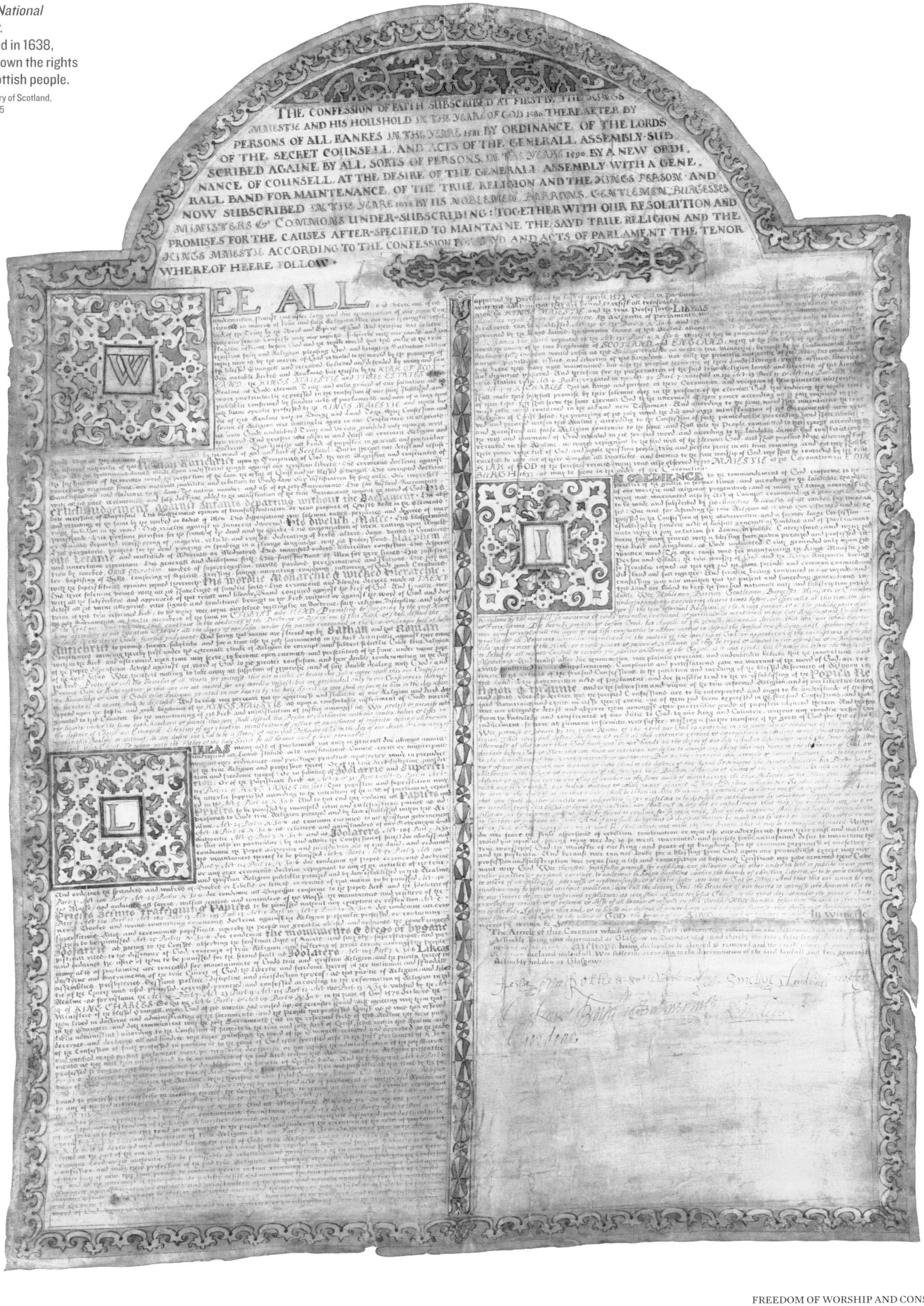
THE CONFESSION OF FAITH SUBSCRIBED AT FIRST BY THE KINGS MAIESTIE AND HIS HOUSHOLD IN THE YEARE OF GOD 1580 THEREAFTER BY PERSONS OF ALL RANKES IN THE YEARE 1581 BY ORDINANCE OF THE LORDS OF THE SECRET COUNSELL AND ACTS OF THE GENERALL ASSEMBLY SUBSCRIBED AGAINE BY ALL SORTS OF PERSONS IN THE YEARE 1590 BY A NEW ORDINANCE OF COUNSELL AT THE DESIRE OF THE GENERALL ASSEMBLY WITH A GENERALL BAND FOR MAINTENANCE OF THE TRUE RELIGION AND THE KINGS PERSON AND NOW SUBSCRIBED IN THE YEARE 1638 BY US NOBLEMEN BARRONS GENTLEMEN BURGESSES MINISTERS & COMMONS UNDER-SUBSCRIBING: TOGETHER WITH OUR RESOLUTION AND PROMISES FOR THE CAUSES AFTER-SPECIFIED TO MAINTAINE THE SAYD TRUE RELIGION AND THE KINGS MAIESTIE ACCORDING TO THE CONFESSION FORSAYD AND ACTS OF PARLAMENT THE TENOR WHEREOF HEERE FOLLOW

Plots and Pleas

The Gunpowder Plot saw a backlash against Catholics and religious dissenters. It was a period when all non-conformists suffered, but the early Baptists and Quakers stood their ground and made bold pleas for religious freedom.

When James VI of Scotland also became King of England (as James I) in 1603, there were several leading Catholics who believed he might be more sympathetic to their religion. But the opposite was true. Early in his reign he reinforced legislation passed by Queen Elizabeth that made it treason for any Jesuit or seminary priest to remain in England or for anyone to give them shelter. It was this and threats of further restrictions that led to the infamous Gunpowder Plot when Robert Catesby and his co-conspirators, including Guy Fawkes, tried to blow up Parliament in November 1605. Their plan had been to destroy Parliament and start a full-scale Catholic rebellion. Catesby was chased across England and killed. In the end all thirteen conspirators died or were executed. Guy Fawkes was executed in the Old Palace Yard, Westminster on 31 January 1606. He was so weak that he could scarcely climb the steps to the scaffold, but he had the strength to leap as he was hanged so that his neck broke and he died quickly.

Guy Fawkes's severed head was displayed on London Bridge, as depicted here in the 1617 volume *Mischeefes Mysterie.*
BL, G.1603

The failure of Catesby's plot was a disaster for Catholics. Thereafter, they could not hold any professional position and needed a special licence to travel. They had some respite during the reigns of Charles II, who had married a Catholic, and James II, who converted fully to Catholicism, but after the overthrow of James II the restrictions were tightened. By 1699 Catholics were not allowed to own or inherit land. It would be another century before Catholic worship was legitimised.

Protestant dissenters also suffered, notably the Baptists. The early Baptist Edward Wightman produced a statement about his beliefs which he presented to James I. He was charged with heresy and was the last person in England to be burned at the stake as a

The Pope-burning ceremony
Before we burnt effigies of Guy Fawkes on Bonfire Night, Protestants burnt effigies of the Pope. Anti-Catholic sentiments were particularly volatile at the end of Charles II's reign and Pope-burning ceremonies were organised in London on three successive years, from 1679-81. It was a parody of the Papal Coronation and the procession ended at Temple Bar where the effigy was burned. This depicts the Pope-burning on 17 November 1679, the anniversary of Queen Elizabeth's accession. It attracted crowds of up to 200,000.
British Museum, 1849,0315.68

Guy Fawkes signed two confessions. The first, shown here, reveals a barely readable signature "Guido". He had almost certainly been tortured, as sanctioned by the King.
National Archives, SP14/216

heretic in April 1612. Thomas Helwys, who founded the first Baptist Church in London in 1612, composed a pamphlet, *A Short Declaration of the Mystery of Iniquity*, which has been called the earliest plea for religious freedom. He wrote:

... is it not most equal that men should choose their religion themselves, seeing they only must stand themselves before the Judgement seat of God to answer for themselves, when it shall be no excuse for them to say we were commanded or compelled to be of this religion by the King ...

Helwys sent his pamphlet to the King accompanied by a note saying: *The King is a mortal man and not God, therefore has no power over the mortal souls of his subjects to make laws and ordinances for them, and to set spiritual lords over them.*

Considering James believed he ruled by Divine Right, this was a brave, even suicidal comment. Helwys was arrested and cast into prison where he died four years later. It would be another seventy years before the religious freedom he wanted was granted.

Also of importance in the story of rights is the Society of Friends, or Friends of the Truth as they began, but popularly known as the Quakers. This was founded by George Fox in the early 1650s. Fox was a pacifist and fundamental to the Quaker creed was the refusal to take up arms. In 1659 Fox presented a manifesto, "Fifty-Nine Particulars", to Parliament, detailing various reforms. It included this plea for freedom of worship: "Let none be persecuted and prisoned as vagabonds who are moved of the Lord to speak abroad his Word freely and faithfully."

From 1660, non-conformists such as Baptists or Quakers could be imprisoned for preaching without a licence. This happened to the Baptist John Bunyan. He spent almost twelve years in prison, plus a further six months in 1675 when he wrote *The Pilgrim's Progress*. However, in 1689 Parliament issued an Act of Toleration which allowed freedom of worship to non-conformists, provided they acknowledged the Trinity. The Act did not extend to Catholics.

Freedom of the Press

When the printing press was first invented it became one of the greatest enemies of both State and Church, which were determined to control it. But there were freedom fighters such as John Lilburne who were just as determined to be heard.

AREOPAGITICA;
A
SPEECH
OF
Mr. JOHN MILTON
For the Liberty of UNLICENC'D PRINTING,
To the PARLAMENT of ENGLAND.

Euripid. Hicetid.

Ex Dono Authoris

This is true Liberty when free born men
Having to advise the public may speak free,
Which he who can, and will, deserv's high praise,
Who neither can nor will, may hold his peace;
What can be juster in a State then this?
Euripid. Hicetid.

Novemb: 24. LONDON,
Printed in the Yeare, 1644.

John Milton's *Areopagitica*. In 1644, Milton took a stand against the State control of printing.
BL, C.55.c.22.(9.)

State control of printing had been introduced by Henry VIII. From November 1538, all new books had to be approved by the Privy Council. In May 1557, Queen Mary gave authority to the Company of Stationers to control the publication of books and to seek out and destroy seditious ones. This continued into Elizabeth's reign, switching Catholic for Protestant.

Further controls were issued by the Star Chamber in 1586 and 1637 over the number of printing presses. The Star Chamber judged cases that threatened national security and often ignored aspects of Common Law. However, it met its match with the brave defiance of John Lilburne. In April 1638 Lilburne was arrested for importing seditious books. Brought before the Star Chamber, he was asked to state under oath how he pleaded. Lilburne refused until told the charges, arguing that it was a free-born person's right not to accuse himself. He was fined £500 for contempt and flogged for the two miles from the Fleet Prison to the pillory. Despite the savage beating, Lilburne told all who lined the route about his treatment. He was imprisoned but continued to have propaganda smuggled out and published.

Parliament abolished the Star Chamber in 1641 and had Lilburne released. Printers took advantage of this new freedom and the host of radical pamphlets that appeared caused Parliament to clamp down again in June 1643 with a Licensing Order that restored all previous controls. John Milton protested in a pamphlet, *Areopagitica*. It was an impassioned plea for free speech, reminding Parliament that when God created Adam He gave him "the freedom to choose". Milton added:

Ye cannot make us now lesse capable, lesse knowing, lesse eagarly pursuing of the truth, unlesse ye first make your selves, that made us so, lesse the lovers, lesse the founders of our true liberty.

Though powerfully argued, no one took any notice. In fact controls were reinforced after the Restoration with a new Licensing Act in 1662. Total control over the approval of books was invested in Roger L'Estrange, the Witchfinder General of the Printing trade. He censored and edited many books. In 1664, printer John Twyn was hanged, drawn and quartered for publishing material suggesting that the monarch was accountable to his subjects.

L'Estrange's office ceased after the "Glorious Revolution" of 1688 and by 1695 the Licensing Act was allowed to lapse. With that there was a blossoming of newspapers and provincial presses.

Free-born John

John Lilburne was a defiant individual who endured all manner of punishment in the cause of freedom. He was arrested and tried many times. His pamphlet, *England's Birthright Justified* of 1645, was written while he was in prison for denouncing Members of Parliament for not taking their part in the Civil War. He attacked the state control of printing and argued for the freedom of the press.

The Star Chamber had been in existence since 1421 and was the most feared inquisitorial court of its day.
BL, G.4099

Image from The Triall of Lieut. Collonell J. Lilburne. Published by 'Theodorus Verax' [Clement Walker] in 1649. John Lilburne was tried for treason in October 1649, having claimed in his book *Legall Fundamentall Liberties* that the new Parliamentarian government was not legal. The jury, named in the top right rosette, found him innocent.
BL, C.37.d.51.(5)

Censorship and the Theatre

The state found it harder to control the theatre as not only did they need to license plays, but the actors also had to be held in check. It led to the Licensing Act of 1737 which imposed censorship on the theatre, and which would remain for 231 years.

The popularity of the theatre grew during the Elizabethan era. The Master of the Revels licensed plays by judging their suitability and had the authority to censor them and arrest actors. The playwright Ben Jonson was imprisoned in 1597 for his play *The Isle of Dogs*. It was suppressed and no copies survive. It was claimed to be lewd and seditious and may have satirised the Queen. Ben Jonson was arrested again for anti-Scottish references in *Eastward Hoe*, which offended James I. The Act to Restrain Abuses of Players in 1606 forbade any blasphemous or profane references to God or Christ – actors were fined £10 for each profanity. It led to revisions of certain plays such as Marlowe's *Faust* and Shakespeare's *King Lear* (the oath "By heaven" was replaced by "Alas").

The ultra-Puritan pamphleteer William Prynne was so incensed by the depravity of the theatre that he wrote *Histriomastix* (1632), in which he condemned plays as "sinfull, heathenish, lewde, ungodly spectacles...". Some of his comments were interpreted as attacks on Charles I's queen, Henrietta, who had appeared in a few masques. He was fined £5,000, imprisoned for life and had his ears clipped. He continued to produce his pamphlets in prison so had the rest of his ears removed and his head branded. He was released in 1640.

Theatres were closed by the Puritans from 1642 and restored, along with the monarchy, in 1660, when women were allowed to perform for the first time. Censorship remained, controlled by the King through the Master of the Revels. Curiously, although plays were revised or even banned, their texts were still published often with the offending phrases intact. It was the *performance* that mattered, and how the actor interpreted the text.

The birth of pornography
A case in 1727 established that obscenity was punishable under common law as a breach of the peace. Edmund Curll was fined and imprisoned for publishing a translation of *The Nun in Her Smock*, about the sexual relationship between two nuns. It was seen as pornographic because it had no moral message. It established a legal precedent for obscenity and led to other prosecutions. The best known was John Cleland's *Fanny Hill* in 1749. This was regarded as pornographic because it had "no redeeming social value". The book was withdrawn and was not printed legally in Britain until 1970. The above engraving, ascribed to Hubert Gravelot, is from the original "corrected" edition of *Fanny Hill*.
BL, P.C.30.k.27

There was a growing view, however, that the theatre was too licentious. The Society for the Reformation of Manners was established in 1691 by various churchmen, including nonconformists. They became the nation's moral watchdog, with informers who reported on any transgression, and lawyers who pursued the cases through the courts. There were branches in several major cities including Edinburgh, where Daniel Defoe was a member. Most of its attention was on brothels, drunkards and Sabbath-breakers, but it also kept an eye on the theatre and brought a number of prosecutions. Jeremy Collier attacked the theatre in *A Short View of the Immorality and Profaneness of the English Stage* (1698) and playwrights, notably William Congreve, John Dryden and Henry Fielding, found it increasingly difficult to write with the moral freedom they

HISTRIO-MASTIX.
THE
PLAYERS SCOVRGE,
OR,
ACTORS TRAGÆDIE,
Divided into Two Parts.
Wherein it is largely evidenced, by divers *Arguments*, by the concurring Authorities and Resolutions of *sundry texts of Scripture*; of the *whole Primitive Church*, both under the *Law and Gospell*; of 55 *Synodes and Councels*; of 71 *Fathers and Christian Writers*, before the yeare of our Lord 1200; of above 150 *foraigne and domestique Protestant and Popish Authors*, since; of 40 *Heathen Philosophers, Historians, Poets*; of many *Heathen*, many *Christian Nations, Republiques, Emperors, Princes, Magistrates*; of sundry *Apostolicall, Canonicall, Imperiall Constitutions*; and of our owne *English Statutes, Magistrates, Universities, Writers, Preachers.*

That popular Stage-playes (the very Pompes of the Divell which we renounce in Baptisme, if we beleeve the Fathers) are sinfull, heathenish, lewde, ungodly Spectacles, and most pernicious Corruptions; condemned in all ages, as intolerable Mischiefes to Churches, to Republickes, to the manners, mindes and soules of men. And that the Profession of Play-poets, of Stage players; together with the penning, acting, and frequenting of Stage-playes, are unlawfull, infamous and misbeseeming Christians. All pretences to the contrary are here likewise fully answered; and the unlawfulnes of acting, of beholding Academicall Enterludes, briefly discussed; besides sundry other particulars concerning *Dancing, Dicing, Health-drinking, &c.* of which the *Table* will informe you.

By WILLIAM PRYNNE, *an Vtter-Barrester of* Lincolnes Inne.

Cyprian. De Spectaculis lib. p. 244.
Fugienda sunt ista Christianis fidelibus, ut iam frequenter diximus, tam vana, tam perniciosa, tam sacrilega Spectacula: quæ, etsi non haberent crimen, habent in se et maximam et parum congruentē fidelibus vanitatē.
Lactantius de Vero Cultu cap. 20.
Vitanda ergo Spectacula omnia, non solum ne quid vitiorum pectoribus insideat, &c. sed ne cuius nos voluptatis consuetudo delineat, atque à Deo et à bonis operibus avertat.
Chrysost. Hom. 38. in Matth. Tom. 2. Col. 299. B & Hom. 8. De Pœnitentia, Tom. 5. Col. 750.
Immo vero, his Theatralibus ludis eversis, non leges, sed iniquitatem evertetis, ac omnem civitatis pestem extinguetis.: Etenim Theatrum, communis luxuriæ officina, publicum incontinentiæ gymnasium; cathedra pestilentiæ; pessimus locus; plurimorumque morborum plena Babylonica fornax, &c.
Augustinus De Civit. Dei, l. 4. c. 1.
Si tantummodo boni et honesti homines in civitate essent, nec in rebus humanis Ludi scenici esse debuissent.

LONDON,
Printed by *E. A.* and *W. I.* for *Michael Sparke*, and are to be sold at the Blue Bible, in Greene Arbour, in little Old Bayly. 1633.

Frontispiece of *Histriomastix* by William Prynne, which attacked the corruptive nature of the theatre. Although dated 1633 the pamphlet appeared at the close of 1632.

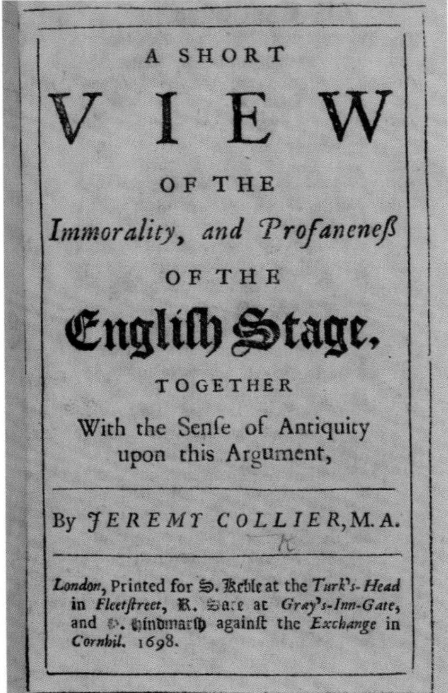
A SHORT
VIEW
OF THE
Immorality, and Profaneness
OF THE
English Stage,
TOGETHER
With the Sense of Antiquity upon this Argument,

By JEREMY COLLIER, M.A.

London, Printed for S. Keble at the *Turk's-Head* in *Fleetstreet*, R. Sare at *Gray's-Inn-Gate*, and H. Hindmarsh against the *Exchange* in *Cornhil*. 1698.

Jeremy Collier also attacked the immorality of the stage in *A Short View* in 1698, which led to an outcry from the playwrights he attacked.

had in the Restoration period.

Instead playwrights changed their stance and used their wit to satirise prominent individuals. Robert Walpole, who was the first Prime Minister from 1721, was a special target for their barbs. In retaliation, Walpole introduced the Licensing Act in 1737 which gave the Lord Chamberlain total control over the licensing of plays and theatres. Lord Chesterfield made a rousing speech against the Bill, calling it "nothing less than an attack on fundamental liberties". He argued: *A Power lodged in the hands of one single man, to judge and determine without any limitation, without any control or appeal, is a sort of Power unknown to our Laws, inconsistent with our Constitution.*

The Act stifled free expression for generations, remaining in force until 1968. The Lord Chamberlain's powers were increased by the Theatre Act of 1838, when he could ban any play that might offend "good manners, decorum, or the public peace".

Wilkes and Liberty

John Wilkes, who became an MP in 1757, was arrogant and ill-mannered, but his very irreverence and determination made him the people's champion against authority. In the process he struck several blows for liberty.

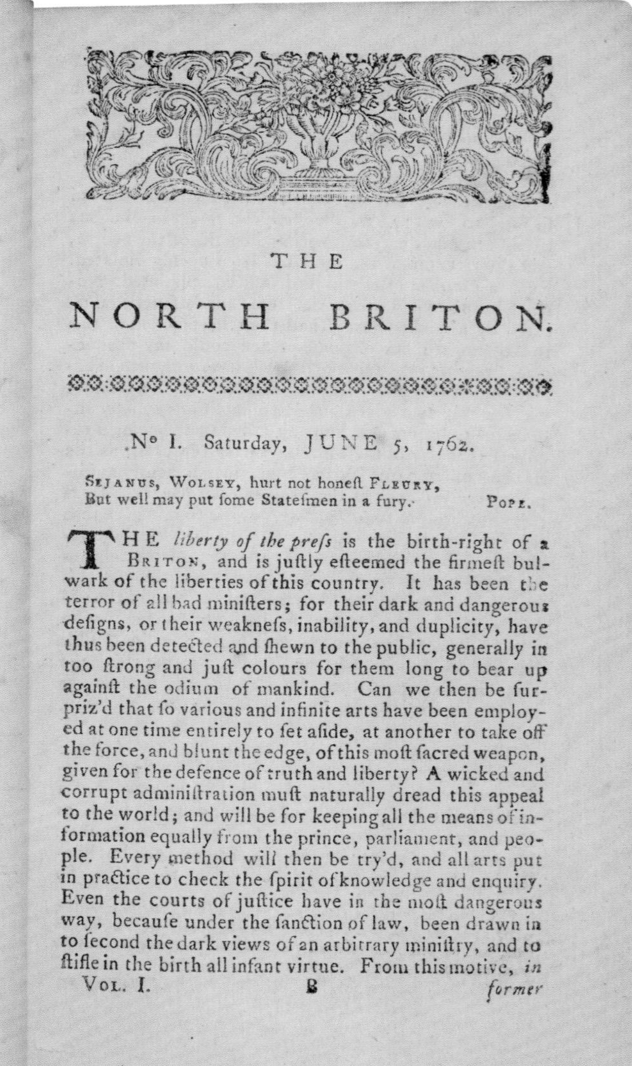

THE

NORTH BRITON.

No I. Saturday, JUNE 5, 1762.

SEJANUS, WOLSEY, hurt not honeſt FLEURY,
But well may put ſome Stateſmen in a fury. POPE.

THE *liberty of the preſs* is the birth-right of a BRITON, and is juſtly eſteemed the firmeſt bulwark of the liberties of this country. It has been the terror of all bad miniſters; for their dark and dangerous deſigns, or their weakneſs, inability, and duplicity, have thus been detected and ſhewn to the public, generally in too ſtrong and juſt colours for them long to bear up againſt the odium of mankind. Can we then be ſurpriz'd that ſo various and infinite arts have been employed at one time entirely to ſet aſide, at another to take off the force, and blunt the edge, of this moſt ſacred weapon, given for the defence of truth and liberty? A wicked and corrupt adminiſtration muſt naturally dread this appeal to the world; and will be for keeping all the means of information equally from the prince, parliament, and people. Every method will then be try'd, and all arts put in practice to check the ſpirit of knowledge and enquiry. Even the courts of juſtice have in the moſt dangerous way, becauſe under the ſanction of law, been drawn in to ſecond the dark views of an arbitrary miniſtry, and to ſtifle in the birth all infant virtue. From this motive, *in*

VOL. I. B *former*

The first issue of *The North Briton*, written and edited anonymously by John Wilkes. It championed the free press, calling it "the firmest bulwark of the liberties of this country".

BL, P.P.3585

In May 1762 George III appointed his favourite, the Earl of Bute, as Prime Minister. This direct involvement by the King upset many, not least because Bute was Scottish – indeed, the first Scottish Prime Minister – and there was still much distrust of the Scots so soon after the Jacobite rising. He also had little Parliamentary experience.

John Wilkes was the MP for Aylesbury, with a gift of the gab and a delight in making mischief. He disliked Bute and fed the public disfavour through his newspaper, the *The North Briton*. He attacked Bute at every opportunity. The increased unpopularity weakened Bute's resolve and he resigned in April 1763. That same week in *The North Briton* Wilkes accused the King of lying in his speech on the Treaty of Paris.

Bute's successor, George Grenville, thought Wilkes had exceeded his Parliamentary privilege. Because the paper was anonymous, a general warrant, which carried no names, was issued for the arrest of all those involved. Wilkes's home was broken into and ransacked.

Imprisoned in the Tower, Wilkes fought back on two fronts. Firstly he argued that he was entitled to say whatever he wanted on the grounds of Parliamentary privilege. The judge agreed and he was released. He then argued that because no one was named in the warrant, the arrests were illegal and the vandalism of his property was trespass. All those arrested sued the officials who had issued the warrant, and won. The judge ruled that such warrants were "totally subversive of the liberty of the subject" and "contrary to the fundamental principles of the constitution". They were eventually made illegal.

Wilkes was literally carried away with his success, borne shoulder high by the public with cries of "Wilkes and Liberty". He reprinted the offending issue of *The North Briton* and when asked how far the freedom of the press went in England, replied, "I cannot tell, but I am trying to find out." Parliament voted the reprinted issue of *The North Briton* a seditious libel and ordered it be publicly burned. Another item printed by Wilkes, "Essay on Woman", was declared obscene, a libel and a breach of privilege. The Commons expelled Wilkes from the House. As his privilege no longer applied, Wilkes fled to France. He was tried in his absence, found guilty and declared an outlaw.

After four years in France and deep in debt, Wilkes returned to England. Surprisingly, he was not arrested. He stood for re-election and was returned to Parliament. He then turned himself in and voluntarily went to prison. In June 1768 Lord Mansfield removed the charge of outlawry in order that Wilkes could be fined and sentenced to prison for libel.

Wilkes continued to write in prison, pursuing a pardon. Again his invective raised the hackles of Parliament. Again he was charged with seditious libel and again expelled from Parliament. He was

Society of the Bill of Rights

In February 1769, Wilkes's friends organised the Society of Supporters of the Bill of Rights. Its objective was to "maintain and defend the liberty of the subject, and to support the laws and constitution of the country", and it started by paying Wilkes's debts. The Society also fought for wider Parliamentary reform but failed, and ceased in 1775.

The TRIUMVERATE or BRITANIA in *DISTRESS*.

TO THE

Glorious SONS of FREEDOM, at the LONDON-TAVERN,

Who nobly defended the Rights of their Country againſt an Arbitrary Adminiſtration,

This PLATE is humbly INSCRIBED,

By their humble Servants,

When John Wilkes's election to Parliament was overturned three times, the electors of Middlesex and London presented a petition in protest to the King. This broadside produced at the time glorifies the scene and relates it to when Henry III was also pressed into accepting a charter of rights. Wilkes is on horseback leading the procession delivering the petition.
British Museum, 1868,0808.4436

re-elected three times and expelled three times, the Commons going so far as to call Wilkes "incapable" of standing for election. They even declared his opponent the winner. The decision rode roughshod over the electoral process as Wilkes was no longer an outlaw, and led to a rise in public protests.

To defuse the situation Wilkes was released from prison, accompanied by bells ringing throughout England, and even in America when news reached there. Wilkes turned his attention to the City of London, rising to the position of Lord Mayor in 1774.

Wilkes took advantage of his position as a magistrate to use the privileges of the City. Parliament had resented newspapers printing reports of its debates, and had ordered the arrest of several printers. Wilkes, always more cunning than ministers, cited the arrests of freemen of the City as illegal and secured the printers' release. Wilkes's popularity was so great that Parliament dared not move against him and he won the day. In 1774 John Almon, one of the printers Wilkes had helped, began the *Parliamentary Register*, the forerunner of Hansard. It was a victory for the press and for freedom of access to public information.

An enamel snuff-box of John Wilkes made in Birmingham around 1770.
British Museum, PY1895, 0521.21

Religious Tolerance

Although Great Britain was becoming a haven for religious refugees, it was still many years before Catholic and Jewish emancipation became a reality, and even then it came as a last resort.

The first Jewish synagogue was opened at Bevis Marks near Aldgate in 1701. Each year they give a gift to the Lord Mayor of London to protect their position. This Silver Salver by John Ruslen was presented in 1702.
The Jewish Museum, London. JM 656

The White Cockade was a symbolic design worn in the headgear of the Jacobite supporters. This cockade was found on the field after the Battle of Culloden (1746) and bears the inscription, "With Charles, our brave and merciful, we'll greatly fall or nobly save our country."
BL, Add. MS 35889, f.108

Jews had been resettling in Britain in small numbers since 1656, and had established their first synagogue in London in 1701. But there were limits. The Jewish Naturalization Act of 1753, which offered British nationality to Jews who had been resident in Britain for three years, caused such an outcry that it was promptly repealed.

The 1709 General Naturalisation Act had bestowed British status on Protestant refugees on taking certain oaths and paying one shilling. Over 13,000 German Protestants flocked to England to escape persecution. It proved difficult to house them in London so most were shipped to Ireland or the colonies thus frustrating the Act's purpose. It was repealed in 1712.

Anti-Catholic legislation stayed in force. There had been a backlash following the Jacobite rising of 1745-6 under the Catholic claimant to the throne, "Bonnie Prince Charlie". Although the threat of a further uprising had diminished after his defeat at Culloden, anti-Catholic sentiment remained. When the Papist Act was passed in 1778, relaxing certain restrictions on inheritance and schooling, it led to the Gordon Riots. Lord George Gordon raised a petition and marched on Parliament in June 1780, drawing huge crowds. Matters got out of hand with rioting lasting for a week. The army was called and nearly 300 rioters killed. This brought some sympathy for Catholics and the Catholic Relief Act was eventually passed in 1791. It legitimised Catholic worship, allowed Catholic schools and for Catholics to practise law.

At the time the number of Catholics in Britain was relatively small, but the Union with Ireland in 1801 changed that. Now the number of Catholic freeholders with the vote could significantly affect an election. Many Irish Catholics had supported the Act of Union, believing it would hasten their emancipation, but it still took nearly thirty years. In 1828 Daniel O'Connell, the leading Irish activist for Catholic reform, won a by-election but was unable to take his seat at Westminster because this was denied Catholics. The Prime Minister the Duke of Wellington realised they would have to capitulate and in 1829 the Catholic Relief Act was passed, removing almost all remaining obstacles for Catholics.

Jewish emancipation eventually followed. In 1845 Jews were allowed to hold public office, although Moses Montefiore had been Sheriff of London already and was knighted by Queen Victoria in 1837. However, attempts to pass a Bill through Parliament failed, even after Baron de Rothschild was elected MP for the City of London in 1847. He tried to take his seat but because he could not swear the Christian oath he was dismissed. It was not until 1858, following the Jewish Emancipation Act, that Baron de Rothschild at last entered Parliament.

A Jewish or Catholic Prime Minister?
There has yet to be a Jewish Prime Minister. Although Benjamin Disraeli was Jewish by birth and upbringing, he was baptised a Christian in 1817. There has also never been a Catholic Prime Minister: Tony Blair, whose wife and children are Catholic, entered the Catholic faith in December 2007, six months after retiring.

“No Popery” engraving by James Gillray depicting an image of the Gordon Riots in 1780. In the background Newgate prison burns. The man may be Ned Dennis, the hangman of Newgate, whom Dickens portrayed in *Barnaby Rudge*. He wears a cockade in his hat, mocking those worn by the Jacobites.

British Museum, 1851,0901.34

British or Alien?

Today everyone has a right to a nationality. Yet as legislation developed, it was possible to be reclassified overnight from a British citizen to an alien, and become "undesirable" in your own country.

Graffiti in Notting Hill soon after race riots had erupted there in August and September 1958. The Notting Hill Carnival was started in 1959 to help foster better race relations.

Britain had been receptive to refugees since the plight of the French Huguenots in the seventeenth century. In the 1890s mass migration affected Britain with the arrival of large numbers of refugees, mainly Jews, escaping persecution in Russia. The Jewish community rose from around 60,000 to 300,000 between 1880 and 1914.

Though these numbers were not as high as propaganda implied, they were enough to create support for the British Brothers' League, formed in 1901 by MP William Evans-Gordon. He influenced the government to set up a Royal Commission, leading to the Aliens Act of 1905. This established a legal basis for those seeking political or religious asylum, but also allowed the deportation of any "alien" deemed undesirable, including the poor. Gerald Balfour, President of the Board of Trade, said: "We have a right to keep out everybody who does not add to the industrial, social and intellectual strength of the community."

Kenyan Asian arriving with his British Passport in February 1968.

It raised the question of how to know whether you were British or an alien. British nationality was defined by the 1914 British Nationality and Status of Aliens Act. It confirmed that you were British if born on British soil (or ship) or had a British father and owed allegiance to the Crown. British soil included the British Empire, which at that time covered a quarter of the globe.

You could of course also be a "naturalised" Briton. The 1870 Naturalisation Act required applicants to have been resident in Britain for five years, though a non-British woman became British upon marrying a British national. However, if a British woman married a foreigner she took on her husband's nationality and lost her British status. She had to reapply for British nationality when her husband died, an anomaly not rectified until 1933.

Anti-German prejudice
Ludwig Becker, Professor of Astronomy at Glasgow University, though born in Germany, had been a naturalised British subject since 1892. Because of anti-German hysteria he was removed from the University and interned. Even after the War the government demanded that he be compulsorily retired, but as passions calmed, he returned to his work and formally retired in 1935.

With the outbreak of the First World War, the government passed the Aliens Restriction Act. This placed limits on the activities of all aliens, not just "the enemy". All had to register with the police. Although Germans who had been naturalised were exempt, not all were treated equally and many were interned. By 1918, anti-German feeling was so high that a rally organised by former suffragette Emmeline Pankhurst in Hyde Park led to a petition demanding that all naturalisation for Germans should be revoked. It did not happen, but Lloyd George put through an Act granting that power.

A new Aliens Act, passed in 1919 with its subsequent Orders,

Jewish immigrants in Stepney in 1903. These images come from *The Alien Immigrant* by William Evans-Gordon, who founded the British Brothers' League and campaigned against immigration. The image below was labelled 'An alien fishwife' in the book.
BL, 08275.aaa.17

discriminated between British nationals. Racial prejudice had grown in ports and factories because of post-war unemployment levels. The 1920 Aliens Order and 1925 Coloured Alien Seamen Order limited the rights of "coloured" workers. Sailors had to produce passports to prove their nationality but passports were relatively new and sailors had not previously needed them. As a consequence thousands of sailors, mostly Asians, who were British by right, were regarded as aliens – along with their families. The government tried to repatriate many, knowing they could not deport those who were rightly British, but few wished to go. In similar fashion the 1935 British Shipping Act (which gave the shipping industry subsidies if they employed British – meaning "white" – seamen), openly discriminated between white and black British nationals.

With the Second World War and the years following, there was demand for labour, and migration to the UK from the colonies was encouraged. The 1948 British Nationality Act created citizens of the United Kingdom and the Colonies, and conferred the status of British citizen on all Commonwealth subjects if they chose to register. It also recognised their right to work and settle in the UK with their families, and this encouraged a rise in immigration.

It led to an increase in racial discrimination, especially against black immigrants. The so-called "colour bar" arose where black people were barred from entering or being served in certain places. Despite attempts by Reginald (later Lord) Sorenson to introduce legislation in 1950, and by Fenner Brockway eight times from 1956 to 1963, it was not until 1965 that the first Race Relations Act made discrimination illegal. However, it was only with the 1976 Act, which set up the Commission for Racial Equality, that it could be said that discrimination was outlawed. In 1981 the British Nationality Act removed British status from Commonwealth subjects. It meant that non-British wives of British citizens ceased to have a right of entry to Britain, even if they were Commonwealth citizens.

Casualties of War

Whilst truth may be the first casualty of war, rights and liberties must be a close second. During the First World War men were compulsorily conscripted for the first time unless they proved the genuineness of their conscience.

Conscientious objectors were often prescribed hard labour, and are shown here building a road, from *The Illustrated London News*, 23 August 1916.

There had been no shortage of British volunteers to sign up at the start of the First World War in August 1914: over three million in the first two years. However the alarming death toll on the Western Front forced the government to consider conscription. The former Prime Minister Lord Rosebery said in a recruitment speech at the start of the War that whilst Britain had never opted for conscription, "by the common law of Great Britain, every man valid and capable of bearing arms is bound at the call of his country to do so."

Compulsory conscription came with the Military Service Act in January 1916. It called up all men aged between nineteen and 41, provided they were unmarried and had no dependent children. Men in Holy Orders were excluded, and those who were seriously ill or with exceptional obligations were granted exemptions. Another exemption was for Conscientious Objectors (COs), which was unique to the United Kingdom and called "the slackers' charter" by maverick extremist MP William Joynson-Hicks.

"Daddy, what did YOU do in the Great War?" A recruitment poster published in 1915.
Imperial War Museum, PST 0311

16,000 men requested that exemption. They had to obtain a certificate issued by a tribunal made up of local officials and at least one army representative, which tested their sincerity. Tribunals were told to respect individual's beliefs but most were harsh, treating COs as cowards unless they could prove firm religious reasons. Fenner Brockway (later one of the founders of CND) set up the No-Conscription Fellowship to support COs. He was imprisoned both for these anti-conscription activities and as a conscientious objector.

Some COs who were not absolutist were assigned alternative war work, but the Fellowship discovered that some were being forced to fight and many that resisted were court-martialled and imprisoned. Some were sentenced to death, but this was commuted to ten-years' imprisonment. Of the 16,000 who sought exemption, over 6,000 were arrested and over 800 of these spent two years or more in prison. Those in prison discovered they were being assigned war work. Some 73 COs died from the treatment meted out to them.

Most COs were kept in prison until long after the War finished, the last being released in August 1919. Some had gone on hunger strike over their situation and had been force-fed.

Conscription ended in 1919 but was reintroduced in 1939 in advance of the Second World War. The same process applied for COs, though this time the Tribunals were rather more humane. Nevertheless, of the 60,000 COs who applied for exemption some 6,000 were imprisoned, including the composer Michael Tippett in 1943. This time there was a formally recognised body to help individuals, the Central Board for Conscientious Objectors, organised once again by Fenner Brockway. Conscription did not end with the War, but continued until December 1960, creating a further 10,000 COs. By the time it finished some twelve million men had been called up.

Battle of the Bogside, Londonderry, 12 August 1969.

was also stacked against Catholics. Suffrage was based on ratepayers and was not universal. It could also be biased towards Protestants by how council houses were allocated. These and other factors showed the inequality in Northern Ireland.

In 1964, the Campaign for Social Justice was formed by Dr Conn McCluskey and his wife, Patricia, to tackle the problem of housing allocation. Out of this grew the Northern Ireland Civil Rights Association (NICRA) in 1967, composed chiefly of Catholics. They wanted an end to discriminatory practices and to establish universal suffrage. They planned strategic marches in major towns, but these were banned by the Northern Ireland Parliament at Stormont. Each march saw a clash between protesters and police, most notably in Londonderry in October 1968 where over 70 people were injured. This gave rise to People's Democracy, a student protest organisation for political reforms.

The activities of these organisations took place against a background of growing militancy. The Irish Republican Army (IRA) had split in 1969 into the Official IRA, which opted to follow a non-violent course, and the Provisional IRA, which retained a militant approach. This was partly in response to the creation of the loyalist paramilitary Ulster Volunteer Force (UVF) in 1966. Reaction to the violent opposition to the civil rights movement saw confrontation escalate. The Battle of the Bogside in Londonderry in 1969 saw seven people killed, a hundred wounded and over 3,000 families driven from their homes.

The Prime Minister Harold Wilson, sent the British Army into Northern Ireland in August 1969. Stormont was ordered to make all possible changes to meet the civil rights' movement's demands. By the end of the year the electoral system was reviewed, fairer housing allocation implemented, and the police force reconstituted. Hereafter, the civil-rights movement became subsumed within the wider conflict between republicans and loyalists, both on political and military fronts.

In an attempt to quash the rise in terrorist activities, Northern Ireland's Prime Minister, Brian Faulkner, reinstigated internment in August 1971. Over 2,000 people were arrested in the first six months, though many were innocent of paramilitary activities. 1,600 were later released, but by then internment was seen as an indiscriminate prosecution of Catholics. No Protestants were interned until February 1973, and by the time internment ceased in December 1975, over 90% of those arrested had been Catholic.

The Republic of Ireland took the issue of internment to the European Court of Human Rights. In December 1977, the Court ruled that the UK government was guilty of "inhuman and degrading treatment" and that internment was in violation of the Convention.

Bernadette Devlin, now Bernadette McAliskey, was one of the founder members of People's Democracy. In 1969 she was the youngest woman to be voted into Parliament, when she was 21. Her book, *The Price of My Soul*, drew attention to the discrimination against Catholics in Northern Ireland.

The Rights of the Individual

In the conflict between the English Parliament and Charles I, thoughts about a formal constitution raised questions about individuals' rights. The Agreement of the People raised such issues as the freedom of worship, the fairness of trials and equality under the law. Others began to consider the true nature of an individual's rights, though it was not until after the Revolution of 1688, and the Bill of Rights, that thinkers felt sufficiently free to express their views without fear of persecution. Their ideas contributed to a growing understanding of political and human rights that would prove fundamental in both the American and French Revolutions and would lead one day to a Universal Declaration of Human Rights.

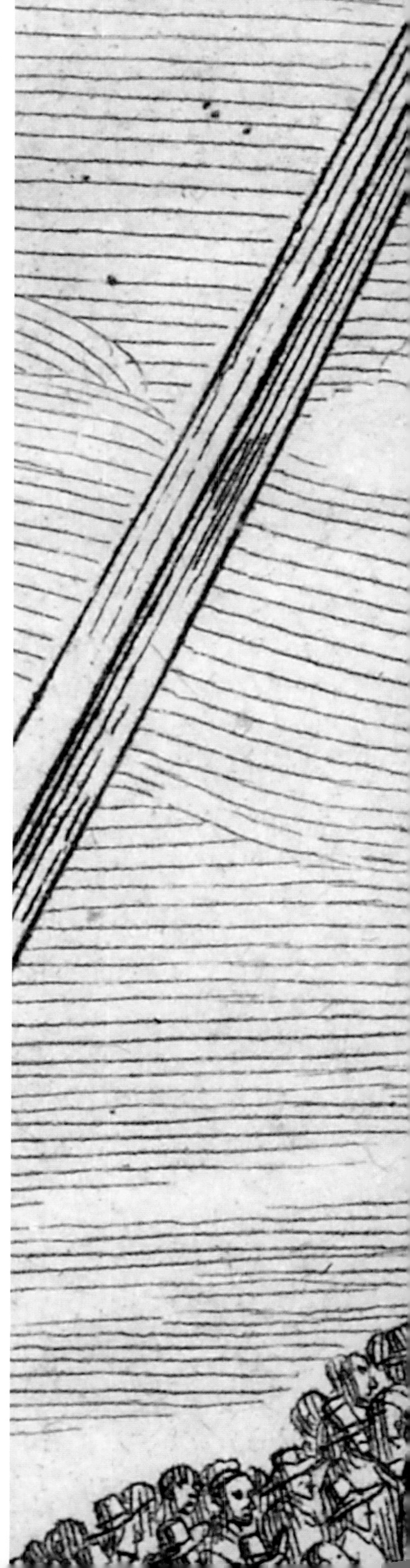

Detail from Thomas Hobbes's *Leviathan*, showing a giant figure composed of all the bodies of its subjects and having command over all it surveys.

Dreams and Ideals

Despite the Restoration of the monarchy the Age of Enlightenment was only just dawning, and those who promoted ideas about rights and freedoms could find their lives in danger. Their thoughts contributed to an understanding about the very nature of rights and their place in society.

TWO
TREATISES
OF
Government:
In the former,
The false Principles, and Foundation
OF
Sir ROBERT FILMER,
And his FOLLOWERS,
ARE
Detected and Overthrown.
The latter is an
ESSAY
CONCERNING THE
True Original, Extent, and End
OF
Civil Government.

LONDON,
Printed for Awnsham Churchill, at the Black Swan in Ave-Mary-Lane, by Amen-Corner, 1690.

John Locke's *Two Treatises of Government*, published at the end of 1689, in which he laid down the basic inalienable human rights.
BL, C.107.c.89

The writings of Thomas Hobbes, a royalist and tutor to the nobility, who fled to Paris at the start of the Civil War, proved fundamental in considering the relationship between a government and its people. He brought his ideas together in *Leviathan*, published in 1651, but elements feature in earlier tracts completed before the outbreak of the Civil War. Hobbes proposed that the natural basic state of humankind is one of anarchy with the strong dominating the weak, so that our one natural right is of self-preservation. In order to remove that basic fear between individuals or groups, Hobbes suggested that people would "contract" with a protector as their sovereign. Under this social contract individuals abnegate all rights, whilst that of the protector is absolute. He did not, though, believe in divine right. Hobbes's key point was that the protector was there by specific agreement with his subjects.

Hobbes's concept of a social contract was taken up by others, who developed it in another direction. Algernon Sidney, son of the Earl of Leicester, would sacrifice his life for his view. In 1683 Sidney was charged with complicity in the Rye House Plot to assassinate Charles II and the Duke of York. His trial was before the notorious Judge Jeffreys. Sidney denied any involvement, but Jeffreys used as evidence Sidney's unpublished manuscript *Discourses Upon Government*. This had been written to rebut the Divine Right of Kings. Sidney, who was against absolutism, argued that man was born free with a natural right to liberty, but that brought potential conflict with another's liberty. A government was needed to ensure balance, but one that governed by consent not divine right. Like Hobbes, Sidney saw this arrangement as a contract. If the King broke that, through tyranny, the people had a right to depose him. It was this that Jeffreys pounced on as proof of Sidney's treason, and for that Sidney was executed in December 1683.

Judge Jeffreys became Lord Chief Justice and presided over the trials of those involved in the Monmouth Rebellion in 1685, where all manner of punishments were meted out. These were the Bloody Assizes. One of the victims was Elizabeth Gaunt, who became the last woman in England to be burned at the stake for treason.
British Museum, P,5.267

Sidney's ideas were similar to those of John Locke. He was physician and private secretary to Lord Ashley, later Earl of Shaftesbury, founder of the Whigs. Shaftesbury had fallen out of favour with Charles II, who suspected his loyalty, and Locke was in similar danger by association. Locke also knew some of the people implicated in the Rye House Plot, so when Sidney was arrested, Locke fled abroad. Locke had already composed several political tracts, but these were not published until after the accession of William and Mary. In *Two Treatises of Government* (1689) Locke rejected Hobbes's natural state of anarchy, but agreed that the political state is a human artifice brought together by common consent. Locke argued that, in God's eyes, everyone was created free and equal, but that individuals give up some of that in exchange for the benefits of a governed society. He believed that the basic (i.e. inalienable) human right was to property, which covered life, liberty and possession (or "estates"). In *An Essay Concerning Human Understanding* (1690) Locke also argued that no one is born with any basic beliefs or understandings but that everything is learned by experience. There are, though, certain innate feelings, notably a desire for happiness and an aversion to misery.

In his books Locke developed the following principles:

- Everyone is created free and equal but relinquishes some of this for the protection of society
- All individuals have a right to life, liberty and property
- Slavery is not a natural state but may be suffered by those who break the natural laws
- All individuals have a natural desire to pursue happiness
- There should be religious tolerance
- A government should be based on popular consent
- There is a right to rebel if government does not protect life, liberty, and property.

Locke kept his authorship of these works anonymous and they received only limited attention when published, but the importance and readership grew with time not just in Great Britain and Ireland, but also in the American colonies.

Frontispiece of Thomas Hobbes's *Leviathan*, published in 1651. The illustration is usually attributed to Wenceslaus Hollar.
BL, C.175.n.3

Liberty Exported

At this same time, the British colonies in America were developing their charters and constitutions and were influenced by the thinking of Sidney and Locke.

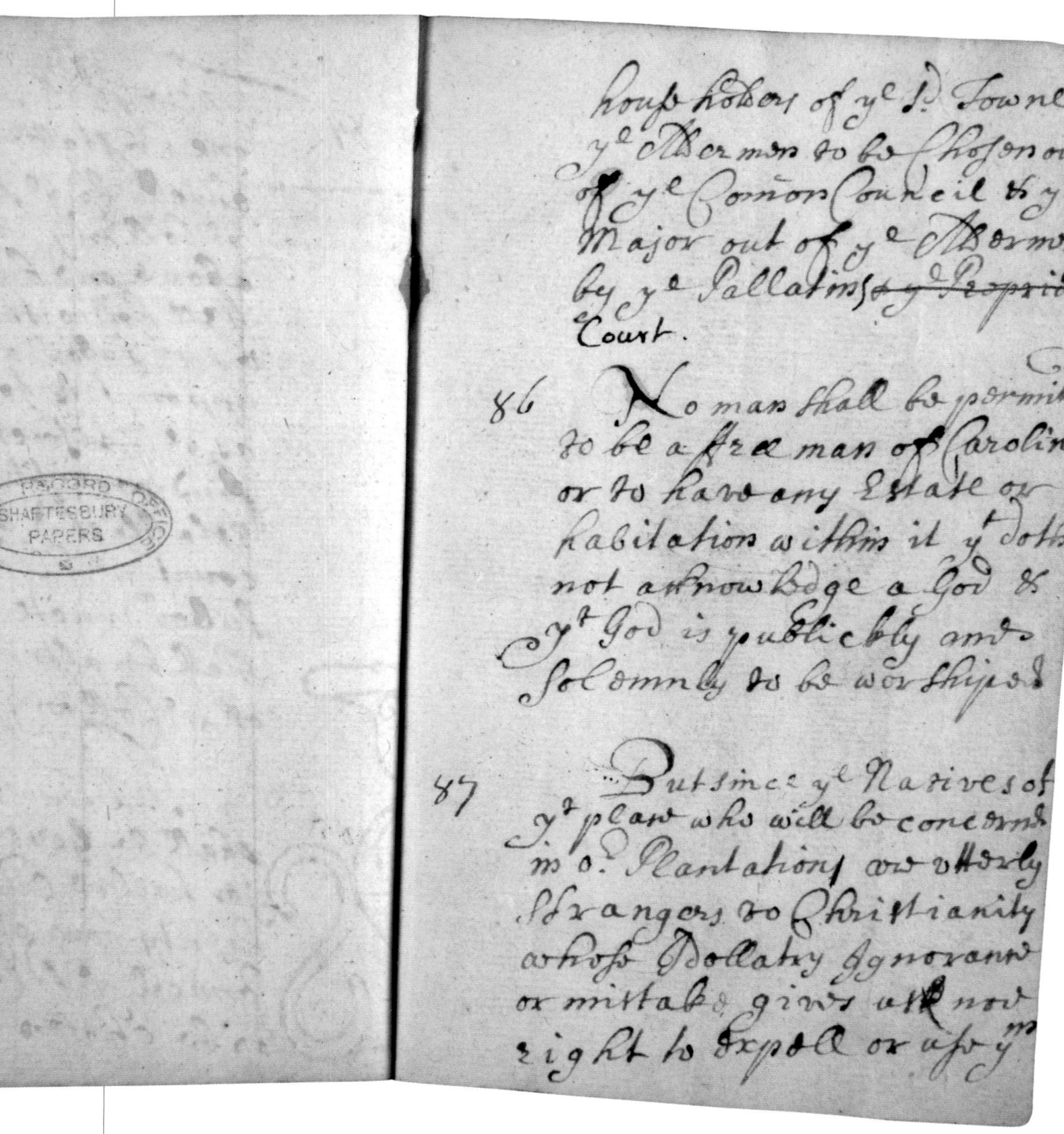
housholders of ye sd Towne is
ye Aldermen to be chosen out
of ye Common Council & ye
Major out of ye Aldermen
by ye Pallatins ~~or ye Proprietors~~
Court.

86 No man shall be permitted
to be a free man of Carolina
or to have any Estate or
habitation within it yt doth
not acknowledge a God &
yt God is publickly and
solemnly to be worshiped

87 But since ye Natives of
yt place who will be concerned
in or Plantations are utterly
Strangers to Christianity
whose Idollatry Ignorance
or mistake gives us noe
right to expell or use ym

An extract from John Locke's draft Constitution of Carolina which states that "No man shall be permitted to be a freeman of Carolina, or to have any estate or habitation within it, that doth not acknowledge a God."
National Archives, PRO 30/24/47/3

The first charter of liberties in the American colonies was by an English Puritan clergyman, Nathaniel Ward, who had emigrated in 1634. He wrote the *Body of Liberties* in 1641 and it was adopted by the colony of Massachusetts. It focused mostly on legal rights and did not advocate religious freedom, as anyone convicted of worshipping "any god but the Lord God" would be put to death. Nevertheless it was unusual for its time in considering at least some rights of children and animals.

In 1669, the Earl of Shaftesbury, then one of the Proprietors of the new colony of Carolina, involved John Locke in drafting that colony's constitution. In addition to clauses that were derived from developments in England, such as freedom of worship, trial by jury, biennial Parliaments, and even specific protection against double jeopardy, were other factors that the home country had not had to consider. Firstly there were the native Americans, who were recognised as "strangers to Christianity" through no fault of their own and therefore the settlers had "no right to expel them or use them ill". Secondly there was the matter of slaves. The document stated: "Every freeman of Carolina shall have absolute power and authority over his negro slaves."

Perhaps the most innovative of the colonies' constitutions was that created by the Quaker William Penn. On his father's death, Penn inherited a claim on a debt owed by Charles II. The King settled the debt in 1681 by granting Penn a significant area of land in America, which became Pennsylvania (named after Penn's father). Penn also negotiated fair treaties with the native Delaware Indians from whom he purchased quitclaims on the land. In consultation with Algernon Sidney, Penn drafted a "Frame of Government" in May 1682 in which he stated a basic tenet of freedom within society: "for liberty without obedience is confusion, and obedience without liberty is slavery." In addition to clauses on religious liberty, a free press, trial by jury and strict limitations on the death penalty, there were other clauses ahead of anything in England such as damages for wrongful imprisonment, compensation for victims of crime and reward for scientific endeavour.

Penn revised the Frame four times, and the final one, issued in 1701, was

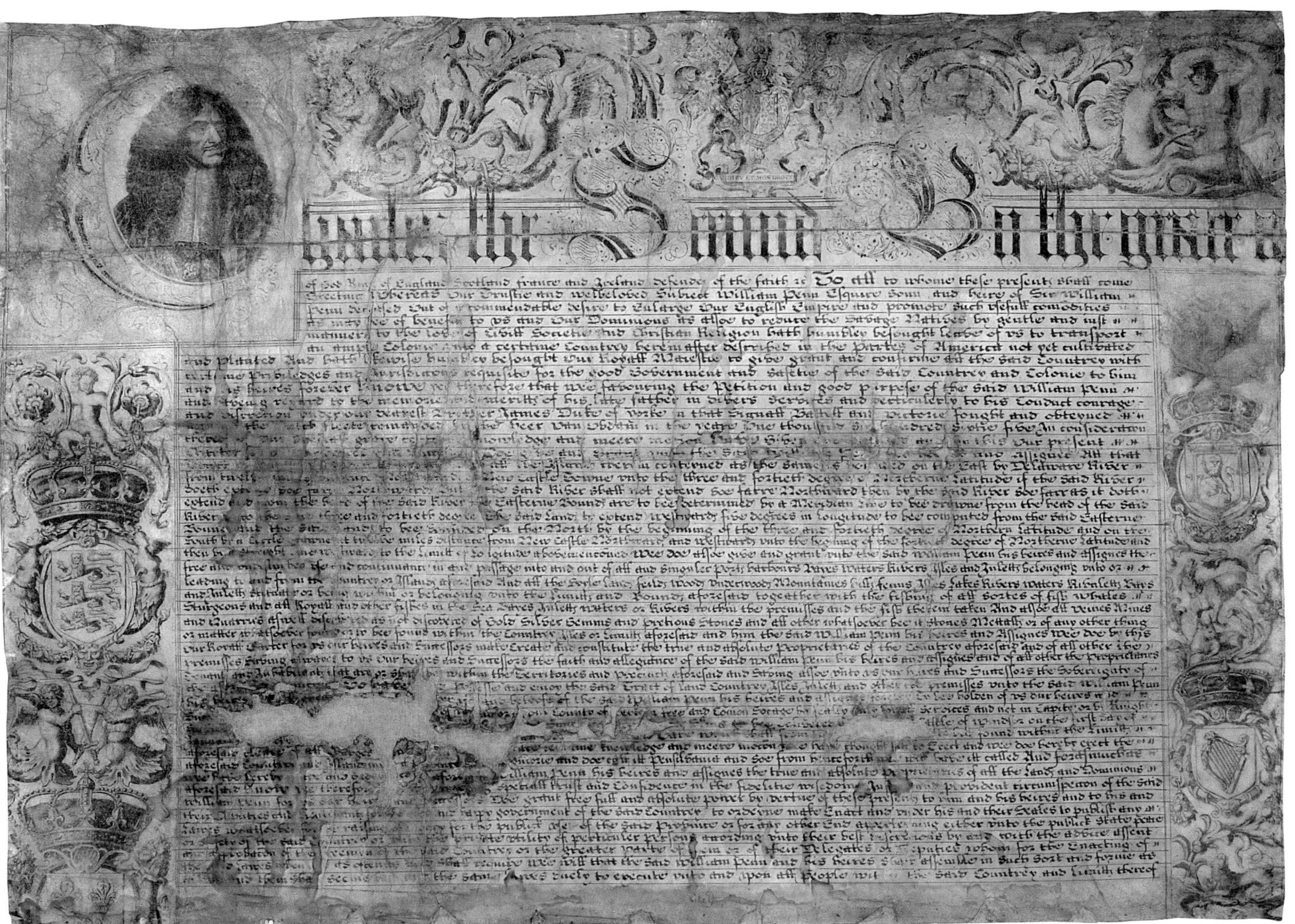

King Charles's charter of land to William Penn.
Pennsylvania State Archives

the Charter of Privileges which remained in force until the creation of the United States. In this version Penn went so far as to state that the clause relating to religious freedom, "shall be kept and remain, without any Alteration, inviolably for ever".

The influences of Sidney and Locke were most evident in the American Declaration of Independence and the subsequent Bill of Rights. Increasing dissent by many of the colonists towards the British government, notably over what was seen as unfair taxation without political representation, escalated into war in April 1775. The revolutionary government, the Continental Congress, set up in Philadelphia, agreed the Declaration of Independence on 4 July 1776.

Locke's basic principles are evident from the start of the Declaration, which states:

We hold these truths to be self-evident, that all men are created equal, that they are endowed by their Creator with certain unalienable Rights, that among these are Life, Liberty and the pursuit of Happiness.

The Declaration was written mostly by Thomas Jefferson together with John Adams and Benjamin Franklin. The American Constitution, adopted in 1787, was chiefly the work of James Madison and he also drafted the first ten amendments, known as the Bill of Rights, which came into force in December 1791. This was clearly influenced by earlier English documents like Magna Carta and the 1689 Bill of Rights, and included the right to bear arms, freedom of speech, freedom of the press, the right to petition government and the right to a trial by jury and the sure process of law.

Writing in 1825, Thomas Jefferson acknowledged the overriding source for American rights and liberties:

... as to the general principles of liberty and the rights of man, in nature and in society, the doctrines of Locke, in his 'Essay concerning the true original extent and end of civil government' and of Sidney in his 'Discourses on government', may be considered as those generally approved by our fellow citizens of this, and the United States.

The case that changed history

In 1670, William Penn was arrested for preaching to an unlawful assembly. Penn challenged the basis of the charge and when the judge refused to be specific Penn argued there was no case to answer. The jury ignored the judge's advice and found Penn simply "Guilty of Speaking". The judge discarded this and told the jury to reconsider. They decided Penn was "Not Guilty." Furious, the judge fined the jury and sent them to prison in default of payment. The jury requested a writ of *habeas corpus* and had their case heard before the Court of Common Plea, where they were upheld. This set the precedent that a jury's verdict is final and cannot be changed by pressure from the judge.

IN CONGRESS, JULY 4, 1776.

The unanimous Declaration of the thirteen united States of America,

When in the Course of human events, it becomes necessary for one people to dissolve the political bands which have connected them with another, and to assume among the powers of the earth, the separate and equal station to which the Laws of Nature and of Nature's God entitle them, a decent respect to the opinions of mankind requires that they should declare the causes which impel them to the separation. — We hold these truths to be self-evident, that all men are created equal, that they are endowed by their Creator with certain unalienable Rights, that among these are Life, Liberty and the pursuit of Happiness. — That to secure these rights, Governments are instituted among Men, deriving their just powers from the consent of the governed, — That whenever any Form of Government becomes destructive of these ends, it is the Right of the People to alter or to abolish it, and to institute new Government, laying its foundation on such principles and organizing its powers in such form, as to them shall seem most likely to effect their Safety and Happiness. Prudence, indeed, will dictate that Governments long established should not be changed for light and transient causes; and accordingly all experience hath shewn, that mankind are more disposed to suffer, while evils are sufferable, than to right themselves by abolishing the forms to which they are accustomed. But when a long train of abuses and usurpations, pursuing invariably the same Object evinces a design to reduce them under absolute Despotism, it is their right, it is their duty, to throw off such Government, and to provide new Guards for their future security. — Such has been the patient sufferance of these Colonies; and such is now the necessity which constrains them to alter their former Systems of Government. The history of the present King of Great Britain is a history of repeated injuries and usurpations, all having in direct object the establishment of an absolute Tyranny over these States. To prove this, let Facts be submitted to a candid world. — He has refused his Assent to Laws, the most wholesome and necessary for the public good. — He has forbidden his Governors to pass Laws of immediate and pressing importance, unless suspended in their operation till his Assent should be obtained; and when so suspended, he has utterly neglected to attend to them. — He has refused to pass other Laws for the accommodation of large districts of people, unless those people would relinquish the right of Representation in the Legislature, a right inestimable to them and formidable to tyrants only. — He has called together legislative bodies at places unusual, uncomfortable, and distant from the depository of their public Records, for the sole purpose of fatiguing them into compliance with his measures. — He has dissolved Represe[n]tative Houses repeatedly, for opposing with manly firmness his invasions on the rights of the people. — He has refused for a long time, after such dissolutions, to cause others to be elected; whereby the Legislative powers, incapable of Annihilation, have returned to the People at large for their exercise; the State remaining in the mean time exposed to all the dangers of invasion from without, and convulsions within. — He has endeavoured to prevent the population of these States; for that purpose obstructing the Laws for Naturalization of Foreigners; refusing to pass others to encourage their migrations hither, and raising the conditions of new Appropriations of Lands. — He has obstructed the Administration of Justice, by refusing his Assent to Laws for establishing Judiciary powers. — He has made Judges dependent on his Will alone, for the tenure of their offices, and the amount and payment of their salaries. — He has erected a multitude of New Offices, and sent hither swarms of Officers to harrass our people, and eat out their substance. — He has kept among us, in times of peace, Standing Armies without the Consent of our legislatures. — He has affected to render the Military independent of and superior to the Civil power. — He has combined with others to subject us to a jurisdiction foreign to our constitution, and unacknowledged by our laws; giving his Assent to their Acts of pretended Legislation: — For Quartering large bodies of armed troops among us: — For protecting them, by a mock Trial, from punishment for any Murders which they should commit on the Inhabitants of these States: — For cutting off our Trade with all parts of the world: — For imposing Taxes on us without our Consent: — For depriving us in many cases, of the benefits of Trial by Jury: — For transporting us beyond Seas to be tried for pretended offences — For abolishing the free System of English Laws in a neighbouring Province, establishing therein an Arbitrary government, and enlarging its Boundaries so as to render it at once an example and fit instrument for introducing the same absolute rule into these Colonies: — For taking away our Charters, abolishing our most valuable Laws, and altering fundamentally the Forms of our Governments: — For suspending our own Legislatures, and declaring themselves invested with power to legislate for us in all cases whatsoever. — He has abdicated Government here, by declaring us out of his Protection and waging War against us. — He has plundered our seas, ravaged our Coasts, burnt our towns, and destroyed the lives of our people. — He is at this time transporting large Armies of foreign Mercenaries to compleat the works of death, desolation and tyranny, already begun with circumstances of Cruelty & perfidy scarcely paralleled in the most barbarous ages, and totally unworthy the Head of a civilized nation. — He has constrained our fellow Citizens taken Captive on the high Seas to bear Arms against their Country, to become the executioners of their friends and Brethren, or to fall themselves by their Hands. — He has excited domestic insurrections amongst us, and has endeavoured to bring on the inhabitants of our frontiers, the merciless Indian Savages, whose known rule of warfare, is an undistinguished destruction of all ages, sexes and conditions. In every stage of these Oppressions We have Petitioned for Redress in the most humble terms: Our repeated Petitions have been answered only by repeated injury. A Prince, whose character is thus marked by every act which may define a Tyrant, is unfit to be the ruler of a free people. Nor have We been wanting in attentions to our Brittish brethren. We have warned them from time to time of attempts by their legislature to extend an unwarrantable jurisdiction over us. We have reminded them of the circumstances of our emigration and settlement here. We have appealed to their native justice and magnanimity, and we have conjured them by the ties of our common kindred to disavow these usurpations, which, would inevitably interrupt our connections and correspondence. They too have been deaf to the voice of justice and of consanguinity. We must, therefore, acquiesce in the necessity, which denounces our Separation, and hold them, as we hold the rest of mankind, Enemies in War, in Peace Friends. —

We, therefore, the Representatives of the united States of America, in General Congress, Assembled, appealing to the Supreme Judge of the world for the rectitude of our intentions, do, in the Name, and by Authority of the good People of these Colonies, solemnly publish and declare, That these United Colonies are, and of Right ought to be Free and Independent States; that they are Absolved from all Allegiance to the British Crown, and that all political connection between them and the State of Great Britain, is and ought to be totally dissolved; and that as Free and Independent States, they have full Power to levy War, conclude Peace, contract Alliances, establish Commerce, and to do all other Acts and Things which Independent States may of right do. — And for the support of this Declaration, with a firm reliance on the protection of divine Providence, we mutually pledge to each other our Lives, our Fortunes and our sacred Honor.

John Hancock

Button Gwinnett
Lyman Hall
Geo Walton.

Wm Hooper
Joseph Hewes,
John Penn

Edward Rutledge 1.

Thos Heyward Junr.
Thomas Lynch Junr.
Arthur Middleton

Samuel Chase
Wm. Paca
Thos. Stone
Charles Carroll of Carrollton

George Wythe
Richard Henry Lee
Th Jefferson
Benj Harrison
Thos Nelson jr.
Francis Lightfoot Lee
Carter Braxton

Robt Morris
Benjamin Rush
Benj. Franklin
John Morton
Geo Clymer
Jas. Smith
Geo. Taylor
James Wilson
Geo. Ross
Caesar Rodney
Geo Read
Tho M:Kean

Wm Floyd
Phil. Livingston
Frans. Lewis
Lewis Morris

Richd. Stockton
Jno Witherspoon
Fras. Hopkinson
John Hart
Abra Clark

Josiah Bartlett
Wm. Whipple
Saml Adams
John Adams
Robt Treat Paine
Elbridge Gerry
Step. Hopkins
William Ellery
Roger Sherman
Samel Huntington
Wm. Williams
Oliver Wolcott
Matthew Thornton

W. J. STONE SC. WASHn

The American Declaration of Independence.

Thomas Paine

One name that is linked with both the American and French Revolutions is that of Thomas Paine, whose vision not only called for Republicanism but for a system of social welfare that was generations ahead of its time.

This 1791 caricature by James Gillray shows Paine measuring the crown in order to make a new pair of breeches. Paine had apprenticed as a corset-maker, a fact which cartoonists set upon in various satires of his achievements.
British Museum, 1868,0808.6057

Thomas Paine was born in Thetford, Norfolk, in 1737. Raised a Quaker, he spent the first half of his life in a series of failed jobs and two unfortunate marriages but, armed with a letter of introduction from Benjamin Franklin, he emigrated to America in 1774. He turned to journalism, becoming increasingly radical – one essay attacked the very basis of slavery. In January 1776 he published *Common Sense*. It took the colonies by storm. There were mixed reactions but a growing enthusiasm for Paine's rallying call to revolution and independence.

Common Sense set out why the general populace is not best served by a despotic government or monarchy. He wrote, "Of more worth is one honest man to society ... than all the crowned ruffians that ever lived." He felt it was impractical for America to be governed from so distant a country as Britain, and no benefits arose by remaining under British yoke. Neither did he see the colonies as especially British, since it had been the refuge of many nationalities. Rather, he saw them as the asylum of liberty, as stated in his oft-quoted rally:

Painting of Thomas Paine by Laurent Dabos in *c.*1791.
The National Portrait Gallery, London. NPG 6805

Freedom hath been hunted round the globe. Asia and Africa have long expelled her. Europe regards her like a stranger, and England hath given her warning to depart. O! receive the fugitive, and prepare in time an asylum for mankind.

Paine's Quaker origins made him opposed to violence, but he believed that the only cause for which one might take up arms was liberty.

Paine remained in America throughout the War of Independence. He returned to England in 1788 and was there when the French Revolution began in June 1789. He was supportive from the start and took the first opportunity to visit France and acquaint himself with events. He had already started on *Rights of Man*, but when Edmund Burke published an attack on the Revolution, Paine reworked his book as a response. He contrasted the governments of post-Revolution America and France with Great Britain's. He explored how government should support not only mankind's natural rights (life, liberty, free speech, freedom of conscience) but its civil rights (relating to security and protection). He highlighted the imbalance between those who paid taxes and those who were allowed to vote. Using detailed calculations, Paine showed how a tax system, ncluding a form of income tax, could provide social welfare in support of those civil rights. He outlined a plan covering widespread education, child benefit, pensions for the elderly, poor relief and much more. He concluded: *When it shall be said in any country in the world, my poor are happy; neither ignorance nor distress is to be found among them; my jails are empty of prisoners, my streets of beggars; the aged are not in want, the taxes are not oppressive; the rational world is my friend, because I am the friend of its happiness: when these things can be said, then may that country boast its constitution and its government.*

Rights of Man was published in two parts in March 1791 and February 1792. It sold in its thousands, becoming one of the most widely read books in the western world at that time. When the second part appeared, the Government sought to suppress it and indicted Paine for seditious libel. Paine fled to France and was tried *in absentia*. The hand-picked jury were guaranteed a dinner and two guineas each if they found him guilty. Paine was outlawed in Britain and never returned. In France he was not only offered French citizenship but a place on the National Convention. He even contributed to the drafting of what proved to be an abortive French constitution.

At the trial of Louis XVI Paine voted against the King's execution. This tarnished Paine's reputation and led to him being regarded as a supporter of Jacques Brissot, a revolutionary who was now believed to be working against the revolution. Paine was imprisoned under Robespierre's regime and narrowly escaped execution. His health failed. He returned to the United States in 1802 where he died in 1809, virtually forgotten. John Adams wrote, "Without the pen of Thomas Paine, the sword of Washington would have been wielded in vain."

The French Declaration of the Rights of Man and the Citizen

On 26 August 1789 the National Assembly adopted and issued the *Declaration of the Rights of Man and the Citizen*. It drew upon the theories of John Locke and the French philosophers Jean-Jacques Rousseau and the Baron de Montesquieu. It also showed the influence of the American Declaration of Independence. Its main features are:

- Men are born free and remain free and equal in rights
- These rights are liberty, property, security and resistance to oppression.
- Liberty consists in the power to do anything that does not injure others
- The law has only the rights to forbid such actions as are injurious to society
- Law is the expression of the general will.

Amongst other rights is the first overt statement that every man is presumed innocent until proven guilty. Like other constitutions it called for religious tolerance and freedom of expression. Taxes would be apportioned according to individual's means. For the first time a declaration of rights not only proclaimed the freedom of individuals, but based a new government on that assumption.

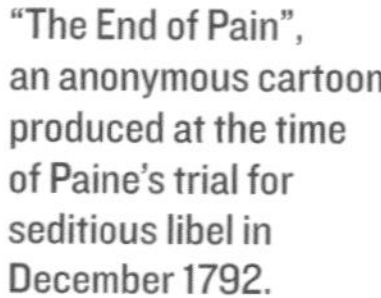

"The End of Pain", an anonymous cartoon produced at the time of Paine's trial for seditious libel in December 1792.
British Museum, 1868/0808/6325

The French Declaration of the Rights of Man and the Citizen.

Archives nationales, Paris. AE II, 3701

DECLARATION DES DROITS DE L'HOMME ET DU CITOYEN

Le Peuple français convaincu que l'oubli et le mépris des droits naturels de l'hoṁe ſont les ſeules cauſes des malheurs du monde, a réſolu d'expoſer dans une déclaration ſolemnelle ces droits ſacrés et inaliénables, afin que tous les citoyens, pouvant comparer ſans ceſſe les actes du gouvernement avec le but de toute inſtitution ſociale, ne ſe laiſſent jamais opprimer et avilir par la tyrannie; afin que le peuple ait toujours devant les yeux les baſes de ſa liberté, de ſon bonheur, le magiſtrat la regle de ſes devoirs, le légiſlateur l'objet de sa miſſion.

En conſéquence il proclame, en préſence de l'Etre ſuprême la déclaration ſuivante des droits de l'homme et du citoyen

ART. 1er Le but de la ſociété eſt le bonheur commun.

Le gouvernement eſt inſtitué pour garantir à l'homme la jouiſſance de ſes droits naturels et impreſcriptibles.

II. Ces droits ſont l'égalité, la liberté, la sûreté, la propriété.

III Tous les hommes ſont égaux par la nature et devant la loi.

IV. La loi eſt l'expreſſion libre et ſolemnelle de la volonté générale; elle eſt la même pour tous, ſoit qu'elle protége, soit qu'elle puniſſe; elle ne peut ordonner que ce qui est juſte et utile à la ſociété: elle ne peut déffendre que ce qui lui eſt nuiſible.

V. Tous les citoyens ſont également admiſibles aux emplois publics. Les peuples libres ne connoiſſent d'autres motiſs de préférence dans leurs élections que les vertus et les talens.

VI. La liberté eſt le pouvoir qui appartient à l'homme de faire tout ce qui ne nuit pas aux droits d'autrui: elle à pour principe, la nature; pour règle la juſtice; pour ſauve-garde, la loi; ſa limite morale eſt dans cette maxime, *ne fais à un autre ce que tu ne veux pas qu'il te soit fait*.

VII. Le droit de manifeſter ſa penſée et ſes opinions, ſoit par la voie de la preſſe, ſoit de toute autre maniére le droit de s aſſembler paiſiblement le libre exercices des cultes ne peuvent être interdits.

La néceſſité d'énoncer ces droits ſuppoſe ou la préſence, ou le ſouvenir récent du deſpotiſme.

VIII La sûreté consiſte dans la protection accordée par la ſociété à chacun de ſes membres, pour la conſervation de ſa perſonne, de ſes droits et de ſes propriétés.

IX. La loi doit protéger la liberté publique et individuelle contre l'oppreſſion de ceux qui gouvernent.

X Nul ne doit être accuſé, arrété, ni détenu, que dans les cas déterminés par la loi et ſelon les formes qu'elle à preſcrites; tout citoyen appellé ou ſaiſi par l'autorité de la loi doit obéir a l'inſtant; il ſe rend coupable par la réſiſtance.

XI. Toute acte exercé contre un homme hors des cas et ſans les formes que la loi détermine, eſt arbitraire et tyrannique: celui contre lequel on voudroit l'exécuter par la violence à le droit de le repouſſer par la force.

XII. Ceux qui ſolliciteroient, expédieroient, ſigneroient, exécuteroient ou ſeroient exécuter des actes arbitraires, ſont coupables et doivent être punis.

XIII. Tout homme étant préſumé innocent juſqu'à ce qu'il ait été déclaré coupable; s'il est jugé indiſpenſable de l'arrêter, toute rigueur qui ne ſeroit pas néceſſaire pour s'aſſurer de ſa perſonne, doit être ſévèrement réprimée par la loi.

XIV. Nul ne doit être jugé ni puni, qu'après avoir été entendu ou légalement appelé, et qu'en vertu d'une loi promulguée antérieurement au délit. La loi qui puniroit des délits commis avant qu'elle éxiſtat, ſeroit une tyrannie: l'effet retroactif donne à la loi ſeroit un crime.

XV. La loi ne doit decerner que des peines strictement et évidemment néceſſaires: les peines doivent être proportionnées au délit et utiles à la ſociété.

XVI Le droit de propriété eſt celui qui appartient à tout citoyen de jouir et de diſpoſer à ſon gré de ses biens, de ſes revenus, du fruit de son travail et de ſon induſtrie.

XVII. Nul genre de travail, de culture, de commerce, ne peut être interdit à l'induſtrie des citoyens.

XVIII. Tout homme peut engager ſes ſervices, ſon tems; mais il ne peut ſe vendre ni être vendu. Sa perſonne n'est pas une propriété aliénable. La loi ne reconnoit point de domeſticité; il ne peut exiſter qu'un engagement de ſoins et de reconnoiſſance entre l'homme qui travaille et celui qui l'emploie.

XIX. Nul ne peut être privé de la moindre portion de sa propriété, ſans ſon conſentement, ſi ce n'eſt lorsque la néceſſité publique légalement conſtatée l'exige, et ſous la condition d'une juſte et préalable indemnité.

XX. Nulle contribution ne peut être établie que pour l'utilité générale. Tous les citoyens ont droit de concourir à l'établiſſement des contributions, d'en ſurveiller l'emploi, et de s'en faire rendre compte.

XXI. Les ſecours publics ſont une dette ſacrée. La ſociété doit la ſubſiſtance aux citoyens malheureux, ſoit en leur procurant du travail, ſoit en aſſurant les moyens d'exiſter à ceux qui ſont hors d'état de travailler.

XXII. L'inſtruction eſt le beſoin de tous. La ſociété doit ſavoriſer de tout ſon pouvoir les progrés de la raiſon publique et mettre l'inſtruction à la portée de tous les citoyens.

XXIII. La garantie ſociale conſiſte dans l'action de tous, pour aſſurer à chacun la jouiſſance et la conſervation de ſes droits; cette garantie repoſe ſur la ſouveraineté nationale.

XXIV. Elle ne peut éxiſter, ſi les limites des fonctions publiques ne ſont pas clairement determinées par la loi, et ſi la responsabilité de tous les fonctionnaires n'eſt pas aſſurée.

XXV. La ſouveraineté réſide dans le peuple. Elle eſt une et indiviſible impreſcriptible et inaliénable.

XXVI. Aucune portion du peuple ne peut exercer la puiſſance du peuple entier; mais chaque section du ſouverain aſſemblée doit jouir du droit d'exprimer ſa volonté avec une entière liberté.

XXVII. Que tout individu qui uſurperoit la ſouveraineté ſoit à l'instant mis à mort par les hommes libres.

XXVIII. Un peuple à toujours le droit de revoir, de reformer et de changer ſa constitution. Une génération ne peut aſſujétir à ſes lois les générations futures.

XXIX. Chaque citoyen à un droit égale de concourir à la formation de la loi, et à la nomination de ſes mandataires ou de ſes agens.

XXX. Les fonctions publiques ſont eſſentiellement temporaires; elles ne peuvent être conſidérées comme des diſtinctions ni comme des récompenſes, mais comme des devoirs.

XXXI. Les délits des mandataires du peuple et de ſes agens ne doivent jamais être impunis. Nul n'a le droit de ſe prétendre plus inviolable que les autres citoyens.

XXXII. Le droit de préſenter des pétitions aux dépoſitaires de l'autorité publique, ne peut, en aucun cas, être interdit, ſuspendu ni limité.

XXXIII. La réſistance à l'oppreſſion eſt la conſéquence des autres droits de l'homme.

XXXIV Il y a oppreſſion contre le corps ſocial, lorſqu'un ſeul de ſes membres eſt opprimé. Il y a oppreſſion contre chaque membre, lorſque le corps ſocial eſt opprimé.

XXXV Quand le gouvernement viole les droits du peuple, l'inſurrection eſt pour le peuple, et pour chaque portion du peuple, le plus ſacré des droits et le plus indiſpenſable des devoirs.

Signé COLLOT-D'HERBOIS *Préſident* *DURAND MAILLANE, DUCOS, MEAULLE, CH. DELACROIX, GOSSUIN, P.A. LALOY, Secretaires.*

The Abolition of Slavery

The opposition to the slave trade was as much, if not more, a humanitarian issue as a question of rights. Even so, those with a vested interest sustained the trade despite the biggest public campaign Parliament had ever seen. It required a complete reform of Parliament before the slave trade was abolished.

Portrait of Granville Sharp included in *Memoirs of Granville Sharp, Esq.* published in 1828.
BL, 135.b.1

England's involvement in the slave trade started in 1562 when John Hawkins conveyed African slaves to the West Indies. Prior to this, England had no slave culture. William the Conqueror had banned the export of slaves from England and in 1102, at the Council of Westminster, the Church had outlawed slavery.

With no common law as precedent, the justice system had to create its own rules about slaves. In 1701 Lord Chief Justice Sir John Holt ruled, "as soon as a Negro comes into England, he becomes free: one may be a villein in England, but not a slave." Not all agreed. A court case in 1677 had stated that black slaves could be treated as "goods" because "negroes were infidels". It implied that if a slave were baptised he was free, but a legal judgment in 1729 stated that a slave's status did not change when they came to England and they could not be freed by baptism.

Often quoted for setting legal precedent is the case of *Somerset v Stewart* in 1772. Stewart had come to England with his slave Somerset, who escaped but was recaptured and chained onboard ship ready for return to Virginia. His plight was noted by abolitionists who applied for a writ of *habeas corpus*, allowing Somerset to be brought before the courts. Lord Mansfield, who was well aware of the potential minefield, ruled that all the time a slave was in England he was subject to English law, not colonial law, and as such could not be forcibly removed. Somerset was freed. The case was interpreted as meaning slavery was not legal in England, although Mansfield had sidestepped that issue.

The Somerset case had been championed by Granville Sharp. He produced many pamphlets and joined forces with former slave Olaudah Equiano. In 1783 they were involved in the case of the slave ship *Zong*, whose captain had thrown 133 ill slaves over-board, because they were worth more under insurance than as cargo. Yet the judge – Lord Mansfield again – did not see this as mass murder because slaves were property.

In 1786 Sharp worked with the Committee for the Relief of the Black Poor, to help destitute black slaves. They decided to repatriate them to a colony in Sierra Leone, West Africa, named Granville Town after Sharp. The scheme failed because of disease and local hostilities, but also because it was not a voluntary resettlement. Though paved with good intentions, the scheme failed to recognise the slaves' own wishes.

In 1787 the Society for Effecting the Abolition of the African Slave Trade was established. Its membership was mostly Quakers, but it also included Granville Sharp as chairman, Thomas Clarkson, Josiah Wedgwood and the MP William Wilberforce. Clarkson was the most tireless worker against slavery. He has been called "the first great propagandist and single-issue campaigner". He travelled extensively, drawing up petitions and collecting

Was slavery legal?

The Somerset case was used in 1775 by Scottish slave Joseph Knight. He had been baptised and had a family but worked as a "perpetual servant" to John Wedderburn, who stated that Knight could obtain his freedom if he returned to Jamaica. Knight wanted to stay in Scotland and appealed to the Courts. At the Court of Sessions the judge stated that as the laws of Jamaica did not apply in Scotland, Wedderburn "had no right to the Negro's service for any space of time, nor to send him out of the country against his consent." Knight was freed.

Clarkson's African Box. During his travels Thomas Clarkson acquired evidence of the violence and savagery of the slave trade which he stored in a special box and displayed during his speeches and meetings.
Wisbech and Fenland Museum

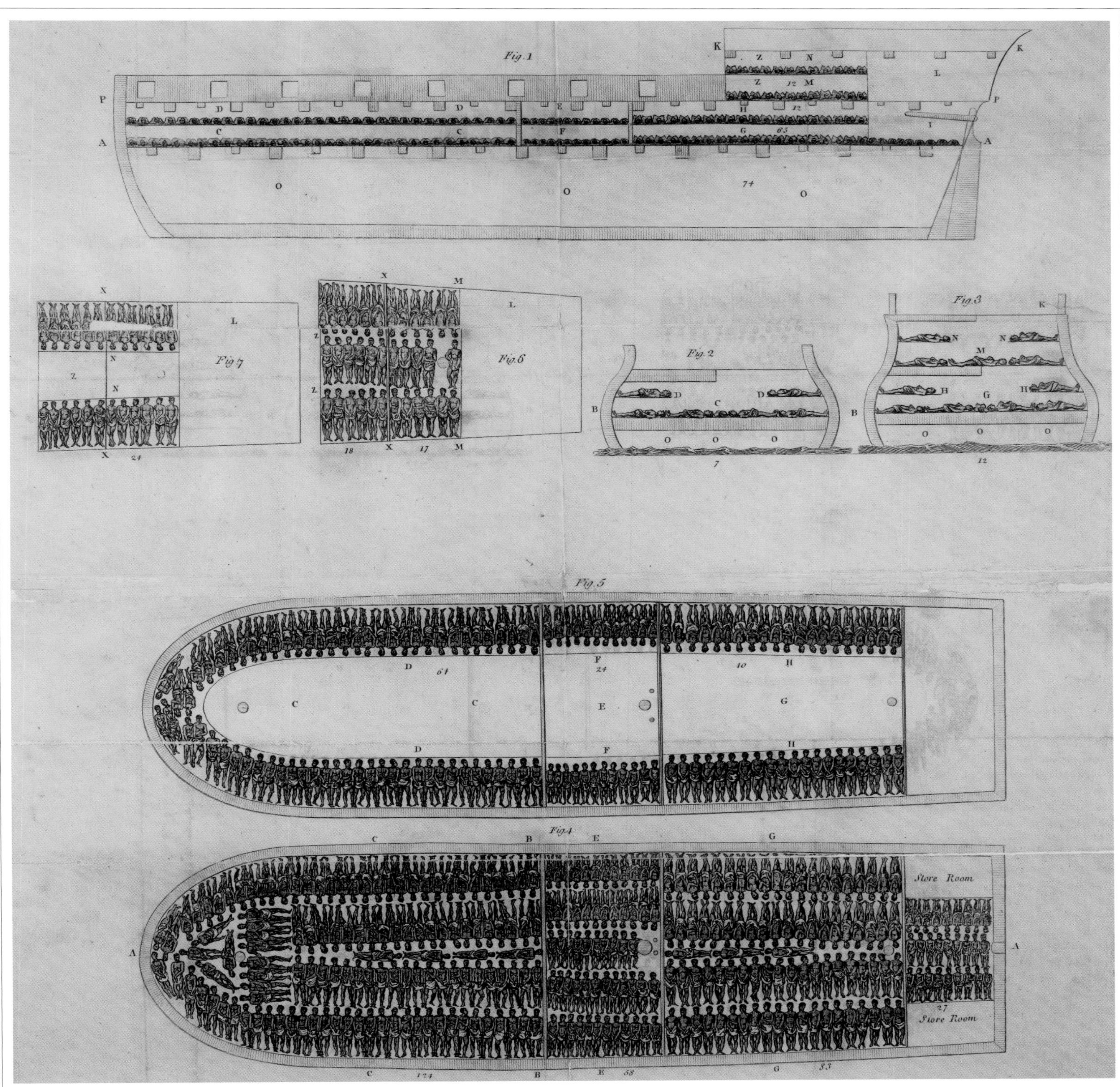

This picture of the slave-ship *Brookes* was reproduced on posters, in magazines and books, and did much to win support for the abolition cause.
BL, 522.f.23

material. After a speech he gave in Manchester in 1787, his petition was signed by 11,000 people, a fifth of the city's population. Thanks to Clarkson, the petitions sent to Parliament were on an unprecedented scale. Inevitably those with vested interests – traders, merchants, ship owners and the like – also lobbied Parliament to protect the slave trade.

Equiano and Clarkson produced a diagram of the ship *Brookes* showing how 482 slaves were crammed into the hold of the ship. At times it carried up to 740 slaves. In 1788 William Dolben pushed an Act through Parliament restricting how many slaves could be transported per ship. Equiano's autobiography about his experiences as a slave became very popular.

Despite their work, the first abolition Bill introduced in 1789 led only to a Parliamentary review. When discussed in 1791 it lost by 163 votes to

The birth of Freetown

During the American Revolution the British promised freedom to any slaves who deserted their rebel masters and fought for the loyalists. After the War some returned to England, but many held fast in New York. In 1783 most were shipped to the colony of Nova Scotia in Canada, but local resentment led to riots. Some black settlers chose to return to Africa and were taken to Sierra Leone in 1792, where they resettled the abandoned Granville Town as Freetown.

AM I NOT A MAN AND A BROTHER

Opposite:
This jasperware anti-slavery medallion issued by Josiah Wedgwood in 1787 is modelled after the Seal for the Committee for the Abolition of Slavery, and bears the inscription, "Am I Not a Man and a Brother?"
British Museum, PY 1887,0307.1.683

The Black Man's Lament, a poem by reformist, abolitionist and Quaker Amelia Opie, published in 1826 and depicting the slavery petitions signed throughout Britain.
BL, T.1271.(2)

THE

BLACK MAN'S LAMENT.

THE PETITION FOR ABOLISHING THE SLAVE-TRADE.

COME, listen to my plaintive ditty,
Ye tender hearts, and children dear!
And, should it move your souls to pity,
Oh! try to *end* the griefs you hear.

THE BLACK MAN'S LAMENT. 3

SUGAR-CANE.

There is a *beauteous plant* *, that grows
In western India's sultry clime,
Which makes, alas! the Black man's woes,
And also makes the White man's crime.

* "A field of canes, when standing in the month of November, when it is in arrow or full blossom, (says Beckford, in his descriptive account of the Island of Jamaica,) is one of the most beautiful productions that the pen or pencil can possibly describe. It, in common, rises from three to eight feet, or more, in height; a difference

88. Wilberforce introduced Bills almost annually over the next decade, but all failed. By 1800 Britain had been responsible for transporting nearly three million slaves – over a third of the trade.

In 1806 the campaign was joined by maritime lawyer James Stephen, who devised a new approach. He suggested a Bill that banned the British dealing in slaves with France or its colonies. With Britain at war with France, it was difficult to argue against, and the Bill was passed in May 1806, even though it restricted over half the British slave trade.

This gave the abolitionists new hope. William Pitt had died in January 1806 and his successor, Lord Grenville, was not only in support of abolition but could fight the cause from within the House of Lords. Clarkson encouraged another campaign and in 1807 Wilberforce introduced the Slave Trade Bill to prohibit the trade throughout the British Empire. It passed.

The battle was only half-won. Slave ships continued to operate. Parliament lobbied other governments to cease the trade in slaves. Captains were fined £100 per slave, but this only increased the likelihood of the more unscrupulous traders throwing slaves overboard if discovered.

Wilberforce and Clarkson continued to campaign vigorously. They founded the Society for the Mitigation and Gradual Abolition of Slavery (later the Anti-Slavery Society) in 1823. With Wilberforce's health failing he retired from Parliament in 1825 and his role was taken on by Thomas Buxton. Women were also active in the campaign. Unable to make an impression on the Anti-Slavery Society, the women formed their own Ladies Society for the Relief of Negro Slaves. Their most active advocate, Elizabeth Heyrick, wanted a complete and immediate ban. Starting in Birmingham, they established a network of women's abolition societies. By 1830 they and Wilberforce's campaign were working closer together.

The Reform Act of 1832 and subsequent elections changed the face of Parliament. When the Slavery Abolition Bill was presented to Parliament, under the government of Earl Grey, it was debated for three months. When passed in July 1833, it was not without a price. Only slaves under six years old were freed immediately. Others had to work for four years as unpaid apprentices. This form of indenture was slavery by another name. However, on 1 August 1838 some 800,000 slaves were freed with compensation of £20 million paid to slave owners.

Wilberforce learned on his deathbed that slavery was abolished after 46 years of campaigning. He died three days later.

Olaudah Equiano depicted on the frontispiece of his autobiography, *The Interesting Narrative of the Life of Olaudah Equiano, or Gustavus Vassa, the African*, published in London, 1789.
BL, 1489.g.50

Free the World

Slavery was the first major humanitarian rights issue that Britain pursued beyond its borders. It led Britain to patrol the seas to intercept slave ships and negotiate treaties with other countries. Yet even today there is still slavery and human trafficking.

Capture of the Slave Schooner Bolodora by HM Schooner Pickle, 6th June, 1829, painted by Edward Duncan, 1831. The Spanish *Bolodora* left Africa in October 1828 and encountered the British HMS *Pickle* just off Cuba. After an exchange of gunfire, the *Bolodora* surrendered with a cargo of 335 slaves.
British Museum, 1983,U.241

With the passing of the 1833 Act there were those who believed that the job was done, and the Anti-Slavery Society was laid to rest. Others felt strongly that it should not be tolerated anywhere and in April 1839 the British and Foreign Anti-Slavery Society was founded by Joseph Sturge. Other founder members included Thomas Buxton and Thomas Clarkson, who was still active after fifty years. The Society organised a National Convention in London in June 1840 attended by delegates from all over the world. The Convention was chaired by Thomas Buxton with Prince Albert as President. Thomas Clarkson, then aged 80, gave a moving speech which brought men and women to tears.

There remained problems within Britain's territories. The sale of slaves was prohibited in India under the Indian Slavery Act of 1843, but slavery itself was not forbidden until the Indian Penal Code of 1860. In Ceylon slave owners had to register their slaves but, because it cost three shillings per slave, few bothered. Non-registration meant they forfeited the slave and, as few were registered, in 1845 Lord Stanley issued an order abolishing slavery.

The situation in Africa was a bigger problem. In 1812 the Admiralty created a West Coast Anti-slavery Squadron, operated by the Royal Navy, initially based at Freetown, Sierra Leone. Its purpose was to patrol the African coastline, to intercept any slave ships and free the slaves. The Squadron also negotiated treaties with local chiefs.

It was no easy task and many ships eluded the Squadron. By 1860 they had seized 1,600 ships and freed some 150,000 Africans. Alas, at least another two million slaves were still transported during that period. It wasonly as Britain annexed various territories, as the Empire grew, that it could gain more control over the trade. This included the Gold Coast [Ghana] in 1874 and Northern Nigeria in 1885, though it was not until 1928 that slavery became illegal in Ghana.

David Livingstone reported on the problems of slavery in South and East Africa in 1858. In Zanzibar, over 80% of the population were slaves brought from the African interior. In 1873 Livingstone's friend, John Kirk, became Consul-General to Zanzibar. Along with Sir Henry Bartle Frere, the former Governor of Bombay, Kirk was able to negotiate a slave treaty with the new sultan, Seyyid Barghash, though only under threat of a naval blockade. It came into force just weeks after Livingstone's death. Even then a form of disguised slavery continued with freed slaves signing oppressive work contracts. It was not until 1897 that slavery was outlawed in Zanzibar. Ironically Sierra Leone, which began as a refuge for freed slaves, still operated slavery legally within its borders until 1927. Northern Nigeria was the last territory then under British rule to abolish slavery in 1936.

Trafficking or slavery?

Although slavery is abolished in Britain, it has become a primary destination for human trafficking. Many are women brought to Britain for sexual exploitation. Migrant workers, including children, are also trafficked for forced labour. In 2000, 58 Chinese illegal immigrants were found suffocated in a lorry arriving at Dover from the Netherlands. In 2004, 19 immigrant Chinese workers died when they were trapped by fast-rising tides while collecting cockles in Morecambe Bay. The tragedy led to the Gangmasters (Licensing) Act to control gangmasters and safeguard the workers.

The Anti-Slavery Convention held in June 1840. Thomas Clarkson's moving speech was captured in this painting by Benjamin Haydon.
The National Portrait Gallery, London. D12546

The slave market in Zanzibar was opened in 1811 by the Sultan of Muscat. Slaves were sold to work in the clove industry. It was closed in 1873 and a church was erected on the site. Picture from *The Illustrated London News*, 8 June 1872.

The Rights of Women

In the eyes of the law a married woman had no property, no vote and no rights to her children. It was a long struggle for them to achieve their rights as individuals and the struggle still continues for many women to achieve full equality with men.

In 1865 Elizabeth Garrett found a loophole to take the examination for the Society of Apothecaries. Despite many obstacles she qualified as a doctor, although the Society rapidly closed the loophole.
The National Portrait Gallery, London. x8446

By the eighteenth century the feudal state of "coverture" was enshrined as common law. It regarded a husband and wife as a single entity, but all rights belonged to the husband. Whilst single or widowed women could own money, property and run businesses, married women had no equivalent right without pursuing expensive legal settlements.

In 1836 Caroline Norton, granddaughter of the playwright Richard Brinsley Sheridan, lost access to her children when her violent husband took them away. Fighting on her behalf, the MP Thomas Telfourd secured the Custody of Children Act in 1839, which allowed mothers not guilty of adultery to have custody of children under seven and access to older children. Norton supported herself by writing and a small legacy from her mother, but her husband argued this money was rightfully his. Again Norton fought the law and helped establish the Matrimonial Causes Act in 1857. This allowed deserted or separated wives to keep any money they acquired directly. It was not until the Married Woman's Property Act of 1870, and subsequent legislation, that married women were allowed to keep money they earned directly and have ownership of property acquired before or after marriage.

Caroline Norton, whose family problems led eventually to the law being changed in favour of married women.
BL, 1508/1657

Although there were a few elite businesswomen, most jobs held by women in the nineteenth century were either as domestic servants, in agriculture or in the textile industry. In May 1833 the card setters at a mill in Scholes, near Leeds, became the first women to go on strike for a better piece-rate. They were the exception rather than the rule, though Robert Owen was advocating equal pay in his Grand National Consolidated Trades Union. Women's trades unions, encouraged by the Women's Protective and Provident League, founded in 1874 by Lady Dilke and Emma Paterson, made little progress. Unions argued that it was men who earned the family wage, and women working in similar jobs undercut men's wages.

University education was also denied women who could thus not pursue professional careers. In 1869 Emily Davies established Girton College, the first university college for women, relocated to Cambridge in 1873. The London School of Medicine for Women was founded in 1874, chiefly through the determination of Sophia Jex-Blake who had been frustrated at her attempts to gain a medical education. London University was the first to award women degrees on the same terms as men in 1878.

The 1870 Education Act allowed women to vote and serve on School Boards, and the 1894 Local Government Act allowed married women the right to vote and sit on municipal councils. In 1919 the Sex Disqualifications (Removals) Act allowed women, including married women, to hold certain professional posts. The first woman magistrate,

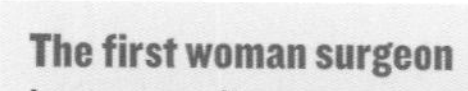

The first woman surgeon

It was not discovered until after her death that the army surgeon James Barry was in fact a woman: the Irish-born Margaret Bulkley. She was disguised as a boy from the age of 10 and passed her whole adult life as a man, studying at medical school in Edinburgh and qualifying as a doctor in 1812 and as a surgeon in 1813. It would be another century before Eleanor Davies-Colley became the first recognised woman surgeon in 1911.

Members of the National Association of Women Civil Servants, the National Union of Women Teachers and St Joan's Alliance march in protest in 1955 as part of the EPCC's campaign against the government's refusal to grant equal pay to women in public services.

"Better citizens"

Mary Wollstonecraft, the wife of William Godwin and mother of the future Mary Shelley, wrote one of the first books on female emancipation, *A Vindication of the Rights of Women*, in 1792. She emphasised how much women could contribute to society if only they were allowed. She wrote: "Would men but generously snap our chains, and be content with rational fellowship, instead of slavish obedience, they would find us more observant daughters, more affectionate sisters, more faithful wives, more reasonable mothers— in a word, better citizens."

Ada Summers, was sworn in on 31 December 1919; the first woman barrister, Helena Normanton, took up her practice in 1922, as did the first woman solicitor, Carrie Morrison.

During the First World War women did many jobs previously undertaken by men. In July 1918 a five-shillings-a-week war bonus was paid to male tram-drivers, but not to women. The women went on strike and their action spread to the London Underground. After seven weeks they won.

Equal pay, however, remained elusive. In 1943 the Equal Pay Campaign Committee (EPCC) was established under Mavis Tate and Edith Summerskill. Their research revealed that for trades where data was available, the average hourly rate for women in October 1938 was 9/- (45p) compared to 17/4d (87p) for men. The government set up a Royal Commission in 1944 which reported in 1946. It advocated equal pay for teachers and certain civil servants, but nothing was done. Women teachers did not receive equal pay until 1961, whilst equal pay for civil servants was phased in over seven years starting in 1955.

In 1954 the EPCC organised a massive petition of over 680,000 signatures demanding equal pay. Amongst those presenting the petition to Parliament was Barbara Castle. She became the first female Minister of State in 1965 when she became Minister of Transport. In 1970 as Employment Secretary she introduced the Equal Pay Act, which was fully implemented from January 1976, at the same time as the Sex Discrimination Act. It was intended that the two would establish a basis for fairness at work. Equal pay remains elusive, however. In 2003 women's pay, for full-time workers, was still only 82% of men's pay.

Gay Rights

Homosexuality amongst men was a crime for over 400 years, punishable for most of that time by hanging or long-term imprisonment. If discovered it could result in the ruin of men's careers and reputations.

Male homosexuality was made a capital offence in England under the Buggery Act of 1533. Female homosexuality was never specified. The first man to be convicted was playwright and schoolmaster Nicholas Udall in 1541, who was imprisoned for a year. The law became permanent in 1563 until replaced by the Offences Against the People Act of 1828. The death penalty was the punishment until 1861 (1889 in Scotland), though it was only exacted a few times, such as when Methuselah Spalding was hanged for sodomy in 1804. Thereafter punishment became imprisonment for between ten years and life. The law became more strict. The 1885 Criminal Law Amendment Act made any homosexual act illegal, even in private. Amongst the prosecutions was, most famously, that of Oscar Wilde in 1895.

Arrests and prosecutions for homosexuals increased in the 1950s. The trial of Lord Montagu of Beaulieu made headlines in 1954. He was found guilty and imprisoned for "gross offences", though he always maintained his innocence. This and other cases led the Conservative government to set up a Departmental Committee under Sir John Wolfenden, Vice-Chancellor of Reading University, to consider both homosexual offences and prostitution. His report, published in September 1957, recommended that homosexuality in private between consenting adults (then 21 or over) should no longer be illegal.

The Report caused much controversy and a polarisation of views. Various individuals, led by Tony Dyson, formed the Homosexual Law Reform Society in March 1958. The government continued to be cautious and a proposal by Kenneth Robinson in June 1960 to enact the Report's recommendations failed by 213 to 99. It was not until February 1966 that Humphrey Berkeley's Sexual Offences Bill was passed in a free vote by 164 to 107. It became law in England and Wales in July 1967. Homosexuality was not legalised in Scotland until 1980 and Northern Ireland until 1982. The age of consent has since been reduced and is now 16 in England, Wales and Scotland, and 17 in Northern Ireland.

In July 1977 Mary Whitehouse, the campaigner for moral standards on TV and in the press, brought a successful prosecution for blasphemy against *Gay News* for publishing a poem about a centurion's homosexual feelings towards Christ on the cross. It led to a major demonstration along the King's Road in London.

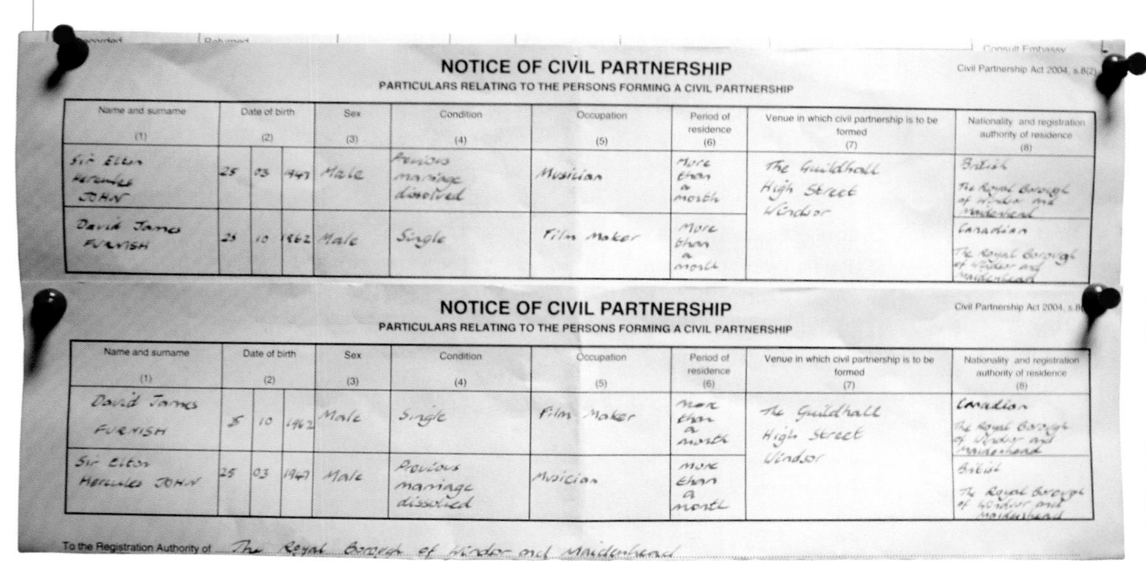

NOTICE OF CIVIL PARTNERSHIP

Civil Partnership Act 2004, s.8(2)

PARTICULARS RELATING TO THE PERSONS FORMING A CIVIL PARTNERSHIP

Name and surname (1)	Date of birth (2)			Sex (3)	Condition (4)	Occupation (5)	Period of residence (6)	Venue in which civil partnership is to be formed (7)	Nationality and registration authority of residence (8)
Sir Elton Hercules JOHN	25	03	1947	Male	Previous marriage dissolved	Musician	More than a month	The Guildhall High Street Windsor	British The Royal Borough of Windsor and Maidenhead
David James FURNISH	25	10	1962	Male	Single	Film Maker	More than a month		Canadian The Royal Borough of Windsor and Maidenhead

NOTICE OF CIVIL PARTNERSHIP

Civil Partnership Act 2004, s.8

PARTICULARS RELATING TO THE PERSONS FORMING A CIVIL PARTNERSHIP

Name and surname (1)	Date of birth (2)			Sex (3)	Condition (4)	Occupation (5)	Period of residence (6)	Venue in which civil partnership is to be formed (7)	Nationality and registration authority of residence (8)
David James FURNISH	25	10	1962	Male	Single	Film Maker	more than a month	The Guildhall High Street Windsor	Canadian The Royal Borough of Windsor and Maidenhead
Sir Elton Hercules JOHN	25	03	1947	Male	Previous marriage dissolved	Musician	more than a month		British The Royal Borough of Windsor and Maidenhead

To the Registration Authority of The Royal Borough of Windsor and Maidenhead

The notice of Civil Partnership for Sir Elton John and David Furnish displayed at Maidenhead Town Hall on 5 December 2005. The 2004 Civil Partnership Act allows same-sex couples who unite in a civil partnership to receive the same pension and tax benefits, property, inheritance and immigration rights as married couples.

Victimised
Alan Turing, the cryptographer who helped break the German Enigma code and is generally recognised as the father of modern computer science, was victimised for his homosexuality. Charged with "gross indecency", he had to choose between prison or hormone treatment. He also lost his job. His death in June 1954 was treated as suicide.

The trial of Oscar Wilde as reported in the *Illustrated Police News* for 20 April 1895.

BL, 1895, LON 182 NPL

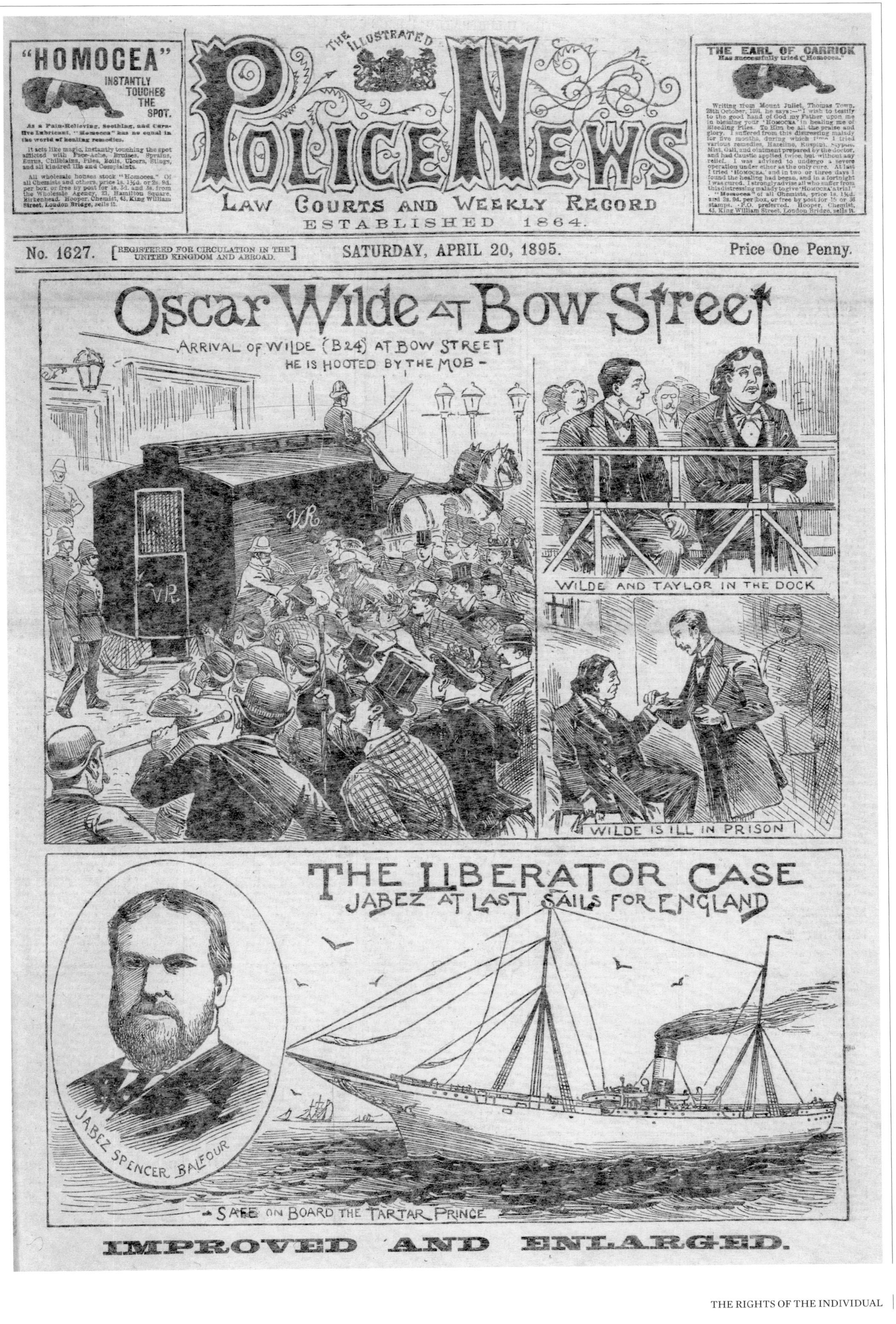

"HOMOCEA" INSTANTLY TOUCHES THE SPOT.

As a Pain-Relieving, Soothing, and Curative Lubricant, "Homocea" has no equal in the world of healing remedies.

It acts like magic, instantly touching the spot afflicted with Face-Ache, Bruises, Sprains, Burns, Chilblains, Piles, Boils, Ulcers, Stings, and all kindred Ills and Complaints.

All wholesale houses stock "Homocea." Of all Chemists and others, price 1s. 1½d. or 2s. 9d. per box, or free by post for 1s. 3d. and 3s. from the Wholesale Agency, 21, Hamilton Square, Birkenhead. Hooper, Chemist, 43, King William Street, London Bridge, sells it.

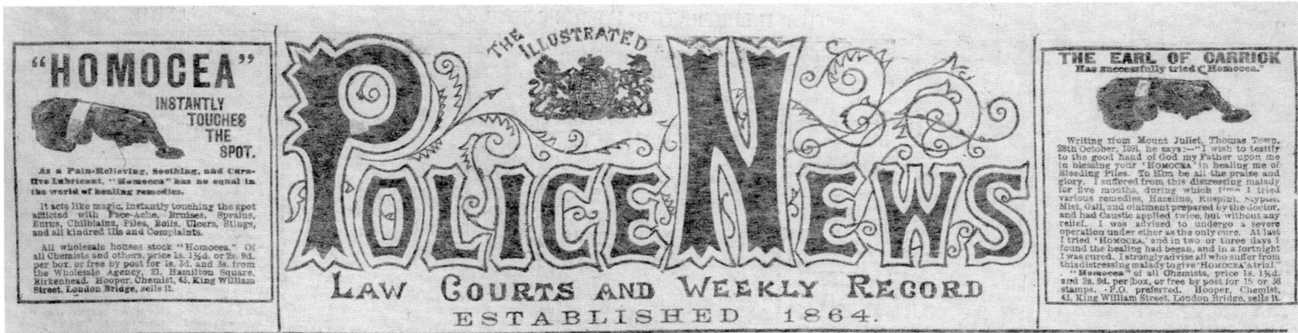

THE ILLUSTRATED POLICE NEWS

LAW COURTS AND WEEKLY RECORD

ESTABLISHED 1864.

THE EARL OF CARRICK Has successfully tried "Homocea."

Writing from Mount Juliet, Thomas Town, 28th October, 1891, he says:—"I wish to testify to the good hand of God my Father upon me in blessing your 'HOMOCEA' in healing me of Bleeding Piles. To Him be all the praise and glory. I suffered from this distressing malady for five months, during which time I tried various remedies, Hazeline, Ruspini, Styptic, Mist, Gall, and ointment prepared by the doctor, and had Caustic applied twice, but without any relief. I was advised to undergo a severe operation under ether as the only cure. At last I tried 'HOMOCEA,' and in two or three days I found the healing had began, and in a fortnight I was cured. I strongly advise all who suffer from this distressing malady to give 'HOMOCEA' a trial."

"Homocea" of all Chemists, price 1s. 1½d. and 2s. 9d. per box, or free by post for 15 or 36 stamps. P.O. preferred. Hooper, Chemist, 43, King William Street, London Bridge, sells it.

No. 1627. [REGISTERED FOR CIRCULATION IN THE UNITED KINGDOM AND ABROAD.] SATURDAY, APRIL 20, 1895. Price One Penny.

Oscar Wilde at Bow Street

ARRIVAL OF WILDE (B24) AT BOW STREET HE IS HOOTED BY THE MOB –

VR

WILDE AND TAYLOR IN THE DOCK

WILDE IS ILL IN PRISON

THE LIBERATOR CASE

JABEZ AT LAST SAILS FOR ENGLAND

JABEZ SPENCER BALFOUR

– SAFE ON BOARD THE TARTAR PRINCE

IMPROVED AND ENLARGED.

International Human Rights

In 1998 Britain passed the Human Rights Act. It recognised in British Law the European Convention on Human Rights which had been ratified by the Council of Europe in 1953, but its origins go back even further.

Promotional advert for H. G. Wells and his "Rights of Man" committee which encouraged discussion in the *Daily Herald* in February 1940.
BL, 1788-2008 LON MLD1 NPL

At the start of the Second World War, H. G. Wells wrote to *The Times*, contributing to a discussion about the aims of the war. He urged the need to plan for world peace which could be underpinned by a Declaration of Rights accepted by all nations. His draft proposal was published in *The Times* on 25 October 1939 and which, he said, "defines the spirit in which the mass of our people are more or less consciously fighting". It was a restatement of many existing Rights, plus such advanced ideas as "the right to roam" and freedom of information.

Wells's proposal encouraged others. A committee was created and the Declaration was revised and redrafted. It was also translated into over a dozen languages. Wells included different drafts in various books, including the *Rights of Man* (1940). He also lectured in the USA in October 1940 and corresponded with President Roosevelt. How much he influenced Roosevelt is uncertain, but Roosevelt's State of the Union speech to Congress in January 1941 outlined "Four Freedoms": freedom of speech, freedom of worship, freedom from want and freedom from fear. They were incorporated into the Atlantic Charter in August 1941.

Winston Churchill's wartime speeches inspired Britain through its darkest and finest hours with many references to freedom and liberty. After the War, conscious of the "iron curtain" which had descended across eastern Europe, Churchill delivered his "Sinews of Peace" speech in the USA in March 1946. Referring to Magna Carta, *habeas corpus* and others, he said:

... we must never cease to proclaim in fearless tones the great principles of freedom and the rights of man which are the joint inheritance of the English-speaking world.

The newly established United Nations set up a Human Rights Commission, chaired by Roosevelt's widow, Eleanor. After eighteen months of considerable deliberation it drafted a Universal Declaration of Human Rights (UDHR), adopted by the UN on 10 December 1948. The British representatives involved in the drafting were frustrated that a Covenant, giving the Declaration a legal basis, had not also been prepared. As it stood, the

Our rights under the Human Rights Act, 1998

- the right to life
- freedom from torture and degraded treatment
- freedom from slavery and forced labour
- the right to liberty
- the right to a fair trial
- the right not to be punished for something that wasn't a crime when you did it
- the right to respect for private and family life
- freedom of thought, conscience and religion
- freedom of expression
- freedom of assembly and association
- the right to marry or form a civil partnership and start a family
- the right not to be discriminated against in respect of these rights and freedoms
- the right to own property
- the right to an education
- the right to participate in free elections

Eleanor Roosevelt with the Universal Declaration of Human Rights at Lake Success, New York in 1949. The initial draft was prepared by Canadian scholar John Humphrey, whilst the French jurist René Cassin led the work on the final draft.

Winston Churchill and Franklin D. Roosevelt signed the Atlantic Charter, incorporating the Four Freedoms, upon a warship anchored in Ship Harbour, Newfoundland on 14 August 1941.

Declaration had a moral but no legal obligation. It was not until 1976 that the International Covenant on Civil and Political Rights came into force, giving a legal status to most of the UDHR.

Meanwhile, a Congress of Europe had met in May 1947 in The Hague under the honorary presidency of Winston Churchill. He proposed a European Charter of Human Rights. Discussions began when the Council of Europe was established in May 1949. The British government was involved from the start, although the Foreign Secretary Ernest Bevin was concerned how the Charter (which soon became a "Convention") would relate to the colonies, and how the proposed European Court of Human Rights would affect British sovereignty on legal matters. The debates over the Convention were long, arduous and often heated, but the final document was signed in Rome in November 1950. Britain was the first to ratify it on 8 March 1951. It came into force in September 1953. The enforcement process, via the European Commission on Human Rights, was set up in 1954 and the European Court in 1959. Britain extended the Convention to almost all of its colonies. Since 1998 all individuals can approach the Court direct.

The British Human Rights Act covers all of the articles and additional protocols of the European Convention with only minor amendments. The European Convention contains fewer clauses than the UDHR but covers them in more detail. All standard clauses are in both, such as equality before the law, freedom of speech and worship, right to a fair trial, prohibition of slavery and freedom of assembly. The UDHR has further clauses covering a right to leisure, a right to a cultural life and the right to a nationality.

The Human Rights Act confirmed the abolition of the death penalty. Capital punishment had been abolished in Britain for murder in 1965 but remained for treason until 1998. The last woman to be hanged was Ruth Ellis in July 1955. The last men executed were Peter Allen and Gwynne Owen Evans, in August 1964. The last people executed under British rule were Larry Tacklyn and Erskine Burrows, in Bermuda on 2 December 1977, for killing the island's Governor. The last colony to abolish it was the Turks and Caicos Islands in 2002.

To oversee this Act and others, the Equality and Human Rights Commission was established in October 2007, combining responsibilities of the former Equal Opportunities Commission, Commission for Racial Equality, and the Disability Rights Commission. Its remit is to eliminate discrimination, reduce inequality, protect human rights and to build good relations, ensuring that everyone has a fair chance to participate in society.

United Kingdom challenged

It is ironic that the very first inter-state case brought to the European Court, in 1956, was by Greece against the United Kingdom over punitive action carried out under emergency powers during the insurrection in Cyprus, which was then a British colony. The case was investigated but dropped by mutual agreement in July 1959.

The Right to Vote

Thomas Paine and others had shown how the right to vote was fundamental to liberty, and the root of democracy. Parliament should be representative of the people. However, Oliver Cromwell had regarded the prospect of all men having the vote as leading to anarchy, and much the same view prevailed 150 years later. The aftermath of the French Revolution, the French Wars and the fear of revolution in Britain led to very repressive measures that stopped any political reform. The struggle towards universal suffrage was long, hard and often very violent. Since 1970 everyone over the age of eighteen in Britain (with few exceptions) has been entitled to vote, yet not much more than half exercise that right.

Detail from the original handwritten version of the Great Reform Act, complete with Royal Assent in Anglo-Norman.

Parliamentary Archives, HL.PO.PU/1/1832/ 2&3W4n147

Le Roy le Veult

[So]it baillé aux Seigneurs.

A cette Bille avecque des amendemens les
Seigneurs sont assentus

[A] ces Amendemens les Communes
sont assentuz —

Whereas it is expedient to take
[e]ffectual measures for correcting divers
[a]buses that have long prevailed in
[t]he choice of members to serve in
[t]he commons house of parliament
[to] deprive many inconsiderable places
[of] the right of returning members
[to] grant such privilege to large po-
[p]ulous and wealthy towns to in-
[cr]ease the number of knights of
[t]he shire to extend the elective
[fr]anchise to many of his majesty's
[s]ubjects who have not heretofore
[en]joyed the same and to diminish

Radicals and Repression

The 1790s saw the rise of Corresponding Societies and other organisations intent on lobbying for political reform. However, the declaration of war between Britain and France in February 1793 led to repressive measures in Britain that dashed hopes of any Parliamentary reform.

The French Revolution in 1789 had increased thoughts of political reform in Britain. In 1792, with the overthrow of the monarchy, the First French Republic was declared with the National Convention elected by universal male suffrage. Such democracy would not last long, but in Britain, where only 10% of the adult male population had the vote, it must have stirred hopes for change.

In Britain elections were neither representative nor balanced. There was a two-tier system of counties and boroughs. At county level all adult men could vote if they owned land worth 40 shillings. At borough level it depended where you lived. In a few places all men could vote, but mostly it depended on whether you owned property or paid certain taxes. In some boroughs no one had a vote and the Corporation chose the MPs. Some towns, such as Birmingham and Manchester, had no MPs at all.

The size of the boroughs varied. There were the notorious "rotten" boroughs, like Old Sarum at Salisbury, which still had two MPs but only seven voters. There were also "pocket" boroughs, owned by major landowners who chose their own MP. Moreover, with no secret ballot, voters were easily bribed or intimidated.

Following the French Revolution a number of societies emerged in Britain seeking political reform. The three major societies were: *The Society for Constitutional Information* (SCI), originally created by John Cartwright in 1780 out of the Bill of Rights Society. It was revived in 1791 by John Horne Tooke as a more militant force. It was composed of intellectuals, with wealthy patrons, and sought to influence at all levels through radical propaganda. *Society of the Friends of the People* (SFP), split from the SCI in April 1792. It was less radical and consisted mostly of Whig MPs, including

The Contrast. John Reeves's Association produced this pamphlet by Thomas Rowlandson comparing liberty in Britain, represented by a majestic Britannia, with post-Revolution France where Liberty is a frightening Medusa
British Museum, 1861,1012.47

John Thelwall speaking at a Corresponding Society Meeting at Spa Fields in London, 1795, depicted by James Gillray. Thelwall continued to preach reform despite the change in the law. His meetings were frequently broken up by the local militia and attempts were made on his life.

The National Portrait Gallery, London. NPG 599

Charles Grey – the future Earl Grey (of 'tea' fame). It wanted to broaden the franchise and stop corrupt election practices. *London Corresponding Society* (LCS), founded by attorney John Frost and shoemaker Thomas Hardy in January 1792. It was composed mostly of workers and artisans, and encouraged affiliates in other cities: some branches were called Patriotic Societies. They soon had over 30,000 members. They wanted universal male suffrage, annual Parliaments and paid MPs.

These organisations put their weight behind a proposal for reform put before Parliament by Charles Grey in April 1792. The motion failed because of the strength of the anti-reform Tories under William Pitt, who cited the French Revolution to show what might happen in Britain if the "lower classes" were allowed to vote.

To stop further thoughts of reform, Pitt issued a Royal Proclamation on 21 May 1792 outlawing seditious meetings and writings. Any open discussion of reform could now be considered treason. Various anti-reform societies emerged, such as the Association for Preserving Liberty and Property against Republicans and Levellers, organised by lawyer John Reeves. People flocked to join, afraid that revolutionaries would destroy their livelihood. The radical atheist William Godwin caused more agitation with *An Enquiry concerning the Principles of Political Justice* in February 1793, which sought not to reform Parliament but to abolish it, promoting instead individualism for the good of all, a form of benign anarchy.

The network of Corresponding Societies planned several meetings, culminating in the British Convention in Edinburgh in 1793. The government infiltrated the organisation and, in January 1793, arrested five members in Scotland for sedition. They were tried by Lord Braxfield, who maliciously revised the meaning of sedition as "violating the peace and order of society". He also declared: "The British constitution is the best that ever was since the creation of the world, and it is not possible to make it better." The five "martyrs" were sentenced to fourteen years' transportation to Australia, and no amount of campaigning saved them. Their counterparts in London were more fortunate. Thomas Hardy, John Horne Tooke and John Thelwall were

The Spencean Philosophers

Thomas Spence ran a bookshop in Holborn called the Hive of Liberty, where one branch of the London Corresponding Society met. He was frequently imprisoned for selling seditious works, including Paine's *Rights of Man*. In addition to universal suffrage, he believed, like the Diggers, in the communal ownership of land. He died in 1814 but his followers, the Spencean Philosophers, continued his cause, with increasing militancy.

The Peterloo Massacre, Manchester, 16 August 1819. The original engraving of this event was acquired by a former weaver, John Jenkins, who painted in colours to identify the yeomen (in red) and the protesters (in blue).

National Archives, MPI 1/134, no.18 (1819)

Commemorative jug of Francis Burdett after his imprisonment in the Tower in 1810.

People's History Museum, NMLH.1995.91.5

charged with treason for planning a convention and publishing leaflets. Neither judge nor jury was convinced and all three were acquitted, to rapturous public acclaim. Unfortunately the trials had a withering effect. Reformers realised nothing would prevail against Pitt, and membership of the societies faded.

The relationship between Britain and France worsened after the execution of Louis XVI in January 1793. A war with France was increasingly likely in order to protect European interests, but it was the French who declared war on Britain in February 1793. This allowed Pitt to introduce greater restrictions. He suspended *habeas corpus* in 1794-5 and again for three years from April 1798. The Treasonable Practices Act made it an offence to bring the King or Government into contempt. The Seditious Meetings Act restricted public meetings to no more than 50 people to be held only in specially licensed premises. The Combination Act forbad political agitation amongst workers; the Unlawful Societies Act, made it illegal for any society to meet in secret; and the Corresponding Societies Act banned the LCS and its cohorts. It would be decades before Parliamentary reform was seriously considered.

Ironically, the process some wanted to reform, such as the rotten and pocket boroughs, occasionally allowed radical MPs into Parliament. One such was Francis Burdett. His father-in-law, the banker Thomas Coutts, bought the borough of Boroughbridge in 1796 and gave the seat to Burdett. Initially his career was unfocused, but between 1809 and 1819 he doggedly pursued electoral reform. He wanted male ratepayer franchise, equal electoral districts, single-day elections and shorter Parliaments. In 1810 he was imprisoned in the Tower for publishing his speech where he objected to the House of Commons imprisoning a man for protesting against the exclusion of reporters during a debate. There was a huge wave of public support for Burdett, and it regenerated interest in Parliamentary reform.

Burdett's lack of success caused the Spenceans to take stronger action. They organised meetings at Spa Fields, Islington, in November

"The Mask of Anarchy"

When the poet Shelley heard of Peterloo, he penned *The Mask of Anarchy*, a long poem which attacked government repression. It ended with this call to arms:

Rise like Lions after slumber
In unvanquishable number –
Shake your chains to earth like dew
Which in sleep had fallen on you –
Ye are many – they are few.

When *habeas corpus* was suspended in 1817 George Cruikshank showed "Liberty Suspended".
British Museum, 1868,0808.8364

The arrest of the Cato Street Conspirators drawn by George Cruikshank from an eye-witness account.
British Museum, 1862,1217.554

and December 1816, with Henry Hunt as speaker. Hunt, known as "Orator", drew crowds of 10,000 of more. He wore a white top hat, representing the purity of his cause, and flourished a Cap of Liberty on top of a pikestaff. The first meeting was peaceful but the second degenerated into a riot. When the Prince Regent's coach was attacked in January 1817, the usual repressive measures were introduced: *habeas corpus* was suspended, seditious meetings banned and printers of seditious material arrested.

John Cartwright had, since 1812, set up a series of Clubs named after the Civil War leader, John Hampden. He wanted to unite radical reformists, like Hunt, with moderates, like Burdett. The Manchester Hampden Club organised a meeting at St. Peter's Fields in August 1819, to deal with Parliamentary reform. Hunt was the main speaker. Estimates of the crowd-size vary but it was upwards of 60,000. The magistrate, fearing a riot, ordered the local yeomen to arrest Hunt. The crowd resisted and the yeomen charged, killing eleven people and wounding 400. Local reporters soon called it the Peterloo Massacre.

Francis Burdett wrote an open letter to his constituents showing his indignation. "Is this England?" he wrote, "This a Christian land? A land of freedom?" He planned a protest meeting, challenging Parliament to interfere. "Whether the penalty of our meeting will be death by military execution, I know not; but this I know, a man can die but once, and never better than in vindicating the laws and liberties of this country."

The Tory Government under Lord Liverpool reacted with the "Six Acts" to suppress radical newspapers and seditious meetings and reduce the chance of an armed uprising. The government infiltrated the extremists. In February 1820 the Spenceans, acting under false information, plotted to assassinate members of the government whom they believed were dining at the home of Lord Harrowby. When they assembled in nearby Cato Street they were arrested. Five were transported whilst five others were hanged and beheaded.

By 1820 Parliamentary reform was no further advanced.

The First Reform Act

It was not until 1832 that a number of factors finally led to the first Reform Act. Yet it was a major battle to get the Bill through Parliament and the delaying tactics led to rioting across Britain and a threat of revolution.

Commemorative medal of the Reform Act depicting Lord Grey at the despatch box.

People's History Museum, NMLH.1995.91.59

For over 30 years the Tories remained opposed to Parliamentary reform, but by 1830 many recognised that some change was necessary. A number of factors contributed. There was a new Revolution in France. The country had reverted to a hereditary monarchy after the downfall of Napoleon in 1814, but in July 1830 Charles X was ousted for his despotism. In just three days the July Revolution showed that "people power" still worked. Meanwhile in Britain, George IV had died in June 1830 and was succeeded by his more tolerant brother, William IV. George's death meant that Parliament was dissolved and new elections called. The Tories won again, but with a reduced majority.

Also agitating for reform was the Birmingham Political Union, formed by Thomas Attwood in January 1830. Other political unions sprung up in other cities. Attwood gave speeches to crowds of up to 200,000, emphasising the importance of the "industrious classes" in a capitalist society. Fellow reformer Francis Place came to regard Attwood as "the most influential man in England".

Most Tories had not forgiven the Duke of Wellington passing the Catholic Relief Act in 1829, and a group of them believed that a reformed House of Commons would not have supported Catholic emancipation. Although the Prime Minister, the Duke of Wellington, remained defiantly against reform, he was forced out of office. William IV asked the Whig Earl Grey to form an administration. This was the same Charles Grey who nearly 40 years before had tried to introduce a Reform Bill. Now was his chance.

The Reform Bill planned to:

- drop all the rotten and pocket boroughs and other boroughs with under 2000 people
- redistribute seats to enfranchise large towns and populations previously not covered
- give the vote in boroughs to male owners of property valued at £10 per annum but keep the 40-shilling freehold franchise for counties
- retain the public vote rather than a secret ballot.

When the details of the Bill were revealed in March 1831, it was learned it would reduce the number of MPs but almost double the number of voters. Few Tories supported it. Not even all radicals liked it. It scraped through its second reading by one vote, but was amended in the committee stage. Grey saw this as a defeat and asked the King to dissolve Parliament. The King reluctantly agreed. The new election, in April 1831, strengthened Grey's majority. However, the Bill was still rejected by the Lords. There was rioting in towns across Britain. In Bristol riots lasted for three days. Over 100 were killed and many more wounded.

Grey was determined to reintroduce the Bill before Christmas

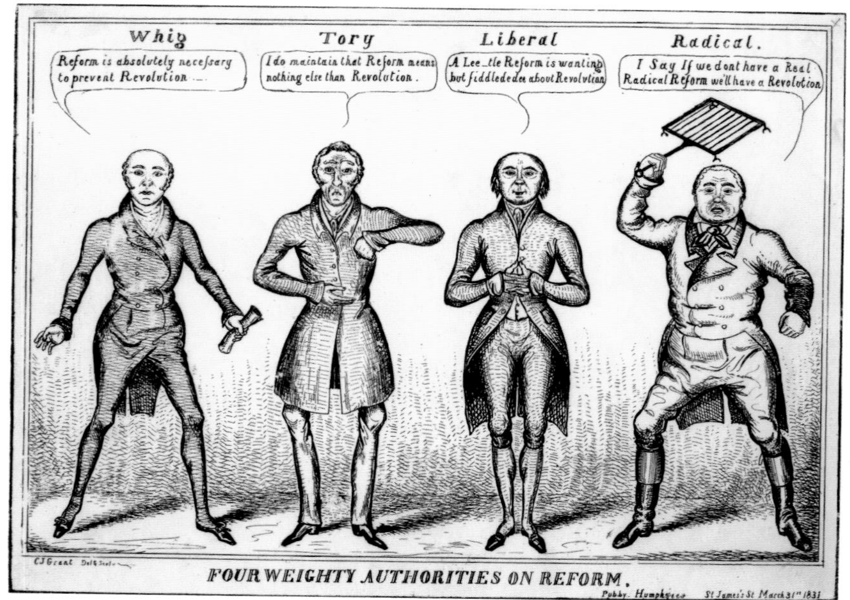

C. J. Grant's "Four Weighty Authorities" produced in 1831 showed the different political attitudes to reform.

British Museum, 1868,0808.9353

Canvassing for Votes, 1757. The second of four prints by William Hogarth portraying the corruption of the electoral process.
British Museum, S,2.131

This banner was made by the Shoemakers' Union to celebrate the passing of the Reform Act in 1832. It bears the inscription: "The Battle's Won – Britannia's Sons Are Free, and despots tremble at the Victory. We are True to the Last."
People's History Museum, NMLH.1997.7.1

and made only minor concessions, restoring some of the smaller boroughs and the number of MPs. The Bill passed through the Commons and nearly passed through the Lords but proposed revisions halted progress. Grey rejected the revisions and threatened to resign unless the King created enough new peers to ensure the Bill's passage. The King was reluctant so Grey resigned on 9 May 1832. Once again Britain erupted in protest. "Every man you met seemed to be convulsed with rage," wrote William Cobbett. Francis Place and Thomas Attwood headed a campaign of civil disruption via the political unions, with mass meetings, petitions, and advocating the withdrawal of money from banks to cause financial chaos. Attwood even advocated a call to arms. After a tense week William IV recalled Grey, who would only return if the King guaranteed to create new peers. In the end he did not have to. The threat was enough. The Lords allowed the

Reform Bill through on 4 June 1832.

In its final form the Reform Act increased the electorate from around 366,000 to 650,000, about 18% of the total adult-male population in England and Wales. In Scotland the electorate increased from 4,500 to 64,447, about 12% of the adult male population.

The Act also brought Thomas Attwood into Parliament as the first MP for Birmingham.

The People's Charter

Whilst Parliament may have thought its job was done, the Reformists saw the 1832 Act merely as a starting point. The demand for universal suffrage continued with the rise of the Chartist movement.

The Chartist meeting on Kennington Common on 10 April 1848. This is apparently the earliest known photograph of a crowd.

In 1836 Cornish cabinet-maker William Lovett formed the London Working Men's Association, along with publisher Henry Hetherington and printers John Cleave and James Watson. Besides disseminating information for the good of the working classes, the Association wanted "to seek by every legal means to place all classes of society in possession of their equal, political, and social rights".

With the help of Francis Place, Lovett composed a six-point Charter, all of which had been advocated by John Cartwright in 1776. These were: (1) a vote for all men over 21; (2) a secret ballot; (3) electoral districts of equal size; (4) no property qualification to become an MP; (5) payment for MPs; and (6) annual elections for Parliament.

It became known as the People's Charter, and its promoters the Chartists. Presented as a popular style Magna Carta, it rapidly gained support across the country. It was launched in Glasgow in May 1838 at a meeting attended by an estimated 150,000. A petition, assembled at Chartist meetings across Britain, was brought to London in May 1839 for Thomas Attwood to present to Parliament. It boasted 1,280,958 signatures, yet Parliament voted not to consider it.

The People's Charter. This was the original "outline" of the proposals produced to promote the Charter. It depicts an example of a secret ballot box.

People's History Museum, LHASC. VIN/6

"PERFECT" EDITION.] [PRICE ONE PENNY.

THE PEOPLE'S CHARTER:

Being the Outline of An Act to provide for the Just Representation of the People of Great Britain and Ireland in the Commons' House of Parliament:

EMBRACING THE PRINCIPLES OF

Universal Suffrage; No Property Qualification; Annual Parliaments; Equal Representation; Payment of Members; and Vote by Ballot.

Prepared by a Committee of Twelve Persons: Six Members of Parliament, and Six Members of the "London Working Men's Association;" and addressed to the People of the United Kingdom.—Re-printed from the Third Edition, Revised and Corrected, from Communications made by many Associations in various parts of the Kingdom.

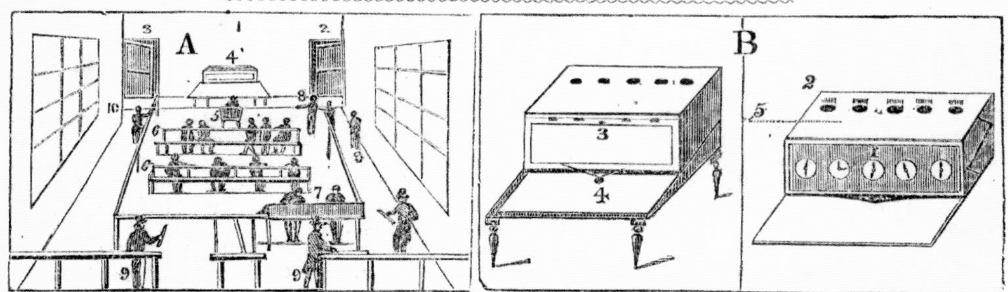

Schedule A, the Balloting Place.—1. The space separated off by a close partition, for the purposes of Secret Voting. 2. The entrance to the Ballot Box, where the voter gives his vote. 3. The door by which the voter retires. 4. The front of the Ballot Box, placed on a stand with an inclined plane, down which the balloting ball descends, to be ready for the next voter. 5. The seat of the Deputy returning Officer. 6. The seats of the Agents of the Candidates. 7. The desk of the Registration Clerk and his Assistant. 8. The Assistant, who delivers the balloting ball to the voters. 9. Assistants and Constables at the doors and barriers, who examine the certificates, and let the voter pass on to the ballot. 10. A Constable, to stop any voter who may vote unfairly.

Schedule B, the Ballot Box.—1. The front of the Ballot Box, with the lid down, shewing five dials (or any number that may be necessary), on which are engraven (or otherwise) numerals, from one to any number of thousands that may be required, with hands (like the minute and hour hands of a clock) to register the number of votes. 2. The apertures with the Candidates' names opposite, through which each voter drops a Brass Ball, which, falling in a zig-zag direction, touches a clock-work spring, which moves a pinion on which the hands are fastened, and thus registers one each time a person votes. 3. The front of the Ballot Box, with the lid up and sealed. 4. The Stand, with the Ball running down. 5. The line of the partition which makes the two rooms.

N.B.—We understand that a Ballot Box of this description, has been invented by Mr. Benjamin Jolly, 19, York-street, Bath, and it is so constructed that not more than one ball can be put in at a time by any voter.

The Working Mens' Association to the Radical Reformers of Great Britain and Ireland.

FELLOW COUNTRYMEN,—Having frequently stated our reasons for zealously espousing the great principles of Reform, we have now endeavoured to set them forth practically. We need not reiterate the facts and unrefuted arguments which have so often been stated and urged in their support. Suffice it to say, that we hold it to be an axiom in politics, that self-government by representation is the only just foundation of political power—the only true basis of Constitutional Rights—the only legitimate parent of good laws:—and we hold it as an indubitable truth, that all government which is based on any other foundation, has a perpetual tendency to degenerate into anarchy or despotism, or to beget class and wealth idolatry on the one hand, poverty and misery on the other.

While, however, we contend for the principle of self-government, we admit that laws will only be just in proportion as the people are enlightened, on which, socially and politically, the happiness of all must depend; but as self-interest, unaccompanied by virtue, seeks its own exclusive benefits, so will the exclusive and privileged classes of society ever seek to perpetuate their power, and to proscribe the enlightenment of the people. Hence we are induced to believe that the enlightenment of all will sooner emanate from the exercise of political power by all the people, than by their continuing to trust to the selfish government of the few.

A strong conviction of these truths, coupled, as that conviction is, with the belief that most of our political and social evils can be traced to corrupt and exclusive legislation—and that the remedy will be found in extending to the people at large, the exercise of those rights, now monopolized by a few, has induced us to make some exertions towards embodying our principles in the following Charter.

We are the more inclined to take some practicable step in favour of Reform, from the frequent disappointments the cause has experienced. We have heard eloquent effusions in favour of political equality, from the hustings and the senate-house, suddenly change into prudent reasonings on property privileges, at the winning smile of the minister. We have seen depicted, in glowing language, bright patriotic promises of the future, which have left impressions on us more lasting than the perfidy or apostacy of the writers. We have seen one zealous Reformer after another desert us, as his party was triumphant, or his interests served. We have perceived the tone of those whom we have held as champions of our cause, lowered to the accommodation of selfish electors, or restrained by the slavish fear of losing their seats. We have, therefore, resolved to test the sincerity of the remainder, by proposing that something shall be done in favour of those principles they profess to admire.

In June last, we called a general meeting of our members, and invited to attend that meeting all those Members of Parliament who, by their speeches and writings, we were induced to believe were advocates of Universal Suffrage. Several did attend, and after some discussion, another meeting was proposed, at which several Members of Parliament pledged themselves by resolutions signed by their

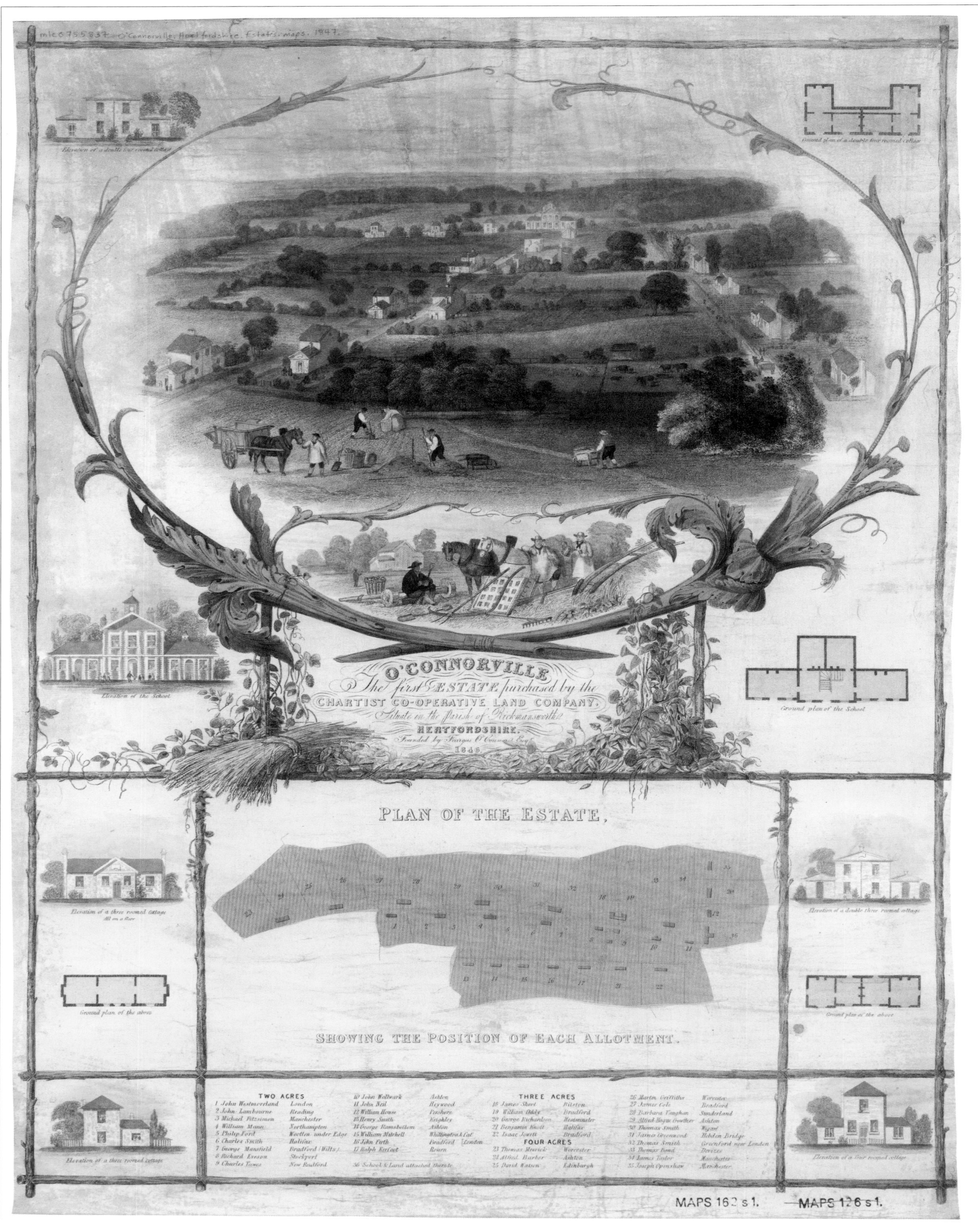
O'CONNORVILLE
The first ESTATE purchased by the
CHARTIST CO-OPERATIVE LAND COMPANY,
Situate in the Parish of Rickmansworth
HERTFORDSHIRE.
Founded by Feargus O'Connor Esq.
1846.
Elevation of the School
Ground plan of the School
PLAN OF THE ESTATE,
SHOWING THE POSITION OF EACH ALLOTMENT.
Elevation of a three roomed Cottage
Ground plan of the above
Elevation of a double three roomed cottage
Ground plan of the above
Elevation of a four roomed cottage
TWO ACRES
1 John Westmoreland London
2 John Lambourne Reading
3 Michael Fitzsimon Manchester
4 William Mann Northampton
5 Philip Ford Wootten under Edge
6 Charles Smith Halifax
7 George Mansfield Bradford (Wilts)
8 Richard Eveson Stockport
9 Charles Tawes New Radford
10 John Wellwark Ashton
11 John Neil Heywood
12 William House Pershore
13 Henry Smith Keighley
14 George Ramsbottom Ashton
15 William Mitchell Whittington & Cat
16 John Firth Bradford
17 Ralph Kerfoot Rouen
36 School & Land attached thereto
THREE ACRES
18 James Short Bilston
19 William Oddy Bradford
20 George Richardson Westminster
21 Benjamin Knott Halifax
22 Isaac Jowett Bradford
FOUR ACRES
23 Thomas Mewick Worcester
24 Alfred Barber Ashton
25 David Watson Edinburgh
26 Martin Griffiths Worcester
27 James Cole Bradford
28 Barbara Vaughan Sunderland
29 Alfred Hague Crowther Ashton
30 Thomas Smith Wigan
31 James Greenwood Hebden Bridge
32 Thomas Smith Greenford near London
33 Thomas Bond Devizes
34 James Taylor Manchester
35 Joseph Openshaw Manchester
MAPS 162 s 1.
MAPS 126 s 1.

Above:
The chartist Ernest Jones was imprisoned in 1848 for seditious behaviour. His prison drawing 'The Grecian City' and 'The English Town', contrasted an idealised community with the nightmarish vision of a northern industrial town.
BL, Add. MS 61971, ff. 28v-29

Opposite:
By 1845 Feargus O'Connor believed the future lay in land reform and established the Chartist Land Company. He acquired land for housing which workers could apply for. One site was near Rickmansworth, Hertfordshire, which became O'Connorville. Although a few houses and facilities were built the scheme was undercapitalised and was wound up in 1851.
BL, Maps 162.s.1

This annoyed the more extreme Chartists led by former Irish MP Feargus O'Connor. He caused a division within the Chartists between those who favoured "physical force" and those, like Lovett, who preferred "moral 'suasion", at least at first. Militants called for rebellion, and there were riots in Newcastle, Birmingham and elsewhere, where leading Chartists were arrested.

The only armed uprising was in Newport, Wales, in November 1839. This was partly a show of force by local miners dissatisfied with working conditions, partly an intention to release recently arrested Chartists, and partly an attempt to establish a Silurian Republic. It went badly wrong. When Chartists stormed a hotel where they believed their colleagues were held, the troops were ready and twenty Chartists were killed. The three leaders of the rebellion, John Frost, Zephaniah Williams and William Jones, were all sentenced to death but, after major public protests, this was commuted to transportation to Australia. All three were later pardoned but only Frost, a former mayor of Newport, returned to England. Williams later made his fortune when he discovered coal in Tasmania.

The Chartist movement was strong in Scotland where it developed an evangelical dimension with the growth of Chartist churches, seeking greater fellowship amongst the poor. These prospered because the established church, which was generally hostile to Chartism, was not seen as helping the poor.

Another petition was compiled by May 1842, bearing over three million signatures (many suspect) and weighing over 300kg. It included many Irish names because the Irish were a major part of the Chartist movement, believing it would help in their hopes for Home Rule. The petition included a demand about the "many grievances borne by the people of Ireland, and contend that they are fully entitled to a repeal of the legislative union". This would not have endeared the petition to Parliament, which voted not to hear the petitioners. This was one of the factors that triggered Britain's first General Strike.

The Chartists split into several splinter groups each trying to further the cause but none advancing significantly. The last major attempt to influence the government came with a meeting arranged at Kennington Common in April 1848, to be followed by a procession to Westminster to present another petition. The Prime Minister Lord John Russell allowed the meeting but advised against the procession and petition. There was a massive police and military presence. In the end the meeting was peaceful, with a crowd estimated by some at 150,000. The petition was signed with nearly two million signatures, not all genuine. Feargus O'Connor had, by now, been elected as an MP and he proposed a motion for the People's Charter to be considered, but once again it was defeated heavily.

The Vote Expands

Reformists continued to protest to gain any further consideration of Parliamentary reform, and it was only by continued pressure that more men acquired the vote and that the ballot box was introduced. But just how representative did Parliament become?

Opposite: Reform League demonstration at Hyde Park in July 1866.

Right: Secret ballot in use at the 1880 General Election with the rich and poor on an equal footing.

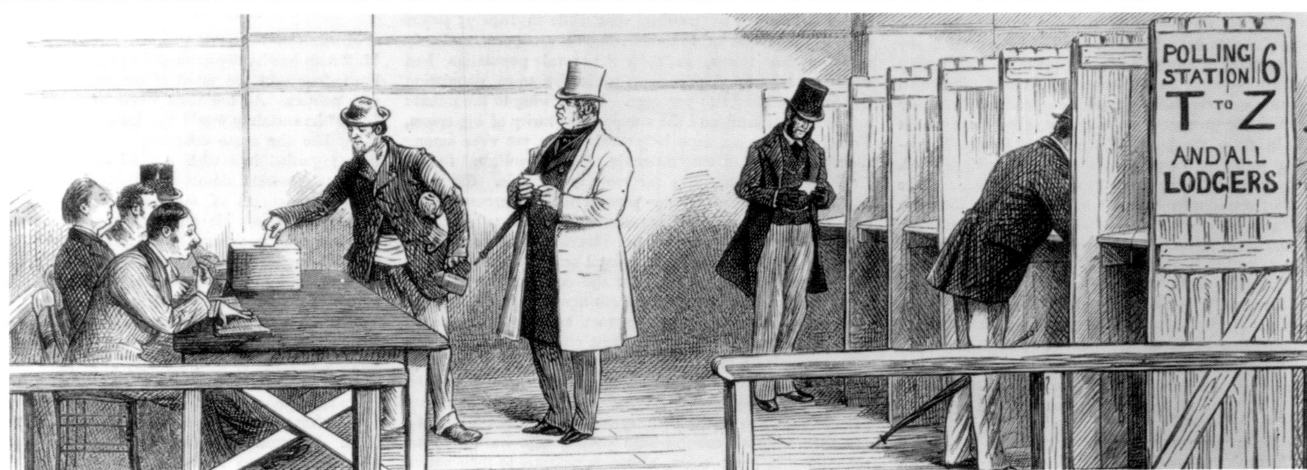

The National Charter Association was wound up in 1860, but the cause was taken up by the Reform League in February 1865. It was led by barrister Edmond Beales, and included such populist figures as the MP John Bright and John Bedford Leno, known as the "Poet of the Poor". Its aims were universal manhood suffrage, voting by ballot, triennial Parliaments and a fair distribution of electoral districts.

Also in 1865 the Prime Minister, Lord Palmerston, died. He had been against reform, but his successor Lord John Russell was in its favour. He had tried to push a Reform Bill through Parliament in 1860 without success. He tried again in June 1866, hoping to enfranchise the "respectable working man", meaning skilled labourers, but a group within the Liberal Party (which had emerged from the old Whig Party) sided with the Conservatives and the Bill failed. Russell resigned. The new Liberal leader was William Gladstone, who had already declared his intention to promote reform. However, Lord Derby became Prime Minister with a minority Conservative government. The Conservative Chancellor of the Exchequer, Benjamin Disraeli, was in favour of reform and convinced Lord Derby that Reform was inevitable and, if well managed, could help shore up the Conservative administration.

The government and the Reform League had several altercations. In July 1866 the League planned a meeting in Hyde Park but it was banned and the gates locked. It led to disturbances at Hyde Park and Trafalgar Square. In May 1867 another meeting was planned and again it was not permitted. Beales challenged the Home Secretary, Spencer Walpole, to explain why the public could not hold a meeting in a public park. Walpole agreed to the meeting, which passed peacefully but, for allowing it, he had to resign.

The new Reform Bill was passed in August 1867 and enfranchised a total of two million men. Now all male heads of household over 21 in boroughs could vote, as well as lodgers paying £10 rent a year. But it still represented only 13% of the total adult population.

The Act seemed to unlock doors and gradually other barriers fell. In 1872 Gladstone pushed through the Ballot Act, at last ensuring voting was in secret. This had been a major demand of the Chartists. In 1884 the Third Reform Act extended the qualification of the 1867 Act to the countryside so that almost two-thirds of men had the vote. In order to gain the Conservative support for that Bill, Gladstone also passed the Redistribution of Seats Act. This simplified the electoral map by creating a predominance of single-member constituencies. Throughout these reforms, women were still excluded. That battle had yet to conclude.

Speakers' Corner

There is no fundamental right to meetings in any public park or open space. The 1872 Parks Regulation Act allowed the right of assembly in London parks and recognised Hyde Park's Speakers' Corner as the first place in Britain where anyone may protest without first obtaining permission, provided they are not obscene, blasphemous or incite a breach of the peace. Here the crowd gather to hear the famous 'Charlie' speaking in September 1933.

Is Parliament representative today?

If you compare the proportion of seats in Parliament at the 2005 General Election with the votes cast and reallocate the seats accordingly the results for the major parties are listed below. Ten parties are represented (excluding Independents and the Speaker). If seats were allocated by votes five more parties would be represented, including UKIP, the Green Party and the BNP. Would this strengthen or weaken Parliament? A form of proportional representation called the "mixed member" system is used to elect the members of the Scottish Parliament and the Welsh National Assembly.

Party	Seats (%)	Votes (%)	Seats based on votes
Labour	356 (55%)	9,566,618 (35.3%)	227
Conservative	198 (30.6%)	8,785,941 (32.3%)	209
LibDem	62 (9.6%)	5,985,414 (22.1%)	142

Votes for Women

The demand for universal suffrage had always related to men. Female suffrage was scarcely considered and many women agreed with that, making it difficult to gain any attention for the movement at the outset. It was the lack of progress that prompted the rise of the militant Suffragettes, but despite all they did women were still denied the vote.

Emmeline Pankhurst, who led the militant suffragette movement, pictured here in the early 1900s.

The first women's suffrage organisation, the Sheffield Female Reform Association, was formed in 1851 thanks to Anne Knight, a Quaker from Essex. The Association compiled a petition which the Earl of Carlisle presented to the House of Lords. Despite their efforts it achieved nothing, but was noted in the essay "The Enfranchisement of Women" published soon after. The essay revealed the prejudice against women in Britain and the hypocrisy of Chartists calling for universal suffrage – but only for men.

The essay, attributed to John Stuart Mill, had actually been written by Mill's new wife Harriet Taylor. By her first marriage, Harriet had a daughter, Helen, who continued to work with her stepfather after her mother's death in November 1858. Together they wrote *The Subjection of Women*, completed in 1861, stating, "the legal subordination of one sex to the other is wrong itself, and now one of the chief hindrances to human improvement."

In 1865 Helen Taylor helped establish the Kensington Society to further women's rights. Its members included Emily Davies (who campaigned successfully for women to enter for the Oxford and Cambridge local examinations), Deborah Beale (headmistress of Cheltenham Ladies' College), Barbara Bodichon (who helped change the law on divorce) and Elizabeth Garrett (the first woman to be licensed by the Society of Apothecaries). They set up a Women's Suffrage Committee and petitioned Parliament with the help of MPs Henry Fawcett and John Stuart Mill. They hoped to influence the new Reform Bill but neither this, nor another petition presented in April 1867, gained any ground. Mill's proposed amendment, to replace references to "man" by "person", was rejected by 194 votes to 73.

John Stuart Mill being presented with the Women's Suffrage Committee petition in 1867.
BL, PP.5270

The early work of the suffrage committees centred upon drawing up petitions, but they needed to co-ordinate their efforts across the country. This came about when Helen Taylor and others created the National Society for Women's Suffrage in November 1867. It had a Central Committee, based in London, which included men.

There was one small triumph for female suffrage in November 1867. By accident the name of Lily Maxwell, a widowed shopkeeper in Manchester who paid rates, ended up on the electoral register. She thus became the first woman in England to vote in a local by-election. Other women registered, but an official removed their names. This resulted in the court case *Chorlton v Ling*, which decided that the 1867 Reform Act did not apply to women and that all were denied the vote.

Defending the rights of women in the *Chorlton* case was Richard Pankhurst. In 1869 he scored a significant achievement in amending the Municipal Franchise Act. This allowed women rate-payers the vote in local council elections, although it did not allow them to stand for office.

Petition of June 1884 asking for women to be included in the Third Reform Bill.
BL, Add. MS 44799, f.102

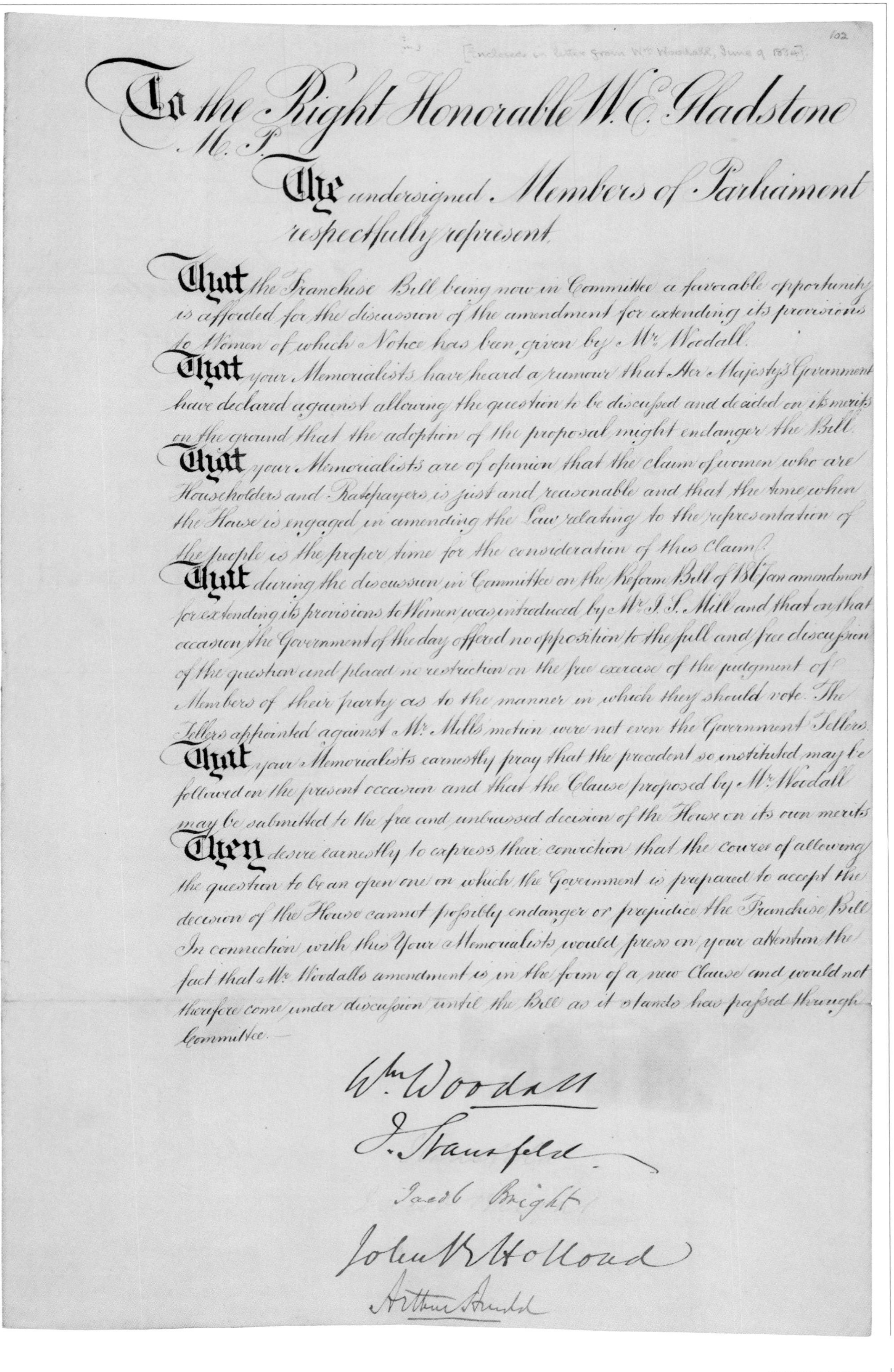

102

[Enclosed in letter from Wm Woodall, June 9 1884]

To the Right Honorable W. E. Gladstone M. P.

The undersigned Members of Parliament respectfully represent

That the Franchise Bill being now in Committee a favorable opportunity is afforded for the discussion of the amendment for extending its provisions to Women of which Notice has been given by Mr Woodall.

That your Memorialists have heard a rumour that Her Majesty's Government have declared against allowing the question to be discussed and decided on its merits on the ground that the adoption of the proposal might endanger the Bill.

That your Memorialists are of opinion that the claim of women who are Householders and Ratepayers is just and reasonable and that the time when the House is engaged in amending the Law relating to the representation of the people is the proper time for the consideration of this Claim.

That during the discussion in Committee on the Reform Bill of 1867 an amendment for extending its provisions to Women was introduced by Mr J. S. Mill and that on that occasion the Government of the day offered no opposition to the full and free discussion of the question and placed no restriction on the free exercise of the judgment of Members of their party as to the manner in which they should vote. The Tellers appointed against Mr Mills motion were not even the Government Tellers.

That your Memorialists earnestly pray that the precedent so instituted may be followed on the present occasion and that the Clause proposed by Mr Woodall may be submitted to the free and unbiassed decision of the House on its own merits.

They desire earnestly to express their conviction that the course of allowing the question to be an open one on which the Government is prepared to accept the decision of the House cannot possibly endanger or prejudice the Franchise Bill. In connection with this Your Memorialists would press on your attention the fact that Mr Woodalls amendment is in the form of a new Clause and would not therefore come under discussion until the Bill as it stands has passed through Committee.

Wm Woodall

J. Stansfeld

Jacob Bright

John K Holland

Arthur Arnold

Elsie Duval's Hunger Strike Medal. Duval was only 19 when arrested for her first suffragette offence, obstructing the police. Thereafter she committed a series of offences and was each time imprisoned and force fed. She was the first to be released and then rearrested under the Cat and Mouse Act.
The Women's Library, London Metropolitan University, 7EWD/M25

Stung by the *Chorlton* case, Pankhurst drafted the Women's Disabilities Removal Bill which stated that any reference to men in the Reform Act should equally apply to women. Jacob Bright, who became the advocate for women's suffrage in Parliament after John Stuart Mill lost his seat, presented the Bill in 1870 and it passed its second reading by 124 votes to 91. However, Gladstone saw women's suffrage as a "practical evil" and scuppered the Bill in the committee stage. What seemed like progress shuddered to a halt.

On 18 December 1879 Richard Pankhurst married 21-year-old Emmeline Goulden after a whirlwind romance. Emmeline Pankhurst would soon become the best-known name in the women's suffrage movement. Intriguingly, on her mother's side Emmeline was half Manx: in 1880 the Tynwald Parliament of the Isle of Man was the first to grant women the vote. During the debate on an Election Bill to grant the vote to all adult males, the Speaker removed the word "male" and thereby also granted suffrage to women. It was not until 1893 that New Zealand allowed women the vote and 1902 before Australia did (and they excluded aboriginal men and women). But in Britain the battle was only just beginning.

Hopes were high when a new Reform Bill was considered in 1884. The Liberal MP William Woodall proposed the standard amendment for any reference to "men" to include women. It would have given the vote to 100,000 or so wealthy women, and the Conservatives, thinking they may benefit from this, supported it. But Gladstone rejected it again.

It was a major blow to the movement and caused much dissension with several splinter groups forming, divided by whether to petition for suffrage for all or only unmarried women. Of these only the Women's Franchise League, run by Elizabeth Wolstenholme, achieved anything. They pursued women's rights at local level and in 1894 were triumphant when the Local Government Act allowed married women the equal right to both vote for and sit on municipal councils. This united the campaigners into striving for universal suffrage.

The figurehead at this time was Millicent Fawcett, the sister of Elizabeth Garrett, and widow of MP Henry Fawcett. She united the movement under the National Union of Women's Suffrage Societies in 1897. These were the suffragists who believed in the peaceful, if rather drawn-out, process of petitioning Parliament in the hope of success.

Emmeline Pankhurst and her daughters were not prepared to wait. In 1903 they launched a new organisation, the Women's Social and Political Union, with a view to more active lobbying. They persuaded the Liberal MP Bamford Slack to present a new Bill to Parliament in May 1905, but this did not get as far as a vote. Pankhurst's protest outside Parliament marked the start of her militant campaign.

In October 1905 Christabel Pankhurst and Annie Kenney heckled the MP Sir Edward Grey. They were dragged from the meeting and because Christabel spat at a policeman she was charged with assault and fined. They refused to pay and were imprisoned for

The National Union of Women's Suffrage Societies was established by Millicent Fawcett in 1897 on the 30th anniversary of the founding of the original Women's Suffrage Committee in 1867.
BL, 8413.k.5

The Daily Herald

No. 346. [Registered at the G.P.O. as a Newspaper.] SATURDAY, MAY 24, 1913. ONE HALFPENNY.

McKENNA

This image from *The Daily Herald* for 24 May 1913 treats lightly the force-feeding of suffragettes, but is rather more chilling than intended.

BL, 1911-1914 LON MLD5 NPL

a week. This received headline news and soon the newspapers were calling them "suffragettes".

The militant campaign gathered pace in 1906 when Anne Cobden-Sanderson and other high-profile women protested in the Lobby of the House of Commons and were imprisoned for a month. Their action encouraged others. Emmeline Pankhurst was herself imprisoned for obstruction in February 1908 and again in October for inciting a riot. A month earlier protesters in Downing Street had started the tactic of chaining themselves to the railings.

When Marion Dunlop was imprisoned in 1909 she adopted a new tactic and went on hunger strike. Fearing she might become a martyr the authorities released her, but others soon followed so the authorities force-fed prisoners, a humiliating and dangerous process. Emmeline's sister, Mary, was force-fed and died soon after she was released. She was proclaimed the first "martyr" for the cause. The MP George Lansbury accused the Prime Minister of having "tortured innocent women". In 1913 the Government passed what became called the Cat and Mouse Act whereby hunger strikers were released and imprisoned again once they'd recovered.

The scale of militant action escalated when further proposed legislation was rejected. There were arson and other attacks on public buildings and MPs' houses. Pillar boxes were polluted or destroyed. Works of art were slashed. The most shocking incident was the death of Emily Davison when she ran in front of the King's horse at the 1913 Derby.

Yet still Parliament did not concede. With the outbreak of War in August 1914 the suffragettes agreed to stop their campaign provided all prisoners were freed.

The contribution made to the war effort by millions of women may have done more to convince MPs to grant women the vote than any protests. The Representation of the People Bill passed through both Houses in 1917 and became law in 1918. It gave the vote to the majority of men over 21 and to all women over 30 – over eight million women. Soon after, the law also allowed women to stand for Parliament. The first woman elected was Countess Markievicz, a Sinn Fein MP, but she did not take her seat because Sinn Fein had boycotted Parliament and she was in prison. Nancy Astor, who was American by birth, was the first woman to enter Parliament in December 1919. It was not until July 1928 that the Equal Franchise Act gave the vote to all adult women. Emmeline Pankhurst had died just two weeks before.

Emily Davison's purse in which was a return ticket from the Derby.

The Women's Library, London Metropolitan University, 7RMB/A24

The Right to Welfare

The United Nations Declaration of Human Rights states that everyone has a right to "an adequate standard of living". Setting such a standard is not simple as there has long been different standards depending on an individual's class, gender or ethnicity. Support came mostly from charities and philanthropists rather than government. Well-meaning though they were, this tended to isolate the less fortunate rather than help them to achieve their potential. In the 1790s Jeremy Bentham had advocated a philosophy of utilitarianism, defined as ensuring "the greatest happiness of the greatest number", and he believed this should be the guiding principle of all legislation. Although the Victorians took Bentham's ideas to their heart, it was not until the 1940s that the concept of a universal welfare state took shape.

Gustav Doré's portrayal of the poor of London in 1872.
BL, WF.1.1856

Rights for the Poor

According to the CIA's World Fact Book, in 2006 an estimated 14% of people in Britain had insufficient income to maintain an adequate standard of living. This compared to 7% in the Republic of Ireland and 6% in France. The same data is not available for the Victorian era, but surveys in Manchester and London at the time suggest that as much as 60% of the population could be defined as poor.

Satirical hand-coloured lithograph of Captain Swing, the imaginary leader of riots by agricultural labourers, published by Orlando Hodgson in 1830.
British Museum, 1997,0928.30

Opposite:
Anti-Poor Law poster drawn in 1837 highlighting the horrors of the workhouse system.
National Archives, HO44/27

In Tudor England the enclosure of land for sheep farming, rather than arable use, led to many peasants being displaced and even whole villages deserted. Legislation in 1489 tried to restrict enclosure but it continued, leading to several rebellions, the last in Northamptonshire in 1607. Thomas More had linked enclosures and the poor. His novel *Utopia*, written in 1516, portrayed a disciplined society where there was welfare for the old and infirm and no private ownership. Most theft had been eradicated because people were not poor. They had work, as land was available to all.

The situation deteriorated in England after the Dissolution of the Monasteries. They had provided shelter and charity which ceased when they closed. The problem shifted to the parish, with provisions made under various Acts, culminating in the 1601 Poor Law. Each parish had Overseers to raise money from the parish, administer those funds for the poor and find suitable work where possible. Any able-bodied pauper who tried to claim relief and refused to work could be sent to a "House of Correction". A later Act extended that to any man who abandoned his wife and children to the parish by refusing to find work. Though amended over time, parts of the 1601 Act remained in force for over 300 years.

Workhouses began to appear from the mid-seventeenth century and at the outset were seen as beneficial. They provided work where none was previously available. However, the parish soon saw this as a way to cut costs and Edward Knatchbull's Workhouse Test Act of 1723 made it obligatory for the poor to enter a workhouse before being entitled to poor relief.

The Speenhamland system, introduced in the Berkshire village of Speen in 1795, allowed low wages to be topped up by poor relief. The idea spread during the Napoleonic Wars but did not become law. It unfortunately encouraged employers to pay low wages and put a strain on parish funds. The position was aggravated by the Corn Laws, which kept the price of corn high to protect landowners whilst taxing the import of foreign corn.

Matters came to a head in 1830 with the Swing riots, named after Captain Swing, the revolt's mysterious figurehead. Like the Luddites in the towns, agricultural labourers found their livelihood diminished by mechanisation and further enclosures. Riots began in Kent and soon spread, the largest popular uprising since the Peasants' Revolt.

Meanwhile, the cost of administering poor relief had risen more than ten times since the 1750s. A Royal Commission was set up in 1832 and its recommendations led to the 1834 Poor Law Amendment Act. This set up a Poor Law Commission to administer the system through Poor Law Unions spread across the parishes. The Act did not solve the problem of poverty, but simply contained the genuinely poor. Some relief was still paid, but the emphasis shifted to the workhouse. To

discourage idlers, the regime was stern and unwelcoming. Able-bodied paupers were set to work crushing bones for fertiliser, breaking rocks or picking oakum. Worst of all, sexes were segregated and families split up.

There was a scandal at Andover Workhouse in 1845 where it was discovered that the Master was frequently drunk and would attempt to seduce or rape the female inmates. Food was rationed and men and children resorted to sucking the marrow from the bones they crushed. Such abuses led the government to take more control. The Poor Law Commission was replaced by the Poor Law Board in 1847. From 1871 the Board was subsumed within local government. Although conditions improved, workhouses remained an ever-present threat and were not abolished until 1930, and even then many lingered on for years.

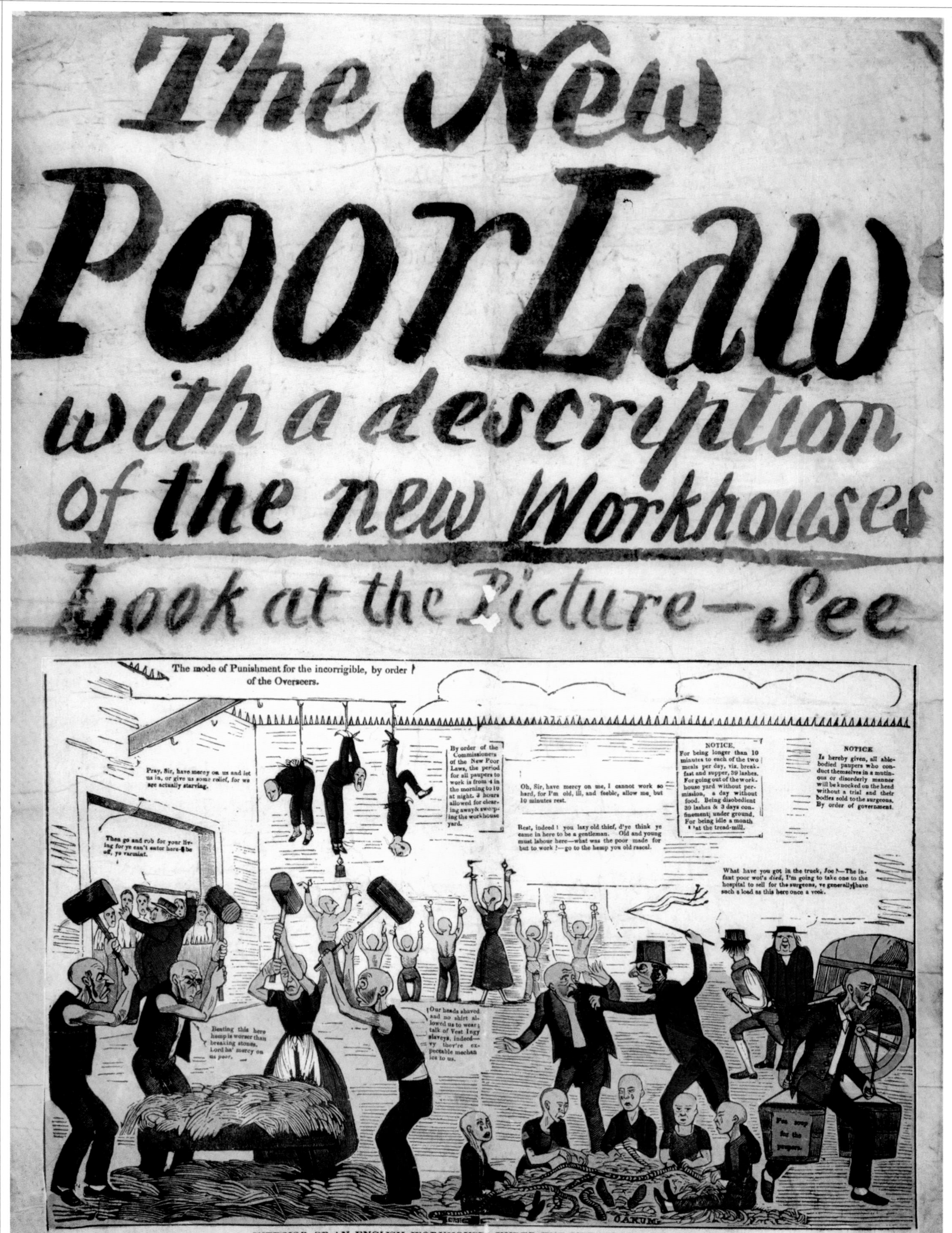

INTERIOR OF AN ENGLISH WORKHOUSE UNDER THE NEW POOR LAW ACT.

Child Labour

The plight of children in the nineteenth century is well known through its portrayal in such books as Charles Dickens's *Oliver Twist* and Charles Kingsley's *The Water Babies*. Children had few legal rights and many were treated little better than slaves.

This illustration by George Cruikshank is from *Oliver Twist* by Charles Dickens, published in 1838 and written specifically to attack the new Poor Law. One of the best-known scenes in all of English literature is when Oliver Twist in the workhouse dares to ask for more food.
BL, K.T.C.105.B.6

Though society now places children first, such axioms as "children should be seen but not heard" and "spare the rod and spoil the child" still resonate from the recent past. Children's legal rights were seldom considered. The first law passed to regulate child labour was the 1788 Chimney Sweepers Act which forbad children under eight being used as climbing boys.

With the rise of cotton mills, children were put to work up to fifteen hours a day, six days a week in a closed environment. Often a third of the workforce in mills were children, usually pauper apprentices, bought in cheaply from the workhouse. They were seldom paid more than a shilling a week and were in danger of being maimed or killed. Workers were fined if they were late or sick, and even for whistling or opening a window.

One of the major mill owners of the day was Robert Peel, father of the future prime minister. He was aware of his own shortcomings in employing children and when he became an MP in 1790 he lobbied for greater protection for vulnerable workers. The result was the Health and Morals of Apprentices Act of 1802. It applied only to pauper apprentices in cotton mills. It limited the working day to twelve hours and placed an onus on employers to improve conditions, provide clothing and religious education. It was a start but the Act was not monitored and was frequently ignored.

Robert Owen urged Peel for better legislation. Owen had acquired the mills at New Lanark in Scotland in 1799 and, despite opposition from his partners, improved conditions. He employed only local children aged ten or over, built new housing for workers, introduced a local shop and used the profits to build a school. This not only provided education for children – Owen was one of the first to promote infants' schools – but pioneered adult education. Owen contributed evidence to a committee of Peel's to investigate child labour, but many of Owen's proposals were discarded in the 1819 Cotton Mills and Factories Act. This prohibited children under nine, and those between nine and sixteen were limited to twelve hours a day.

It was not until Lord Ashley's Coal Mines Act in 1842 that women and children under ten stopped working underground.

The need for reform continued. The radical MP John Hobhouse proposed his own Factories Act in 1830, although only a watered-down version made it onto the statute book. Its main benefit was to stop night work for those under 21. Richard Oastler, whose work had encouraged Hobhouse, now inspired Michael Sadler who proposed a Bill limiting the working day to ten hours for those under eighteen. It was unsuccessful but Sadler chaired a Parliamentary Committee, which included Hobhouse, and which interviewed many workers (some of whom were sacked because of their involvement). His report was published in January 1833 and the findings horrified readers with its stories of children being whipped for absconding, being forced to work extreme hours, and of their illnesses and injuries.

Drawing by Auguste Hervieu from Frances Trollope's groundbreaking novel *Michael Armstrong: Factory Boy*. Published in 1839 and called the first industrial novel, it was based on the life of Robert Blincoe, a pauper from the workhouse who was taken as a seven-year-old to work in a cotton mill in Nottingham. Blincoe succeeded and became a self-made man.

BL, YA.1994.a.7128

A Victorian chimney sweep with a barefoot climbing boy, small enough to fit inside narrow passages.

Sadler lost his seat in the 1832 election and Lord Ashley (the future Lord Shaftesbury) took up the campaign. Though his Bill was defeated, the government put through its own Factory Act in 1833, covering all textile factories. This reduced the working day for those between nine and thirteen to nine hours, but those over thirteen still worked a twelve-hour day. No one under eighteen worked nights. For the first time inspectors were appointed. The ten-hour day for women and children was finally introduced in 1847.

Further Acts chipped away at child labour. From 1840 no child under 21 was allowed to sweep chimneys, though it was not until 1864 that this was monitored and any infringement fined. In 1875 twelve-year-old George Brewster died when trapped up a chimney. It caused an outcry and led to all sweeps being licensed.

The Education Act of 1870 legislated for the education of children between five and twelve via new School Boards, though it was not made compulsory until 1880. Thereafter the employment of children was regulated in accordance with school age and attendance. In fact the 1878 Factory Act, which consolidated all previous legislation, was the first to stipulate compulsory education for children up to age ten.

Looking after the Child

Although there was a growing recognition of the need for children to be educated in schools rather than at home, very little was done to protect the child from abuse within the family or in society. Rather than the Government, it was down to philanphropists and charities to lead the way.

Philanthropists such as Robert Owen provided schools in the communities they were building for their workers. Here, the pupils are learning to dance at Owen's school at New Lanark in 1825.

Before the rise of compulsory state education, many children were instructed by religious foundations or philanthropists. In 1731 the Welsh minister Griffith Jones began a scheme in Carmarthen where he spent three months in one town teaching people to read and then moved on. His "circulating schools" idea spread throughout Wales. In 1780 Robert Raikes began his first Sunday school in Gloucester for the children of chimney sweeps.

In 1818 John Pounds, a shoemaker in Portsmouth, started free lessons for poor children in his shop. Thomas Guthrie developed the idea in Scotland, and by the 1840s there were many such "ragged schools" across Britain. A visit to a ragged school inspired Dickens to write *A Christmas Carol* in 1843. Lord Ashley established the Ragged School Union in 1844, with generous contributions from Angela Burdett-Coutts, the daughter of Francis Burdett.

The 1834 Poor Law Amendment Act required workhouses to provide at least three hours' schooling each day. So when William Forster introduced his Education Act in 1870, he was essentially encouraging the new School Boards to fill in the gaps across the country.

What was needed, however, was more care and protection of children. In 1867 Thomas Barnardo was so overcome by the scale of destitution in London, worsened by a recent cholera epidemic, that he set up a Ragged School in the East End. He followed this in 1870 with his first home for destitute boys in Stepney.

The Waifs and Strays' Society was founded in 1881 by Edward Rudolf, a Sunday school teacher and civil

The shadow of illegitimacy

The legal status of children born out of wedlock goes back to the Statute of Merton in 1235. The Church proposed such children should be legitimate (that is, able to inherit) if their parents married. The Barons disagreed and so an illegitimate child had no rights in England. In Wales they would inherit if accepted by the father. In 1926 the Legitimacy Act made a child legitimate if the parents subsequently married. Only in 1969 did the Family Law Reform Act allow an illegitimate child to inherit as of right. Scotland's laws were harsher and until 1835 someone of illegitimate birth could only make a will if they had children of their own.

1850 etching by George Cruikshank of a Ragged School at West Street, Smithfield.

Right:
In 1858 the magazine *Town Talk* asked the question whether children should be educated or allowed to turn to crime.
BL, P.P.5267

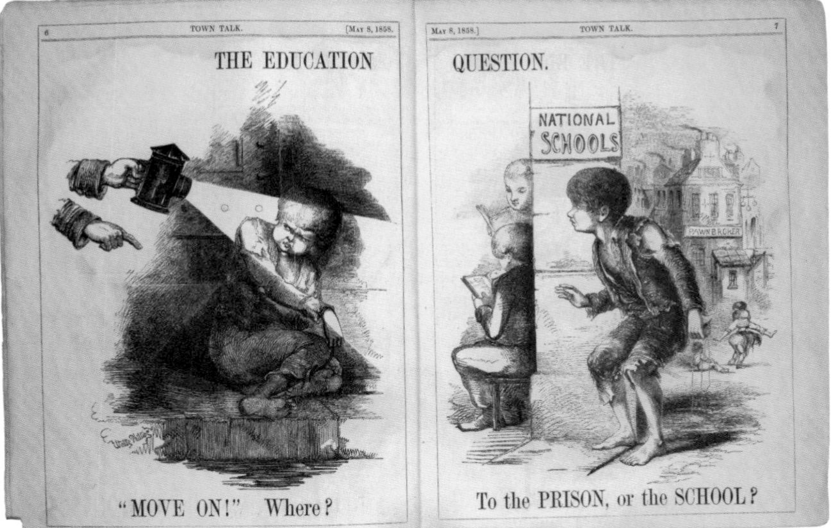

servant. With his brother Robert he gained the support of the Church of England and set up their first home in Dulwich. Like Barnardo's they also ran small cottage homes and arranged for foster care. It continues today as the Children's Society.

Edward Rudolf was also one of the founders of the London Society for the Prevention of Cruelty to Children in July 1884, with Lord Shaftesbury as President. The principal driving force, however, was Benjamin Waugh, a Yorkshire minister who had worked for years in the slums of Greenwich. He, Dr Barnardo and Rudolf, were all critical of the workhouse system which encouraged destitution. Under Waugh the Society flourished and by 1889, with 32 branches throughout Britain, it became a National Society (the NSPCC). Each branch had an inspector who investigated claims of child abuse or neglect. A separate Scottish society (now called Children 1st) was also founded that year. The objective of the NSPCC was to educate good parenthood and help support the family.

The government regarded children as their parents' property and would not intervene in cases of cruelty. The NSPCC worked with the reformist MP Anthony Mundella, a former Chartist, to develop the Prevention of Cruelty to, and Protection of, Children Act. It was passed despite opposition in August 1889, and made the ill-treatment of children an offence punishable by a fine of up to £100 or two years in prison. It also gave magistrates the power of search, though it was not until 1904 that the Prevention of Cruelty Act gave powers to NSPCC inspectors to remove children from their parents if there was evidence of danger. Now the responsibility of Social Services departments, it remains a challenging issue regarding the rights and welfare of both children and parents.

Barnardo's dilemma

Barnardo (who qualified as a doctor in 1876) was deeply affected in 1874 when he turned away an eleven-year-old boy called 'Carrots'. A few days later the boy died from hunger and exposure. Barnardo wrote: "Poor forlorn little lad! I think I see him on that sad, sad evening of a bright May Day, creeping supperless into the empty cask, his heart crushed with its sense of loneliness and dire need. I wonder whether Carrots cried as most children do when distressed? Or had the feelings of a child been long banished from that young breast in its grim struggle for life?" Soon after Barnardo adopted the slogan, "No Destitute Child Ever Refused Admission".

The Elderly

Although the workhouse scheme had originally been designed for the able-bodied poor, by the second half of the nineteenth century it had become the last dreaded refuge of the elderly. Something needed to be done to keep them out of the workhouse.

Life expectancy, especially in cities, dropped during the nineteenth century. In the eighteenth century about 8.5% of the population (one in twelve) lived to be over 60, but by the nineteenth century this had dropped to 6.5% (one in fifteen).

Not all elderly were poor, but those who were dreaded spending their final years in a workhouse. Those who could afford it, paid into a Friendly Society. These had been legally recognised since 1793, and provided the sick with a payment based on contributions. Since many elderly were also sick, they received regular payments which were tantamount to a pension. By the 1870s there were 30,000 such societies with over four million members. These were almost all men, about two-thirds of the working population. However, most poor people could not afford the high level of contributions.

In 1878 Canon William Blackley, who had spent some years in the poorest parts of London where he nearly died of cholera, became the first to propose a scheme called National Provident Insurance. He suggested that those who had just started work, aged between seventeen and twenty, pay heavily into the equivalent of a State Friendly Society so that money would gain the most interest and provide a pension of eight shillings a week until aged 70, and then four shillings. His scheme aroused attention but no action, until Bismarck introduced a national insurance scheme in Germany in 1883. Then a House of Commons Select Committee spent two years exploring Blackley's idea before dropping it as impractical.

Blackley did not let the idea go and in the 1890s his cause was taken up by Joseph Chamberlain. A Parliamentary committee considered the matter, but dismissed the idea of a state-funded scheme as too expensive. As for a contributory scheme, Chamberlain was not convinced a sufficient level of income could be achieved. The committee gave way to a Royal Commission in 1893 to consider a proposal from social reformer Charles Booth for a five-shilling weekly pension for the over 65s. This would cost £21 million in public funds but when the great social reformer Octavia Hill gave evidence, she declared the scheme "inadequate" and destructive of family responsibility to the elderly.

The fight was taken up by the Revd. Francis Stead, brother of W. T. Stead. Working with the Amalgamated Society of Engineers, which had recently introduced a superannuated pension scheme for its members, Stead organised a series of public talks across Britain, starting in December 1898. Charles Booth was the chief speaker. Although he thought that pensions should start at 65 years of age, he realised the cost may be

The Bournville revolution
George Cadbury, of the famous chocolate firm, was always at the forefront of social welfare. When he built the village of Bournville near Birmingham for his workers in 1895, he included not only schools and shops but sports and medical facilities, and almshouses for the elderly. He supported the campaign for old-age pensions and introduced a contributory scheme for his own employees in 1906, paying in £60,000 to kick-start it.

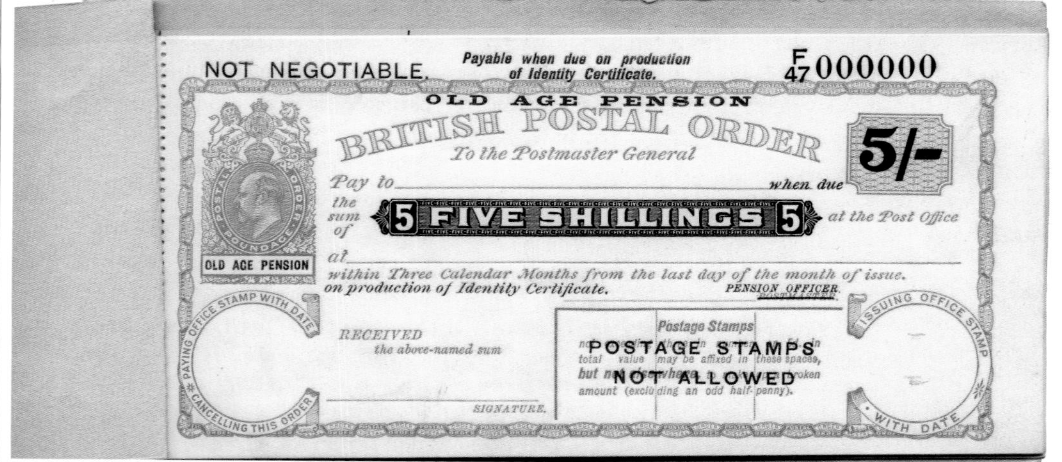

NOT NEGOTIABLE. Payable when due on production of Identity Certificate. F 47 000000

OLD AGE PENSION

BRITISH POSTAL ORDER

To the Postmaster General

5/-

Pay to ______ when due

the sum of 5 FIVE SHILLINGS 5 at the Post Office

at ______

OLD AGE PENSION

within Three Calendar Months from the last day of the month of issue. on production of Identity Certificate. PENSION OFFICER.

PAYING OFFICE STAMP WITH DATE CANCELLING THIS ORDER

RECEIVED the above-named sum

SIGNATURE.

Postage Stamps

POSTAGE STAMPS NOT ALLOWED

ISSUING OFFICE STAMP WITH DATE

Original Old Age Pension postal order from 1909.
The British Postal Museum & Archive

A London post office on 1 January 1909 when the very first old-age pensions were paid (from *The Graphic*, 9 January 1909).

insurmountable so revised his scheme to start at 70. Booth and Stead organised a National Committee of Organised Labour (NCOL), composed chiefly of trade unionists and representatives of Friendly Societies, and half-funded by the Quaker philanthropist George Cadbury.

The NCOL kept pressure on government and when the Liberal Party returned to power in 1906, Herbert Asquith, as Chancellor of the Exchequer, proposed a new non-contributory scheme. By reviewing indirect taxes the Treasury found £7 million. To fit within this, Asquith's proposals fell back on Booth's suggestions of starting the scheme at 70 and of making it means-tested. The full weekly pension was five shillings (25p) for those earning less than £21 a year, falling to one shilling (5p) where the annual income was £31-10-0 (£31.50). Asquith juggled the Budget, and it was as Prime Minister that he saw it through in August 1908. The first pensions were paid on 1 January 1909 (2 January in Scotland).

At a thanksgiving service held on 3 January, Frederick Rogers, secretary of the NCOL, acknowledged the considerable work of Charles Booth and added, "Pensions were given to the aged, not as a charity, but as a right." Every effort had been made to ensure they did not carry the stigma of poor relief. Take-up in the first week was over 50% and continued to grow.

Disabilities

For centuries the disabled relied upon charities for help and assistance. Whilst legislation helped support people with disabilities it also isolated them within society. In the end the disabled fought back for their own equality.

People with a learning disability deserve the right to have their say.

Disabilities cover a broad spectrum, both physical and mental, and society has long had difficulties dealing with the more extreme cases. Such individuals were usually isolated from society, often in special institutions. It was uncommon for any to be integrated in society, although "visiting" societies would help the blind in their homes. Special alphabets, such as Braille or the Moon system, helped the blind to read and be more self-sufficient.

A Royal Commission set up in 1886 to consider "the Blind, the Deaf and the Dumb" broadened its remit to investigate all "handicapped" children, leading to the Elementary Education (Defective and Epileptic Children) Act of 1899 which started the development of special needs' schools and facilities. Whilst these schemes were important in recognising special needs they still isolated the disabled from society, making them more dependent. Even though the 1944 Education Act recommended disabled children should be educated in mainstream schools, little of that happened. The National Assistance Act of 1948 promoted services for the disabled rather than encouraging them to help themselves. It was an ethos that became firmly entrenched, stigmatising rather than enabling the disabled.

In 1972 Paul Hunt, frustrated by how disempowered and institutionalised he was in a residential home, joined with similar individuals to form the Union of the Physically Impaired Against Segregation (UPIAS), the first disability liberation group in Britain. They highlighted the fact that society had created the problems for the disabled by actively excluding them – it was society that did the disabling, not the individual's impairment. Together with Vic Finkelstein and Mike Oliver, the group developed the Social Model of Disability which was adopted by Disabled People's International (DPI) in 1981. The representative organisation of DPI in Britain was the Disabled People's Council (DPC), run by disabled people and unifying similar such groups across the country.

UPIAS was disbanded in 1990 and its philosophy continued by the DPC. The DPC led the campaign to alter society's view of the disabled which resulted in the Disability Discrimination Act of 1995. This enforced changes upon society to provide a more level playing field in terms of access to facilities, employment and health rights, education, mobility and equality of opportunity.

Thomas Armitage, who founded the forerunner of the Royal National Institute for the Blind in 1868, researched the many systems developed to help the blind read. His committee favoured the Braille system.

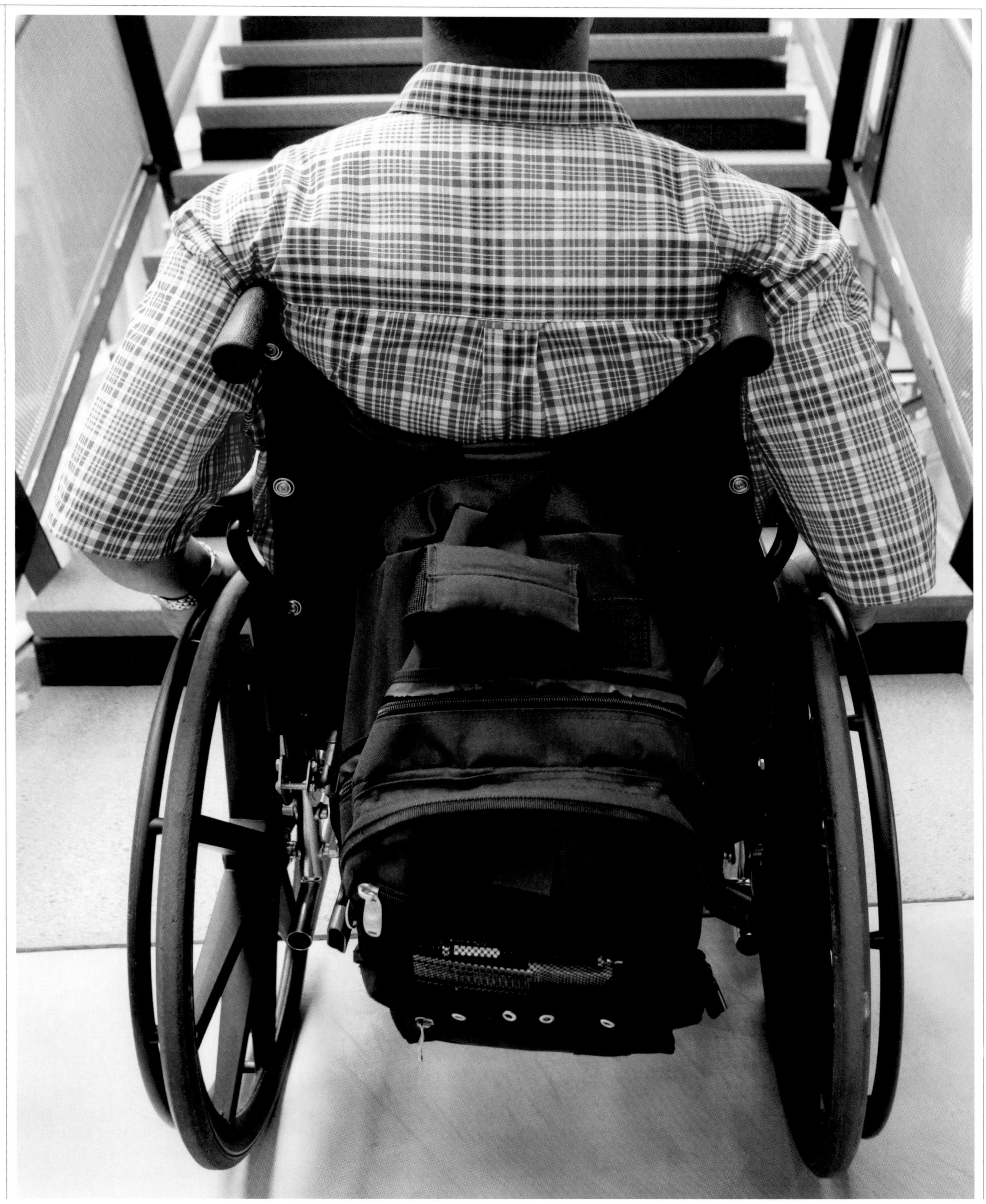

Workers' Rights

Employers frequently rode roughshod over workers, with no thought to any rights. It took years of sacrifice before trade unions became legal and could fight for the worker. There were several pioneering strikes that boosted support for unskilled workers.

This copy of the pamphlet *The Story of the Dockers' Strike* was owned by John Burns, the future MP, who supported the dockers throughout the strike and did much to sustain their morale.
BL, Add. MS 74265B

Any form of political agitation amongst workers was forbidden by the Combination Acts of 1799 and 1800. Though repealed in 1824, a series of strikes led to a new Act. This allowed wage-bargaining but anything beyond that was regarded as conspiracy, with harsh penalties.

Wages had not kept pace with costs and varied considerably across the country. The rising costs were a major factor in the eruption of the Swing Riots of 1830, increasing the government's fear of rebellion. It was this background that contributed to the fate of the Tolpuddle Martyrs. In November 1833 George Loveless established a Friendly Society of Agricultural Workers to negotiate their wages, then seven shillings (35p) a week but likely to fall to six shillings (30p). They wanted ten shillings (50p). A local landowner informed the Home Secretary about the society. Whilst it was entirely legal, Loveless and five others were prosecuted under Pitt's 1797 Illegal Oaths Act that made any society where members took oaths, illegal. Found guilty, all six were transported to Australia. They were pardoned in 1836.

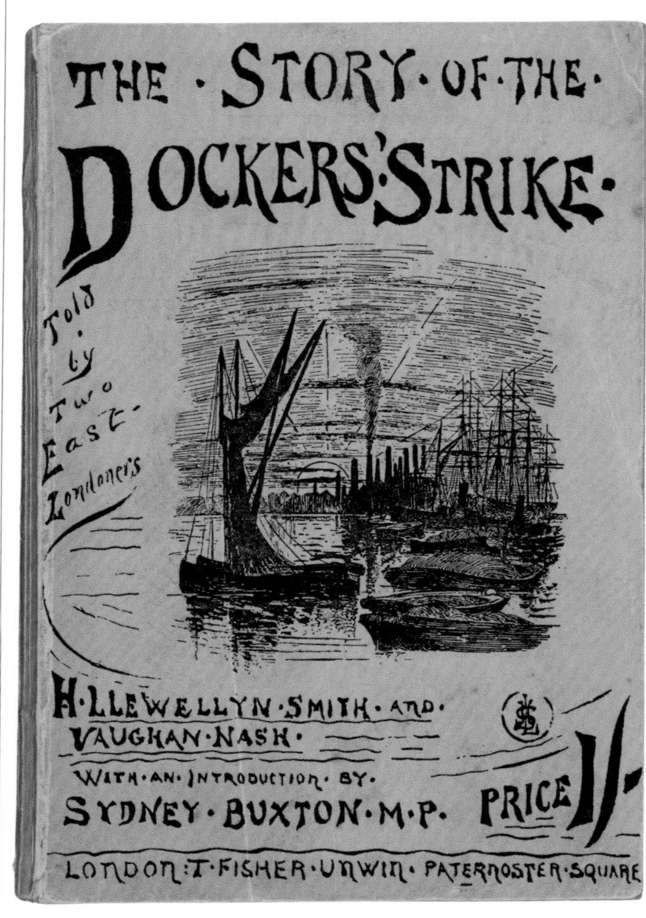

The prosecution cast a cloud over other unions, such as Robert Owen's Grand National Consolidated Trades Union, which he had set up in 1833. Owen wanted to unite existing unions as a co-operative, but the political climate saw its collapse.

Owen's co-operative ideas did bear fruit. A group of weavers and artisans in Rochdale got together in 1844 to buy and sell food they could not otherwise afford. They developed a set of rules, the "Rochdale Principles", which have formed the basis of the co-operative movement ever since. The Co-operative Wholesale Society grew from this in 1863.

Unrest erupted following the rejection of the People's Charter in 1842. By August over half a million workers were on strike, mostly in northern England, in what was the first General Strike, known as the Plug Riots. There were over 1,500 arrests and 79 transportations.

Change came slowly but with greater prosperity in the 1850s, thanks to industrialisation, unions became more organised. The Scot, William Allan, helped create the Amalgamated Society of Engineers, the first successful national union, uniting 121 societies and charging sufficient dues to have full-time officers and provide benefits, like the friendly societies. Other large unions followed and combined forces as Trades Councils in the major towns, leading to the Trades Union Congress in 1868.

Generally unions acted responsibly. Following a Royal Commission which reported favourably in 1871, the Trade Union Act became law, giving unions a legal status. The unions also developed a political base when two members, Thomas Burt and Alexander McDonald, became MPs in 1874.

The effectiveness of the unions was tested in three crucial strikes: the matchgirls in 1888, and the dockers and gasworkers, both in 1889. It was the gasworkers' strike led by Will Thorne that established an eight-hour working day with three shifts.

Women at Bryant & May's match factory worked up to fourteen hours a day for five shillings (25p) a week. Money was deducted for lateness, talking or going to the toilet without permission. Annie Besant highlighted their conditions in an article "White Slavery in London". Bryant & May's

The Fabian Society

The Fabian Society had been established in 1884 as an intellectual, non-aggressive society to promote social reform. It included such influential people as George Bernard Shaw, Sidney and Beatrice Webb, Edith Nesbit, Hubert Bland, Eleanor Marx and Emmeline Pankhurst.

The Political Drama. No. 32.

Most Gracious King, Most Sacred Monarch, Most Sovereign Lord and Divine Master, gifted with grace from God, to rule with Paternal Love over millions of Human Beings, your *Slaves and Subjects*—have Mercy upon us as you hope for Mercy hereafter.—Remember Sire, your Coronation *Oath* strictly enjoins you to *Temper Justice with Mercy.* We have committed no moral sin against God or Man. Forget not, Sire, that millions of your Sacred Majesty's Loyal subjects are bound by *Oaths* in their different Societies to protect themselves from unjust encroachments on their Rights. Are not these, Royal Sir, as culpable as ourselves? The *Conservatives, Freemasons, Orange Lodges, and Government Spies,* Gracious Sire, are all bound by Oaths to protect their *Orders,* however *unlawful* they may be; are not these also as culpable as us? O! King! We only bound ourselves for the just protection of our Miserable Earnings—they for *Oppression, Monopoly,* and *Plunder.*—Oh! Sire! have *Mercy* on poor *Humanity.*

Humanity!—Who the hell's he? Come cut your sticks—I'm damn'd if you dont smell of *Rebellion, Poverty,* and *Parish Soup,* as strong as Stink pots in a sea fight.—Mercy indeed—dont you wish you may get it—here, take it—*over the left.*

(Aside)—Blast me, they talking about *Oaths* makes me recollect well when I was in Sarvice (for they always send the greatest *Fool* in a family to sea), I used to Swear worse than a Ship Parson,—Shiver me; I never Ate, Drank, or had a Woman without prefacing it with a gallus good Oath—that was something like "Flare up!"

Pilly, turn your *Donkey* to 'em, de horrid *Paupers,* if you give 'em de smallest hopes you shall have no peace for vun month.

Guards, turn the *Slaves* out they must be *Transported,* my duty to the Capitalists, Landholders, the Tories and my nine hundred & ninety-nine Cousins demand it

THE DORCHESTER UNIONISTS IMPLORING MERCY!!! OF THEIR KING,

"He who trusts in Princes shall be thus rewarded".

Printed and Published by G. Drake, 12, Houghton Street, Clare Market.

This cartoon was part of the campaign to support the Tolpuddle Martyrs. It shows the King turning his back on the Martyrs, because he was more interested in landowners, the rich and his relatives.

National Archives, HO44/27

reaction was to get workers to sign a statement of satisfaction and sack those who refused. The women went on strike. They were supported by the press, the Salvation Army and the Fabian Society, of which Annie Besant was a member. Within three weeks Bryant & May gave in.

The Dockers' strike lasted four weeks during August 1889. Many dockers were casual labourers with no guaranteed work. They could wait all day for one hour's work and be paid 5d (2p). They demanded a minimum of four hours' work and 6d an hour (the "docker's tanner"). The employers thought they could starve them out but the dockers were supported by the Fabians, the Salvation Army and the large unions in Britain and Australia. This and the Matchgirls' strike were triumphs for unskilled workers and a massive boost for the union movement. Union membership rose from 750,000 in 1888 to 6.5 million in 1918.

The Matchgirls' strike in 1885 was the first triumph for unskilled workers over an uncaring employer.

Strife

The years between the First and Second World Wars were dominated by the Great Depression and unemployment. There was the General Strike and hunger marches were organised to demand attention to the needs of the unemployed.

Under the 1911 National Insurance Act, Asquith's government provided cover for both sickness and unemployment. It was a compulsory scheme with contributions from each worker, employer and the state and allowed seven shillings (35p) benefit a week for men (six shillings for women) for a fixed period (initially up to fifteen weeks) of forced unemployment. At the start the scheme covered only those industries with seasonal fluctuations, such as the building trade, and affected about two million workers, but was extended to all wage-earners after the War, when the benefit was also increased. By 1920, however, unemployment had risen sharply, with figures complicated by numbers of returning servicemen. There were protests in many cities, including the notorious "Battle of Whitehall" in October 1920 when police baton-charged men and women, seriously injuring up to 40 people.

Various economic factors, including the aftermath of the War, led to a Depression across Europe and the USA. Unemployment shot to 12.2% in 1921. Though it dropped in 1922, it remained high. The National Insurance scheme had been based on an average unemployment rate of 4.6%. At the start, and during the War, the actual rate was well below that, so by 1920 the scheme was substantially in profit. But soon after, that profit evaporated and the scheme was in debt. Restrictions were introduced especially for those "not actively seeking work", where benefits were stopped. Many individuals had to fall back on poor relief (renamed Public Assistance from 1929) with all the associated stigma.

The financial climate also led to the General Strike which began in May 1926, though its cause goes back much further. During the War the government had taken over the mines and working conditions had improved, including a seven-hour day introduced in 1919. The mines were in need of modernisation, though, and when they were returned to private ownership in March 1921, the mine owners proposed wage cuts and longer hours to meet the

A queue of unemployed men outside a labour exchange in October 1924.

London's Great Food Convoy during the General Strike guarded by armoured cars and troops.

Workers in the North-East of England demonstrating during the General Strike.

Slum housing in Liverpool in 1933.

cost. The miners went on strike but were not supported by their colleagues in the rail and transport unions. The miners had to accept wage cuts and local pay bargaining, and soon there were wage cuts in other industries.

In 1925 Winston Churchill restored the pound to the gold standard which strengthened the pound and made exports more expensive. Economic recovery slowed and once again the mine owners announced further wage cuts. This time the TUC pledged support for the miners. The Government agreed to subsidise the mines but a Royal Commission under Herbert Samuel, which reported in March 1926, urged the withdrawal of subsidies as counterproductive to modernisation. It suggested that the cost of improvements could be met by a short-term wage cut. The miners were adamant: "Not a penny off the pay, not a second on the day."

Negotiations between the TUC and the Government were cut short when printers refused to run an editorial in the *Daily Mail* stating that the strike was "... a revolutionary move which can only succeed by destroying the government and subverting the rights and liberties of the people". The TUC called out workers in two phases starting with the transport, printing, building, metal and chemical trades from 3 May 1926.

The response was virtually unanimous with some 1.8 million workers on strike at its peak. The Government used volunteers, the police and the army to maintain essential services. After a week the strike began to falter. The National Sailors' and Firemen's Union, which did not want to be called out, sought a court injunction. Justice Astbury ruled that the General Strike was illegal because there was no trade dispute other than amongst the miners.

This put the TUC in a difficult position and on 12 May it called off the Strike. The miners continued for another seven months but without success. They had to accept wage cuts and return to the eight-hour day. The Government brought in the Trade Disputes and Trade Unions Act in 1927 which remained in force until 1971. It made sympathetic strikes illegal and restricted picketing and secondary action.

The Stock Market crash in New York in 1929 ushered in the Great Depression of the 1930s. Countries limited their imports and demand for British products dropped. The major export industries had to reduce output, resulting in unemployment doubling in 1930. Over one third of the 2.5 million unemployed were from the iron and steel, shipbuilding, cotton and engineering industries. The Government set up a Commission to review national expenditure. The report's recommendations included severe public sector cuts, mostly in unemployment benefits. The 1931 Anomalies Act and National Economy Act reduced benefits by 10%, cut the period of benefit and then means-tested those who applied for Public Assistance. Under these Acts over 700,000 people had their benefits denied or reduced.

Housing conditions for the unemployed were also appalling. Although there was a massive programme between the Wars, building over four million new homes, and some 300,000 slum houses cleared, this benefited mostly the middle class and those in employment. Even if moved to new housing, the unemployed could not afford the increased rents or rates and they needed increased government subsidies to alleviate their plight.

It was in this climate that the National Unemployed Workers Movement (NUWM) became a notable force. It was started in April 1921 by Wal Hannington, a member of the newly formed British Communist Party. Its purpose was to campaign on behalf of the unemployed and to abolish capitalism, which it saw as the main cause of unemployment. Its most memorable activities were the hunger marches it organised. It suffered in the eyes of many because it was seen as an arm of the Communist Party, but in the early 1930s its membership increased significantly. In October 1932, 2,000 marched on London to present a petition of one million signatures to Parliament but they were denied this, leading to skirmishes with the police and many arrests.

The most famous of the Hunger marches was from Jarrow in October 1936. It was one of the few not organised by the NUWM but by Ellen Wilkinson of the Labour Party and the local council. It was well organised, seeking a new steelworks at Jarrow following the closure of the shipbuilding yard. Some 207 men marched the 300 miles to London with a petition of 12,000 signatures. The government were more sympathetic to this march and the petition was accepted. Although no immediate action was taken, a steelworks and other industrial sites were established at Jarrow in 1938-9.

Few of the hunger marches achieved much, but the images have become iconic and serve as reminders of the poverty of the inter-war years.

Opposite: The Jarrow Hunger march in 1936.

JARROW
CRUSADE

The Welfare State

Most of the building blocks of the Welfare State existed before William Beveridge's 1942 report. His skill was to unite them in a comprehensive "cradle-to-grave" scheme that helped promote a spirit of post-war optimism.

William Beveridge, the architect of the Welfare State.

In 1941 William Beveridge, one of Britain's leading economists, was asked by Winston Churchill's government to look at the problem of building a post-war Britain. Beveridge had also been asked to consider how the various social security schemes could be harmonised. Beveridge had been the Director of Labour Exchanges in 1909 and had advised Lloyd George on pensions and national insurance. He brought all these threads together in his report "Social Insurance and Allied Services" in December 1942. His approach was based on two simple, overriding principles: universality and comprehensiveness. In other words the scheme applied to everybody, with no "means test", and just one payment covered all the benefits.

The report tackled the five threats to society: want, ignorance, disease, squalor and idleness. Churchill's coalition government took the opportunity to tackle "ignorance" first with the 1944 Education Act. This raised the school-leaving age to sixteen and established the system of primary, secondary and further education. It also helped make university entrance easier to new students with government subsidies.

Churchill's brief 1945 caretaker government also sneaked in the Family Allowance Act, which provided a weekly payment for all children after the first. The scheme had been promoted for some years by former leading suffragette Eleanor Rathbone. She was furious that the Bill planned to make the payment to the father rather than the mother, and threatened to resign unless it was changed.

The main implementations were carried out by the Labour government under Clement Attlee with the National Insurance and National Health Service Acts of 1946. The first provided workers with unemployment, sickness, maternity and widows' benefits and old-age pensions. It was funded by compulsory contributions of 4/11d (just under 25p) a week for all people in work, except married women, plus contributions from employers and the state.

The second Act, seen through by the Minister of Health Aneurin Bevan, introduced a national health service

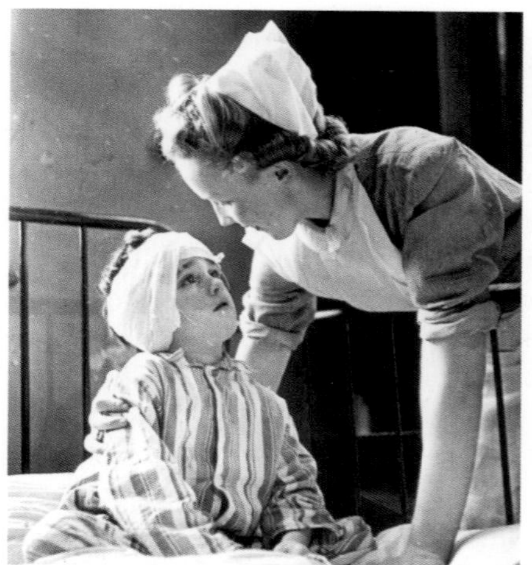

A nurse and child at the miners' hospital at Tredegar in South Wales at the time the National Health Service was introduced. Workers paid twopence out of every pound they earned into the Workmen's Medical Aid Society to cover their medical, dental and optical services. This scheme purportedly inspired Aneurin Bevan in developing his National Health Service.

Two of the pamphlets produced to promote aspects of the Welfare State.
BL, 1899.ss.11 (9)
BL, 1899.ss.18 (74)

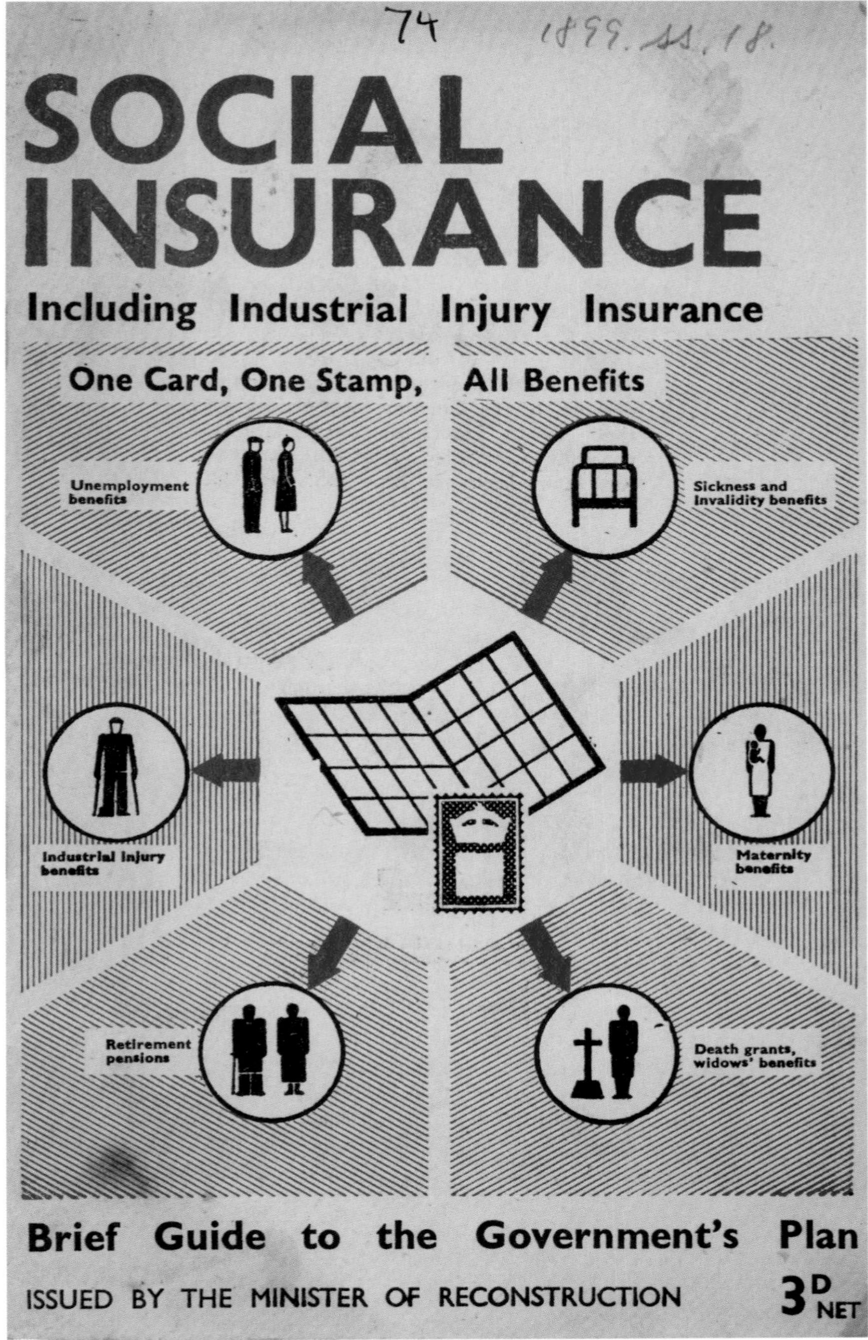

free to all, including dental and opthalmic services. This was seen through Parliament despite sizeable opposition from the British Medical Association, who did not want doctors to become "salaried servants of the state". When the BMA conducted a survey in early 1948, 90% of respondents were against the scheme. A compromise was reached and the scheme came into operation in July 1948.

The public took full advantage of the National Health Service, and the cost of delivery rose. The government proposed prescription charges in 1951, along with dental and ophthalmic charges. Incensed, Bevan resigned. The Labour Party lost the next election before charges were introduced and it was the Conservatives who brought in the charge at 1 shilling (5p) per prescription. Charges were abolished by Labour in 1965 but were reintroduced in 1968. By 2008 the charge was £7.10 per item in England. In Scotland it was reduced to £5 to be phased out by 2011. In Wales the charge was abolished in 2007.

The 1948 National Assistance Act looked to provide support for those unable to help themselves, chiefly the elderly, the critically ill or disabled and the homeless. It did away once and for all with Poor Law relief.

Finally, the 1948 Children's Act looked not only to child protection but the nurturing and development of each child's character and abilities. There had been several driving forces for the Act, such as the fear that not all wartime evacuated children would have a home or family to return to. There was also the case of Dennis O'Neill, a 13-year-old malnourished foster child, who was beaten to death in February 1945. To try and avoid this happening again, local authorities created Children's Departments with responsibility for child welfare.

Often overlooked in Beveridge's report was that he favoured a level of benefit set at subsistence level only, as he did not want to take away individual initiative. "Management of one's income is an essential element of a citizen's freedom," he wrote. But he also regarded social welfare as an individual's right. He summarised his scheme by saying: "It is, first and foremost, a plan of insurance – of giving in return for contributions benefits up to subsistence level, as of right and without means test, so that individuals may build freely upon it."

Beveridge wanted to ensure people had the basics of life as of right. It was a reminder of John Locke's three inalienable rights first stated 300 years before.

Rights Under Threat

Issues affecting our human and political rights never stop. New technologies, the threat of terrorism, globalisation, identity theft and other advances in science all challenge our accepted views of privacy and freedom.

Having struggled for centuries to win our rights, recent years have seen them increasingly under threat. According to the human rights organisation Liberty, over 60 Acts of Parliament since 1997 have created over 3,000 new offences. They range from the extreme, causing a nuclear explosion, to the minor, such as failing to nominate a key-holder if you have an audible intruder alarm. Whilst many of these laws have sought to protect the public from an increasing diversity of threats, they also affect our liberties and the sheer mass of legislation makes it difficult to know just what we may be gaining or losing.

A few examples will demonstrate the diversity. The invasion of privacy is frequently in the news. There is in fact no right to privacy under English law, although the 1998 Human Rights Act states: "Everyone has the right to respect for his private and family life, his home and his correspondence." Celebrities have been battling against the paparazzi and the media for privacy, and rulings in Europe are starting to have an effect, but it is not just celebrities who are at risk. There are reportedly over four million CCTV cameras in Britain, one for every fifteen people, although this figure may not be reliable. Authorities must show that CCTV cameras are "in the interests of national security, public safety or the economic well-being of the country, for the prevention of disorder or crime, for the protection of health or morals, or for the protection of the rights and freedoms of others." Whilst some statistics suggest that CCTV does reduce crime, the case is not yet proven.

Also of concern is the amount of data recorded and retained about individuals for commercial purposes. Access to details, especially that provided by our credit cards and internet useage, contribute to fraud and identity theft and raise questions about the security of Identity Cards. The presumption is that by fighting technology with technology, the use of biometric data will improve personal security and reduce identity theft.

In England and Wales, the 2001 Criminal Justice and Police Act allowed for DNA details taken during a criminal investigation to be kept on file, whereas in Scotland they are deleted if there is no conviction. As a result it has been

In his 1949 book *1984*, George Orwell coined the phrase 'Big Brother is Watching You', a prophecy which may well have come true.

assessed that the national DNA database now holds the details of over four million people, or over 7% of the population. The counter-argument to this apparent invasion of privacy is that the database has helped solve previously unsolved crimes including, since 2001, 114 murders and 116 rapes.

Related to privacy is the question of protecting our homes. Ever since the case in 1999, when farmer Tony Martin was convicted of murder after killing an intruder in his home, there has been an issue about the right of self-defence and protection of property. The 2008 Criminal Justice and Immigration Act clarified previous laws on self-defence and "reasonable force" to provide greater legal protection to victims of crime.

Freedom of speech linked with religious and racial discrimination remains controversial. It was put to the test when a *fatwa* was issued on Salman Rushdie in 1989, for the offence caused to Muslims who regarded his book *The Satanic Verses* as blasphemous. This forced Rushdie into hiding for a decade. Christian blasphemy was still a crime in Britain, but had not been enforced since the *Gay News* trial of 1977 and the law was abolished in 2008. The issue remains, however, of how to ensure respect for the rights and beliefs of other religious groups. The 1998 Crime and Disorder Act broadened discrimination to include racially aggravated offences, and was extended to cover religiously aggravated crimes in 2001. However, the 2006 Terrorism Act, drafted in reaction to the 7 July bombings in 2005, made it illegal to "glorify terrorism". This, along with the 2006 Racial and Religious Hatred Act and the 2005 Serious Organised Crime Act, have the potential to limit our freedom of speech and the right to protest.

Perhaps most challenging are those affecting the basic freedoms of our personal liberty: of being presumed innocent until proven guilty and of the right to a fair trial. The 2003 Anti-Social Behaviour Act allowed local authorities to establish curfew zones and any child under sixteen found in those zones after 9.00pm could be escorted home by the police, whether or not they were up to mischief. One fifteen-year-old challenged the ruling in the High Court as infringing his rights under the European Convention, and won his case.

The 2003 Criminal Justice Act included the option of dispensing with trial by jury where jury-tampering may be suspected, or where the length or complexity of a trial may prove too burdensome for a jury. Along with Section 44 of the 2000 Terrorism Act, this act also increased the stop-and-search powers of the police. The 2005 Prevention of Terrorism Act introduced "control orders" which allowed the Home Secretary to limit the freedom of an individual suspected of terrorism with only limited right of appeal.

Most controversial has been the government's proposed Counter Terrorism Bill, which will allow police to detain terrorism suspects for up to 42 days without charge if it becomes law, which some consider will be a major infringement of *habeas corpus*. It is argued that these more extreme measures have built-in controls. No one would be held under the 42-day clause, for instance, without the agreement of a judge every seven days.

Surveys amongst the public have revealed that in general they support those measures if they improve personal safety and security, but it is evident that those same measures are challenging our personal liberties. We are just a decade into the 21st century and already some of our oldest freedoms are seriously at risk. They may only be upheld by further controls with potentially new risks leading to a downward spiral. In a speech in June 2008, Gordon Brown said: "These issues ... how we maintain our security and advance our freedoms, are some of the biggest questions governments have to face." The thousand-year battle to protect our rights has entered a new era.

Key Dates

The following provides a selective chronology to the key dates in the development of our individual and national rights and freedoms. It is divided into the same individual sections as the book.

Part 1	**The Roots of Liberty**
1086	Domesday Book: completed in two volumes by 1088
1164	Constitutions of Clarendon: Henry II codifies legal rights of church and state
1166	Assize of Clarendon
1215	Magna Carta
1217	Charter of the Forest
1220s	Jury system develops as primary form of judgement
1235	Statute of Merton legislates for enclosure of land and defines illegitimacy
1297	Edward I enshrines Magna Carta in English law
1337-1453	The Hundred Years War
1348	The Great Plague (Black Death) reaches Britain
1381	The Peasants' Revolt
1628	The Petition of Right
1679	Habeas Corpus Act

Part 2	**National Liberties**
949/950	Death of Hywel Dda, who established the first Welsh law code
979	First meeting of the Tynwald, Parliament of the Isle of Man
1264	Simon de Montfort calls the first English Parliament with elected representatives
1265	De Montfort defeated and killed at Evesham
1284	Statute of Rhuddlan brings Wales under English control
1295	Edward I creates a "model" Parliament
1297	William Wallace declared Guardian of Scotland; English set up Parliament in Ireland
1301	Edward I invests eldest son as Prince of Wales
1305	William Wallace captured and hanged
1314	Edward II defeated by the Scots at Bannockburn
1317	Irish chiefs remonstrate to Pope against English rule
1320	Declaration of Arbroath
1328	Treaty of Northampton: England recognises Scottish independence
1406	Owain Glyn Dŵr appeals to King of France against English control
1536	An act of union with England imposed upon Wales
1542	Crown of Ireland Act: Henry VIII acknowledged as King of Ireland
1604	Treaty of Union: aborted plan to unite Scottish and English parliaments
1628	Charles I accepts Petition of Right
1638	Scottish National Covenant introduced
1642-1649	Civil War
1647	The Putney Debates; Agreement of the People of England first drafted
1649	Execution of King Charles I
1653	Instrument of Government – first formal constitution for England, Scotland and Ireland
1657	The Humble Petition replaces the Instrument of Government; invests Oliver Cromwell as Lord Protector of England, Scotland and Ireland
1658	Oliver Cromwell dies
1661	Restoration of the Monarchy under Charles II
1689	Bill of Rights; accession of King William III and Queen Mary II of England
1701	Act of Settlement determines rights of succession to English throne; excludes Catholics
1706	Treaty of Union between England and Scotland
1707	England, Wales and Scotland formally unite as the Kingdom of Great Britain
1801	Union of Ireland Act creates United Kingdom of Great Britain and Ireland
1922	Southern Ireland becomes the Irish Free State
1927	New Act of Union to create the United Kingdom of Great Britain and Northern Ireland
1998	Establishes a National Assembly for Wales and a Scottish Parliament; Belfast Agreement sets out plans for devolved government in Northern Ireland

Part 3	**Freedom of Worship and Conscience**
1290	Edict of Expulsion of all Jews from England
1380	John Wyclif completes translation of New Testament
1401	*De haeretico comburendo*: heresy made a capital crime
1476	William Caxton sets up first printing press in England
1526	German-printed English translation of bible by William Tyndale reaches London
1534	Act of Supremacy, establishing Henry VIII as head of the Church of England
1536	Tyndale captured and burned at the stake
1536-1540	Dissolution of the English monasteries
1540	Henry VIII approves the Great Bible, an English translation
1549	Act of Uniformity: Book of Common Prayer introduced
1556	Thomas Cranmer burned at stake
1572	St. Bartholomew's Day Massacre of Huguenots in Paris
1603	James VI of Scotland becomes King of England as James I
1605	Gunpowder Plot
1638	Scottish National Covenant introduced
1638	John Lilburne arrested for importing seditious books
1641	Parliament abolishes Star Chamber
1643	Licensing Order controlling printing
1644	John Milton publishes *Areopagitica*
1656	Petition to Cromwell, asking permission for Jews to have right to practise their religion
1689	Act of Toleration extends freedom of worship to non-conformists
1737	Licensing Act gives Lord Chamberlain control over licensing of plays and theatres
1762	John Wilkes MP launches *The North Briton*, a satirical weekly paper
1764	John Wilkes found guilty of seditious libel and obscenity
1774	First edition of the Parliamentary Register, forerunner of Hansard
1778	Papist Act mitigates against official Roman Catholic discrimination in Great Britain
1780	The Gordon Riots, an uprising against the Papist Act
1829	Catholic Emancipation Act allows Catholics to have a seat in Parliament
1858	Jewish Emancipation Act allows Jews to have a seat in Parliament
1905	Aliens Act safeguards right of political asylum for immigrants
1914	British Nationality and Status of Aliens Act
1916	Military Service Act: conscription with exemption for Conscientious Objectors
1948	British Nationality Act: all Commonwealth subjects to have status of British citizens
1965	Race Relations Act prohibits public racial discrimination
1967	Northern Ireland Civil Rights Association

Part 4	**The Rights of the Individual**
1651	Thomas Hobbes publishes *Leviathan*
1669	John Locke helps draft the Constitution of Carolina
1682	William Penn with Algernon Sidney drafts a "Frame of Government" for American colony of Pennsylvania
1683	Algernon Sidney executed for treason in the Rye House Plot
1689-1690	John Locke publishes *Two Treatises of Government* and *An Essay Concerning Human Understanding*
1772	The case of *Somerset v Stewart* which frees the slave Somerset in England
1776	The Declaration of Independence agreed by the Continental Congress in Philadelphia
1787	Society for Effecting the Abolition of the African Slave Trade established
1789	Start of the French Revolution
1789	The National Assembly in France adopts the "Declaration des droits des hommes et du citoyen"
1790	Edward Burke publishes *Reflections on the Revolution in France*
1791	Thomas Paine publishes first part of *Rights of Man*
1807	Slave trade abolished in all British possessions
1828	Offences Against the People Act makes any male homosexual act illegal, even in private
1834	Slaves throughout British Empire become legally free
1839	Custody of Children Act
1859	John Stuart Mill writes *On Liberty*
1869	Emily Davies establishes Girton College, the first university college for women
1895	Criminal trial of Oscar Wilde for gross indecencies
1940	H. G. Wells publishes *Rights of Man*
1943	Equal Pay Campaign Committee established
1948	United Nations adopts a Universal Declaration of Human Rights (UDHR)
1950	European Convention on Human Rights signed in Rome
1957	Report of the Wolfenden Commission
1965	Capital punishment abolished in Britain for murder
1967	Sexual Offences Bill legalising homosexuality becomes law in England and Wales
1976	Equal Pay Act fully implemented
1976	International Covenant on Civil and Political Rights gives legal status to most of UDHR
1998	Human Rights Act becomes law in Britain
2007	Equality and Human Rights Commission established

Part 5	**The Right to Vote**
1792	London Corresponding Society founded for parliamentary and social reform
1794-1800	William Pitt introduces a series of repressive measures that curtail any chance of political reform
1819	Peterloo Massacre: yeomanry attack crowd campaigning for reform in Manchester and kill eleven
1832	Great Reform Act extends franchise to include all upper-middle class
1836	William Lovett founds London Working Men's Association
1837	London Working Men's Association proposes a six-point "Charter"
1838	The People's Charter published and launched in Glasgow
1839	First Chartist Petition presented to Parliament
1845	Feargus O'Connor establishes the Chartist Land Company
1867	Second Parliamentary Reform Act enfranchises nearly all men in towns
1872	The Ballot Act ensures voting is in secret, a major demand of the Chartists
1884	Third Reform Act ensures the franchise is extended to men in the countryside
1897	National Union of Women's Suffrage Societies founded by Millicent Fawcett
1903	Women's Social and Political Union founded by Emmeline Pankhurst
1909	Suffragettes begin hunger strikes
1913	Emily Davison runs in front of King's horse at Derby to publicise women's suffrage
1914-1918	First World War
1918	Representation of the People Act gives vote to majority of men over 21 and women over 30
1928	Equal Franchise Act gives vote to all women over 21
1969	Representation of the Peoples Act lowers voting age for men and women to eighteen

Part 6	**The Right to Welfare**
1516	Thomas More writes his novel *Utopia*
1601	The Poor Law places administration of the poor and destitute with the parishes
1723	Workhouse Test Act obliges the poor to enter a workhouse
1788	Chimney Sweepers Act forbids children under eight being used as climbing boys
1795	Magistrates at Speenhamland, Berkshire, devise a sliding scale for poor relief
1819	Cotton Mills and Factories Act sets limits on child labour
1830	Captain Swing agrarian riots against enclosures and threshing machines
1833	Tolpuddle Martyrs transported to Australia after trying to negotiate a fair wage
1834	Poor Law Amendment Act shifts emphasis to the workhouse where conditions are harsh
1838	Charles Dickens publishes *Oliver Twist*, written to attack the new Poor Law
1842	First General Strike across Britain
1867	Thomas Barnardo sets up a Ragged School in the East End
1878	Factory Act legislates for compulsory education for children up to age ten
1884	London Society for the Prevention of Cruelty to Children founded, later a national society
1884	Fabian Society established to educate public in socialist ideas
1889	Great Dock Strike: 130,000 workers call for a fair wage; Gasworkers' Strike brings in eight-hour day
1899	Elementary Education (Defective and Epileptic Children) Act
1909	First payment of old age pensions
1911	Lloyd George introduces National Insurance scheme
1926	General Strike involves 1.8 million workers at its peak
1929	Wall Street Crash in America marks onset of worldwide economic depression
1936	Jarrow Hunger March
1939-1945	Second World War
1942	Beveridge Report tackles threats to society: want, ignorance, disease, squalor, idleness
1944	Education Act raises school-leaving age to sixteen
1945	Family Allowance Act provides weekly payment for all children after the first
1948	National Health Service launched
1995	Disability Discrimination Act

Further Information

Further Reading

G. E. Aylmer, *The Struggle for the Constitution 1603-1689*, fourth edition (London: Blandford Press, 1975).

Arthur H. Cash, *John Wilkes: The Scandalous Father of Civil Liberty* (New Haven: Yale University Press, 2006).

Andrew Clapham, *Human Rights, A Very Short Introduction* (Oxford: Oxford University Press, 2007).

David Colclough, *Freedom of Speech in Early Stuart England* (Cambridge: Cambridge University Press, 2005).

Linda Colley, *Britons, Forging the Nation 1707-1837*, second edition (New Haven: Yale University Press, 2005).

Elizabeth Crawford, *The Women's Suffrage Movement, A Reference Guide 1866-1928* (London & New York: Routledge, 2001).

Howard Davis, *Human Rights and Civil Liberties* (Cullompton: Willan Publishing, 2003).

H. T. Dickinson, *Liberty and Property, Political Ideology in Eighteenth-Century Britain* (London: Weidenfeld & Nicolson, 1977).

Peter Berresford Ellis, *Hell or Connaught!: The Cromwellian Colonisation of Ireland 1652-1660* (London: Hamish Hamilton, 1975).

K. D. Ewing and C. A. Gearty, *The Struggle for Civil Liberties* (Oxford University Press, 2000).

J. E. S. Fawcett, *The Application of the European Convention on Human Rights* (Oxford University Press, 1987).

Kim Feus (editor), *The EU Charter of Fundamental Rights* (London: Federal Trust for Education and Research, 2000).

Conor Foley with Liberty, *Human Rights, Human Wrongs* (London: Rivers Oram Press, 1995).

John Garrard, *Democratisation in Britain: Elites, Civil Society and Reform since 1800* (London: Palgrave Macmillan, 2001).

Elizabeth M. Hallam, *Domesday Book Through Nine Centuries* (London & New York: Thames & Hudson, 1986).

Robert Hargreaves, *The First Freedom. A History of Free Speech* (Stroud: Sutton, 2002).

Christopher Hill, *Liberty Against the Law* (London: Allen Lane, 1996).

Thomas Hinde, *The Domesday Book: England's Heritage, Then and Now* (London: Century Hutchinson, 1985).

Adam Hochschild, *Burying the Chains. The British Struggle to Abolish Slavery* (London: Macmillan, 2005).

Julian Hoppit, *A Land of Liberty? England 1689-1727* (Oxford: Oxford University Press, 2000).

Anne Hudson, *The Premature Reformation* (Oxford: Oxford University Press, 1988).

Lynn Hunt, *Inventing Human Rights* (New York: Norton, 2008).

Micheline R. Ishay, *The Human Rights Reader* (Routledge, 1997).

Micheline R. Ishay, *The History of Human Rights* (Berkley: University of California Press, 2004).

Paul Johnson (editor), *20th Century Britain: Economic, Social and Cultural Change* (London: Longman, 1994).

John Keane, *Tom Paine, A Political Life* (London: Bloomsbury, 1995).

Anthony King, *The British Constitution* (Oxford: Oxford University Press, 2007).

Anthony Lester and Geoffrey Bindman, *Race and Law* (London: Longman, 1972).

T. O. Lloyd, *Empire, Welfare State, Europe: English History, 1906-1992* (Oxford: Oxford University Press, 1993).

Rodney Lowe, *The Welfare State in Britain since 1945* (London: Palgrave Macmillan, third edition 2004).

Edward Miller and John Hatcher, *Medieval England. Rural Society and Economic Change, 1086-1348* (London: Longman, 1978).

Frank O'Gorman, *Voters, Patrons and Parties: The Unreformed Electorate of Hanoverian England, 1734-1832* (Oxford & New York: Oxford University Press, 1989).

Melanie Phillips, *The Ascent of Woman* (London: Little, Brown, 2003).

Roy Porter, *Enlightenment. Britain and the Creation of the Modern World* (London: Allen Lane, 2000).

David Prior, John Stewart & Kieron Walsh, *Citizenship: Rights, Community & Participation* (London: Pitman, 1995).

R. C. Richardson and G. M. Ridden, editors, *Freedom and the English Revolution* (Manchester University Press, 1986).

A. W. Brian Simpson, *Human Rights and the End of Empire* (Oxford: Oxford University Press, 2001).

Michael J. Turner, *The Age of Unease. Government and Reform in Britain, 1782-1832* (Stroud: Sutton Publishing, 2000).

Randolph Vigne & Charles Littleton, *From Strangers to Citizens. The Integration of Immigrant Communities in Britain, Ireland and Colonial America, 1550-1750* (Brighton: Sussex Academic Press, 2001).

Jeffrey N. Wasserstrom, Lynn Hunt and Marilyn B. Young (editors), *Human Rights and Revolutions* (Lanham, MD: Rowman & Littlefield, 2000).

Eric Williams, *Capitalism and Slavery* (London: Andre Deutsch, 1964).

Addresses and Websites

Citizens Advice, www.citizensadvice.org.uk

Equality and Human Rights Commission, 3 More London Riverside, Tooley Street, London SE1 2RG, www.equalityhumanrights.com

Liberty, 21 Tabard Street, London SE1 4LA, www.yourrights.org.uk

Liberty Library of Constitutional Classics, www.constitution.org/liberlib.htm

The Online Library of Liberty, oll.libertyfund.org

Parliamentary Archives, www.publications.parliament.uk

The UK Statute Law Database, www.statutelaw.gov.uk

Index

Certain categories, such as Acts of Parliament, Kings and Queens and Rights are grouped under those headings rather than indexed separately.

200 Surefire Ways to Eat Well & Feel Better

200 Surefire Ways to Eat Well & Feel Better

Dr Judith Rodriguez

A QUARTO BOOK

Published in 2014 by
New Burlington Books
6 Blundell Street
London N7 9BH

ISBN: 978-0-85762-133-7

Conceived, designed and produced by
Quarto Publishing plc
The Old Brewery
6 Blundell Street
London
N7 9BH

QUAR.FTTE

Senior editor: Katie Crous
Copy editor: Ruth Patrick
Proofreader: Liz Jones
Designer: Karin Skånberg
Design assistant: Martina Calvio
Photographer: Simon Pask
Illustrator: Justin Gabbard
Picture researcher: Sarah Bell
Art director: Caroline Guest

Creative director: Moira Clinch
Publisher: Paul Carslake

Colour separation in Hong Kong by Cypress Colours (HK) Ltd

Printed in China by 1010 Printing International Ltd

10 9 8 7 6 5 4 3 2 1

Contents

Eating smart, losing weight and keeping the weight off does not have to be difficult. With some personalized and convenient changes to your diet, physical activity and lifestyle, you will soon be feeling good and living better.

This book is organized into five sections, each of which addresses an aspect of daily life: At home, Shopping, Restaurants and parties, Diets and eating plans, and Special health concerns. As a step in the right direction, try to adopt a few tips from each of the sections. Once those tips have become a healthy habit, adopt a few more. If you select a tip and find it is not working, come back to the book and look for some others to try instead. Pick the tips you think are relevant and applicable to you.

When trying to implement food, physical activity and lifestyle changes you can easily become overwhelmed. But the research shows that taking small steps can help you succeed in your attempts. Being healthy is achievable if you take an honest look at all aspects of your lifestyle, know what and how to change, and stay motivated. This book will help you do all of these things.

Judith C Rodriguez
PhD, RDN, LD/N, FADA
Chairperson and Professor, Department of Nutrition and Dietetics, Brooks College of Health, Florida

Jenna Braddock, MSH, RDN, CSSD, is an Instructor at the University of North Florida and a Nutrition Consultant.
• Start the party right – appetizers 82 • Enjoy the party – right! Main dishes 84–85 • Detox diets 96–97 • Fuelling the athlete 130–131

Kate Chang, MS, RDN, is an Adjunct Instructor at the University of North Florida and a Nutrition Consultant.
• Dinner: The healthy option 30–33
• Shopping for snacks 60–61
• Healthy dining at restaurants: Japanese cuisine 77

Catherine Christie, PhD, RDN, is Associate Dean at the University of North Florida.
• Cooking for many 22–25 • Calories and serving sizes 62–63 • Healthy dining at restaurants: Italian cuisine 76 • Nutrigenomics: What's in it for you? 94–95 • The Paleo diet 106–107 • Food and mood 132–133

Alireza Jahan-mihan, PhD, RDN, is an Assistant Professor at the University of North Florida.
• Ageing well 122–123
• Nutrition for men 126–127

Shahla Khan, PhD, is an Adjunct Instructor at the University of North Florida and Jacksonville University.
• Getting and staying active 36–41

Corinne Labyak, PhD, RDN, is an Assistant Professor at the University of North Florida.
• High blood pressure 116–117
• Nutrition for children 128–129

Jamisha Laster, MS, RDN, is an Adjunct Instructor at the University of North Florida and a Senior Public Health Nutritionist.
• Healthy dining at restaurants: Soul food 74

Alexia Lewis, MS, RDN, is a Wellness Dietitian at the University of North Florida and a Nutrition Consultant.
• Snacks: Boosting your nutrition 34–35 • The raw food diet 100–101 • The vegan diet 102–103
• The DASH diet 104–105
• Heart disease 118–119 • Gluten sensitivity 136–137

Jen Ross, MSH, RDN, is an Instructor at the University of North Florida and a Nutrition Consultant.
• Cooking and baking made easy 14–17
• Cooking for one 18–21

Claudia Sealey-Potts, PhD, RDN, is an Assistant Professor at the University of North Florida.
• Healthy dining at restaurants: Chinese cuisine 75
• Be ingredient savvy 64–65
• Diabetes 114–115

Jackie Shank, MS, RDN, is an Instructor at the University of North Florida.
• Nutrition for women 124–125
• Food allergies 134–135

Zhiping Yu, PhD, RDN, is an Assistant Professor at the University of North Florida.
• Shopping for vegetables 48–49
• Shopping for fruit 50–51
• End the party right – sweets 83
• Enjoy the party – right! Main dishes 84–85 • Healthy drinking practices 86–87

About this book

The five chapters in this book each address a key aspect of eating well – whether it's in your home or out and about, or adopting specific dietary changes in order to meet your specific needs and desires for a healthier lifestyle.

Chapter 1: At home, pages 10–41

Perhaps the easiest – and most important – place to make a start is in your own home. This chapter looks at how you can make the most of your time in the kitchen, preparing and cooking the right kind of meals, and staying active without even leaving your front door.

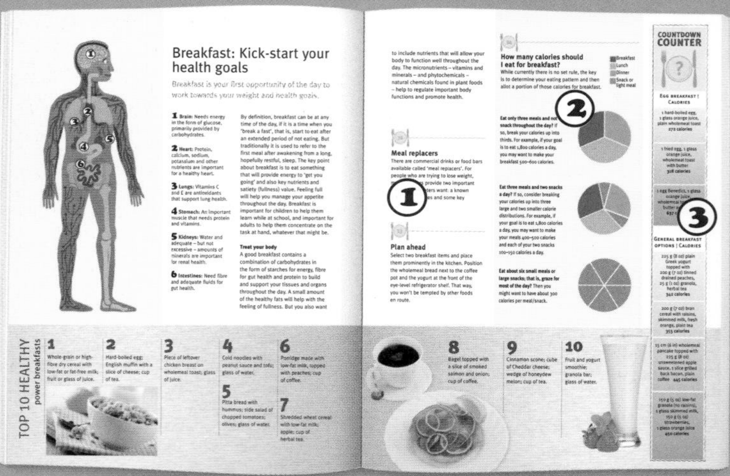

1 Hints and tips
Concise snippets of information and advice for making changes towards a healthier lifestyle.

2 Reference charts
Easy-to-digest charts show important facts and figures.

3 Countdown counters
Comparative lists of foods in ascending order of calories or descending order of specific nutrients (check the individual Counter heading). Calories and nutritional values are an indication only; both will vary greatly depending on how the food is made and the serving size.

Chapters 2 and 3: Out and about: Shopping, pages 42–67; Restaurants and parties, pages 68–87

In Chapter 2 you'll find plenty of tips for shopping for all food types, comparing calories and serving sizes, understanding the ingredients on labels and buying snacks. Then be guided through the maze of fast-food menus and popular ethnic dishes available at restaurants. Finally, whether hosting or attending, parties are often a time when you may find it difficult to make healthy choices and this section can help you through those dilemmas.

Chapter 4: Diets and eating plans, pages 88–109

Discover the rationale behind popular diets and the strength of the science behind them. Assess the pros and cons and take a look at some sample menus before you decide on the best option for you.

Chapter 5: Special health concerns, pages 110–137

Common chronic diseases, such as diabetes, and food allergies and/or sensitivities can be better managed with appropriate dietary changes. Women, men, children, the elderly and athletes all have specific needs and this section will help you identify issues and gain the maximum benefit from food.

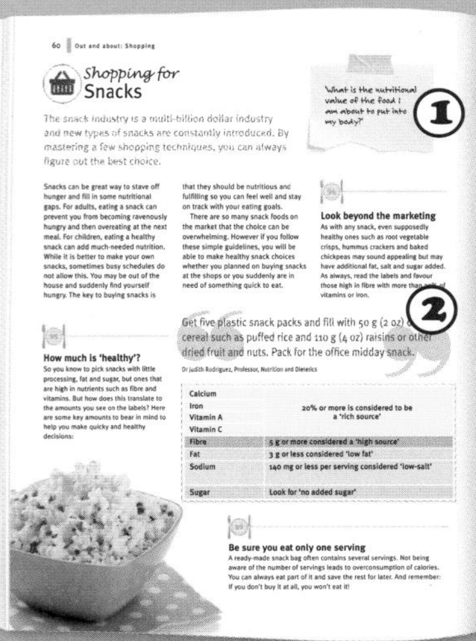

1 Fridge magnet mantras
Motivating boosts to write down and place in a prominent location.

2 Expert quotes
Additional insider advice from professionals in the field of nutrition.

3 Top foods
At-a-glance illustrated lists of the best foods available for your dietary needs.

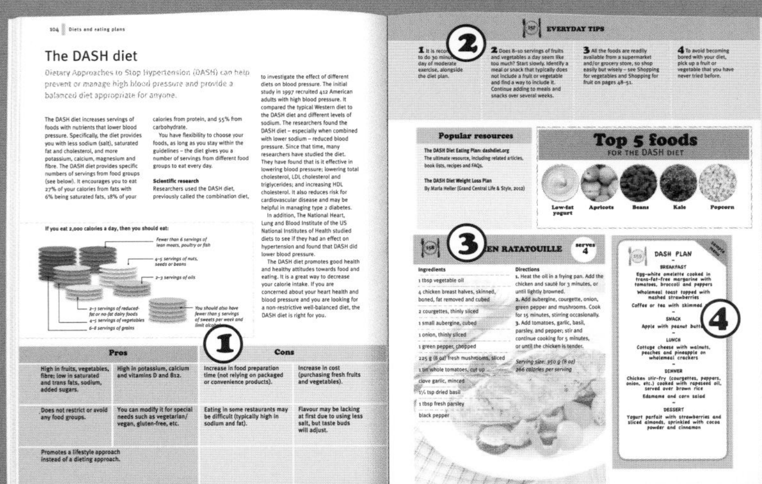

1 Pros and cons
Weigh up the positives and the negatives of each diet.

2 Everyday tips
Small changes you can make to daily life to help you follow each diet.

3 Healthy recipes
Quick and easy recipes – including ingredients and nutritional details – that you can try at home.

4 Sample menus
Guides to the type of meals you can expect to eat when following a specific eating plan.

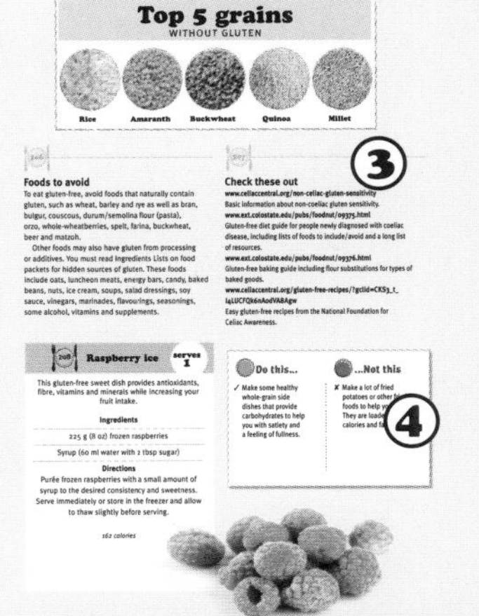

1 Specific guidelines
Follow the advice and manage your health easily and effectively.

2 Meal ideas
Lists of healthy meal enhancers and ingredient substitutions provide plenty of inspiration for mealtimes.

3 Check these out
Websites offering additional information for further reading.

4 Do this/Not this
Identify unhealthy behavioural practices and find alternatives for smarter choices.

At home

A healthy life starts at home

What you learned when growing up at home most likely formed the foundation of what you currently do, whether it's managing your weight, life or work.

Home was your first school. This is where you learned how to interact with others and developed food and physical activity habits. You learned basic life management skills, such as shopping, cooking and how to manage stress and emotions through dialogue and relationships. A home is also where you may have learned behaviours that have become problematic and hard to correct. These may include using food as an emotional outlet when angry or upset, using food to demonstrate love, eating excessively during specific holidays or celebrations or watching television for many hours at a time. To create a healthier lifestyle, begin with small changes at home and turn them into lifelong benefits you can take with you anywhere you go.

Your personality, lifestyle and values are reflected in your home, particularly the kitchen and activity niches. What do your home and colour schemes say about your lifestyle? Key to making lifestyle improvements that support weight loss or maintenance is to work not only on your personal behaviours, but also to create a home environment that supports the goals you are trying to achieve.

Check these out

www.caloriesecrets.net
10 tips on how to develop healthy eating habits.

www.healthcastle.com/healthy_kitchen_staple.shtml
Kitchen staples for healthy family meals.

www.styleathome.com/kitchen-and-bath/kitchen
Eight steps to designing a healthy kitchen.

Four steps to create a supportive home environment

1. Use fruits as a table centrepiece and healthy snack option.
2. Place exercise motivators in key positions, such as a skipping rope in the garage or weights by the sofa.
3. Create a quiet space in which to relax, such as a comfy chair in the bedroom or rocker on the patio.
4. Keep scales by the shower. Use twice weekly.

Get active in the home

Get a pedometer and commit to walking a specific number of steps in the home, say 2,000. Walk around the sofa, step in place, walk up and down the stairs, or run after the dog (or kids). Do it every day and make it fun.

Do this...

✓ Encourage family members to eat until almost but not overly full.

✓ Focus on pleasant conversation and interactions during mealtimes rather than watching TV.

...Not this

✗ Use food to compensate for, or protect against, sad feelings.

✗ Use highly sweetened or fatty foods as a reward or tease for promoting good behaviours in children.

Every home needs one
Fill your fruit bowl with fruit of different colours and shapes for attractiveness, choice and nutrient variety.

Before eating that food, ask yourself: 'Am I really hungry?'

Big on energy, bananas also have potassium, important in heart health, and are the original prepackaged snack.

Pears are packed with antioxidants, fibre and flavour!

Ideal for grazing, grapes contain resveratrol, an antioxidant that helps fight cancer and heart disease.

A common fruit that should never be overlooked, an apple a day cleanses and detoxifies.

Oranges will refresh in the summer or after exercise whilst providing plentiful Vitamin C, which protects against illness and chronic disease.

Remodel your home

Make each room in your home a welcome supporter of your goals. Go to each room and assess the environment. Identify small, cost-free or inexpensive changes you can make.

Den or sitting room: Are there any small dishes containing high-calorie snacks? Replace them with decorative stones or pinecones from your garden.
Exercise room or corner: Place your favourite fitness equipment in a common and popular area to encourage you to use it. Decorate with green accents or walls to give you a feeling of greenery and the outdoors, and decrease the perception of exertion.
Kitchen: Do you have high-fat cream-based dressings or high-sodium/salt condiments in your larder? Replace them with healthier substitutes such as olive oil, flavoured vinegars and garlic powder. Avoid using the colour red on your walls, which may stimulate the appetite, but instead try using smaller red dishes for snack plates. That 'red' may help signal 'stop'.
Shower: Relax with some lavender-, chamomile- or bergamot-scented soaps if you shower at night. Use citrus-, jasmine- or peppermint-scented soaps to help you wake up if you shower in the morning.
Bedroom: Do you have a TV? Replace it with a music system and play some soothing sleep or sea sounds. Use cool blue colours or light pastel shades of blue, grey or green on your walls.

Cooking and baking made easy

Enjoy healthy cooking and eating at home while saving time and calories.

Preparing delicious and healthy foods at home doesn't have to be boring or time-consuming. There are some basic steps you can take to help make cooking at home easy and successful.

Think ahead

Think about your family's meal preferences, budget and time. It's important to work around these to make mealtimes more successful and less stressful. Meal planning is an important tool. Take a look at your weekly schedule and plan accordingly. If you know that one night is particularly hectic, plan for leftovers or a quick meal that night. Gather some familiar recipes plus some new ones to try to choose recipes that are within your cooking level and don't require equipment or time that you don't have. Cookbooks, websites and blogs are great resources for recipe ideas and meal planning.

Broaden your skill set

Online videos are useful for learning new techniques and kitchen skills. If you want to advance your kitchen skills, consider taking a cooking class at a local college. The more flexible you can be with the ingredients you can cook and the methods you can use in the kitchen, the more likely you are to stick with healthy changes.

Shop smart and stock your larder

Make a list of staples to always have on hand to save time and money at the supermarket. If you're trying to cut down on calories, be sure to have some low-sodium stock, vegetables, herbs, spices and whole grains on hand. Acknowledge which ingredients you're more likely to use versus unfamiliar or expensive items. For example, if you find that you're constantly throwing out fresh produce, try buying more frozen vegetables and working some of the fresh in as you have time. See Chapter 2 for more advice on shopping for health.

Preparation is key

Many people are hesitant to cook because they're tired and don't want to think about putting something together after a long day at work. A little time prepping on the weekend can save you a lot of time and calories (not to mention money) during the week. Take an hour or two to plan your meals and pre-prep ingredients for the week. Go ahead and chop the vegetables for the stir-fry, or make the green salad. Put the meat in the refrigerator to defrost. Prepare and store any marinade.

You can't always tell by looking or smelling whether a food has gone bad, so to be safe, always use the mantra 'when in doubt, throw it out'.

Maximizing nutrients

The chart on the right gives the optimum cooking times for popular vegetables. Use it as a guide, as times will vary by size, quantity, type of cut and temperature cooked at.

Food safety first

Food safety is an important consideration when cooking at home.

• **Store raw meats, poultry and seafood separate from other foods in the refrigerator**, preferably on the bottom shelf to keep any juices from dripping onto other items. Or simply freeze these foods if you don't plan on using them within a few days. Avoid cross-contamination and use separate utensils and cutting boards for produce, meat/poultry, seafood and eggs.

• **Thaw your frozen meat and poultry in the refrigerator, in a bowl of cold water, or in the microwave (carefully following instructions for your model).** Do not thaw frozen foods out on the counter at room temperature – unless the packet instructions specify this method – because the food may become contaminated.

• **If storing leftovers, cool as quickly as possible and put in the refrigerator no more than two hours after cooking.** Most leftovers can be safely kept in the refrigerator for two to three days.

Vegetable	Steam (minutes)	Boil (minutes)	Microwave (minutes)	Blanch (minutes)	Bake/roast (minutes)
Artichoke, whole	30–40	30–45	5–7	n/a	n/a
Asparagus	8–10	5–10	4–6	2–3	8–10
Aubergine, diced	15–20	10–20	7–10	3–4	10–15
Beans, green	5–15	10–20	6–12	4–5	n/a
Beets	40–60	30–60	14–18	n/a	60
Broccoli, spears	8–12	5–10	6–7	3–4	15–20
Brussels sprouts	6–12	5–10	7–8	4–5	30–40
Cabbage, wedges	6–9	10–15	10–12	n/a	20–25
Carrots, sliced	4–5	5–10	4–7	3–4	20
Cauliflower, florets	6–10	5–8	3–4	3–4	20–25
Corn, on cob	6–10	4–7	3–4	3–4	30
Courgettes, sliced	5–10	5–10	3–6	2–3	20–30
Kale	4–7	5–10	3–6	4–5	20–25
Mushrooms	4–5	3–4	3–4	3–5	20–35
Onions, whole	25–40	15–20	6–10	4	50–60
Parsnips, whole	30–35	15–25	7–8	3–4	45–60
Peas, green	5–15	10–15	5–7	1–2	60
Peppers	2–4	4–5	2–4	2–3	40
Potatoes, whole	30–45	30–40	6–8	3–5	40–60
Potatoes, cut	30–35	20–30	5–7	3–5	25–30
Spinach	6–12	3–10	3–7	2–3	25–30
Squash, sliced	30–40	20–25	6–7	3	40–50
Tomatoes	10	5–15	4–6	1–2	20–30
Turnips, diced	20–25	15–20	12–14	2–3	30–45

Enhancing baked goods

If you like baked goods but don't like the extra calories, consider baking at home. You can start with a prepackaged mix and reduce the calories by substituting a fruit purée such as apple sauce for the oil.

Also consider ways to boost the nutrition in your baked goods. Adding fresh or frozen fruit, using whole-grain flours, flaxseeds and reducing the fat are all easy ways to increase the nutrition without compromising the flavour.

Additionally, many baked goods can easily be frozen and reheated for later consumption. Replace shop-bought frozen items with homemade muffins, pancakes, waffles and breads as these items are all easy to make at home and freeze well.

8

Nutritional information

Vegetables are a great, easy way to fill up on nutrients. Most vegetables are low in fat and calories but high in nutrients and fibre, which help you stay full for longer. Try to vary your vegetables and eat a range of colours. The different colours signify different phytonutrients, powerful compounds that help fight disease. Cook your vegetables in as little water as possible for the shortest amount of time possible to retain those important nutrients.

The data in this chart represents 200 g (7 oz) of cooked vegetables unless otherwise noted. Percentages of daily values (DV) are based on a 2,000-calorie diet.

Vegetable	Calories	Total fat (g)	Sodium (mg)	Carbohydrates (g)	Fibre (g)	Sugar (g)	Protein (g)	% DV Vitamin A	% DV Vitamin C	% DV Iron	% DV Calcium
Artichoke, medium	60	1	120	13	6	1	4	0	25	9	6
Asparagus	20	0	12	3.5	1.5	1	2	18	12	5	2
Aubergine	20	0	2	5	3	2	1	0	3	1	1
Beans, green	18	0	16	4	1.5	0	1	8	7	6	3
Beets	37	0	65	8.5	1.5	6.5	1	1	5	4	1
Broccoli	27	0	32	5.5	2.5	1	2	24	84	3	3
Brussels sprouts	28	0	16	5.5	2	1	2	12	81	5	3
Cabbage	17	0	6	4	1	2	1	1	47	1	4
Carrots	27	0	45	6	2	2	0.5	266	5	1	2
Cauliflower	14	0	9	2.5	1	1	1	0	46	1	1
Corn on cob, medium	111	1	17	25	2.5	4	3	0	11	3	0
Courgettes	20	0	12	4	1	2	2	5	35	2	2
Kale	33	0	29	7	1	1.5	2	206	134	6	9
Mushrooms	23	0	5	4	1	1	2	0	0	2	2
Onions	64	0	6	15	3	7	2	0	20	2	4
Parsnips	100	0	13	24	7	6	2	0	38	4	5
Peas	117	1	7	21	7	8	8	22	97	12	4
Peppers, bell	30	0	4	7	3	4	1	11	200	3	1
Potatoes	164	0	13	39	5	2	4	0	70	9	3
Spinach	7	0	24	1	1	0	1	56	14	5	3
Squash	18	0	2	4	1	2	1	5	32	2	2
Tomatoes	32	0	9	7	2	5	2	30	38	3	2
Turnips	36	0	87	8	2	5	1	0	46	2	4

TOP 10 Recipe substitutions

1

Apple sauce or other fruit purée is a great substitute for oil in baked goods, at a one-to-one ratio.

2

Use low-sodium stock or stock instead of oil when sautéing to decrease fat and calories.

3

Wholemeal flour can be used to substitute half of the all-purpose flour in baked goods to increase nutrients, including fibre.

4

Substitute yogurt for sour cream as a condiment or for oil in baking.

5

Use herbs and spices instead of added salt as a flavour booster.

Check these out

www.eatingwell.com
Healthy recipes and features such as videos, healthy eating information and meal-planning tools.

www.epicurious.com and **www.cookinglight.com**
Advance your kitchen skills with recipes and videos that range from basic knife skills to preparing a multi-course dinner.

www.nutritionblognetwork.com
A compilation of blogs, with trusted nutrition information by registered dietitians. Search its directory to find the type of blog you're looking for. Categories include diabetes, family nutrition, vegetarian, weight management and many more.

10

The perfect pan

A good non-stick frying pan is easy to clean and an essential tool to make cooking easy. Choose a pan with high enough sides so that you can stir ingredients around easily. Start with some meat and some vegetables and grains for an easy one-pan weeknight meal.

For a fuller tummy, add vegetables to other foods.

- Add extra veggies to soups, casseroles, pasta dishes and even baked goods.
- Add grated carrots and courgettes to muffins and breads.
- Make vegetable purées ahead of time and freeze in ice-cube trays.
- Add the purées to pasta dishes and baked goods (be sure the vegetable is similar in colour to the main dish).

6

Replace up to 50% of the fat in baked goods with cooked bean purées, and use puréed black beans in brownies and puréed white beans in biscuits.

7

Use cooking spray instead of butter or margarine to prevent sticking.

8

Substitute two egg whites for one egg or use one tablespoon of ground flaxseed mixed with three tablespoons of water to replace one egg in a recipe to boost nutrition.

9

Use extra-lean minced beef or minced turkey/chicken breast without skin for recipes that call for minced beef.

10

Reduce up to half of the amount of sugar called for in most recipes without compromising taste or texture.

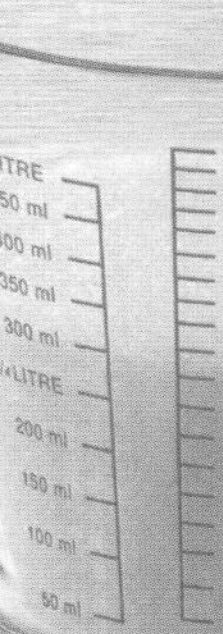

Cooking for one

Save money and calories while preparing nutritious and delicious meals for one at home.

Cooking for one doesn't have to be boring or require complicated maths to scale down recipes designed to serve four or more people. In fact, cooking for one can be very gratifying, and it allows you to explore and experiment with different flavours you may not otherwise try when cooking for others.

You can apply most of the same basic preparation as for Cooking for many (see pages 22–25). The main rules apply:

- Preparation is key and meal planning will save you valuable time during the week.
- Pay close attention to your recipes to avoid those ingredients you won't use often.
- Invest in some cookbooks or find websites and blogs that feature recipes for one.

Shopping for one can be costly, especially if you end up wasting food. Plan your meals (breakfast, lunch, dinner and snacks) for the week. This will help ensure that you are eating a variety of foods. It will also help you save money because you won't buy too much food that will end up spoiling, and it will make eating out less tempting. From your weekly menu, make a grocery list of only the foods that you will need for the meals. Write the list down and take it with you to the supermarket. Sticking to your list will prevent the impulse to overbuy.

Simple and hearty vegetable soup

Stock up on a versatile soup like this one. Mix and match the ingredients with the vegetables and spices you have on hand. Freeze leftovers in single-serve containers for a quick lunch or evening meal.

Ingredients

- 1 tbsp olive oil
- 1 onion, diced
- 3 carrots, diced
- 3 cloves garlic, minced
- 1 stalk celery, diced
- 1 cup shredded cabbage
- 1–2 bay leaves
- 200 g (7 oz) chopped asparagus
- 450 g (1 lb) new potatoes, diced
- 960 ml (32 fl oz) low-sodium vegetable stock

Directions

1. Heat the olive oil in a large pan. Add the onion, stir occasionally, and cook until translucent, about 5 minutes.

2. Add the carrots and garlic and cook for about 5 minutes or until garlic is fragrant. Add the celery, cabbage and bay leaves and cook for another 5 minutes.

3. Add the asparagus, potatoes and stock. Bring to a boil, then simmer uncovered for about 20–25 minutes or until the potatoes are soft enough to pierce with a fork. Season with salt (go easy!) and pepper to taste.

90 calories per serving

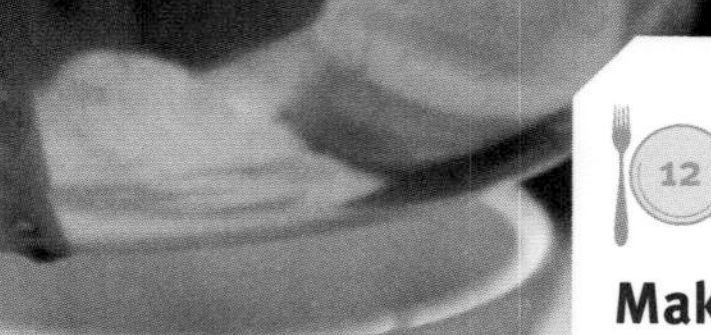

12

Make a vat of soup

If you're feeling adventurous in the kitchen, use a big saucepan to prepare a large quantity of your favourite soup on the weekend and store the leftovers in single-serve containers in the freezer. Reheat the soup for lunch the next day or pair with a sandwich for a quick and easy weeknight meal.

13

Make that sandwich healthier

Add a smear of hummus, drained tinned beans, dark greens, tomato, pepper slices or cucumber slices to your standard lunchtime sandwich. These additions will increase your nutrient and fibre intake.

Cooking in bulk

Bulk cooking and baking can prove to be a real time saver while also ensuring that you always have healthy meals on hand. Prepare larger servings of your favourite healthy foods and use them later in the week as leftovers or store in the freezer for a quick weeknight meal.

In a hurry?

Grab a tin of low-sodium soup or a serving of homemade soup, and add 400 g (14 oz) of mixed vegetables, spinach or carrots to increase its nutritional value and help fill you up. Serve with a cheese sandwich on wholemeal bread.

Do this...

- ✓ Acknowledge that it's okay to prepare a meal for one, and that it can in fact be an enjoyable experience.
- ✓ Plan your meals. Scour the web and cooking magazines for low-calorie, delicious recipes. Variety ensures that you're getting more of the nutrients you need and keeps cooking interesting.

...Not this

- ✗ Fall into the trap of thinking that it's too much work to cook for one and eat convenience and takeaway foods.
- ✗ Wait until hunger strikes to think about what you're going to eat. It's much more difficult to eat healthily if you're not prepared, and chances are you'll reach for the first thing you see!

Leftover veggies or pasta?

Scramble an egg, throw in the leftover veggies or pasta and make a healthy omelette.

Minimize mess

There are some specific cooking methods that solo cooks can use to deliver fast and healthy meals at home without spending time on washing multiple dishes afterwards.

- **Sauté** a piece of meat in a frying pan, add some vegetables and pair with a whole grain such as brown rice for a quick and healthy one-pan meal.
- **Cooking in foil or parchment packets**, a method known as en papillote, uses steam to quickly and gently cook food without adding fat. Take a piece of fish or chicken, season it, add vegetables, and wrap it in foil or parchment. Simply place the packet in the oven and cook at the proper temperature. An added bonus to this method is that there are no pots and pans to clean up.
- **Roasting** is a simple cooking method that can save calories while delivering a healthy and delicious meal. Roast a small chicken or chicken breast, adding some vegetables such as carrots or turnips to the roasting pan.

18

Don't have time for a full dinner?

Enjoy breakfast at dinnertime. Breakfast foods are are good at any time, and are typically quick cooking and easy to prepare for just one person.

Protein-rich time saver
Combine tofu, an excellent source of plant protein, with auberine or other veggies, and stir-fry for a quick and nutritious meal.

Save time throughout the week:

- At the weekend, prepare salad ingredients for an easy lunch or quick weeknight meal.
- Cook extra chicken, beef or other protein and store it in the refrigerator for future use.
- Chop in advance and add when needed dry ingredients such as onions, carrots, beans, etc.
- Keep greens crisp by adding moist ingredients such as tomatoes and dressing only when ready to eat.

Enjoy the process

Enlist some mindful eating techniques, not only to save calories in home-prepared meals, but also to enhance the experience.

Before choosing your food check in and ask yourself what you really want to eat and consider how you want to feel after your meal.

Check ingredients labels: Are there fewer than 10 ingredients? Do you know what they all are and how they contribute to your nutrition intake, or otherwise?

Pause before and during your meal to assess your hunger level.

Pay attention to the colours, smells, tastes and textures of your food.

Put your utensils down a few times during the meal to help you slow down.

> Before you sit down for a meal, do a short breathing exercise to become a more mindful eater. Breathe in for 4, hold for 7 and slowly exhale for 9 seconds. This foundation of being fully aware will help you overcome overeating.
>
> Cindy Guirino, Nutrition Writer and Consultant

Have fun experimenting

When cooking for one, it's important to stay flexible and be prepared. Take note of which recipes work and which ones don't, as well as the flavours you like the most. Since you are cooking for yourself, you have more freedom to experiment. The good news is that you don't have to worry about anyone else liking your dish as you're the only one eating it!

Veggie pitta pizza

We all like pizza. But ready-made pizza can be greasy and too big for one person. Enjoy the winning combination of cheese, dough and tasty veggies with this perfectly sized version.

Ingredients

- 1 large wholemeal pitta bread
- 3–4 tbsp tomato sauce (to taste)
- 30 g (1 oz) shredded part-skimmed mozzarella cheese, chopped
- Assorted chopped vegetables

Directions

1. Preheat oven or toaster oven to 180°C (350°F).
2. Spread the tomato sauce on the pitta and sprinkle with the cheese.
3. Add enough vegetables to cover the pitta and bake for about 10 minutes or until the cheese is melted.

315 calories per serving (may vary based on vegetables used)

A trip around the world in soup form

You can create an easy chicken and egg soup with different international flavours. Just boil 240–480 ml (8–16 fl oz) of chicken stock. Add one whisked egg and lightly heat until the egg is cooked (about one minute). Top with any of the following:

Mexican style Dash of hot pepper, chopped coriander and baked corn tortilla strips.

Greek style Teaspoon of lemon juice, a dash of olive oil and chopped parsley.

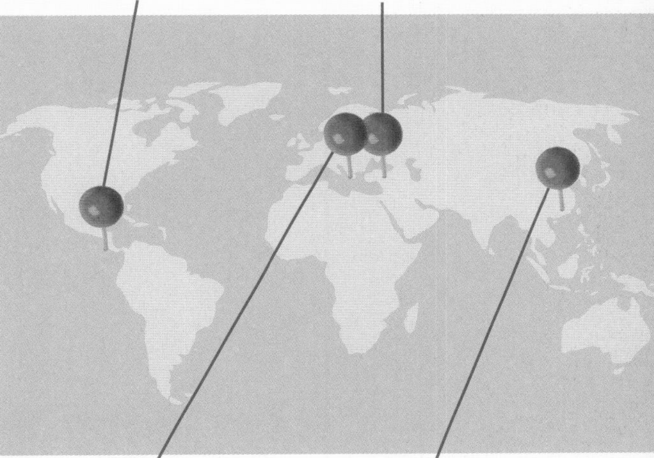

Italian style Chopped tomato, croûtons, oregano and a dash of olive oil and garlic powder.

Chinese style Chopped spring onions and 2 drops of sesame oil just before serving.

Check these out

www.allrecipes.com
Collection of recipes for solo cooks.

www.bbcgoodfood.com/recipes/collection/meals-one
Recipes for one, including cooking time and level of difficulty.

> Buy a whole boneless pork loin when it goes on sale. Have the butcher cut roasts, chops and country ribs so you have a variety and save money.
>
> Linda Eck Mills, Career and Life Coach

Cooking for many

Whether you have a large family or are planning a party, feeding many mouths – healthily – does not have to be a chore.

Cooking for many can be fun with some advance planning. All it takes is planning, preparation and practice. Using those three 'P's will organize your work and guarantee your success in the kitchen – see below for more details.

If shopping to feed a family, stock up when key staples are on sale, buy in bulk where possible and shop with the season to maximize freshness while minimizing cost.

Follow the three 'P's

Step 1: Planning
Think about the event itself and who will be coming. This will direct your efforts from the beginning. If it's a special event, what type of atmosphere do you want to create? Whether formal or informal, fun or serious, business or casual, it all depends on your vision or goal for the event.

Think about what you will prepare, what you might ask friends or family members to prepare and bring and what you can buy that doesn't require much preparation. At what time of day is the event or meal? Timing will greatly influence the type of foods you will serve. Do you need to serve a full meal or will hors d'œuvres suffice? You can save money by preparing some foods yourself but if time is at a premium, it may be worth buying some key elements pre-prepared (beware of 'hidden' or dubious ingredients – see pages 64–67).

How much do you need per person?

Cooked vegetables	Beans	Green or leafy salads
200 g (7 oz) per person if serving two vegetables; 200–275 g (7–10 oz) for one vegetable, or big eaters!	110 g (4 oz) cooked beans per person; 110–200 g (4–7 oz) for vegetarians	110–225 g (4–8 oz) per person (225–350 g/8–12 oz per person if they like greens)

Cupboard staples
Be ready for a crowd and extend your meals with tinned staples of low-sodium beans and veggies, water-packed tuna or chicken and fruits packed in their own juice. Frozen options work well, too, if you have a good freezer.

Fruit, mixed	Grains	Cheese	Meat, poultry or fish
110 g (4 oz) per person (220 g/7 oz if it is a popular item)	110–200 g (4–7 oz) or 25–50 g (1–2 oz) per person (75 g/3 oz for heavy pasta or rice eaters or vegetarians who like grains)	25–50 g (1–2 oz) per person (more for lacto-vegetarians)	75 g (3 oz) per person (175 g/6 oz for people who like meat, poultry and fish); less than 75 g (3 oz) if you are serving more than one type of these items

Step 2: Preparation
Before you start cooking, make a shopping/grocery list and check your larder for staples you may already have on hand like dry pasta, brown or wild rice, barley or buckwheat groats, tinned goods, drinks or snack foods.

Organize your shopping list by the order of things you want to serve so you won't forget anything: appetizers, main dish, side dishes, salads, desserts and drinks. Your time and money are valuable – don't waste them at the market. You want to enjoy your time at home cooking, not looking for ingredients.

Load your larder with staples for quick and easy meals.
For example, with these items:

- low-sodium tinned beans
- low-sodium tinned vegetables
- tomato sauce or paste
- low-sodium chicken stock
- tinned tuna, in water
- tinned chicken, in water
- fruit packed in its own juice

...you can easily prepare any of the following:

1 Bean and veggie burgers
2 Chicken noodle soup
3 Fruit and nut dessert salad or snack
4 Minestrone soup
5 Barley and veggie salad
6 Pasta with marinara and vegetable sauce
7 Buckwheat with vegetables
8 Brown rice and beans
9 Wild rice with vegetables
10 Three-bean salad

Look at your recipes and think about what can be cooked or prepared in advance and where you will store it, and cooking times and methods to make sure you are aware of what you will need to do. Remember to thaw frozen foods a day in advance (in the refrigerator) to make sure they are ready for preparation.

Step 3: Practice
After you have had success with some of your large meals or events, you can recycle the recipes and cook them with confidence. Try variations of your recipes, in particular substituting lower-calorie ingredients or adding some healthy ones.

Examples of variations to try:

- Add flaxseeds, nuts and dried fruit to salads
- Cut the fat by a third in recipes
- Use egg whites instead of whole eggs
- Try baking usually 'breaded and fried' favourites
- Add powdered dry milk to baked goods

Be better equipped

Slow cookers and electric frying pans can give you more flexibility in the kitchen.

1 Leave dishes or sauces to simmer in slow cookers while you get on with something else.

2 Use an electric frying pan for convenient sautéing, grilling or for omelettes and frittatas.

3 Switch to the low-heat function to keep food warm when hosting an event.

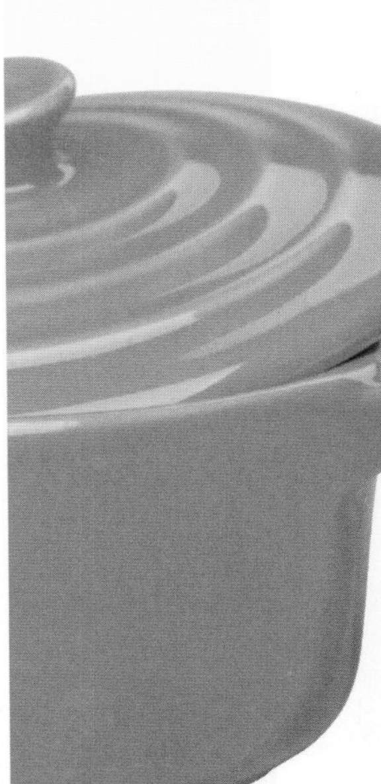

Useful hints and tips when cooking for many

Save time and calories with appetizers and snacks by serving a variety of nuts, raw fruits and vegetables and salads to balance higher-calorie foods to come later in the menu.

Cook sweet potatoes in the microwave. Cool, cut into sticks, toss lightly with cinnamon and brown sugar (just a light scattering) and 'oven-fry'.

Make a large batch of macaroni or other similar-shaped pasta. Lightly sauté fresh chopped kale and mushrooms in olive oil and garlic. Mix and serve.

Stretch the meat money and make dishes healthier by cooking fricassées and stews with a tomato sauce or low-sodium stock base with mostly celery, carrots, onions, tomatoes and potatoes (with skin) and less meat or chicken.

Set up a pizza, taco or other fun 'bar' where your guests can serve themselves. Warm up wholemeal pittas or whole-grain taco shells and set out healthy toppings such as beans, vegetables, low-fat cheese and even fruit.

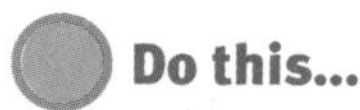

Do this...

✓ Grill or bake meats for more efficient use of your preparation time and to reduce fat and calories.

...Not this

✗ Fry meats. This requires more of your 'watch time' (you have to stand over it constantly) and adds fat and calories.

Three dishes to cook for picky eaters

Pick a base dish and include two or three side items your choosy eaters can select from:

1. **Taco base:** Prepare seasoned lean minced beef served with a choice of soft corn and wholemeal tortillas, leafy greens, chopped tomatoes and peppers, grated low-fat cheese and taco sauce.
2. **Pasta base:** Prepare wholewheat pasta served with a choice of chickpeas, grilled tuna, chicken chunks, cherry tomatoes, chopped fresh herbs and 2–3 low-fat dressings.
3. **Brown rice, barley or quinoa base:** Prepare the rice or quinoa served with a choice of black beans, corn, chopped onions and peppers, olives, chopped parsley or basil, lemon and olive oil.

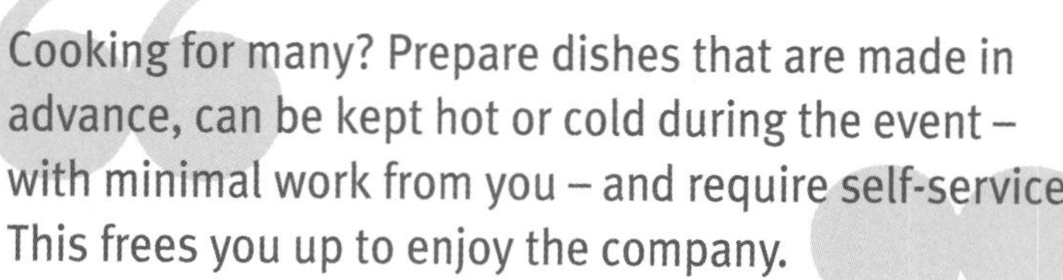

> Cooking for many? Prepare dishes that are made in advance, can be kept hot or cold during the event – with minimal work from you – and require self-service. This frees you up to enjoy the company.
>
> Dr Judith Rodriguez, Professor and Registered Dietitian, University of North Florida

Follow the 80:20 rule when cooking for many. Offer 80% healthy foods and 20% that may not be so healthy – the overall meal will be a satisfying mix of nutrients and treats.

29

Check these out

www.dummies.com/how-to/content/cooking-for-crowds-for-dummies-cheat-sheet.html

Includes a chart to help you find out how much food you need to prepare.

www.pinterest.com/juzt4j/recipes-to-feed-a-crowd

Recipe ideas for crowds, ranging from appetizers to desserts.

30

Three ideas for healthier dishes to make in advance

1. **Make a big batch of chilli con carne** by using more beans than meat and a combination of tofu crumbles and lean minced beef or turkey.
2. **Make a big batch of tortellini or gnocchi** and season with olive oil and fresh herbs. A few hours before serving, toss in washed and chopped broccoli and cauliflower (or a few bags of frozen). Reheat, toss and top with grated cheese before serving.
3. **Make your own meatballs** by mixing half-minced beef and half-moistened wholemeal bread (use stock or water to moisten) with egg whites and seasonings.

31

serves 5

Salad for all seasons

A quick, easy and healthy salad can be made with mixed greens, chopped or dried fruit, nuts and cheese.

Ingredients

- 550 g (1¼ lb) mixed greens
- 50 g (2 oz) chopped dried cranberries, cherries or apricots
- 50 g (2 oz) chopped or sliced walnuts, peanuts or almonds
- 25 g (1 oz) crumbled Gorgonzola cheese

Directions

Put the greens in the bottom of the salad bowl. Sprinkle with the dried fruit, nuts and crumbled cheese. Add the salad dressing (see right) before serving, or serve on the side of the salad.

All-seasons salad dressing

Use one quarter of this dressing for your salad; save the rest for later!

Ingredients

- 120 ml (4 fl oz) orange juice
- 3 tbsp olive oil
- 1 tbsp balsamic vinegar
- ½ tsp pepper
- ½ tsp dill
- 2 packets sugar substitute

Directions

Place the ingredients in a shaker bottle or whisk together in a bowl and pour over the salad.

126 calories per serving of salad with dressing

Breakfast: Kick-start your health goals

Breakfast is your first opportunity of the day to work towards your weight and health goals.

1 Brain: Needs energy in the form of glucose, primarily provided by carbohydrates.

2 Heart: Protein, calcium, sodium, potassium and other nutrients are important for a healthy heart.

3 Lungs: Vitamins C and E are antioxidants that support lung health.

4 Stomach: An important muscle that needs protein and vitamins.

5 Kidneys: Water and adequate – but not excessive – amounts of minerals are important for renal health.

6 Intestines: Need fibre and adequate fluids for gut health.

By definition, breakfast can be at any time of the day, if it is a time when you 'break a fast', that is, start to eat after an extended period of not eating. But traditionally it is used to refer to the first meal after awakening from a long, hopefully restful, sleep. The key point about breakfast is to eat something that will provide energy to 'get you going' and also key nutrients and satiety (fullness) value. Feeling full will help you manage your appetite throughout the day. Breakfast is important for children to help them learn while at school, and important for adults to help them concentrate on the task at hand, whatever that might be.

Treat your body

A good breakfast contains a combination of carbohydrates in the form of starches for energy, fibre for gut health and protein to build and support your tissues and organs throughout the day. A small amount of the healthy fats will help with the feeling of fullness. But you also want

TOP 10 HEALTHY power breakfasts

1

Whole-grain or high-fibre dry cereal with low-fat or fat-free milk; fruit or glass of juice.

2

Hard-boiled egg; English muffin with a slice of cheese; cup of tea.

3

Piece of leftover chicken breast on wholemeal toast; glass of juice.

4

Cold noodles with peanut sauce and tofu; glass of water.

5

Pitta bread with hummus; side salad of chopped tomatoes; olives; glass of water.

6

Porridge made with low-fat milk, topped with peaches; cup of coffee.

7

Shredded wheat cereal with low-fat milk; apple; cup of herbal tea.

to include nutrients that will allow your body to function well throughout the day. The micronutrients – vitamins and minerals – and phytochemicals – natural chemicals found in plant foods – help to regulate important body functions and promote health.

Meal replacers

There are commercial drinks or food bars available called 'meal replacers'. For people who are trying to lose weight, meal replacers provide two important components dieters want: a known number of calories and some key nutrients.

Plan ahead

Select two breakfast items and place them prominently in the kitchen. Position the wholemeal bread next to the coffee pot and the yogurt at the front of the eye-level refrigerator shelf. That way, you won't be tempted by other foods en route.

How many calories should I eat for breakfast?

While currently there is no set rule, the key is to determine your eating pattern and then allot a portion of those calories for breakfast.

Eat only three meals and not snack throughout the day? If so, break your calories up into thirds. For example, if your goal is to eat 1,800 calories a day, you may want to make your breakfast 500–600 calories.

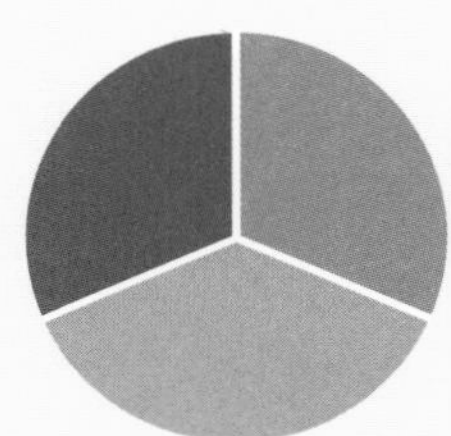

Eat three meals and two snacks a day? If so, consider breaking your calories up into three large and two smaller calorie distributions. For example, if your goal is to eat 1,800 calories a day, you may want to make your meals 400–500 calories and each of your two snacks 100–150 calories a day.

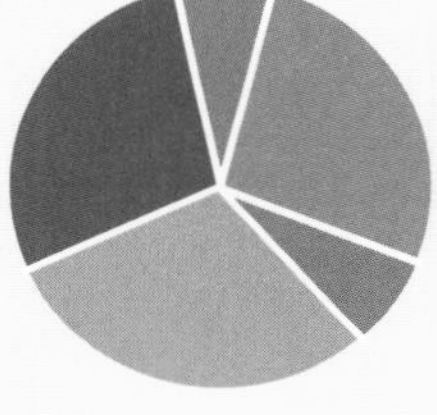

Eat about six small meals or large snacks; that is, graze for most of the day? Then you might want to have about 300 calories per meal/snack.

8
Bagel topped with a slice of smoked salmon and onion; cup of coffee.

9
Cinnamon scone; cube of Cheddar cheese; wedge of honeydew melon; cup of tea.

10
Fruit and yogurt smoothie; granola bar; glass of water.

COUNTDOWN COUNTER

Egg breakfast | Calories

1 hard-boiled egg, 1 glass orange juice, plain wholemeal toast | **272 calories**

1 fried egg, 1 glass orange juice, wholemeal toast with butter | **318 calories**

1 egg Benedict, 1 glass orange juice, wholemeal toast with butter and jam | **637 calories**

General breakfast options | Calories

225 g (8 oz) plain Greek yogurt topped with 200 g (7 oz) tinned drained peaches, 25 g (1 oz) granola, herbal tea | **342 calories**

200 g (7 oz) bran cereal with raisins, skimmed milk, fresh orange, plain tea | **355 calories**

15 cm (6 in) wholemeal pancake topped with 225 g (8 oz) unsweetened apple sauce, 1 slice grilled back bacon, plain coffee | **445 calories**

150 g (5 oz) low-fat granola (no raisins), 1 glass skimmed milk, 150 g (5 oz) strawberries, 1 glass orange juice | **450 calories**

Make time for lunch

Whether you are in a hurry or taking your time, at home or at work, lunch is an important meal that can refuel you.

Lunch is the meal that gets you over that midday 'hump' to provide you with energy until later in the day.

Meals tend to be larger for people with physically demanding jobs such as farm work, and smaller meals are generally consumed by people with sedentary jobs such as office work, but it depends on your eating habits and, in particular, the size and times of your other meals and snacks (see page 27).

Lunch also varies around the world. In some areas, it is a multi-course meal consumed slowly, as a major social event or the main meal of the day. In other areas, it may be light, consisting of bread or other starch and a high-protein food. Brunch has also become popular, describing a late breakfast or early lunch that has the elements of both meals. It is most common on weekends.

What's your goal?
Consider how you want to feel after you eat. Rested? Energized? Avoid skipping the meal, since it will make you feel tired, moody or irritable (it's hard to be nice when you are hungry and have low blood sugar). A combination of complex carbohydrates and proteins will rejuvenate the mind and body. Stimulants such as coffee may perk you up temporarily, especially if combined with sugar, but this is followed by a blood sugar drop, and too much caffeine could make you nervous and irritable.

35

Brown-bag lunch

While some people will eat lunch at restaurants or eateries near their place of work, this pattern is facing competition from the traditional 'brown bag' lunch, when people prepare lunch at home and bring it to work. If you work at a location that has a cafeteria, the food lines may be long, or the food not to your liking – or preferred quality or price range. This may be the same with food from local restaurants, and sitting down in a restaurant may be too time-consuming in the first place. When you brown-bag your lunch, you undoubtedly save money, but you also have more control over flavour and your time, and can feel comforted that you know the quality of the ingredients.

36

Three brown-bag time-saving tips

1. Make five sandwiches at a time, and freeze each in individual freezer bags.
2. Cook a large dinner and set some aside in a lunch container.
3. Include individually wrapped cheese, crackers and fruit cups in small plastic bags.

37

What does lunch mean to you?

Something quick to eat while running errands or working? Watch out for hidden calories in quick-serve pre-prepared foods.

Something low-cost? Try 'brown bagging' meals (see opposite).

The best choice at a fast-food eatery? Focus on the smart choices regarding portion size and side items.

The best choice at your work cafeteria? Try the simple items, like grilled chicken and salad instead of mixed dishes such as casseroles.

Something you eat out while sharing time with friends or colleagues? Consider splitting the meal – and cost – or having an appetizer instead of a full meal.

38

Focus your mind

Interestingly enough, although people may feel that it is a fast meal, lunch actually tends to be one of the longer meals. This may be because people are often distracted talking to friends or working while eating lunch. They may feel like it did not take much time to eat or have a feeling of satisfaction. This mindless eating pattern can lead to overeating. Stop, take time to eat (instead of multitasking) and enjoy the meal and break from work or the day's routine.

> When you sit down to eat, take a couple of deep breaths, relax, look at your food and tell yourself, 'I'm going to relax, eat and enjoy my food.' This can help you slow down, focus on the experience of eating and eat less.
>
> Penny L Wilson, www.eatingforperformance.com

39

Lunch in a jar

Get a 450 g (1 lb) or larger Mason or other preserving jar and add:

- 2 tablespoons of your favourite salad dressing
- Any 'hard' veggies: coarsely chopped carrots, broccoli, cooked beets, etc., or cooked beans
- Any 'medium' veggies: chopped green beans or sugar snap peas, green, yellow or red peppers, etc.
- Any 'light' veggies: chopped greens, cabbage, etc.
- Protein such as chicken pieces (leftovers) or cheese

Directions

Pour the dressing into the Mason jar. Add the hard chopped veggies, followed by the medium, then light veggies. Seal the jar. Just before serving, shake the jar to mix the ingredients. Arrange on a plate and top with the protein.

COUNTDOWN COUNTER

Lunch item | Calories

Steamed broccoli, 200 g (7 oz) | **27 calories**

Turkey breast, 25 g (1 oz) | **34 calories**

Honeydew melon, 200 g (7 oz) | **64 calories**

Beef salami, 25 g (1 oz) | **74 calories**

Medium banana | **105 calories**

Hummus, 50 g (2 oz) | **109 calories**

Cheddar cheese, 25 g (1 oz) | **113 calories**

Medium potato, baked or microwaved | **145 calories**

White bread, 2 slices | **160 calories**

1 pitta bread | **170 calories**

Peanut butter, 2 tbsp | **190 calories**

Berry-flavoured yogurt, 200 g (7 oz) | **233 calories**

Dinner: The healthy option

Dinner is the opportunity to enjoy the last meal of the day and make sure you've had your daily dose of nutrients.

Dinner is usually the last meal of the day, eaten around 6pm or later in the evening in many countries. For most people, dinner is based on convenience but is still more elaborate than breakfast and lunch. Dinner is a great opportunity to get creative with ingredients and flavours but, in reality, people often have limited time to prepare dinner and can feel hungry and tired after a hard day at work, and so may not always make healthy choices.

Build a well-balanced dinner

You should aim to include each food group in your dinner. As with breakfast (see pages 26–27) and lunch (see pages 28–29), a complete meal should consist of carbohydrates, protein and a small amount of healthy fats. All of these macronutrients are needed for energy (carbohydrates, fat) and healthy tissue growth and maintenance (protein, fat). It is recommended that these three key macronutrients are obtained from high-fibre starches, grains, fruits and vegetables (carbohydrates); lean meats, fish, poultry or plant proteins (protein); and heart-healthy oils such as extra virgin olive oil and rapeseed oil (fat). An example of a well-balanced dinner meal is the following:

- 150 g (5 oz) wild rice
- 75 g (3 oz) baked wild salmon
- 225 g (8 oz) steamed green beans

Dinner plate composition

There are several ways of deciding on portion sizes. One easy approach is the New American Plate from the American Institute for Cancer Research. This approach suggests that two thirds (or more) of your plate should be made up of vegetables, fruits, whole grains or beans, and one third (or less) of animal protein. Another similar approach from the United States Department of Agriculture named My Plate is shown to the right. These methods are mere guidelines and you must keep in mind that you may need to adjust your dinner portions depending on what you already ate throughout the day.

Check your food groups

Your dinner portions should be adjusted according to how much of each food group you have already eaten throughout the day. Therefore, dinner is a great occasion for including food groups that you may have missed throughout the day, or an opportunity to cut down on food groups of which you may have already met your limits. For example:

- If you did not have any **vegetables or fruit** for breakfast and/or lunch, catch up at dinnertime. Since fruits and vegetables provide important nutrients such as vitamins, minerals, antioxidants and fibre, which all help ward off diseases, they are recommended to be eaten every day.
- Likewise, if you had a large lunch, which included a foot-long meatball sandwich, it would be best to go easy on the amount of **protein** for dinner. Instead of 75 g (3 oz) of salmon, have only 25 g (1 oz) for dinner, with increased vegetables.

Building blocks of a healthy, complete dinner

Grains and starches for carbohydrates

Brown or wild rice

Wholewheat or whole-grain pasta

Bread, tortillas

Whole-grain quinoa

Red potatoes, with skin

Sweet potatoes

The longer the shelf life, the shorter your life. Eat real food!

Vegetables that are high in carbohydrates

While these vegetables do contain a great amount of nutrition, they also contain as much starch as grains. They should be considered a carbohydrate and not a regular vegetable.

Potatoes

Sweet potatoes

Peas

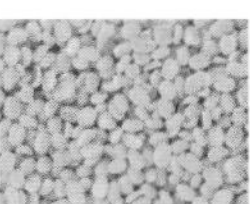
Corn

Pumpkin

Butternut and acorn squash

Yams

Vegetables low in carbohydrates and calories

All of these are good choices. Try to eat as many different vegetables throughout the week as possible. If there are some you have not tried before, give them a try – you might be pleasantly surprised!

Broccoli

Green beans

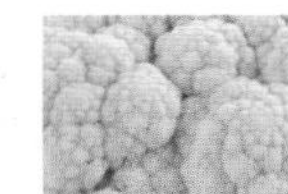
Cauliflower

Cabbage

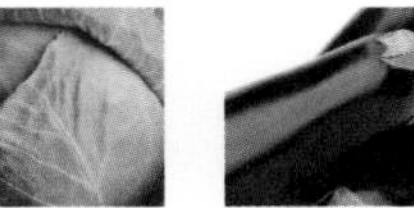

Aubergine

Carrots

Salad greens

Tomatoes

Kohlrabi

Spinach

Peppers

Onions

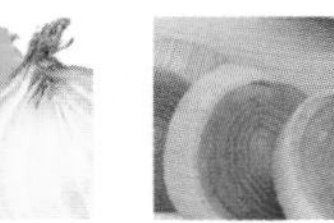
Leeks

Garlic

Mushrooms

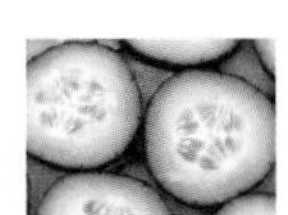
Cucumbers

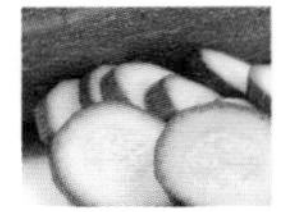
Courgettes

Squash

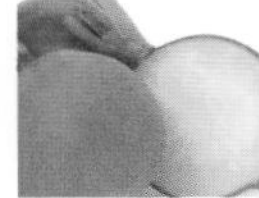
Radishes

Brussels sprouts

Good protein choices

Lean beef, pork, lamb, etc. with all visible fat trimmed off and no marbling. Lean poultry includes chicken and turkey breast, without the skin. Other parts of poultry have a higher fat content. Fish – in particular, fatty fish such as salmon and trout – is a healthy choice since it contains great amounts of omega-3 fatty acids, which are beneficial for numerous body functions, including protection of heart health.

Beef

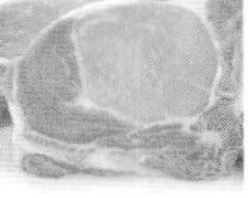
Pork

Lamb

Chicken

Turkey

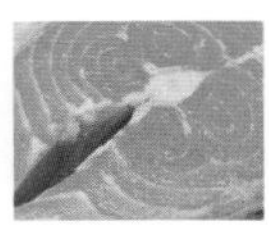
Salmon

Trout

44

Oil-less preparation methods

While fried foods may taste good, they add unnecessary calories and fat. There are many healthy alternative methods to frying such as:

- Baking
- Grilling
- Lightly sautéing
- Steaming

Some of these methods require the use of little or no oil. If some oil is needed, aim for rapeseed or sunflower oil. But use sparingly, as oils contain about 120 calories per tablespoon. You can also use extra virgin olive oil to drizzle over salads or steamed vegetables. According to the American Heart Association, you should avoid coconut oil, palm oil and palm kernel oil. While these are vegetable oils and have no cholesterol, they are high in saturated fat.

45

Eat dinner early

Aim to eat dinner earlier in the evening rather than later whenever you can. Researchers suggest that this will give your body the opportunity to properly digest your food. Unwanted pounds are also less likely to creep up so this strategy may help with weight loss if that is your goal. Furthermore, by eating dinner earlier in the evening you also avoid heartburn, which can be triggered by lying down shortly after eating. According to the National Institute of Health, it is recommended to avoid lying down for at least three to four hours after eating.

46

A light start

Studies have shown that eating a low-calorie soup or salad before the main course results in a significant reduction of energy intake during the remainder of the meal. However, these soups and salads must be light in calories, otherwise you could easily overdo it. Good examples of first-course salads are leafy-green, colourful salads consisting of only vegetables (no protein such as chicken or beans – those salads should be considered a main course). Filling yet energy-light soups are stock or chunky vegetable soup. This is not only an easy way to increase your vegetable and fibre intake, but will also help to avoid overeating with the rest of your dinner because you will feel satisfied more quickly.

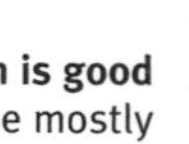
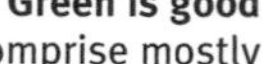

Green is good
A starter salad should comprise mostly greens. Consider adding low-calorie and filling veggies such as broccoli, celery or green beans. Sprinkle with a flavoured vinegar.

TOP 10 TIPS for dinnertime success

1

Make a menu for the week or for several days. Then shop for the required items in one or two trips to avoid having to go out every day.

2

Plan and prepare ahead. Wash and chop ingredients that can withstand being prepped ahead of time (peppers, broccoli, green beans, cabbage, etc) so they are ready to use when needed.

3

Marinate the night before if the recipe calls for it, and also to infuse flavour.

4

Buy certain items in bulk that you can pre-prep and freeze. For example, sauté a quantity of lean minced beef, use half for one dinner and freeze the rest for another night. Or buy a large quantity of chicken breast, trim (if needed), portion out and freeze.

5

Use produce that is in season. It is not only packed with more flavour and nutrients but is also usually cheaper.

6

Keep your larder stocked with staples such as brown rice, wholewheat pasta, tinned beans, tomato sauce, low-sodium soup, fruit cups in 100% juice, etc.

7

Keep some frozen or tinned fruits and vegetables on hand for convenience. Use no-salt-added or low-sodium for tinned vegetables. Rinse before using. Tinned fruits should be packed in water or 100% juice with no sugar added.

A quick way to cook potatoes

Microwave potatoes instead of boiling or baking them. Wash and pierce the potatoes. Microwave them for about three to six minutes (depending on their size and quantity) until they are slightly soft. Then wrap them in foil and let them sit to steam and continue cooking. You can have perfectly cooked potatoes in less time than baking and with more nutrient retention than boiling.

Check these out

www.eatingwell.com/recipes_menus
A treasure trove of healthy recipes, incuding one-pot recipes for easy weeknight meals.

www.realsimple.com/food-recipes
Plenty of ideas for easy weeknight dinners.

www.cookinglight.com/food/quick-healthy
Healthy and fast recipes for busy people.

Versatile chicken
Chicken can be part of many low-calorie dishes. Its protein helps provide satiety.

> The weekend (Friday dinner–Sunday dinner) has over 30% of your meals for the week. Do you want to eat healthily only 67% of the time?
>
> Kathleen Searles, Nutrition Consultant, www.lunchbox-nutritionist.com

COUNTDOWN COUNTER

Chicken dinners	Calories
Grilled chicken breast (with garlic and dried herbs)	**129 calories**
BBQ chicken breast (grilled with bottled barbecue sauce)	**145 calories**
Lemon pepper chicken (pan-fried with cooking spray)	**149 calories**
Herb-baked chicken (oven-baked with olive oil and dried herbs/spices)	**155 calories**
Chicken Alfredo (made with bottled Alfredo sauce)	**263 calories**
Traditional Italian chicken Marsala (with butter and wine)	**316 calories**
Classic chicken Parmesan (breaded and fried)	**410 calories**
Chicken Cordon Bleu (with ham and cheese)	**411 calories**

8

Seek out one-pot meals – you will have less to clean up afterwards when your entire dinner can be prepared in just one pot or pan. Casseroles and slow-cooker recipes can save you lots of time. So try different one-pot recipes such as green bean casserole, pinto bean and chicken sausage stew, tuna noodle casserole and macaroni cheese with a layer of spinach. Many of these kinds of recipes can be found online.

9

Pop to the shops on your way home from work and pick up a rotisserie chicken, bag of pre-washed salad greens, a few tomatoes, 1 small cucumber, baby carrots and a small wholewheat baguette. At home, quickly chop the vegetables and toss with the salad greens with a drizzle of olive oil and vinegar or your favourite dressing with the shredded chicken breast on top. Toast the baguette and lightly dip in extra virgin olive oil sprinkled with dried basil and oregano (or any other herbs or spices you love).

10

Combining snacks to make a meal – when your fridge is almost empty and you are too tired to go to the shops, let alone cook – doesn't mean you have to skimp on nutrition. Have some wholewheat cereal or oats with skimmed or low-fat milk combined with a handful of baby carrots and some fruit, and you have a wholesome meal. Or have your favourite low-sodium soup with some toasted whole-grain bread. Keep a few fruit cups packed in 100% juice for when you are running low on time and energy.

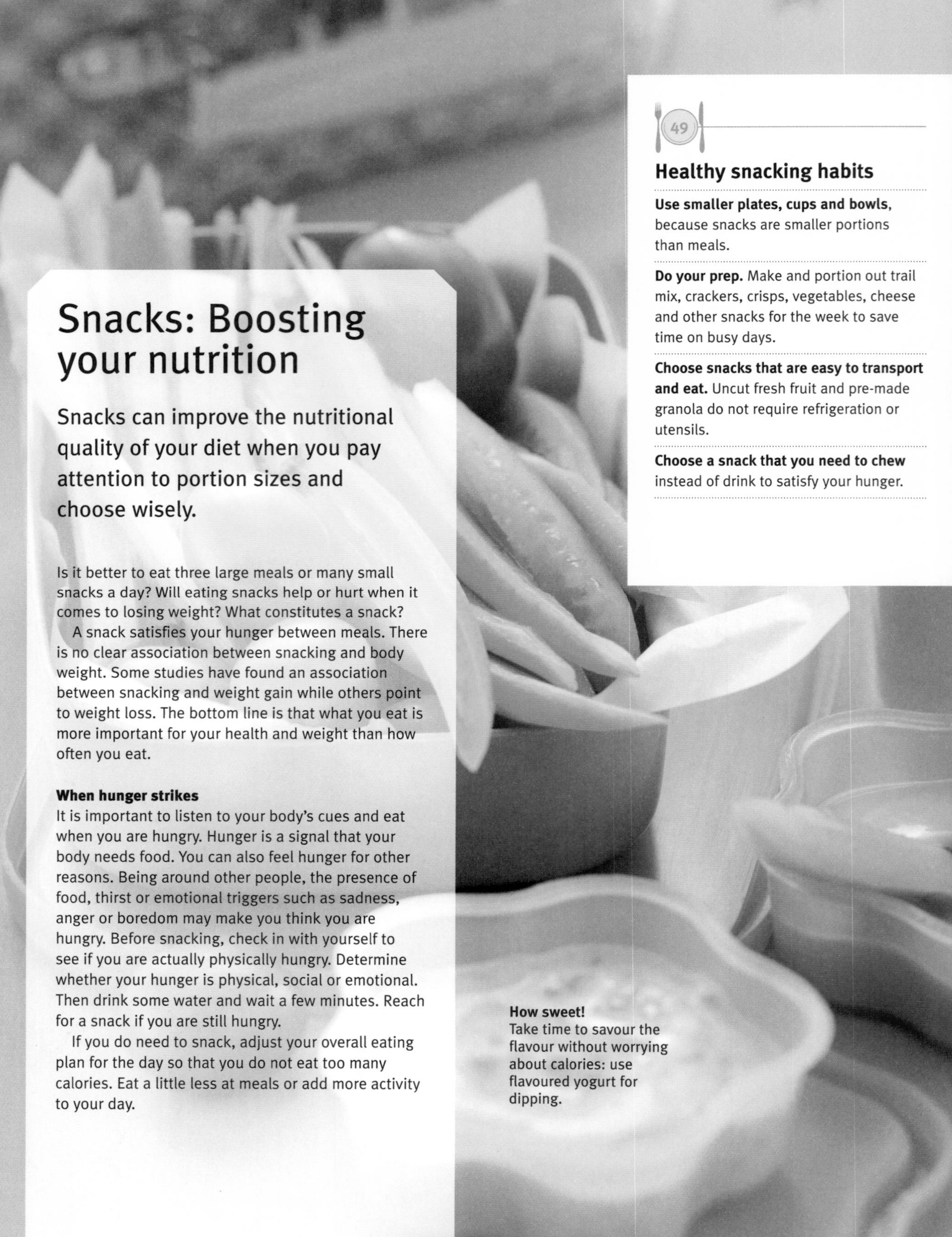

Snacks: Boosting your nutrition

Snacks can improve the nutritional quality of your diet when you pay attention to portion sizes and choose wisely.

Is it better to eat three large meals or many small snacks a day? Will eating snacks help or hurt when it comes to losing weight? What constitutes a snack?

A snack satisfies your hunger between meals. There is no clear association between snacking and body weight. Some studies have found an association between snacking and weight gain while others point to weight loss. The bottom line is that what you eat is more important for your health and weight than how often you eat.

When hunger strikes

It is important to listen to your body's cues and eat when you are hungry. Hunger is a signal that your body needs food. You can also feel hunger for other reasons. Being around other people, the presence of food, thirst or emotional triggers such as sadness, anger or boredom may make you think you are hungry. Before snacking, check in with yourself to see if you are actually physically hungry. Determine whether your hunger is physical, social or emotional. Then drink some water and wait a few minutes. Reach for a snack if you are still hungry.

If you do need to snack, adjust your overall eating plan for the day so that you do not eat too many calories. Eat a little less at meals or add more activity to your day.

49

Healthy snacking habits

Use smaller plates, cups and bowls, because snacks are smaller portions than meals.

Do your prep. Make and portion out trail mix, crackers, crisps, vegetables, cheese and other snacks for the week to save time on busy days.

Choose snacks that are easy to transport and eat. Uncut fresh fruit and pre-made granola do not require refrigeration or utensils.

Choose a snack that you need to chew instead of drink to satisfy your hunger.

How sweet!
Take time to savour the flavour without worrying about calories: use flavoured yogurt for dipping.

Filling the gaps

Use snacks to round out your nutrition. A snack that will satisfy your hunger for longer contains protein, fat and/or fibre. Including at least two of these nutrients in each snack will give you more staying power.

QUICK GUIDE to nutrients

Protein
Meats, dairy products, nuts, beans, seeds

Fats
Oils and spreads, nuts and seeds, avocado

Fibre
Whole grains, beans, fruit, vegetables

COUNTDOWN COUNTER

SNACK | CALORIES
Air-popped popcorn, 450 g (1 lb) | **80 calories**
Reduced-fat Greek yogurt with peach, 150 g (5 oz) | **125 calories**
Roasted chickpeas, 110 g (4 oz) | **135 calories**
12 baked tortilla chips with 2 tablespoons salsa | **140 calories**
Wholewheat cereal, 110 g (4 oz), with handful of raisins | **150 calories**
Dark chocolate, 25 g (1 oz) | **155 calories**
Almonds, 25 g (1 oz) | **160 calories**
14 pitta chips with 2 tablespoons hummus | **195 calories**
Reduced-fat Swiss cheese, 50 g (2 oz), on 6 wholewheat crackers | **200 calories**
2 tablespoons peanut butter on 2 large celery stalks | **230 calories**
Bag of pretzels, 50 g (2 oz) | **280 calories**

> Blend equal amounts of non-fat Greek yogurt with the following to cut calories and fat in half: guacamole, hummus, ranch dressing, blue cheese dressing, mayo in tuna salad or chicken salad or potato salad.

Georgia Kostas, Author, *The Cooper Clinic Solution to the Diet Revolution: Step Up to the Plate!*

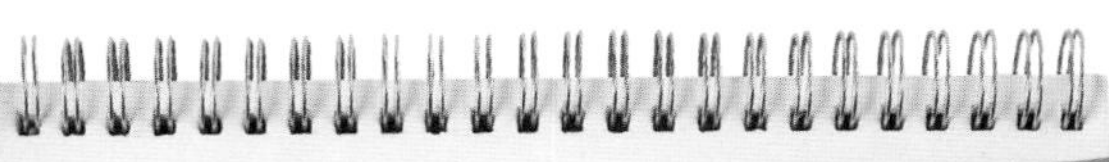

Roasted chickpeas

This recipe is budget-friendly, packed with protein and fibre and provides an easily portable snack.

Ingredients
- Chickpeas, boiled (or tinned, rinsed)
- Your choice of spices (e.g., paprika, cayenne pepper, cumin, garlic powder, salt)
- Non-stick cooking spray

Directions

1. Preheat the oven to 230°C (450°F). Prepare the dried chickpeas as directed and drain, or rinse tinned chickpeas.

2. Place wet chickpeas and spices in a plastic bag, seal, and shake to cover the chickpeas with the spices.

3. Spray a baking sheet with non-stick cooking spray and spread the chickpeas in a single layer on the sheet. Place in the preheated oven and cook until crunchy, approximately 30–45 minutes, shaking the baking sheet occasionally to prevent sticking.

Serving suggestion: Enjoy a 110 g (4 oz) serving on its own or add to homemade trail mix or on top of a salad for a protein-rich crunch.

176 calories, 7 g protein, 6 g fibre per 110 g (4 oz) serving

Tempting treats

Be aware that prepackaged snack foods may be high in calories and low in nutrition. These are typically high in fat and sodium, or salt, and low in vitamins, minerals and fibre. As a smart snacker, do allow yourself to enjoy a snack just for fun – chocolate, crisps or cake – but only have these as occasional treats and keep portions small.

Did you know celery sticks stay crisp for longer after you cut them if you store them in a cup of water in the fridge?

Getting and staying active

Even if you don't have access to a gym or equipment, there are many ways you can still get all the benefits of exercise while at home.

You know it's something you should do. And you probably know why: moving and being active are critical for maintaining good health. Inactivity is as much of a health risk as any of the other major risk factors – such as smoking – for the development of chronic diseases.

The decision to become more active is life-changing. Your quality of life will increase; quite possibly the risk of developing heart disease, diabetes and stroke will diminish; as could the risk of developing high blood pressure and high cholesterol. Physical activity plays an important role in any weight-loss programme; when you exercise, your body uses more calories than you eat and you lose weight. Also, your mood will improve. You will sleep better, have more energy, feel less stress and anxiety, tone your muscles and decrease the risk of osteoporosis. Why wouldn't you want all these rewards and positive feelings in your life?

There are three areas of fitness that you need to focus on:

- Flexibility
- Cardiovascular or aerobic fitness
- Muscular strength and endurance

These three areas of fitness do not require costly gym memberships or even leaving the house. You can do many if not most activities in the comfort of your own home. Some you can even do at work!

> Start small and make it enjoyable. Try to do some fun physical activity every day by making it part of your daily routine. If it's fun, your activity choices will soon become your healthy lifestyle habits.
>
> Chris Robertson, Assistant Professor of Exercise Science, Jacksonville University

53

Consult your doctor

Before you start any kind of exercise regimen, make sure that you consult a doctor for medical clearance. This is especially important if you are a male over 45 years of age or a female over 55 years of age. There is no condition that exercise can worsen, as long as it is the right kind of exercise done in a safe way.

54

Set realistic goals

Once you have been given the all-clear from your doctor, set one or two short-term and long-term realistic goals for yourself.

- **As a short-term goal: less sitting!** Whilst watching your favourite TV show, walk on the spot or do some stretching exercises.
- **As a long-term goal: decrease leisure time spent at the computer** by at least half. You will find yourself with more time for exercising and should also feel less lethargic.

55

Make exercise a lifestyle routine

Make an 'appointment' to exercise. Schedule exercise as you would any other important activity. This will integrate it into your life, making it a lifelong habit.

Get past those relapses: Everyone has relapses. But there's a difference between a relapse and giving up. Not exercising for a month after you've been exercising for three months may be a relapse. It doesn't mean you're a failure and you should not give up. Do not feel guilty – think of it as a time to reflect. Ask yourself, what happened? Why did you stop exercising? Think of ways to get yourself going again. Learn from your relapse so that you can keep on moving towards your goal of staying physically active. It is important to keep at it, even if you slip up or have relapses along the way.

Congratulate yourself! Remember to congratulate yourself for fitting activity into your day. After you finish your exercise, take a few minutes to reflect on how good it made you feel and use this to motivate yourself to continue exercising. When you achieve a long-term goal, give yourself an external reward too, such as treating yourself to a movie, a new outfit, new walking shoes, a pedometer or tickets to a special event.

Exercise effectiveness: Calorie burning

The chart below gives calorie-burning estimates for popular sports and household chores. As you become more fit and do the activity more efficiently you will expend fewer calories. However, as you become more fit you will be able to exercise for longer and more vigorously.

BODY WEIGHT KG/LB	45/100	54/120	64/140	73/160	82/180	91/200	95/210
EXERCISE	calories burned per hour	calories burned per hour	calories burned per hour	calories burned per hour	calories burned per hour	calories burned per hour	calories burned per hour
Aerobics, high impact	332	398	465	531	598	664	697
Aerobics, low impact	228	274	319	365	410	456	479
Aerobics, in water	251	301	351	402	452	502	527
Walking, 3 kmph (2 mph)	128	154	179	205	230	256	269
Walking, 5.5 kmph (3.5 mph)	196	235	274	314	353	392	412
Running, 8 kmph (5 mph)	378	454	529	605	680	756	794
Cycling, 16 kmph (10 mph)	182	218	255	291	328	364	382
Tennis, singles	264	317	370	422	475	528	554
Weightlifting, general	156	187	218	250	281	312	328
Swimming, laps	264	317	370	422	475	528	554
Yoga, dynamic	396	475	554	634	713	792	832
Rowing, stationary	273	328	382	437	491	546	573
HOUSEHOLD CHORE/ACTIVITY							
Cooking	120	144	168	192	216	240	252
Dusting	134	161	188	214	241	268	281
Cleaning	159	191	223	254	286	318	334
Mopping floors	204	245	286	326	367	408	428
Gardening	182	218	255	291	328	364	382
Dancing, energetic	252	302	353	403	454	504	529
Vacuuming	167	200	233	267	300	333	350
Washing car	204	245	286	326	367	408	428
Washing dishes	102	122	143	163	184	204	214

57

Stretches for flexibility

Flexibility is the ability to move your joints and muscles within their entire range of motion. Performing stretching exercises will increase blood flow throughout the body, help burn calories and decrease overall pain while increasing overall flexibility. And, even better news, stretches can be done easily in the home with little or no equipment.

Lower back and hip stretch: Lie on your back. Bring both knees to your chest and roll to the left and right. Bring both legs back to the centre and release them down to the floor. Then pull one knee at a time up to the chest, holding each leg there for about 3 seconds.

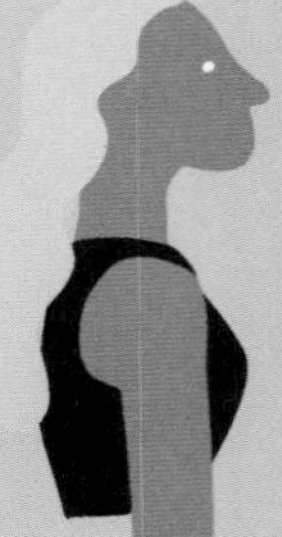

Neck stretch: Slowly lower your chin to your chest. Bring it back to a resting position. Next, move your head to the right and tilt your ear towards that shoulder. Make sure you keep both shoulders down. You will feel the stretch along the left side of your neck. Bring your head back to its resting position then repeat the same motion to the left by tilting your left ear to your left shoulder. Slowly repeat this exercise several times.

58

Aerobic activities to do at home

When you are aerobically fit, your cardiovascular and respiratory system effectively move oxygen around the body. When you are doing aerobic exercise your heart is beating faster and you are breathing harder. For these exercises, wear low-heeled shoes with traction, such as trainers. Continue exercising until you feel slightly out of breath, gradually increasing the amount of time that is spent on the activity.

Stepping: This exercise is ideal on stairs or steps. Lift one foot and place it on the lowest step, then lift the second foot to join the first foot on the step. Make sure you are well balanced or holding onto a stair rail or wall. Return the first foot back to the ground, followed by the second foot. Repeat, gradually increasing your pace.

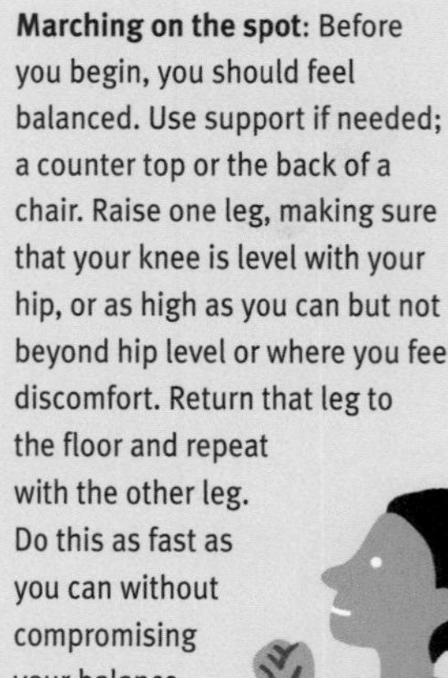

Marching on the spot: Before you begin, you should feel balanced. Use support if needed; a counter top or the back of a chair. Raise one leg, making sure that your knee is level with your hip, or as high as you can but not beyond hip level or where you feel discomfort. Return that leg to the floor and repeat with the other leg. Do this as fast as you can without compromising your balance.

Arm across the chest stretch: Straighten one arm in front of you, grasp it just above the tricep (the muscle on the back of the top half of your arm) with your other hand, and stretch it across the chest. Rest the arm you are stretching in the V (that is, elbow crease) of your other arm. Press both arms into the chest. Make sure that you keep the stretching arm straight. Repeat the same stretch exercise with the other arm.

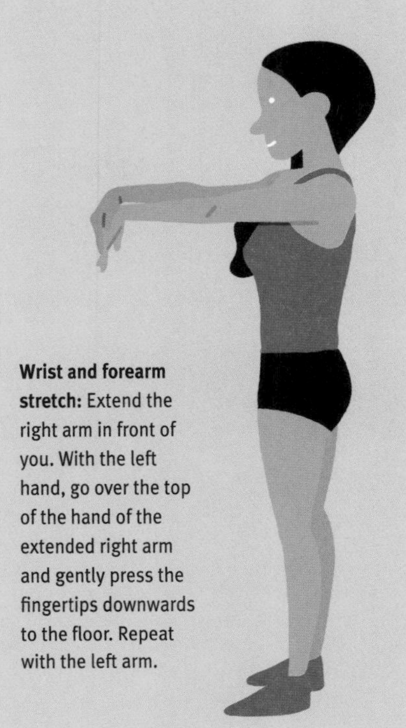

Wrist and forearm stretch: Extend the right arm in front of you. With the left hand, go over the top of the hand of the extended right arm and gently press the fingertips downwards to the floor. Repeat with the left arm.

Jogging on the spot: Before you begin, make sure you feel balanced. Raise one leg so the foot is a few inches off the ground, then return the foot to the floor. At a fast pace, lift the other leg and then return the foot to the floor. Both feet should only be on the floor for a very short time. Visualize this activity as running on the spot at a slow pace. Relax your upper body, and bend your arms at the elbows so that they are in front of your body. As you raise one leg the opposite arm should be raised and move forwards naturally. Do this as fast as you can without compromising your balance.

Jumping jacks: Stand with your arms straight down at your sides. Make sure your legs are straight and close together, knees slightly bent. Jump both legs out so they are wider than your shoulders while clapping your hands above your head in a smooth, rhythmical movement. If you are uncomfortable jumping, have your legs straight and close together, slightly bent knees, then extend one leg out to the side a little further than your shoulder. Quickly return the leg so the feet are together and repeat with the other leg. Do the same movements with the arms.

Cardiovascular or aerobic fitness

Aerobic exercise strengthens your heart and lungs, and makes you feel less fatigued. Aim to do about 2½ hours (a total of 150 minutes) of moderate activity a week or at least 1½ hours (90) minutes of vigorous activity weekly. You can also have aerobic bursts of 10 minutes or more throughout your day.

Moderate activities include raking leaves, vacuuming, pushing a lawn mower or playing with your children.

Vigorous activities include jogging on the spot, using a skipping rope or riding a stationary bike to the point where you are breathing harder.

Exercise equipment

You don't have to spend money to get and stay in shape, but there are some useful pieces of equipment you can buy to use at home if you think you will find it motivational. Some are more expensive than others, in which case be sure that you will use an item before investing, and also measure up to make sure you have adequate space.

- Treadmill
- Stationary bike
- Exercise DVDs
- Skipping rope

Muscular strength and endurance

When you are building stronger muscles, you are developing muscular fitness. If you are increasing how long you can use your muscles, you are developing muscular endurance. You can make muscles stronger by pushing or pulling against them. Try to do strengthening exercises two or more times a week. Focus on working the large groups (such as your arms, legs, back, chest and core abdominals). You can gain muscular fitness by doing exercises like push-ups and leg lifts, or even by doing housework and gardening, such as scrubbing floors or pulling up weeds.

Simple squats: Standing upright with feet hip-distance apart, tighten your abdominal muscles and place your hands on the front of your thighs. Bend the knees as if you are going to sit on a chair, making sure that you cannot see your toes in front of your knees. Hold the position for a few seconds. Over time, increase the duration of the hold.

'Swim' on the floor: Place some kind of padding on the floor for comfort. Lay face down on the floor. Extend your arms straight in front of you, shoulder-width apart, but do not lock the elbows. Extend your legs straight behind you, hip-distance apart. The tops of your feet should be touching the floor. Tighten your abdominal muscles. Raise your right arm and your left foot while keeping your head facing the floor, in line with the spine. Lift your head, but do not tilt it back or forwards. Hold the position for a few seconds. Repeat using the opposite arm and leg.

Lunges: Wear low-heeled shoes with traction, such as trainers. Before you begin, make sure you feel balanced. With both feet on the ground, hip-distance apart, raise one leg and step forwards while still balanced. Bend your front knee as far as you can, making sure your back leg is straight and directly behind you, and that you're on the ball of the back foot. Place your hands on the front of your thigh for support. Make sure your front knee does not go beyond the toes – you may have to move your front foot forwards. Alternate each leg. Start slow and increase the number of lunges over time.

Modified push-ups: Place some kind of padding (an exercise mat, towel or blanket) on the floor to provide comfort and protect the knees. Lie face down, then get up on your knees and place your arms under your shoulders, shoulder-width apart. Your arms should be straight but not locked at the elbows. Separate the knees so they are under your hips and hip-distance apart. Contract your lower stomach muscles and slowly bend your arms, keeping the elbows close to your body, lowering your body towards the floor but between your hands. Use your upper body and abdominals to bring you back up to the starting position. Repeat as many times as you can.

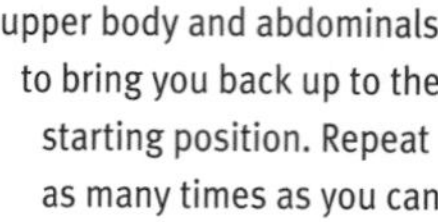

62

Check these out

www.webmd.com/fitness-exercise/guide/fitness-beginners-guide
A beginner's guide to exercise.
www.mayoclinic.com/health/fitness/HQ01543
Tips for staying motivated.
www.webmd.com/fitness-exercise/how-to-stay-active
How to stay active.

Do this...

- ✓ Make time for fitness: Schedule workouts in your calendar. Make exercise an 'appointment' that you must keep. Take 10–15 minutes of computer or sitting breaks. Stand on one foot, stretch or walk in place.
- ✓ Vary your workouts and make them fun and enjoyable. Identify three things you like to do and create a rotation schedule.
- ✓ Start exercise off with low- or moderate-intensity activities. Test yourself: can you talk or sing while doing the activity?
- ✓ Make rest and exercise a routine for health and fun.

...Not this

- ✗ Assume you will find some time to exercise; be inactive or sit by your TV or computer for more than two hours at a time.
- ✗ Get into an activity rut, doing the same things at the same times. You might become bored and give up.
- ✗ Do too much, too fast, too soon. Can't talk? Panting? In pain? Slow down!
- ✗ Exercise just to lose weight.

63

Household props

You may not know it yet, but there are already some useful props for stretching in your home. Consider the following:

Use a bed or desk as a simple prop to do stretches.

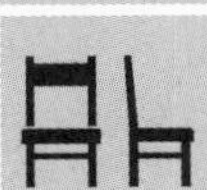

Use a chair or bench for stability to do dips.

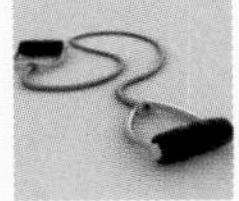

Use resistance bands to help stretch and build strength and flexibility.

64

Simple core strengthener

This exercise can be done anywhere, anytime, so no excuses!

1 Bring your belly button back in towards your spine.
2 Hold this position for 5 to 10 seconds, then relax and repeat several times. Breathe normally and do not hold your breath while you are holding the position.
3 Repeat.

66

Beyond the home

It is most important that you find something that you really enjoy, because you will be more likely to stick to it. Exercising with others outside of the home can be motivational – taking up a team sport makes you accountable for showing up and adds a new social element to your life. Consider giving ballroom dancing or Zumba a try, or simply walk with a friend.

65

Keep a record

Logging the date, time and type of exercise is a great idea. Making others aware of this new venture is also a great motivator – report to your chosen friend or family member every day. Hopefully they will be super-supportive and be a source of encouragement.

Out and about: Shopping

Shopping for health and flavour

A grocery shop or market may seem like a maze, but with a good plan and a strategy you can save money while buying healthy and delicious food.

Where you shop and your shopping style will influence what you purchase and how much money and time you spend at the market. There are many types of food markets. Which do you frequent, and is your choice down to convenience or preference?

Convenience shops are plentiful but have a limited selection of snacks, pre-prepared items and a few staples, usually at high prices. **Grocery shops** are larger and tend to cater to local community preferences, but may also carry some high prices. Some of these may be **ethnic shops** that specialize in particular foods. **Butchers, bakeries** and **fish markets** specialize in specific food items. **Farmers' markets** provide an array of locally produced fruits, vegetables and other foods and trinkets, and support local economies. There is an increase in **gourmet food shops** that sell speciality and ethnic items, and charge prices that reflect their upmarket nature. Then of course there are **supermarkets,** large chain stores stocking thousands of food products and household supplies. Recently there has been an increase in **wholesale markets**, where you become a member and shop for food in bulk.

Know your habits

You likely shop in several types of shops and switch between being a peripheral and a weaver type of shopper (see opposite). The key is to determine the strengths and pitfalls in your shopping style so that you can maximize your time and money while purchasing healthy foods you like and will eat.

If you prefer fresh fruits and vegetables and have time, shopping daily or several times a week can be pleasant and rewarding, especially if you can walk to the market.

However, if you are short on time, find healthy alternatives that allow you to shop less frequently. Frozen vegetables and fruits may be a more practical solution for you. Fresh and minimally processed foods are regarded as 'more natural' and contain fewer secondary ingredients and additives. However, the term 'processed' covers a broad range of items from a bag of pre-cut carrots to a loaf of bread to a frozen TV dinner. In general, the more processed a food is, the longer it may last. But compared to the fresh counterpart it will have more added ingredients and may cost more, although it may not appear that way. Think of a bag of frozen boiled potatoes, a box of dried mashed potato mix or a bag of crisps. How much 'potato' was used to make those products, and how much does that cost compared to one potato?

None left? Is the pencil and notepad shopping list on your refrigerator or pantry door? Write it down before you forget.

Do this...

- ✓ Check out the layout of the shop or supermarket before you start shopping. Review what you need and 'map out' your travel pattern for the shortest route to each section from where you need food.
- ✓ Shop after eating, so you can make decisions with your head and not your stomach!

...Not this

- ✗ Walk into the shop without 'mapping out' the organization and sections of the market. You are more likely to spend more time shopping and purchase things you do not need.
- ✗ Shop when hungry and veer towards high-calorie foods with low nutritional value. You will also be at your most vulnerable to supermarket marketing ploys (see pages 66–67).

67 Five money-saving tips

1. Create a shopping list based on staple foods and recipes for the week ahead.
2. Substitute items with in-store sales. Sometimes frozen or tinned fruits or vegetables cost less.
3. Only buy in bulk if it is something you use frequently or does not spoil quickly.
4. Do not buy it just because you have a coupon.
5. Do you have a friend who grows their own veggies? Consider bartering or trading food, or join a cooperative.

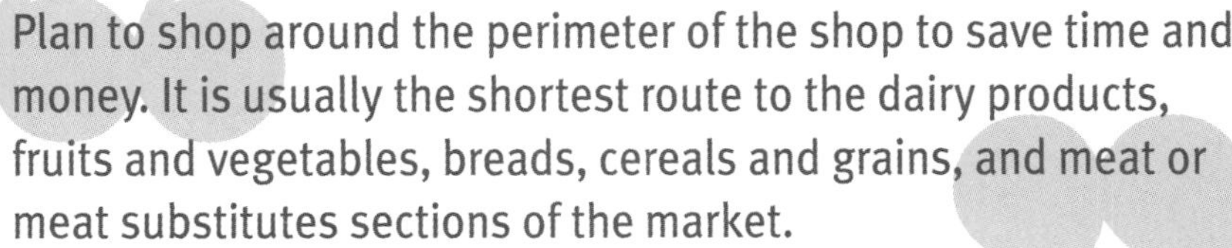

> Plan to shop around the perimeter of the shop to save time and money. It is usually the shortest route to the dairy products, fruits and vegetables, breads, cereals and grains, and meat or meat substitutes sections of the market.
>
> Dr Claudia Sealey-Potts, Registered Dietitian/Nutritionist

68 Don't lose money on food waste

Three easy ways you can 'lose money' on food. Imagine that on Tuesday you:

1. Buy a £2 cup of coffee at work. It sits on your office desk. At the end of the day you discard the leftover half. You threw away 50%, or £1 of your money.
2. Discard one third of a 4.5 kg (10 lb) bag of potatoes for which you paid £3 due to spoilage. You threw away 30%, or £1 of your money.
3. Buy 900 g (2 lb) of fish for dinner for five that cost £10. After dinner you notice you are discarding about 275 g (10 oz), an average waste of about 50 g (2 oz) per person. You threw away 32%, or £3.20.

That equates to a food waste loss of about £5.20 for the day. An average waste of that amount per day equals £1898 per year.

69 Which type of supermarket shopper are you?

Peripheral shopper

'I hate doing this, am running through the major areas so get out of my way, I'm out of here.' You run into the shop, grab the items you think you need, and rush out. On the 'pro' side, you may -shop faster than most other people and spend less time at the supermarket, but are you sure you are spending money effectively and selecting the best products for your needs?

Weaver shopper

'La de da, this is something that I can do for days and will take my time to complete.' You weave through all the aisles and take time to look at many products and labels. On the 'pro' side, you may be taking time to compare information regarding price, ingredients and nutritional value. But are you buying unnecessary items and spending money on foods or things you really do not need or will not completely use?

Shopping for Meat, fish and other proteins

Whether you are a meat eater or a vegetarian, protein is an important nutrient, and there are ways you can get the most for your money when buying this dietary staple.

Fish provides both high-quality protein and healthy fats.

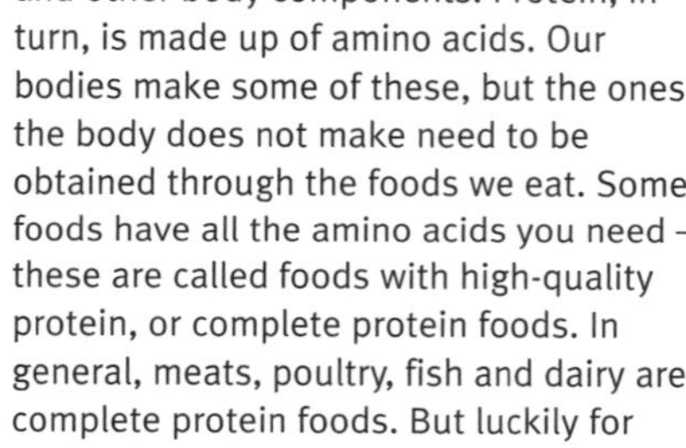

What are meat and meat substitutes, and why are they important? The human body needs protein to grow and repair tissues and other body components. Protein, in turn, is made up of amino acids. Our bodies make some of these, but the ones the body does not make need to be obtained through the foods we eat. Some foods have all the amino acids you need – these are called foods with high-quality protein, or complete protein foods. In general, meats, poultry, fish and dairy are complete protein foods. But luckily for vegetarians, there are also some plant-based foods that are complete protein foods. In addition, even if some foods are not complete proteins, by combining the foods wisely you can obtain all the complete proteins you need.

Eggs	Meats	Poultry
Eggs are the ultimate versatile food! Although you can get chicken, duck and quail eggs, you probably only buy hens' eggs. Buy eggs to eat as part of any quick meal or snack and in cooked or baked foods. Keep a couple of hard-boiled eggs in the refrigerator for a quick snack or as part of a meal, as in chopped in a main salad or a salad sandwich.	Although meats from sources such as pork or beef are high-quality proteins, they also contain fat. In some cases, they might even contain more calories from fat than they do from protein! So, when shopping, look for lean cuts of meat. This includes cuts such as rump, top rump, fillet, topside, silverside and skirt. For pork, this includes tenderloin, loin chops and cuts from the shoulder and leg; and for lamb, lamb shanks or loin chops.	Chicken, turkey, duck and goose are among the foods classified as poultry. You probably buy chicken and turkey most often. Keep it nutritious by removing the skin, which contains most of the fat. Turkey or chicken breast or drumsticks (without skin) are top poultry choices if you want protein and less saturated fat. But remember, a key for any poultry cut is to avoid or limit the skin, and to bake it instead of frying it.

Leaner meat

Look at the meat in the supermarket. Does it contain a lot of visible fat? Can you cut it out prior to cooking to cut back on fat? How much meat will be left?

Before you buy meat check for marbling (see right). That is the white fat globules or lakes of fat between the meat. It will help make the meat tender but add lots of fat to your diet. Skip the buy if there is a lot of marbling.

Lean cuts of meat need to be cooked correctly – avoid high heat or overcooking, which will make the meat tough. Cook using moist methods such as in stews.

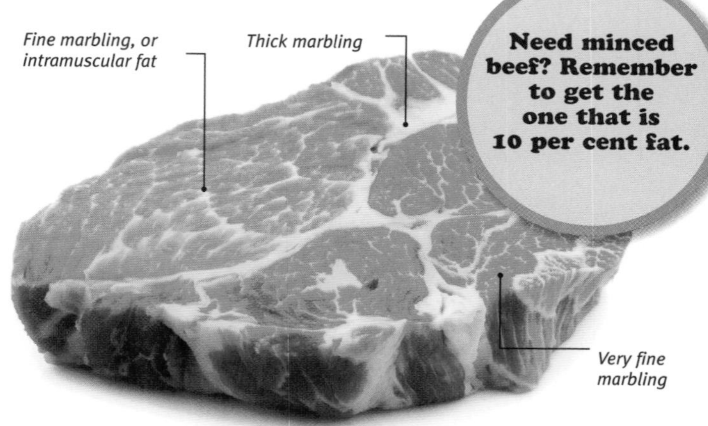

Need minced beef? Remember to get the one that is 10 per cent fat.

71

Buying fish?

Get a variety of both fatty and lean fish. Fatty fish such as salmon will give you some omega-3 oil, and lean fish, such as haddock, cod or grouper, will be lower in fat.

Do this...

✓ Buy high-protein, high-satiety snacks such as roasted soya beans or low-fat cheese sticks.

✓ Use two thirds creamy or coarse-ground mustard and one-third light mayo in your egg salad.

...Not this

✗ Buy bags of crisps or sweets for snacks.

✗ Use only regular mayonnaise in your egg salad.

Fish and seafood	Dairy	Vegetarian options	Nuts and seeds
When buying farmed fish and seafood, try species such as bass, tilapia, trout, clams, mussels and scallops. Other fish to buy are Pacific cod, Atlantic herring or sardines, wild pollock, wild salmon and albacore tuna. If you like fish and buy and eat it regularly but vary it to get a range of nutrients, avoid species that are overfished.	Dairy products are a source of both high-quality protein and also calcium, so purchase these often. This allows you to double-dip your money for two major nutrients from one food group. Buy the best options: reduced-fat milk, fat-free yogurt (especially Greek-style yogurt), Cheddar and low-fat cottage cheese.	If you are a vegan (see pages 102–103), beans – especially edamame – or soya products such as tofu and soya milk are important foods to buy. Shop for staples such as dried and tinned beans and nuts. Some grains, such as quinoa and buckwheat, can be important contributors to your daily protein intake. If you are a lacto-vegetarian or a lacto-ovo-vegetarian (eat dairy or eggs and dairy), these foods will provide high-quality protein, too.	Soya beans, pumpkin seeds, peanuts, almonds, pistachios and sunflower seeds are among the nuts and seeds highest in protein, so get these when buying high-protein snacks. However, watch the portion sizes as they are high in calories.

With so many varieties to choose from, it's always possible to find a low-fat cheese that's big on flavour.

PROTEIN COUNTER

Boiled beans | 1 cup | Protein

Lentils | 8 g

Chickpeas | 14 g

Pinto beans | 15 g

Black beans | 15 g

Haricot beans | 15 g

Pink beans | 15 g

Black-eyed peas | 16 g

White beans | 17 g

Soya beans | 22 g

72

Ditch fat for protein

If used correctly, yogurt can be a versatile, low-fat source of protein. Try these two ideas for tasty treats:

• Instead of soured cream, buy Greek yogurt for a dip base. If you want a thicker spread, first strain the yogurt in a coffee filter for a few hours, before adding your seasonings.

• Mix cold vanilla-flavoured yogurt and fruit juice in a tightly sealed container and shake. Increase protein by adding 1 tablespoon powdered skimmed milk.

73

Milky alternatives

Can't drink milk because of its side-effects? Buy the following:

• Low-lactose or lactose-free milks

• Aged cheeses

• Yogurts with no added milk or cream

All beans are good, so just buy the ones you like most whenever they are on sale. Use them for 'Meatless Mondays'.

Shopping for Vegetables

'Eat your vegetables'. You might have heard it from your Mum. Well, her advice was wise. Start by buying smart!

Save your vitamin C: Wrap fresh washed cauliflower, broccoli, or sugar snap or green beans in plastic wrap and place in the microwave for 3–4 minutes. This quick, waterless cooking technique will help preserve the vitamin C in the vegetables.

Vegetables are naturally low in calories and high in essential nutrients. All vegetables contain some amount of potassium, folate, vitamin A and vitamin C as well as compounds called phytonutrients. These compounds help keep your body working properly and many are antioxidants. Eating more vegetables as part of a healthy diet will not only help you control weight but also promote optimal health and help prevent serious health problems such as heart disease, type 2 diabetes, certain cancers and high blood pressure. Due to their high water and fibre content, vegetables are a great choice for filling you up on fewer calories.

The usual recommendation for vegetables is about 5 servings per day. It sounds like a lot, but it's easier than you think. If you have a large salad at lunch with a cup of a vegetable or tomato soup, and a cup of mixed vegetables and side salad at dinner, you can meet your daily recommendation.

You may wonder if it's better to eat vegetables fresh or cooked. In fact, all fresh, frozen, dried and tinned vegetables contain similar amounts of fibre and minerals, and cooking or drying vegetables does not destroy them. Vitamins that dissolve in fats, including vitamins A and E, are actually more concentrated in processed fruits and vegetables because the mild heat treatment makes the nutrients more available to your body. Cooking carrots or tomatoes can increase the level of phytonutrients available. On the other hand, heat used during the canning process – or the cooking of raw vegetables in water – can reduce the amount of B and C vitamins.

74

Perfectly tossed salad

Place all of your salad ingredients in a clean, unused plastic bag. Add a small amount of your favourite dressing. Toss around, and put in a bowl.

For a low-calorie dressing on fresh greens or cooked veggies, drizzle with a flavoured vinegar.

"A great way to eat your veggies is to roast them, which takes away some of the bitterness. Add a dab of olive oil and seasoning."

Chelsey Millstone, Instructor and Nutrition Counsellor

75

The right quality for the right use saves money

The nutritional value of vegetables will not vary hugely across brand and grade, but the shape, uniformity of colour and size will. If you are making pea soup, buy the less-expensive can or frozen bag of peas. Looks won't matter in a puréed bowl. Making a salad with peas as a centrepiece? Get the fancier ones, where shape, colour and uniform size will make for a beautiful dish.

76

Create a vegetable rainbow

A good way to eat more vegetables is to eat a variety of coloured vegetables. Different colours of vegetables provide different natural phytonutrients that are good for your body and health. Choose vegetables that are green (such as dark leafy greens, broccoli, green pepper, green peas and green beans), red (such as tomato, red pepper and beetroot), orange/yellow (carrot, yellow pepper, pumpkin, squash, corn, sweet potato and yam), purple/blue (aubergine and red cabbage), and white (potato, cauliflower, onion and turnips) to get a wide range and amount of phytonutrients.

77

Stock up your freezer

Many frozen vegetables are a great option because they can be found in their natural form in the freezer section of the supermarket. The advanced processing techniques used today minimize the exposure to time and temperature and prevent the loss of nutrients. Frozen vegetables are picked at the ideal time of peak ripeness and then quickly flash-frozen to prevent spoilage and preserve nutrients.

78

In praise of the potato

A popular dieting trend has been to 'avoid white things', including potatoes. While this may be a good principle for some foods, potatoes have nutritional value to offer for a relatively low number of calories and cost. Don't skip this economical and nutritious vegetable. Just include the skin and go easy with or skip toppings such as butter, soured cream and bacon.

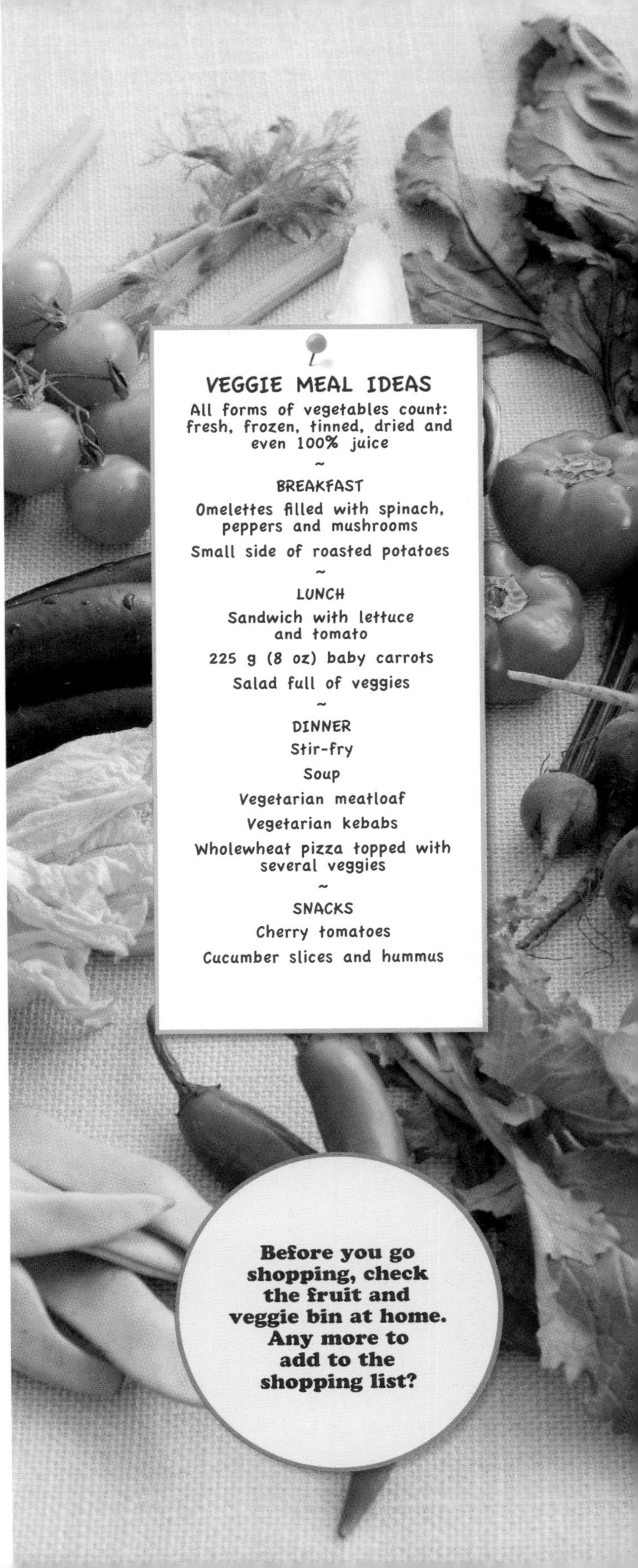

VEGGIE MEAL IDEAS

All forms of vegetables count: fresh, frozen, tinned, dried and even 100% juice

~

BREAKFAST

Omelettes filled with spinach, peppers and mushrooms

Small side of roasted potatoes

~

LUNCH

Sandwich with lettuce and tomato

225 g (8 oz) baby carrots

Salad full of veggies

~

DINNER

Stir-fry

Soup

Vegetarian meatloaf

Vegetarian kebabs

Wholewheat pizza topped with several veggies

~

SNACKS

Cherry tomatoes

Cucumber slices and hummus

Before you go shopping, check the fruit and veggie bin at home. Any more to add to the shopping list?

Shopping for Fruit

Fruits are as important as vegetables. So Mum's advice to eat more vegetables also applies to eating more fruit. You can buy and enjoy fruit in many forms.

Like vegetables, fruits are full of essential nutrients including vitamins, minerals, fibre, phytonutrients and water. Fruit can help you maintain a healthy weight and reduce the risk of chronic diseases. Some people avoid fruit because it contains natural sugar. While the whole fruit is recommended over juices, natural sugar in whole fruit or 100% fruit juice is different from added sugars as it is accompanied by other health-promoting nutrients including fibre, vitamins, minerals and phytonutrients.

The usual recommendation for fruits is about 4 servings (450 g/1 lb) each day. Together with vegetables, that's 9 servings per day. An easy way to meet this goal is to try to fill one half of your plate with vegetables and fruits.

When adding more fruits in your daily diet, try to buy them according to what's in season. This will help lower their cost and ensure peak flavour.

Spring: Apricots, pineapples and strawberries.
Summer: Berries, cherries, grapes, peaches, plums and watermelons.
Fall: Apples and pears.
Winter: Clementines, dates, grapefruit, kiwi, oranges and tangerines.

Many fruits are available throughout the year, but the price will vary based on availability, and although quantity is important, eating a variety of fruits can better contribute to good health. Different fruits offer different nutrients, and eating a range will keep your tastebuds interested.

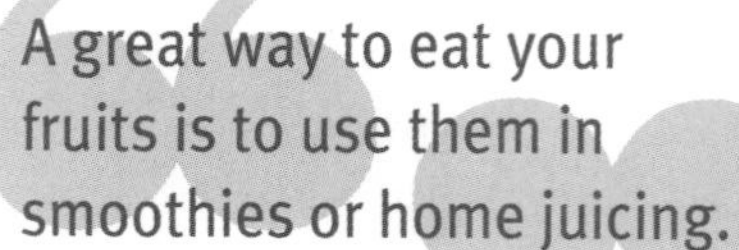

A great way to eat your fruits is to use them in smoothies or home juicing.

Jenna Braddock, Consultant and Sports Dietitian, University of North Florida

In the fridge immediately:
Oranges, lemons, pineapples, berries, cherries, watermelons

OK on the worktop:
Bananas, cantaloupes, honeydews, pears, peaches, plums. (Refrigerate them if cut or they start to overripen and you do not plan to use them immediately.)

79

Frozen and tinned options

Many fruits can be found in their natural form, without added sugar or syrup, in the frozen food section of a grocery shop. Frozen foods have been picked at the peak of ripeness and flash-frozen to preserve nutrients.

Some tinned fruit may have added sugar, in which case, drain and rinse the fruit to reduce sugar content, or choose fruit packed in water or 100% juice.

80

Create a fruit rainbow

Try to eat all the different colours of fruits to help create variety. Green is green grapes, kiwi, honeydew melon and lime. Red is red grapes, cherries, cranberries, strawberries and watermelon. Orange/yellow is apricot, cantaloupe, mango, orange, peach and pineapple. Purple/blue is blackberries, blueberries, plums, and purple grapes. White is bananas, pears and apples.

81

Bought too many?

Fresh fruit should never go to waste. If you think you've got more than you can eat, think ahead and take action to maximize your shopping:

Peel, cut into slices, wrap in plastic wrap and freeze for a cooling treat.

Purée and mix with softened ice cream or yogurt. Put in the freezer and use later as a snack or dessert.

Make your own high-phytonutrient ice pops by half-filling a paper cup with grape, cranberry, pomegranate or blueberry juice and sticking in a popsicle stick. Freeze and enjoy!

82

Once bought, store wisely

General rule: Use before the 'use by' date on the packet if one is included.

Fresh Use within a few days.

Frozen Store at -17°C (0°F) or less and use within six months.

Tinned Store at room temperature – most tinned foods have a shelf life of two years.

Dried Store in a cool dry place – most will last from four months to a year.

FRUITY MEAL ENHANCERS

There is a variety of ways you can enjoy fruit any time of the year by using fresh, frozen, tinned or dried fruit, or 100% juice.

~

AT BREAKFAST

Top cereal or porridge with slices of bananas or peaches

Top pancakes with fresh berries

Drink a glass of 100% fruit juice

~

AT LUNCH

Eat fresh fruit for dessert

~

AT DINNER

Include orange sections or strawberries in a tossed salad

Add fruit like pineapple or peaches to kebabs

Add fruit to some meat dishes, like stir-fry chicken with pineapples or lamb tagine with prunes

Have fruit salad or poached apple or pear

~

AT SNACK TIME

Keep dried fruit in your work desk or bag

Mix fresh fruit with plain fat-free or low-fat yogurt

Fruity fish
Fruit, especially citrus, can enhance the flavour – and appearance – of fish. Try slices or wedges of pineapple, lime or orange in a prawn salad, or a lime-orange sauce drizzled over fish.

Do this...

✓ Choose whole fruits over fruit juices. This is the best way to enjoy their flavour and nutrients for the lowest amount of calories.

✓ Read the ingredients on juice cartons.

...Not this

✘ Drink cartons of fruit juice instead of eating whole fruits. When fruits are juiced, the fibre is removed, leaving sweet juice. It also takes a lot of whole fruit to produce a single serving of juice. This means that the calories in juice could be double or triple the amount in a single serving of whole fruit.

✘ Assume all fruit juice is healthy. Some blends contain concentrates, sugar, colour and flavouring.

83

Stock up on dried fruit when on sale

Add raisins and/or unsweetened dried fruit to cereal, baked goods and some meat or poultry dishes. Mix with peanut butter for your sandwich or have alone as a healthy snack.

Superfoods

Superfoods have exceptional nutritional qualities that both promote good health and help prevent disease. Here, we look at a handful of superfoods found in every grocery shop, and a few more unusual ones.

To avoid smelly garlic breath, chew fresh parsley, which neutralizes garlic odour – and is another superfood.

Garlic

What and why: Garlic is a bulb in the allium family, made up of a number of individual 'cloves'. Antibacterial, antifungal, antiviral and an excellent general tonic, garlic is considered the king of the superfoods and has been found to be effective against a wide range of degenerative and infectious diseases, from cancer to the common cold.

How: Garlic is used as a flavouring in traditional cuisines around the world. It's most efficacious in its raw state, however, and even more so when it's crushed, chopped or chewed to activate the sulphur compound allicin. The one downside to garlic is that it's famously antisocial, the odour lingering long and noticeably on the breath. Look out for fermented black garlic, which has no pungent odour but twice the antioxidants of white garlic and a more mellow flavour.

As well as providing super nutrients, Romanesco cauliflower looks super, too.

Cruciferous vegetables

What and why: Broccoli, kale, cabbage, cauliflower, Brussels sprouts, pak choi, rocket, watercress. Crucifers contain antioxidants, which protect healthy cells from damage caused by free radicals (toxic molecules), and are therefore associated with preventing the development of cancers and heart disease as well as other diseases linked to oxidative stress, such as diabetes, rheumatoid arthritis and Alzheimer's. Each crucifer also has many other benefits—for example, kale is a rich source of iron, calcium, vitamin K (essential for blood-clotting and wound-healing) and lutein, which promotes eye health.

How: Cooking destroys valuable nutrients, so eat raw or do no more than lightly steam these invaluable veggies. It's important to chew thoroughly, as this helps form glucosinolates, the anticancer compounds. If you have a powerful blender, you can join the Green Smoothie movement – raw kale is especially good for this, blended with fruit such as orange, banana or mango. The blender does all the chewing for you!

Eat apples with the skin on to benefit from all the nutrients.

Apple

What and why: An apple is a fruit – old-fashioned, pure and simple. There's an old saying that an apple a day keeps the doctor away, and this still holds true. Apples contain pectin, which helps stabilize cholesterol levels and also binds to heavy metals such as lead and removes them from the body, which is helpful in our polluted modern environment. Apples also aid digestion and are therefore ideal accompaniments to fatty foods such as cheese or rich meats.

How: Choose organic apples where possible (or at least rinse non-organic apples), so that you can safely eat the skin, and eat them raw. It's best to eat an apple whole, chewing it well, but if you have digestive problems, grate it and eat it immediately. Apple juice is delicious but deprives you of the pectin-rich fibre.

4

Oily fish

What and why: Mackerel, salmon, tuna, herring, anchovies, sardines. Whereas the oil in white-fleshed fish is concentrated in the liver, with oily fish it's distributed throughout, making the omega-3 fatty acids readily available in their natural form. Omega-3 is essential for heart health and for brain and immune system function. Oily fish are also a good source of vitamin D, the 'sunshine' vitamin, essential for maintaining strong, healthy bones and for muscle function.

How: Oily fish is available fresh or tinned, so it's very easy to consume the optimum three servings a week without getting bored – a pan-fried salmon steak, baked mackerel stuffed with herbs and a tinned tuna salad, and you're there.

Salmon is among the best sources of Vitamin D.

Continued next page

5 Seeds

What and why: Pumpkin, sunflower, sesame, flax, chia. An excellent source of protein and plant-based omega-3 fatty acids, seeds provide many other nutrients – they are, after all, literally the seed of a new plant – including important minerals such as magnesium, manganese, potassium, zinc and copper. Seeds are anti-inflammatory and antioxidant and assist in hormone balance. Flax and chia seeds become mucilaginous when soaked in water and are excellent for maintaining a healthy digestive tract. Pumpkin-seed butter makes a good alternative to butter, and sunflower lecithin is a GMO-free alternative to soya lecithin as a nutritional supplement.

How: Pumpkin and sunflower seeds are an instant snack, but the nutrients are more bio-available if the seeds are first soaked in water and then dried in a very low oven. Sesame seeds are tiny, so sprinkle them on salads or oatmeal or make hummus or dressings from tahini. Unsoaked flax and chia seeds can also be sprinkled, but because they are so mucilaginous it's essential to drink plenty of water.

6 Avocado

What and why: Avocado is a fruit that's more usually used in a savoury context than a sweet one. Anti-inflammatory and antioxidant, avocado is a good source of heart-healthy monounsaturated fat, promotes absorption of nutrients and contains generous levels of fibre, potassium and B vitamins.

How: Avocados are the ultimate healthy fast food – simply halve lengthwise and season with a little sea salt and freshly ground black pepper; blend into a guacamole dip; or crush onto crispbread and sprinkle with sunflower seeds. To make an instant superfood 'ice cream', blend avocado with frozen apple slices; no sweetener required.

Use mashed avocado in place of mayo or butter in sandwiches.

New superfoods on the block

'New' superfoods are introduced on a regular basis, although usually their usefulness has been known to the local population for centuries. Those listed below are currently enjoying a high profile.

Name	Origin	What and why	How
Quinoa (keen-wah)	Andes	Tiny pseudo-cereal grain; contains all nine essential amino acids; gluten-free	Serve as a side instead of rice; add to soups; cool and use in salads
Goji berries	Himalayas	Bright red dried berries; contain B and E vitamins, minerals and carotenoids	Mix with pumpkin seeds for an instant snack or whizz them in smoothies and desserts
Moringa	Africa, Asia	Powdered leaves of the Moringa oleifera tree; high-protein, low-fat, and carbohydrate; rich source of vitamins and minerals	Blend into green smoothies or add to water or juice
Cacao powder	Amazon	Seed of Theobroma cacao ('cacao, the food of the gods'); good source of minerals, fibre and essential fatty acids; stimulates endorphin release	For optimal health benefits, add raw cacao powder to smoothies and raw desserts

Goji berries are a quick and convenient snack food.

Shopping for Fats and sweets

We all eat fats and sugars. The key is knowing which ones to buy, which ones to consume and how much.

Fat-free, sugar-free, natural, or organic does not mean low-calorie. Read the label for calories per serving.

Do this...

✓ Buy foods with zero trans fat.

✓ Buy foods with zero saturated fat.

...Not this

✗ Buy foods that have more than 1 gram of trans fat.

✗ Buy foods that have more than 5 g of saturated fat per serving (try to eat less than about 20 g in total per day).

Fats are bad! Sugar is bad! But we all eat them. How can we buy and eat them wisely?

Types of fat

There are visible fats and invisible fats. **Visible fats** include butter, margarine, oils, lard, hydrogenated fats and cream cheese. **Invisible fats** are already in the foods you eat, so it is hard to know how much you are eating or to know if it is a healthy or an unhealthy fat. Common sources of invisible fats are whole milk, cheese, cakes, biscuits, flaky pastries, some breads, pie crusts, cakes, pancake or waffle mixes, fried foods, doughnuts, some sweets, chocolates, crisps, packaged popcorn or frozen foods.

From a chemical and nutrition perspective, monounsaturated fats have one double-bonded (unsaturated) carbon in the molecule. Polyunsaturated fats have more than one double-bonded carbon in the molecule. Both fats (which are actually oils) can help reduce bad cholesterol levels and risk for heart disease. Although all these fats have about the same number of calories, some are more important in health promotion (monounsaturated and polyunsaturated fats) than others (saturated fats, hydrogenated fats, lard and trans fats). So it is important to read the ingredients label to know what type of fat is in the food, and to read the nutrition label to know how much you are getting in a serving.

Sugar and other sweeteners

Most people buy **granulated sugar**, which is sucrose. Did you know that icing sugar is the same thing, just more finely ground? **Brown sugar** tends to contain more molasses than granulated sugar, but that does not mean it is less refined. In some cases, the granulated sugar (made by removing the top layer of molasses) has had molasses re-sprayed onto granulated sugar to make brown sugar. **High-fructose corn syrup**, or corn syrup, is used in many commercial foods. **Honey** is made by bees, and is essentially a mixture of sugars such as dextrose, levulose, fructose and sucrose in a water solution. (Notice that chemically most sugars end in 'ose'? Look for that on the label.) Some people prefer honey over granulated sugar because it is made 'by nature'.

Sugar substitutes include aspartame, saccharin, stevia and sucralose. In commercial food processing, any one or any combination of these may be used. Other products may also be added (such as fibre) to provide some of the textural qualities found in sugar and needed in the food when a sugar substitute is used.

Fat and sugar provide flavour and important characteristics to food, such as browning or texture. But we tend to eat too much of both. So, by finding ways to cut, not totally eliminate, fat and sugar, you can enjoy their benefits in moderation.

Sweet nothings

Don't assume that brown sugar is healthier than white – both types are in fact very similar and have little nutritional value.

Granulated, the popular refined sugar—16 calories per tsp

Brown has a more robust flavour than granulated sugar due to the small amount of molasses – 17 calories per tsp.

A convenient form of packing and serving sugar, a sugar cube is equal to a teaspoon measure.

What are omega-3 and omega-6?

Omega-3 and omega-6 are polyunsaturated essential fatty acids. In the body, omega-3 fatty acids are converted to important substances called EPA and DHA. Omega-3 fatty acids are found in cold-water fish such as salmon, sardines, herring and mackerel. Walnuts and flaxseeds also contain EPA and DHA.

Vegetable or rapeseed?

If the label says 'vegetable oil', it is usually a combination of different oils. Although vegetable oil will cost less and can be used interchangeably with rapeseed oil in recipes, buy the rapeseed oil, which contains more omega-6 and omega-3, healthy fatty acids.

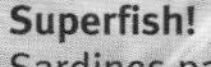

Superfish!
Sardines pack small in a tin but are big nutritionally. They are a source of high-quality protein, healthy fats, calcium, vitamin D and other nutrients. If tinned, favour those packed in olive oil.

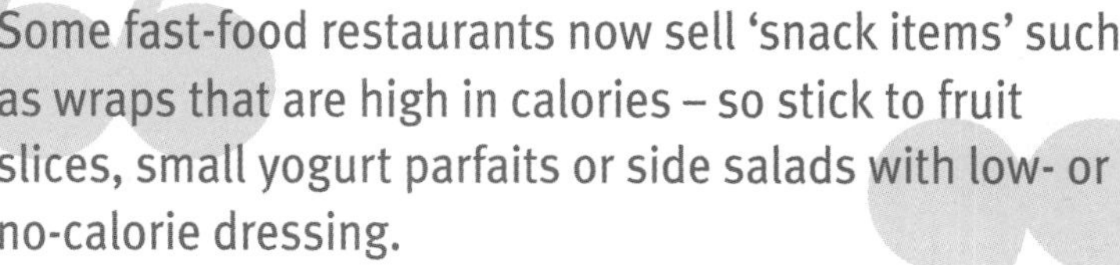

> Some fast-food restaurants now sell 'snack items' such as wraps that are high in calories – so stick to fruit slices, small yogurt parfaits or side salads with low- or no-calorie dressing.
>
> Dr Judith Rodriguez, Professor and Registered Dietitian, University of North Florida

5 easy ways to cut fats not flavour

1 Mix mashed cauliflower and chicken stock with your mashed potatoes, not butter.

2 Use apple sauce and cinnamon or mashed bananas in your cake or muffin recipe instead of oil.

3 Use two egg whites instead of one egg for baking or your omelette recipe.

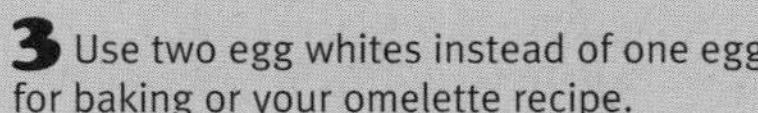

4 Use fat-free chicken, vegetable or beef stock for your rice instead of water and oil.

5 Chill your soup or stew, then remove the fat layer on top before reheating and serving.

5 easy ways to cut sugar not flavour

1 Add a dash of lemon or lime, or a slice of fruit to cold sparkling water and enjoy in place of soda or fruit punch.

2 Top pancakes, waffles or cereal with flavoured yogurt or apple sauce.

3 Replace one third of the sugar in recipes with sugar substitute.

4 Use ricotta cheese with flavoured extract, or chopped or puréed fruit as your filling instead of jam.

5 Top a cake with an array of naturally sweet, naturally colourful fruit rather than sugary frosting.

88

Read all those labels!

The Ingredients List will inform you of the ingredients in descending order, by weight, if there is more than one ingredient. The Nutrition Facts panel provides information about the caloric value and nutrients in a serving of the food. For the true picture of the healthiness of the food you are buying, you will need to consult both lists. For example, sometimes manufacturers use a combination of sugars, so while 'sugar' may not be listed as the first or top ingredient on a label, the cumulative use of these sugars will make the product high in sugars overall, in which case you'd be better informed by also looking at the Nutrition Facts label (see right).

Very important! If you eat more than the specified serving remember that you are getting more than is listed below.

Avoid foods with anything other than zero trans fats.

Nutrition Facts

Serving Size 1Tbsp (14g)

Amount Per Serving	
Calories 80	Calories from Fat 80
	% Daily Values*
Total Fat 8g	**12%**
Saturated Fat 2.5g	**13%**
Trans Fat 0g	
Polyunsaturated Fat 3g	
Monounsaturated Fat 2.5g	
Cholesterol 0mg	**0%**
Sodium 85mg	**4%**
Total Carbohydrate 0g	**0%**
Dietary Fiber 0g	**0%**
Sugars 0g	
Protein 0g	**0%**

Vitamin A 15%	Vitamin D 15%
Vitamin E 15%	Vitamin B6 35%
Vitamin B12 20%	

*Percent Daily Values are based on a 2,000 calorie diet. Your Daily Values may be higher or lower depending on your calorie needs.

	Calories	2,000	2,500
Total Fat	Less than	65g	80g
Sat Fat	Less than	20g	25g
Cholesterol	Less than	300mg	300mg
Sodium	Less than	2400mg	2400mg
Total Carbohydrate		300g	375g
Dietary Fiber		25g	30g

Select foods that are a good source of fibre, 2.5–4.9 g per serving.

Look for high vitamin values (20% or above for at least one vitamin). Avoid foods with values of 5% or under, as these are considered to be low in vitamins.

89

Avoid saturated fats

Avoid fats that have cholesterol (from animal sources) or saturated fats, which may be naturally occurring or the result of processing. These include:

- ✗ Butter
- ✗ Coconut oil
- ✗ Hard margarine
- ✗ Hydrogenated fat (vegetable shortening)
- ✗ Lard
- ✗ Palm oil

Shop for healthy fats

Monounsaturated fats, buy:	Polyunsaturated fats, buy:
Canola oil	Corn oil
Olive oil	Soya bean oil
Peanut oil	Safflower oil
Sunflower oil	
Sesame oil	

90

Make your own healthy spread

Don't want to give up the taste of butter? Mix one-third butter and two thirds rapeseed oil. Put in the fridge and use (sparingly) as your soft spread.

91

Beware of 'sugar-free'

Small sweets or other products labelled 'sugar-free' commonly have sugar substitutes known as sugar alcohols (which do not contain alcohol) and include erythritol, glycerol, isomalt, lactitol, maltitol, mannitol, sorbitol and xylitol. Be careful – they are not calorie-free, and eaten in large quantities may act as a laxative.

92

Lower in calories? Not really...

Honey is in a water solution so it is more concentrated. That's why it tastes better than sugar. You are getting more 'sugar' and a few micronutrients per teaspoon.

Sugar: 16 calories per tsp

Honey: 21 calories per tsp, but use less than sugar for the same sweetness and fewer calories

The difference between extra-virgin and regular olive oil is in the intensity of flavour – extra-virgin being the stronger.

Regular olive oil: 40 calories per tsp

Extra-virgin: 40 calories per tsp, but use less than regular oil for more flavour and fewer calories

93

What about plant stanols or plant sterols?

Some spreads contain plant stanols or plant sterols, which are substances found in plants. These substances are similar to cholesterol, but they work to help remove the harmful or 'bad' cholesterol from the body.

Scanning the ingredients

Read the ingredients on the label (see below) to check if the spread you are buying contains stanols or sterols. These are 'heart-healthy' fats – but still be careful with the calorie intake by watching serving sizes.

INGREDIENTS: BUTTER, **OIL BLEND (PALM FRUIT, RAPESEED, PURIFIED FISH OILS)**, WATER, CONTAINS LESS THAN 2% SALT, **PLANT STEROLS**, WHEY, SORBITAN ESTER OF VEGETABLE FATTY ACIDS, NATURAL FLAVOUR, SUNFLOWER LECITHIN, VEGETABLE MONOGLYCERIDES, VITAMIN A PALMIATE, BETA-CAROTENE COLOUR; LACTIC ACID, POTASSIUM SORBATE, TBHQ, CALCIUM DISODIUM EDTA

Add flavour with oil

Dribble a little bit of olive or sesame oil on your salad or dish just before serving, not in high-heat cooking, to maximize flavour and use.

Shopping for Snacks

The snack industry is a multi-billion dollar industry and new types of snacks are constantly introduced. By mastering a few shopping techniques, you can always figure out the best choice.

'What is the nutritional value of the food I am about to put into my body?'

Snacks can be great way to stave off hunger and fill in some nutritional gaps. For adults, eating a snack can prevent you from becoming ravenously hungry and then overeating at the next meal. For children, eating a healthy snack can add much-needed nutrition. While it is better to make your own snacks, sometimes busy schedules do not allow this. You may be out of the house and suddenly find yourself hungry. The key to buying snacks is that they should be nutritious and fulfilling so you can feel well and stay on track with your eating goals.

There are so many snack foods on the market that the choice can be overwhelming. However if you follow these simple guidelines, you will be able to make healthy snack choices whether you planned on buying snacks at the shops or you suddenly are in need of something quick to eat.

94

Look beyond the marketing

As with any snack, even supposedly healthy ones such as root vegetable crisps, hummus crackers and baked chickpeas may sound appealing but may have additional fat, salt and sugar added. As always, read the labels and favour those high in fibre with more than 20% of vitamins or iron.

95

How much is 'healthy'?

So you know to pick snacks with little processing, fat and sugar, but ones that are high in nutrients such as fibre and vitamins. But how does this translate to the amounts you see on the labels? Here are some key amounts to bear in mind to help you make quicky and healthy decisions:

Get five plastic snack packs and fill with 50 g (2 oz) dry cereal such as puffed rice and 110 g (4 oz) raisins or other dried fruit and nuts. Pack for the office midday snack.

Dr Judith Rodriguez, Professor, Nutrition and Dietetics

Calcium	20% or more is considered to be a 'rich source'
Iron	
Vitamin A	
Vitamin C	
Fibre	5 g or more considered a 'high source'
Fat	3 g or less considered 'low fat'
Sodium	140 mg or less per serving considered 'low-salt'
Sugar	Look for 'no added sugar'

96

Be sure you eat only one serving

A ready-made snack bag often contains several servings. Not being aware of the number of servings leads to overconsumption of calories. You can always eat part of it and save the rest for later. And remember: If you don't buy it at all, you won't eat it!

20 Tasty snacks under 150 calories

Medium apple
7.5 cm/3 in diameter, 182 g/6½ oz, 95 kcal

Blueberries
150 g/5 oz, 84 kcal

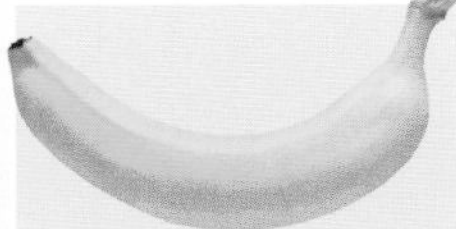

Medium banana
18 cm/7 in long, 110 g/4 oz, 105 kcal

Dried apricots
4 halves, 10 g/½ oz, 136 kcal

Raisins, seedless
25 g/1 oz (approx. 60 raisins), 85 kcal

Prunes, pitted
40 g/1½ oz (approx. 4 prunes), 91 kcal

Dried apple rings
40 g/1½ oz, (approx. 6 rings), 93 kcal

Celery
50 g/2 oz, 8 kcal

Tomatoes, cherry
75 g/3 oz, 13 kcal

Peppers
Raw, sliced, 110 g/4 oz, 29 kcal

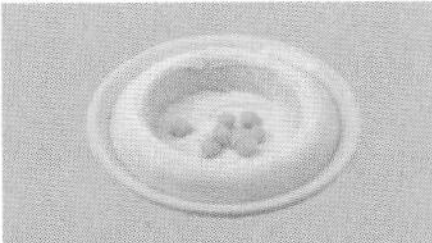

Hummus, home-prepared
3 tbsp/50 g/2 oz, 81 kcal

Chicken breast
Deli, rotisserie seasoned, sliced, prepackaged, approx. 3 slices, 25 g/1 oz, 36 kcal

Roast beef
Separable lean and fat, trimmed to 3 mm fat, all grades, 50 g/2 oz, 124 kcal

Large hardboiled egg
50 g/2 oz, 78 kcal

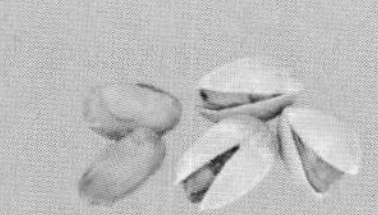

Pistachio nuts
Dry-roasted, no added salt, 10 g/½ oz (approx. 49 kernels), 121 kcal

Greek yogurt
Plain, non-fat, 175 g/6 oz, 100 kcal

Cottage cheese
Reduced fat, 2% milk fat, 110 g/4 oz, 97 kcal

Milk, low-fat
1% milk fat, 240 ml/8 fl oz, 102 kcal

Chocolate almond milk
Sweetened, ready to drink, 240 ml/8 fl oz, 120 kcal

Frozen yogurt
Strawberry, 75 g/6 oz, 80 kcal

Calorie, ingredient and nutrient content may vary by brand.
Always read the Nutrition Facts label and the Ingredients List to verify ingredients, nutrient content and calories per serving.

Calories and serving sizes

The more you know about the foods you routinely eat, the more you can tailor your choices to meet your calorie needs.

When shopping, it's helpful to know what is high and low in calories, as well as the recommended serving sizes – and weigh that up against how much you will actually eat.

Visual guides for portion estimation

Keeping the visual guidelines below in mind will help you quickly estimate how much of a food you are eating and therefore control portions and calories to be able to determine how much to purchase.

Hand measure	Equivalent	Foods
	An average-size fist = 225 g (8 oz)	Whole or cut-up fruit and vegetables, cooked beans, cooked or dry cereal, cooked pasta, rice or other grains
	Your palm = 75 g (3 oz)	Cooked meat, poultry, seafood
	A small cupped handful = 25 g (1 oz)	Nuts, seeds, dried fruit
	A large cupped handful = 50 g (2 oz)	Dry snacks, i.e. pretzels
	Your thumb (from tip to base) = 25 g (1 oz)	Cheese
	Your thumb tip (from tip to first joint) = 1 tablespoon	Peanut butter, hummus, soured cream, salad dressing
	Your fingertip (from tip to first joint) = 1 teaspoon	Butter, margarine, mayonnaise

When shopping, you'll need to look at the number of calories in certain foods and, just as important, the serving size of prepared foods. Then determine how much you are likely to eat, to get a real account of the calories you will be taking in.

Foods that are high in calories, or calorie-dense, tend to be high in fat and/or sugar:
- Casseroles
- Desserts
- Cream soups
- Certain cuts of meat or cheese, either alone or in combination with pasta, rice or another starch

Foods that tend to be low in calories, or less calorie-dense, are:
- Fruits and vegetables
- Low- or non-fat dairy products
- Whole grains

Keep your eye on the size

If buying frozen dinners, you need to look at the serving size to make sure you know how many calories you will eat. For cake mixes, you need to determine what other ingredients will be added. And some prepared items, such as salad dressings, give calories for small serving sizes, such as a tablespoon. So, always read the nutrition label for serving size and calories per serving, and make sure you know how big that serving really is.

Substitute lower-calorie items when possible. Being a calorie hunter will make you aware of places you can cut calories.

Three easy ways to cut calories from your food shop

1 Buy in small amounts or put back anything you are tempted to eat in excess.

2 Look for lower-calorie substitutes for items you usually buy and pick those instead.

3 Walk around one more time before going to the checkout and put back some of the 'naughtier' or unnecessary items.

Don't be fooled!

Look at the serving size. Imagine two 350-g (12-oz) packets of lasagne. A quick glance at 'calories' on the label shows 400 calories for Lasagne A and 500 for Lasagne B. Careful inspection shows a serving size for Lasagne A is 110 g (4 oz) but a serving size for Lasagne B is 175 g (6 oz). Lasagne B is actually lower in calories overall, and probably is a more realistic serving size.

> Love those creamy mashed sweet or white potatoes? Use undiluted evaporated low-fat milk instead of butter to decrease fat and increase calcium.

Dr Judith Rodriguez, Professor and Dietitian, University of North Florida

CALORIE COMPARISONS

Size matters:

Bagel, 7.5 cm (3 in) | **140 calories**

Bagel, 15 cm (6 in) | **350 calories**

Topping matters:

Muffin | **140 calories**

Muffin with 1 tsp each butter and jam | **249 calories**

Ingredients matter:

Baked sweet potato, mashed, 225 g (8 oz) | **114 calories**

Sweet potato casserole, 225 g (8 oz) | **236 calories**

Portion size illusion

Notice how the portions look smaller when the plate or bowl is larger. To make the illusion work in your favour and help prevent overeating, go back to your grandmother's crockery or source some vintage plates.

Be ingredient savvy

Maintaining healthy eating habits requires watchfulness and a keen sense of the types of ingredients in the foods you buy and eat.

It is not sufficient just to look at the pictures on the food packets or to assume that you are purchasing high-quality, nutritious food because it comes from a respectable shop or well-known manufacturer. With many foods consumed on the go and purchased in packaged, ready-to-eat or convenient forms, the Ingredients List is the key to making wise and healthy food choices.

Many convenience or packaged foods contain lots of ingredients that are difficult for consumers to pronounce or understand. Most of these ingredients seem to have been created in a food science lab. It is also important to note that some of the claims on packets require further investigation and can only be verified by reading the Ingredients List. One example: A food packet may claim that there is 'no trans fat'; however, if you read the ingredients list you may find that one of the ingredients listed is partially hydrogenated oil, a source of trans fat.

Resist seduction!
Grocery shopping can be overwhelming for even the most experienced shoppers, and a consumer trend toward purchasing more 'natural' foods has forced marketers to create seductive labels that have added to the confusion. With all of the marketing and advertising tactics used, it is hard to ascertain what is really inside your food. You may come across foods that are labelled 'natural', 'healthy' or 'organic' to entice you to pick the product. Always look beyond clever packaging and select truly nutritious and wholesome foods.

Preservatives
Some food ingredients are added by companies to help preserve the food items. These ingredients may help improve the taste and texture of the products. At times additional ingredients may contribute excessive intakes of calories, fat, sugar and salt, thereby making the food item less desirable as a healthy option.

'Real' fresh foods should contain no hidden ingredients. Buy as many as you will manage to eat or store before they perish.

broccoli £0.98
asparagus £1.78 — *Buy plentiful supplies for vitamins and fibre – a superfood!*
onions £1.14
apples £2.38
strawberries £2.56 — *Make the most of seasonal fruit, for variety throughout the year and top-level nutrition*
bananas £1.54
grape juice £3.22
low-fat milk £1.20
evaporated milk £0.95
Cheddar cheese £2.70 — *Nutritious – with calcium and protein – and versatile for cooking*
low-fat yogurt £0.70
chicken breasts £3.58
tin tuna £0.90
large eggs £1.30 — *A kitchen staple and a source of protein and vitamins*
tin chickpeas £0.70 — *Check no salt has been added; rinse well before using if it has*
fettuccini £2.94
parboiled rice £3.58
French bread £1.43
wholemeal bread £1.89
ice cream £3.59 — *Treats like this are packed with additives and preservatives – limit them to one per grocery shop*
crisps £1.96
biscuits £2.14
diet cola £2.39 — *Fewer calories, but beware the processed ingredients*
chewing gum £0.77
frozen peas £1.07
dry roasted peanuts £2.38 — *Healthy fats; replace with peanuts in the shell for less salt*
malt vinegar £0.95
ginger tea £1.67 — *Aids digestion. Try making your own from root ginger*
tomatoes £1.40
low-salt ham £2.98
mandarin oranges £3.58
apple crumble £3.68
mixed salad £1.75
cream soda £0.60 — *Needless sugar and calories – save money and ditch this!*
Muffins £1.50

Running order

Ingredients lists are a hands-on way to know exactly what is in the food you are planning to consume. To do so you must note that ingredients are listed on the packet in descending order of prevalence. This means that the first ingredient in the packet makes up the highest proportion of the ingredients in that food item. It is also important to note that the first three ingredients are the ones that should matter the most to you.

Do this...

✓ Use all-natural peanut butter, without added sugars and fat. In addition, natural peanut butter is often lower in sodium than the regular alternative.

...Not this

✗ Many brands of peanut butter contain added sugar and hydrogenated oils. These ingredients may change the texture of the final product, but do not have a major impact on flavour.

Quick-glance guide to additives and preservatives

Use the chart below to familiarize yourself with some of the more commonly used extra ingredients that food manufacturers add to their products, so that you will recognize them on food labels.

Give food body, stability, firmness and/or texture	Enhance flavour	Add colour	Make food last longer—common preservatives
Calcium chloride	Autolyzed yeast extract	Annatto extract (yellow)	Ascorbic acid (vitamin C)
Calcium lactate	Hydrolyzed soya protein	Beta-carotene (yellow to orange)	BHA
Carrageenan	Disodium guanylate or inosinate (notice the sodium!)	Caramel (yellow to tan)	BHT
Egg yolks	Monosodium glutamate, or MSG (notice the sodium!)	Dehydrated beetroot (bluish-red to brown)	Calcium propionate
Gelatine	Salt or sodium chloride	Brilliant Blue (E133) and Indigo Carmine (E132)	Calcium sorbate
Guar gum	Citric acid	Citrus Red 2	Citric acid
Mono- and diglycerides	Acetic acid	Fast Green (E143)	Potassium sorbate
Pectin	Sodium citrate	Orange B	EDTA
Polysorbates	Guanosine monophosphate	Erythrosine (E127) and Allura Red (E129)	Potassium sorbate
Sorbitan monostearate	Inosine monophosphate	Tartrazine (E102) and Sunset Yellow (E110)	Sodium benzoate (notice the sodium!)
Soya lecithin	Neotame	Grape skin extract (red, green)	Sodium erythorbate (notice the sodium!)
Whey	Quinine	Ferrous gluconate	Sodium nitrite (notice the sodium!)
Xanthan gum	Stearic acic	Sodium nitrite or nitrate	Tocopherols (vitamin E)

Want to avoid additives?

Shop for your groceries in the following order:

1 Fresh fruits, vegetables, frozen fruits and vegetables, fresh meats, dry beans and plain roasted nuts.

2 Low-fat dairy, tinned foods (drain and rinse to remove added salt or sugar), rice, pasta and bread.

3 Rarely buy pre-prepared commercial mixes, frozen dinners, cured meats, snack foods and baked items.

Simple guidelines for savvy shoppers

Follow these suggestions and you should be able to navigate the challenging environment of snazzy packaging and enthusiastic marketing.

Look for foods with only one or a few ingredients. These products will have gone through minimal amounts of processing.

Look for products featuring the word 'whole', as in wholewheat breakfast cereals, crackers, pasta and breads in your packaged food items, instead of refined grains.

Be mindful of added ingredients such as sugar, salt or sodium and fat. Limit these wherever possible to maintain your healthy eating habits.

Unmasking marketing

Sensational and promotional language and enticing terms can lure the unwary shopper to buy unhealthy 'healthy' foods.

Sometimes it seems that the harder we try to choose the healthy option, the more we're thwarted by marketing and advertising strategies that lure us towards unhealthy foods. However, with practice and armed with a few clues, it's easy to see beyond the marketing smokescreen.

1 No added sugar

This alluring label means that a product contains no sweetener, right? Wrong! It simply means that there is no added natural sugar – that is, the sort derived from sugar cane or sugar beet (sucrose). The product might, however, contain any one of several alternative sweeteners, especially high fructose corn syrup (sweeter and cheaper than 'real' sugar) or sugar substitutes, as well as a whole range of other additives. Remember to check all labels for sugar and sugar substitutes, because they're used in the most unlikely products.

Check the labels on low fat and flavoured yogurts for added sugar and other ingredients.

2 Low-fat

When a dairy product declares itself to be low-fat, that's what it will be. However, fat is where all the flavour is, so in order to make the product palatable, it is usually laden with sugar and possibly other additives instead, which are required to thicken and stabilize the base product. Be particularly wary of those fruit-flavoured low-fat yogurts, which sound like the perfect snack food or dessert but have so much added sugar, starches, stabilizers or flavourings that for your health's sake, you'd be better off adding fresh fruit to a full-fat yogurt.

Always check labels for ingredients that are minimally processed, are in a whole or as a natural state as possible, and leave highly processed products on the grocery-shop shelf.

A simple rule to follow, but an effective one!

3 Only 99 calories

This must be a winner, surely! Not so. There are calories and calories, and to be healthy you should always aim to get your calories from the healthiest source. With this in mind, beware – those low-calorie products are usually packed full of unnecessary additional ingredients. Cereal bars are particular culprits, luring you not only with the promise of low calories but with the magic words 'whole grain', which also aim to convince you of the bar's value to your health. Look out for high levels of sweetener (any type), fats, artificial flavours, additives and preservatives – if it takes you longer than a couple of seconds to read the Ingredients List, give the product a wide berth.

4 Organic

Manufactured products marked 'organic' are not necessarily 100% organic or free of added chemicals – they might contain a mix of organic and non-organic ingredients, so if this is important to you, check the label where the organic ingredients will be identified. When it comes to buying fruit and vegetables, consider freshness and food miles and decide whether it's better to buy a non-organic product grown locally or an organic product flown hundreds of miles before it reaches your table.

5 Grass-fed beef

The healthiest beef comes from animals raised on organic pasture, but for meat that is rich in essential fatty acids (EFAs), especially omega-3, and low in saturated fat, it must be grass-fed until slaughter. However, it's very common for animals to be grass-fed for a few months only, then 'finished' on cereals, greatly reducing the levels of EFAs while raising the saturated fats. To be sure that the beef and other grass-fed meat you buy is most beneficial to your health, look for a reliable local producer – otherwise you might be paying grass-fed prices for cereal-fed meat.

Responsible meat eating
Eat your meat lean and in moderation. Emphasize minimally processed plant proteins instead, such as beans. They are a more ecological alternative and let cows live!

6 MSG

Monosodium glutamate (MSG) is a naturally occurring chemical, identified in the early 20th century by a Japanese chemistry professor, Kikunae Ikeda, as a component of seaweed and various other foods such as Parmesan cheese, tomatoes and mushrooms. It creates the taste sensation now known as 'umami', and it makes your taste buds very happy. So what's the problem with it? Simply this: It is added to manufactured products that we should eat in moderation, such as crisps, encouraging us to eat more of them. And because it's been subject to some bad press, MSG is labelled under a number of other names, such as autolyzed yeast extract, calcium caseinate and names containing 'glut' – monopotassium glutamate, glutamic acid. For the sake of your health, get your umami kick from 'real' foods!

3

Out and about: Restaurants and parties

Healthy choices when eating out

Eating out provides a wide range of choice. The key is selecting restaurants and foods that fit your time, lifestyle and health goals whilst staying within budget.

People are eating out more for many reasons. These may include changes in lifestyle, such as working families, lack of time, the increased availability and access to restaurants or a lack of cooking skills. There is also an interest in trying new foods, so people are going out to enjoy ethnic dishes. No matter where you choose to eat, you want food that is 'priced right' and good-tasting and healthy options that make you feel satisfied about your eating out choices.

Popular eating out trends include:
- Selecting local meats, seafood and produce
- Supporting restaurants that have their own gardens for growing produce
- Selecting foods that are considered 'safe' (prepared hygienically, not linked to any recent food scares, free from unknown ingredients that may provoke allergies, sourced responsibly)
- Buying gluten-free foods
- Selecting healthy meals and drinks for children
- Trying non-traditional or unfamiliar foods
- Selecting more whole grains

When you are trying to decide what to select from a menu and how much emphasis to put on making healthy choices, consider how often you eat out. If it's more than twice a week, knowing how to make healthy choices becomes very important. If you rarely eat out and tend to eat well at home, a treat at a restaurant may not be a bad thing.

Watch your wallet, and your waistline

Eating out may seem easier than cooking food at home, but it can be costly. No matter what your income level, if you eat out, you may be spending the largest amount of your food budget on food away from home. Be careful; if you eat out frequently, just 25% of your meals eaten out can take up 40–50% of your food budget. Eating out may also lead to overeating.

If eating out often is part of your lifestyle, it is important to develop a system that helps cut food costs and enables you to select healthy foods. Like many people who work or lead busy lives, you may not have the time to go home for lunch, prepare food for lunch or have facilities at work where you can keep your lunch. Furthermore, after a long day at work, you may prefer going somewhere to eat instead of cooking at home.

No matter where you choose to eat, you can make eating out healthily a choice, not a chance.

How often do you eat out?

Calculate how many times a week you eat out or eat takeaway food. Is it more than 20% of the time? If so, take action to make eating out healthy. For example:

3 meals + 2 snacks x 7 days a week = 35 food events a week

1 meal + 1 snack as 'eat out' activities x 7 days a week = 14 'eat out' events a week

That is **40%** of food events that involve eating out (14 divided by 35 = 40%). It's time to check the cost and nutritional contribution of these activities!

Don't overeat

Portion control is critical when eating out. When food is delicious and plentiful, it is very easy to overeat. To avoid this, use a smaller plate (your side plate, for example), or ask the waitress/waiter to box up half of your food to enjoy at home the next day.

Enjoy yourself, sensibly

If you're out with a group and fancy a drink, why not start with a glass of sparkling Prosecco instead of wine? At just 69 calories per glass, Prosecco is lower in calories than both red and white wine (125 and 122 calories per glass). Also, ordering by the glass is one way to think twice before drinking more, because it's easier to keep track; sharing bottles between groups often results in over-drinking. See pages 86–87 for more advice on limiting your alcohol intake.

Want to limit calories from dressings? For a reduction of about 70–100 calories, choose light dressings instead.

Do this...

✓ Go onto the website or get a calorie card or handout from your favourite restaurant, then create a calorie budget such as 'every meal will be 600 calories or less' and carry this with you.

✓ Have an appetizer as a main meal.

...Not this

✗ Rely on your instincts about what might be high or low in calories and order based on this.

✗ Eat bread and butter or appetizers before the meal.

Healthy eating at fast-food restaurants

It is unrealistic to decide to totally give up eating at fast-food outlets. So the key is to make informed decisions about what you eat.

The hurried life that is emerging worldwide is fuelling the use of fast-food restaurants. What makes this type of dining outlet so popular?

- They make food available quickly: you can get your meal in a few minutes, with little or no wait.
- They are relatively inexpensive: compared to more formal restaurants, the prices are generally lower for similar foods.
- They serve familiar and popular items: you usually know what they serve anywhere you go, especially if they are popular chain restaurants.
- They have standardized processes: there is consistency of experience in ordering, payment and serving, and procedures tend to be the same everywhere you go.

There are some foods that are especially popular choices at fast-food restaurants. These include French fries, burgers, pizza, fried chicken, grilled chicken, tacos, burritos, hot dogs, ice cream, sundaes, bagels, baked potatoes, fried fish, coffee and kebabs.

The common critique about fast-food restaurants is that the food is high in calories, fat and salt. But many of these eateries have healthier alternatives that you can select, provided you are aware of them.

A large fizzy drink can add anywhere from 150 to 555 calories, depending on the size.

Check in advance

Look up the fast-food restaurant's website, have a read through the menu, and plan two possible healthy meals you could have there before going out to eat. By thinking of two, you have a backup if you change your mind or something's not available.

TOP 10 CALORIE CUTTERS

1

Breakfast sandwiches Ask for plain rolls or wholemeal bread instead of croissants or flaky biscuits; back bacon instead of streaky bacon or sausage.

2

Hot cereals Opt for plain porridge. Add milk instead of cream, and sugar substitute or cinnamon instead of sugar. Skip the nuts and raisins to save a few calories.

3

French fries Ask for a small portion or share with a friend, or replace with a side salad.

4

Burger Order the regular size, plain or with lettuce and tomato. Drop all the 'creamy toppings'. Do you dare to do half the bun?

5

Fried chicken Get grilled chicken instead, which is also among the top fast foods.

Make sure your salad is healthy
Salads with chicken can be a healthy, low-calorie, widely available choice when eating out, but make sure the chicken is grilled, not fried, and that you are careful with your choice and amount of dressing.

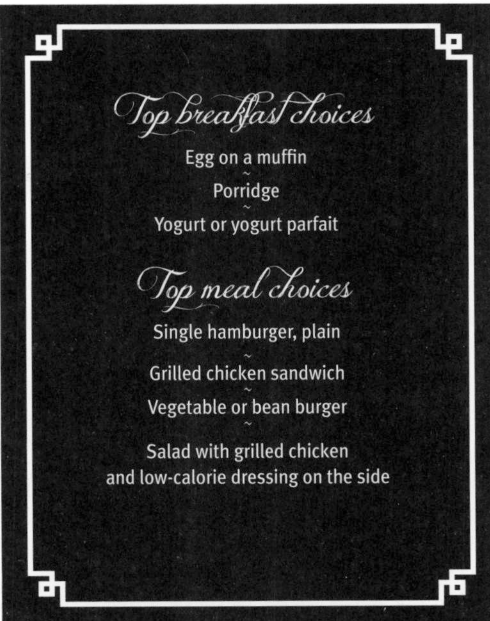

Slow down

Just because it is called a fast-food restaurant and you get the food fast, this does not mean you have to eat it fast. Take time to savour the food so you focus on quality, not quantity. You might find that you go off some of your favourite fast-food restaurants or dishes in favour of healthier, tastier options.

Pizza | Calories

Thin-crust cheese pizza slice | **230 calories**

Thick-crust cheese pizza slice | **312 calories**

Hamburger | Calories

Regular hamburger; single, plain | **232 calories**

Double regular hamburger with condiments | **575 calories**

French fries | Calories

French fries, 1 small serving | **323 calories**

French fries, 1 large serving | **497 calories**

6

Taco Order a soft corn taco, add lots of salsa and skip the soured cream. Got to have guacamole? Only a small dab.

7

Hot dog Ask for the regular-size hot dog, add mustard or ketchup and skip the other toppings. Do you dare to do half the bun?

8

Lemonade Ask for water and a few wedges of lemon instead. Squirt lemon juice into the water. Add your own calorie-free sweetener if desired, and you have your own, healthy lemonade, with added vitamin C!

9

Dressings and sauces There's no way round these – omit or, at the very least, limit all trimmings such as dressings, soured cream, mayonnaise and ketchup.

10

Pizza Opt for thin crust with a vegetable topping. Avoid stuffed crusts and pizzas dripping in greasy cheese. If the pizza is large, take home half of it and eat it for lunch or dinner the next day.

Healthy dining at restaurants

By eating out more, you become familiar with different foods. But, how do you know if your menu choice is healthy, or how it can be made into a healthier one?

No matter which country's cuisine you choose to sample, the main watchpoints for dining away from home remain the same:

• Saturated fat, salt and sugar levels are harder to monitor when you haven't cooked the food yourself.

• You can easily end up eating more than you would have done by serving your own portions.

• The temptation to throw caution to the wind and ignore your healthy eating practices can be hard to resist when faced with a delicious and plentiful array of food and when surrounded by people who may not be dining out with the same health concerns as you.

But forearmed with a few key strategies and some background knowledge of the cuisine and the type of foods likely to be on offer, you can easily stick to your principles while enjoying the benefits of dining out. After all, even healthy people need a social life!

Nourishing food for the soul

African-American cuisine, commonly known as 'soul food', is a comfort to all, with its hearty meals full of flavour and great-tasting desserts. Traditional soul food tends to be high in sugar, fat and salt due to the cooking methods and sauces/gravies used. But, there are ways to enjoy some popular dishes without losing touch with nutrition.

Choose vegetables – one of the great aspects of soul food is that there are so many great and tasty vegetables to choose from, such as okra and green beans.

Opt for collard greens instead of candied yams. Collard greens prepared without additional fat are low in calories (70 calories per serving) and fat and are a great source of vitamins A, C and K, but candied yams (206 calories per serving) are often prepared with an abundance of sugar and fats.

If having meat, stick with grilled, baked or grilled lean meats such as poultry and fish. Choose entrées such as grilled chicken breast or baked turkey wings to ensure that you are not ordering meat that is high in fats and calories.

Consider beans for your portion of protein, since they are a great source of this nutrition group but have much less fat and cholesterol compared to meat. Choose from green peas, black-eyed beans and lima beans, among others.

Watch out for foods that use words such as 'creamy', 'fried' or 'smothered'. Although tasty, these foods tend to be higher in fats and calories because ingredients such as butter, vegetable oil and/or double cream are used in preparation. Instead, choose foods with the words 'grilled', 'baked' or 'light', because these choices are prepared with rapeseed oil instead of lard or vegetable oil.

SAMPLE HEALTHY SOUL FOOD MENU

~

BREAKFAST

Egg white omelette with cheese

Watermelon salad

Fresh berries

~

LUNCH

Hoppin' John (rice and peas)

Collard greens with smoked turkey necks

~

DINNER

Oven-fried chicken

Ribs, with sauce on the side

Green beans

Baked sweet potato

Buttermilk corn bread

~

DESSERT

Peach crisp

Sweet potato pie

Hoppin' John

Hoppin' John is a traditional southern US dish, similar to Caribbean rice and peas. The basics are black-eyed beans, rice, onions, bacon, salt and spices. Try low-fat beef stock instead of bacon and reduce the salt. Eat with collard greens (made without bacon) for a healthy, inexpensive dish.

Exercising caution with commercial Chinese food

To maintain your healthy eating goals, there are areas of caution in Chinese feasting, including the fat, sodium and calorie content of the dishes you select. Deep-fat frying is a common cooking technique for many menu items. Some foods are stir-fried in large amounts of oil and two of the most frequently used flavouring ingredients are monosodium glutamate (MSG) and soy sauce, both of which are high in sodium. However, Chinese cuisine can be enjoyed as part of a sensible diet. Many of the standard dishes consist of noodles or rice built around a variety of vegetables that provide fibre, beta-carotene, vitamin C and phytonutrients. Tofu or soya bean curd provide low-fat, low-cholesterol protein options. Many selections can be steamed, roasted and simmered, and can form part of your healthier options when on the go.

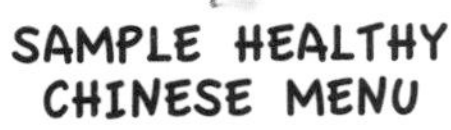

SAMPLE HEALTHY CHINESE MENU

~

APPETIZERS

Spring rolls
Egg drop soup

~

MAINS

Bean curd with sautéed mixed vegetables

Grilled chicken stir-fry with brown rice

~

DRINKS

Green tea

Tailor your order
When ordering a chicken stir-fry, ask the restaurant to go light on the oil (for stir-frying), heavy with the veggies and hold the MSG.

Pick dishes with these key terms:
Jum – means poached
Kow – means roasted
Shu – means barbecued

Choose spring rolls instead of egg rolls for your appetizer. Both carry similar flavours, but spring rolls will provide fewer calories.

Do not assume that the vegetarian dishes are lower in fat or calories. Many dishes are of the deep-fried varieties. Steamed mixed vegetables will provide vitamins and minerals without the calories. Consider also dishes made with steamed chicken, fish or prawns.

The Cantonese variety of Chinese cuisine tends to be lighter because fresh ingredients are part of the tradition. Choose that regional cuisine as much as you can.

Be sensible with sauces. Because sauces can add extra calories, fat, sugar and salt to your meal, ask for the sauce on the side so you can decide how much can be added to your meal. Select hoisin, plum, hot mustard or sweet-and-sour instead of lobster, soy, oyster and bean sauces. Remember, commercial sauces vary, and some may be higher in calories and sodium than listed, right.

Keep them separate
Asking for steamed veggies? Ask for no added oil and for any sauces to be served on the side.

THE LOWDOWN ON SAUCES (PER TBSP)

Soy
Fat: n/a
Sodium: 1006 mg
Calories: 11

Hoisin
Fat: 1 g
Sodium: 258 mg
Calories: 35

Plum
Fat: n/a
Sodium: 102 mg
Calories: 35

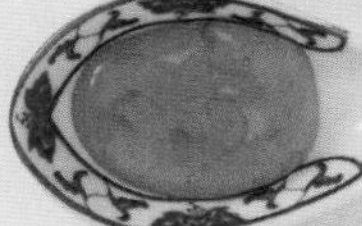

Hot mustard
Fat: n/a
Sodium: 70 mg
Calories: 10

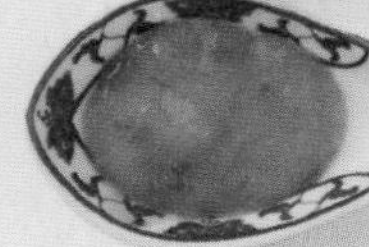

Sweet and sour
Fat: n/a
Sodium: 97 mg
Calories: 22

Black bean
Fat: 1.3 g
Sodium: 500 mg
Calories: 30

Oyster
Fat: n/a
Sodium: 492 mg
Calories: 9

Making Italian meals healthier

Portion sizes are not large and if you choose to eat in the Italian style, the fundamentals of the diet are healthy: high consumption of beans and legumes, fruit and vegetables, grains and extra virgin olive oil; moderate consumption of wine and dairy products; low consumption of red and processed meat, cream and pastries.

Superfood your spaghetti dish by opting for vegetarian versions, such as marinara (185 calories per 225 g/8 oz) or primavera (223 calories) rather than bolognese (450 calories).

Watch the portion sizes for pasta – 110–225 (4–8 oz) per person, especially when it is a side dish to meat, poultry or fish.

Choose extra virgin olive oil instead of light. This has a stronger flavour, so you can consume less.

Bean-based pasta dishes are both filling and nutritious. Try cannellini in your main dish.

Make your pizza a thin-crust vegetarian at 300 calories, so there's no need to sacrifice this restaurant favourite.

SAMPLE HEALTHY ITALIAN MENU

~

BREAKFAST

Roll with prosciutto

Fresh fruit salad

~

LUNCH

Bruschetta with tomatoes and olive oil

Prawn primavera

~

DINNER

Minestrone, Tuscan or Florentine soup

Vegetarian lasagne

~

DESSERT

Biscotti

Fruit tart

More than a slice of bread
Olive oil imparts flavour and healthy monounsaturated fats; tomatoes provide vitamins C and A and the antioxidant lycopene – great ways to make your bruschetta healthier and delicious.

SAMPLE HEALTHY JAPANESE MENU

~

Sashimi

Teriyaki chicken or beef

~

SUSHI ROLLS

California roll: A makizushi-type roll filled with cucumber, avocado and real or imitation crabmeat

Rainbow roll: Variation of the California roll with sashimi (salmon, white fish and prawns) on top

~

GRAIN-BASED DISHES

Donburi: Rice topped with meat or seafood, cooked or raw

Yakisoba: Grilled or fried Chinese-style noodles with meat, cabbage, carrots or other vegetables, and garnished with red ginger

Key benefits of Italian cuisine:

- Low saturated fat levels
- High in fibre, omega-3 fatty acids, antioxidants, vitamins and minerals
- Thought to be protective against heart disease, metabolic syndrome and type 2 diabetes.

Smart choices with Japanese cuisine

Japanese food is often thought to be healthy since it does not bring heavy, greasy fried foods to mind. But the kind of Japanese food that is served outside of Japan can be vastly different from traditional food. With an emphasis on soya beans and rice, it can be a healthy option if you know what to choose and what to avoid.

Watch the condiments and sauces for sodium – only 1 tablespoon of soy sauce – even the light version – contains almost half the recommended amount of sodium for an entire day.

Pass on rolls and sauces with certain Western ingredients such as cream cheese and mayonnaise.

Limit the 'fancy' sushi rolls. The more elaborate rolls such as spider, dynamite or dragon rolls usually have more than four extra ingredients, as they are often rolled with tempura crumbs or flakes, fish roe, sesame seeds and drizzled with some kind of sauce. Order two plain, lower-calorie sushi rolls such as salmon and prawn rolls instead.

Watch your portions – while rice and noodles are staple ingredients, large helpings of them may not be beneficial. Soba noodles are made with buckwheat, while udon noodles are made out of plain white flour. Soba noodles and brown rice are higher in fibre than udon or white rice.

Steer clear of dishes that include the words 'tempura' and 'tonkatsu', which means that food is covered with panko (Japanese breadcrumbs) and deep-fried in oil. Choose a dish with steamed, cooked, baked or grilled ingredients instead.

Commercial Japanese food can have its limitations if you are trying to watch your calorie, sodium and fat intake.

Consider how it's cooked
Teriyaki is a healthy option due to the cooking process, which involves grilling.

Maximizing nutrients at a Spanish restaurant

With vegetables, citrus fruit and seafood at the forefront, Spanish cuisine is an inherently healthy cuisine to turn to for making wholesome dietary choices.

Order two or three tapas for a main meal instead of an entrée. Tapas provide a good opportunity to eat slowly as you chat, so you can be mindful of your appetite as the evening progresses.

Enjoy the many cocidos, or stews with vegetables, popular in Spanish cuisine as a main dish.

Watch the portion size of paella. Often, the waiter will leave the pan with you so you can help yourself. Eat slowly and if you can't resist a second helping, make sure it's smaller than the first, and that it's your last.

If you fancy a meat or tuna pie (empanada) ask the waiter if it can be baked instead of fried.

Sample tomatoes in a variety of ways – drizzled with olive oil as an appetizer, stuffed with rice and vegetables as a main or as part of a rich stew sauce. A key ingredient in Spanish cuisine, tomatoes are excellent sources of vitamins A and C, and contain the antioxidant lycopene, vitamin E, potassium and other minerals.

Go easy on the chorizo (Spanish sausage). Just 225 g (8 oz) contains 1,120 calories and 132% of your daily allowance of fat.

Ahead of its time
Andalusian gazpacho, here topped with a quenelle of black olives, is a cold tomato-based vegetable soup. The veggies may be finely or coarsely puréed. It's a great low-calorie and nutritious appetizer and, it could be said, a precursor to the popular modern-day veggie smoothies.

SAMPLE HEALTHY SPANISH MENU

~

APPETIZERS
Catalan-style beans
Gazpacho

~

MAINS
Baked cod and yellow rice
Fabada (bean stew) or fish stew

~

SIDE DISHES
Steamed spinach
Roasted peppers

~

DESSERTS
Almond biscuit
Flan

SAMPLE HEALTHY MEXICAN MENU

~

APPETIZERS

Salsa with baked corn chips

Caldo de pollo (chicken stock)

~

MAINS

Bean burrito with side salad

Soft corn chicken taco with vegetables

~

SIDE DISHES AND SALSAS

Nopalitos or prickly pear salad

Roasted corn, sweet potato or other vegetables

~

DESSERTS AND DRINKS

Aguas frescas de frutas (fresh fruit drinks)

Rice pudding

Keep an eye on the size
Bean burritos are, on the face of it, a sound option for the health-conscious diner: a flour tortilla filled with mashed beans and rolled, usually with grated cheese and a sauce included inside the wrap. However, control the portion size and accompaniments to avoid excessive calories.

Enjoying the variety of Mexican food

Mexican food is much more than the commonly known tacos, burritos, enchiladas and chilli. It is varied and colourful, with many healthy staples. Corn, which originated in what is now Mexico, is found in grain as corn tortilla, masa harina (fine cornmeal) and other grain forms, but is also eaten as a vegetable. Black and pinto beans are popular cooked, mashed or refried.

Many Mexican dishes are 'stuffed' foods – tacos, flautas, enchiladas, etc. Be careful to monitor the types and amounts of 'stuffings'. That's what adds the calories!

Ask about carnes asadas (grilled or roasted meats) and order one with a side of vegetables such as roasted corn.

Like fish tacos? Make sure the fish is not breaded and fried. Sprinkle the tacos with lime instead of dressing.

Enjoy the fruit pastes, but only in small amounts. They are mostly sugar!

Mexican cuisine includes many different types of cheeses, eaten alone, used as toppings or used in desserts. Weigh up the calorie, fat and calcium content when making your menu choices.

Panela Usually eaten fresh as a snack or over cold dishes. 25 g (1 oz) = 80 calories, 4 g saturated fat, 15% calcium.

Queso blanco A crumbly cheese used as a topping, or creamy when heated. Avoid it in frying. 25 g (1 oz) = 90 calories; 4 g saturated fat, 20% calcium.

Queso fresco A common crumbly Mexican cheese used as a topping and to stuff quesadillas and chillies. 25 g (1 oz) = 87 calories, 4 g saturated fat, 16% calcium.

Crema Like a thick, double or soured cream, used in sauces or toppings. 25 g (1 oz) = 60 calories, 3.5 g saturated fat, 2% calcium.

Healthy choices at parties

Party time should be when you get to savour delicious foods while supporting, not sabotaging, your eating goals. Then you can savour the fun, too.

For many people, party times can be a source of stress and worry, since they may be tempted to deviate from their healthy eating goals. The key to enjoying the celebration and the food is to know what type of event you are hosting or attending, the types of foods and drinks that are likely to be there, and to develop a strategy for enjoying the event.

Be mindful of requirements

If hosting, ask your guests to let you know in advance of any special dietary requirements. Make sure your menu suits all your guests, tailor it to do so, or provide suitable alternatives. For example, if you have nuts as an appetizer (and a person with nut allergies attending), provide popcorn or another item, too. Also keep 'high allergy' foods away from commonly selected items to avoid cross-contamination.

If you're planning to attend a party, ask the host in advance what dishes will be served. If they are not likely to have low-fat and healthy options, or options that cater to your special dietary requirements, offer to bring some to help out. Once there, check out all the tasty treats on offer before eating or drinking anything. Plan on a few items from the major categories – appetizers, main dishes, side dishes, desserts and drinks. Have an idea of portions and maximum limits before digging in.

115

Avoid mindless drinking and eating

At the party, limit what you eat by holding a glass of sparkling water with one hand and a celery stick with the other hand. Your hands will be too full to let you mindlessly eat other higher-calorie foods.

116

Create a theme with the decor

If you want to create a theme, do it through the decorations around the environment rather than the food. For example, a New Year's party with a blue-and-silver colour scheme could have balloons and confetti in blue and silver around small cupcakes instead of cupcakes covered with dark-blue frosting. Or you could serve sponge fingers or sponge cake or sponge topped with blueberries.

Don't leave for the party really hungry! Drink 240 ml (8 fl oz) of water or eat a small apple before leaving the house.

Top 10 quirky, healthy party foods
SOMETHING DIFFERENT
Smoothie or cold soup shot glasses
Lettuce wraps or cups
Mini chicken or fish pies
Smoked salmon appetizer spoons
Cracker pizzas
Beetroot risotto
Spinach dip bread bowl
Polenta wedges
Stuffed potato skins
Rainbow fruit tray

Start the party right – appetizers

Many appetizers are laden with cheese or sauces or fried to a crisp. With a few wise choices, however, appetizers can remain delicious but also be healthy.

Appetizers are a great idea, but unfortunately many are made up of heavy dips or cheese-stuffed items that contain as many – if not more – calories than the meal itself. The good news is that by focusing on unique uses of healthy foods such as fruits, vegetables and low-calorie proteins instead, you can quickly turn the appetizer into a guilt-free, full-flavour home run.

Don't scrimp on the salsa!

Salsa is one condiment that you can always feel good about serving because it's full of flavour and vegetables and low in calories – only 30 per tablespoon. Serve it with fresh vegetable slices, low-calorie crackers or baked chips. Salsa is also versatile because you can use it as a dip – or for a topping on finger sandwiches or other foods. It's an easy way to enhance an appetizer with minimal work.

Serve 'complicated' finger foods

Nuts in their shells, such as pistachios and peanuts, require work to eat and will naturally help you eat less. Other foods that take a little work are molluscs (clams, oysters and mussels), shell-on prawns or edamame.

> When choosing appetizers at a party, rather than putting a little of everything on your plate, look through the whole selection first, and then decide on two to three items to enjoy.
>
> Sarah-Jane Bedwell, author of *Schedule Me Skinny*

Prime position

The placement of your appetizers can be a strategy to help you and your guests make the best choices. Put fruits and vegetables at the front and centre positions in the serving area and set higher-calorie appetizers further away. Research has shown that the further you have to walk for food, the less likely you are to choose it.

Top 3 high-flavour low-calorie appetizer foods
1 Roasted vegetables
2 Raw fruit
3 Grilled prawn skewers

End the party right – desserts

Healthy eating at a party does not mean you should skip the desserts table. It means finding a way to indulge without compromising your health goals.

One strategy for enjoying sweets but avoiding excess is to fill up on healthy snacks and foods before walking to the dessert table so you are not as tempted to overeat desserts. However, you can indulge sensibly with smaller portions or healthier versions of your favourite desserts and still have fun alongside everyone else at the party.

In most recipes, you can decrease the amount of sugar by up to one third or fat by up to a half and still have a delicious treat.

120

Control your ingredients

Think carefully before choosing ready-made sweet rolls, biscuits, pies, cakes and cream-filled desserts. These foods are usually high in sugar and unhealthy fats, such as trans or saturated fats. Making your own desserts means you can lower the amount of added sugar or fats.

121

Chocolate-covered strawberries

Chocolate may reduce the risk of heart disease, and dark chocolate may have better health benefits than milk chocolate. Combine with fruit for added health benefits and taste.

Ingredients

- 20 strawberries
- 175 g (6 oz) dark chocolate, chopped

Directions

1. Melt the chocolate in a glass dish in the microwave, then let it cool slightly and thicken.
2. Hold each strawberry by the stem, then dip and twist the bottom half in the chocolate.

52 calories and 2.6 g fat per strawberry

122

Healthy party desserts

Make your icing with low-fat cream or curd cheese and a small amount of icing sugar instead of a large amount of cream cheese or butter and sugar.

Instead of icing a chocolate cake, place a doily over the cake, sprinkle icing sugar, then remove the doily to reveal an attractive pattern.

Serve small biscottis instead of cakes or biscuits.

Make pies with a lattice top with large open spaces to have less pie crust and fewer calories.

Use liqueur glasses instead of regular glasses for ice cream and provide nut toppings instead of syrups.

COUNTDOWN COUNTER

Sweet	Calories
Butter biscuit, 25 g (1 oz)	132 calories
Vanilla ice cream, 125 ml (4½ oz)	137 calories
Chocolate-chip cookie, 30 g (1 oz)	140 calories
Chocolate ice cream, 125 ml (4½ oz)	143 calories
Milk chocolate, 25 g (1 oz)	152 calories
Dark chocolate, 25 g (1 oz)	155 calories
Apple pie, 100 g (3½ oz)	237 calories
Cheesecake, 100 g (3½ oz)	321 calories
Sponge cake with vanilla frosting, 100 g (3½ oz)	373 calories
Brownies, 100 g (3½ oz)	466 calories

Thyme Chives Oregano Lavender Sage Tarragon

Don't limit yourself to garnishes – use herbs and edible flowers as part of seasonings, in salads or in vinegars for a culinary treat.

Enjoy the party—right! Main dishes

Whether you are providing, bringing or just eating, focus on reducing the fat and calories in main dishes.

With a little effort and forethought, it's nearly always possible to reduce the calories in a dish. However, choosing low-calorie in the first place could make things easier. So why not try soups or stews, for example, and make them stock-based rather than cream-based? Many recipes allow you take advantage of each season's bountiful produce and spices, e.g. vegetable noodle soup in the spring or pumpkin soup in the autumn. Comforting, vegetable-filled casseroles can be a great winter warmer for large gatherings, with brown rice and wholemeal bread to increase fibre intake. Wholemeal vegetarian pizzas are ideal for sharing, and there are many healthy salads that add flavour, texture and nutrients as a side dish or on their own.

Roast veggies for a colourful, healthy dish

For a tasty side dish, toss chopped parsnips, carrots and Brussels sprouts evenly in olive oil and herbs and roast or grill. Roasting vegetables like peppers, jalapeños, carrots, parsnips and aubergine will bring out complex, sweet flavours. Pay attention to presentation by considering colours, herb toppings and serving dishes.

Rely on herbs

Fresh herbs are a wonderful addition to any cold dish because they add vibrant flavour and antioxidants. Because heat tends to amplify flavours, cold dishes really benefit from the extra flavour-boost herbs provide.

Pasta appeal

Often found at parties, a filling, healthy pasta salad can easily be created by using a handful of vegetables and a few splashes of dressing. It can be a surprisingly filling dish: if the salad contains high-fibre grains and beans, such as quinoa, barley, wheatberries, bulgur wheat, black beans or kidney beans in place of pasta, it will fill you up on less quantity and calories. These substitutions are great options for people who need to control their blood sugar or just want to eat low-glycemic-index foods.

126

Serve hot stuffed vegetables

Hot stuffed vegetables such as stuffed peppers, mushrooms and squashes can also make low-calorie tasty party dishes. Stuff the vegetables with rice, spices, chopped vegetables, nuts or lean meats. Use lean minced turkey or beef instead of higher-fat beef to reduce the fat intake. To add a nutty flavour and boost the nutrition even further, substitute white rice with brown rice or wholemeal breadcrumbs.

128

Cooking with cheese

Choose reduced-fat or low-fat cheeses such as skimmed milk mozzarella or Jarlsberg light for casseroles. When trying reduced-fat forms of cheeses such as Cheddar, Brie and Gruyère in cooking, avoid very high temperatures, which may make them – and your dish – rubbery.

129

Healthy substitutions

Instead of...	Try this...
Mayonnaise	Low-fat Greek yogurt
Creamy dressings	Red wine vinegar
Butter	Small amounts of olive oil
Salt, to boost flavour	Fresh herbs

127

serves 10

Wholesome pasta salad

This pasta salad maximizes the use of vegetables and, with plenty of green and red, makes for an attractive dish on your party table.

Ingredients

- 350 g (12 oz) dry whole-grain, short-cut pasta (macaroni, penne, fusilli or farfalle)
- 2 tablespoons extra virgin olive oil
- 4 tablespoons red wine vinegar
- 3 tablespoons minced fresh parsley
- Zest of one lemon
- 200 g (7 oz) chopped cherry tomatoes
- 350 g (12 oz) fresh spinach
- 1 courgette, diced
- 1 red pepper, diced
- 200 g (7 oz) small-cut broccoli florets
- 3 tablespoons diced spring onions

Per serving: 105 calories, 3.2 g fat, 0.4 g saturated fat, 0 g trans fat, 0 mg cholesterol, 16 g carbohydrate, 3.3 g fibre, 1.2 g sugar, 4 g protein

Directions

1. Cook pasta according to the directions on the packet.
2. In a small bowl, whisk together the oil, vinegar, herbs and lemon zest.
3. Drain the pasta, and then put it into a large serving bowl. Add the spinach immediately and toss into the pasta until slightly wilted.
4. Add the remainder of the vegetables, spring onions and dressing, and toss to fully coat.
5. Refrigerate for at least two hours until chilled. Serve cold.

A filling, healthy pasta salad can be created easily by using a handful of vegetables and a few splashes of dressing.

Healthy drinking practices

Sugar-sweetened or alcohol-containing drinks can contribute a surprising number of calories to your diet at party time. Drink smart, and you can still enjoy the good times.

Keep your punch healthy and cold by freezing fruit in diet ginger ale or sparkling water in a mould and inverting into your punch prior to serving.

Whether it is tea, beer, wine, hard liquor or soft drinks, there are three main things you need to watch out for:

- Alcohol
- Sugar
- Calories

There are several strategies you can use to enjoy the party while staying healthy and happy.

Limiting alcohol

If you plan on treating yourself to a glass of alcohol, start with a calorie-free, non-alcoholic beverage such as sparkling water with lime to satisfy your thirst and save you some calories before you have your alcoholic drink. You may have a glass of light beer, wine, whisky, rum, vodka, gin or a mixed drink, but red wine is a slightly better choice: in moderate amounts it provides antioxidants and offers heart-healthy benefits.

To avoid drinking too much, you can dilute alcoholic drinks with water or juice. Ask for a spritzer such as wine with sparkling water or diet ginger ale. You may ask for an addition of antioxidant-high cranberry juice or vitamin C-high lime juice and create your own wine spritzer. Know your limit and drink in moderation – approximately one serving of an alcoholic beverage per hour is the general rate of consumption for adequate metabolism. Having too much alcohol may put you at risk of intoxication and dangerous driving. A general recommendation is a maximum of one drink per day for women and two drinks per day for men.

Beware the empty calories

Having too many sugary drinks will result in taking in lots of empty calories with little or no nutritional value. This becomes especially easy because you may be 'drinking mindlessly'. That is, because you are involved in talking or other activities you are not aware of how much you are drinking. Prior to attending the party, set yourself a limit of sugar-sweetened drinks or alcoholic drinks and be aware of how many calories each contains.

What else can you drink?

If you want to avoid alcohol altogether, there are some tasty and refreshing alternatives you can turn to:

- Plain water, with a slice lemon or lime for a fresh taste
- Sparkling or tonic water with a splash of 100% fruit juice
- 100% fruit juice (a small amount)
- Unsweetened iced tea or sweetened with calorie-free sweeteners
- Diet soda

ALCOHOLIC DRINKS | CALORIES

Irish cream, 100 ml (3½ fl oz) | **327 calories**	Vodka, 100 ml (3½ fl oz) | **231 calories**	Daiquiri, 100 ml (3½ fl oz) | **186 calories**	Martini, 100 ml (3½ fl oz) | **167 calories**	Eggnog, 100 ml (3½ fl oz) | **88 calories**	Wine, 100 ml (3½ fl oz) | **83 calories**

SEASONAL PARTY PUNCH IDEAS

~

SUMMER

Orange juice, pineapple juice, sparkling water, orange slices

~

AUTUMN

Cider, apple juice, diet ginger ale, apple slices

~

WINTER

Grape juice, berry-flavoured tea, sparkling water, berry or pear nectar, apple juice, sparking water, pear slices, cinnamon stick

~

SPRING

Pineapple juice, apricot nectar, sparkling water, raspberries

Explore healthy hot drink options

On some occasions such as parties in the winter, hot drinks keep you warm and healthy. As a host, you may offer some flavoured teas. Tea contains antioxidants and other compounds and may prevent against cancer, heart disease and other diseases. Choose unsweetened brewed tea over sweetened to avoid extra calorie intake from sugar. Another option is herbal teas such as ginger, jasmine and mint. Herbal teas are caffeine-free or lower-caffeine drinks made from herbs, flowers, roots, bark and seeds steeped in hot water. Some may have anti-inflammatory properties.

Drink in moderation

Drink water between alcoholic drinks to dilute the effects of alcohol. Sip alcoholic drinks slowly and leave a gap between glasses.

NON-ALCOHOLIC DRINKS | CALORIES

Champagne, 100 ml (3½ fl oz) | **76 calories**

Beer, 100 ml (3½ fl oz) | **43 calories**

Orange juice, 240 ml (8 fl oz) | **111 calories**

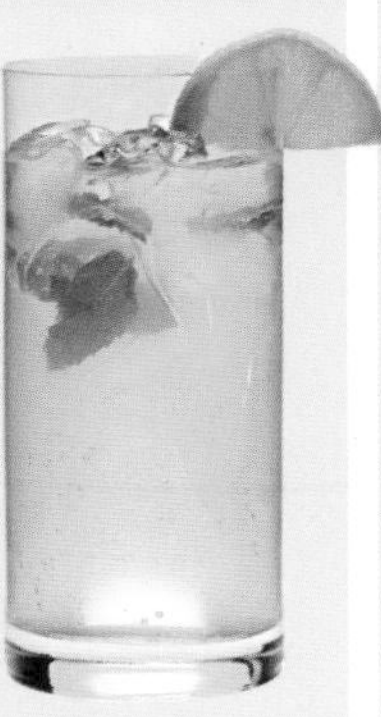

Lemonade, 240 ml (8 fl oz) | **99 calories**

Cola, 240 ml (8 fl oz) | **92 calories**

Unsweetened iced tea, 240 ml (8 fl oz) | **92 calories**

4

Diets and eating plans

Popular diets and plans

OK, you've heard it before. Diets don't work. But you want to try that 'hot' new diet. Should you? Find out if it may work for you, and how to do it safely, if at all.

You may have modified how you eat or bought a weight-loss book in order to lose weight. But think about it: If you spent money on a diet book, did you lose anything permanently other than the money?

Most diets work in the short term because they encourage you to lower your total calorie intake. They do this through a variety of different techniques – see the chart, right.

Keep in mind that because a diet is popular, that does not necessarily mean it is safe or is based on studies of its effectiveness. The best diet for you is the one that was specifically designed for you, and considers your likes and dislikes, your financial limits, your lifestyle and weight and your health goals. A registered or licensed dietitian/nutritionist can help you with this.

No matter the diet and its claims, what you should look for in any diet is its EAT factor:

Ease of incorporation given your eating behaviours, likes, current finances and need for long-term use.

Application to your lifestyle and situation; 'family friendliness'.

Truthfulness of claims – does the science really support that it is safe and is effective?

133

Start small and specific

Start by setting one small goal every two weeks, such as replacing lunchtime French fries with a side salad on Mondays, Wednesdays and Fridays.

134

Don't believe the hype

What is the diet claim? Lose weight fast? Cleanse you? Build muscle without exercise? How much does it cost? You know it's not true. Save your money and follow a free plan instead of buying in to unproven marketing claims.

135

Five diet myths

An informed dieter is a smarter – and therefore more successful – dieter. Make sure you separate fact from fiction. Here are some popular misconceptions about dieting:

1. Skip meals to lose weight.
2. Diet foods are best for weight loss.
3. Starches are fattening.
4. Low-fat or fat-free foods are lower in calories.
5. You cannot eat out when trying to lose weight.

Do this...

✓ Spend your money on a trained professional, such as a registered or licensed dietitian/nutritionist, who can personalize a plan based on your needs.

...Not this

✗ Spend your money on a million-pound bestseller that will collect dust on your shelf.

Technique	Key attributes and practices	Example diets
Behaviour change	Healthy eating, physical activity and behaviour changes; i.e. using smaller plates, cue identification, regular exercise	➤ French women's diet ➤ Intuitive eating ➤ Mindful eating
Consumption of foods in specific combinations or preparation	Eating or not eating specific foods together, or only prepared in specific ways	➤ Fit for life ➤ Raw food diet (pages 100–101)
Consumption of specific foods at set times	Eating or not eating specific foods at specific times	➤ 3-hour diet
Consumption of foods based on typing or classification of population groups	Encouraging you to classify yourself according to groups such as blood type	➤ Eat right for your type
Focus on consumption of one or a few specific foods	Eating a specific food for its 'special qualities'	➤ Grapefruit diet ➤ Cabbage soup diet ➤ Vegan diet (pages 102–103) ➤ Paleo diet (pages 106–107)
Personalized guidance based on lifestyle, health and genetic predispositions (pages 94–95)	Personalizing your plan based on your health goals, lifestyle, preferences and disease risk	➤ Fat is not your fate ➤ Forever young
Restriction of proteins, fats or carbohydrates	Limiting your intake of one or two of the macronutrients	➤ New Atkins diet ➤ Dukan diet ➤ South Beach diet
Purchase and consumption of meal replacements	Using commercial drinks, snacks and/or meal replacements	➤ Jenny Craig ➤ Weight Watchers ➤ Slimfast ➤ Nutrisystem
Total or partial avoidance of foods (pages 98–99)	Encouraging you to fast	➤ Daniel fast ➤ Juice fast diet ➤ Intermittent 5:2 diet
Food groups and exchanges	Selecting foods from categories or groups to create menus or snacks within established limits	➤ Volumetrics ➤ DASH diet (pages 104–105)
Techniques that 'remove toxins or cleanse' (pages 96–97)	Encouraging you to 'detox' by fasting or promoting foods that supposedly eliminate toxins	➤ Green smoothie detox diet ➤ Super cleanse

Working with a registered dietitian/nutritionist

Whether you want to lose weight, eat to manage your diabetes or just learn some healthy food tips to implement in family meals, consider working with a nutrition professional.

Often, you may think you are making the best selections and be unaware of strategies you can use to improve your choices. In much the same way you would see a physician when you are ill, or a dentist for prophylactic care or treatment, you should consider working with a qualified nutritionist such as a registered dietitian/nutritionist who can help you establish and succeed with your food and nutrition goals. Working with a nutrition professional will help you identify your needs and set a course of action that fits your lifestyle and goals.

What should you look for when seeking a qualified professional?
Ask the practitioner if he or she has a degree in nutrition and dietetics. Ask where he or she studied – was it an accredited course? Ask the potential consultant if he or she took courses such as chemistry, anatomy and physiology, food science and food safety, nutrition science, dietetics and medical nutrition therapy. Also, did the practitioner have clinical or internship experience? Does the practitioner belong to a professional organization? Does the professional take regular continuing education courses to stay up to date? What is the practitioner's area of practice? Is it related your counselling needs?

One easy way to find a registered dietitian/nutritionist is through the relevant professional organization, such as the Association of UK Dietitians (BDA), the Academy of Nutrition and Dietetics (in the United States), etc. They can provide you with names of local practitioners who are consultants.

136

Five questions to ask a potential consultant to determine if the nutritionist is qualified to counsel you

1 How long was your programme of study?

2 Did you do an accredited internship or supervised practice programme?

3 Are you registered with a professional body?

4 Are you licensed?

5 What is your practice speciality area?

137

If you answer 'yes' to any of the questions below, you might find it beneficial to work with a dietitian/nutritionist. Do you find it hard to:

- Analyze different diets and diet claims for hype and truth?
- Figure out how to create a weight-loss diet that works for you?
- Figure out what to look for on a food's nutrition label?
- Make sense of the items listed on a food's Ingredients List?
- Plan meals that are quick, healthy and delicious?
- Plan meals that fit your goals but also please other family members?
- Buy foods that help you and your family prevent disease?
- Buy the foods you need for your special diet?
- Buy a range of foods but stay within a budget?
- Make healthy snacks or meals to eat on the move?
- Eat healthily when eating out?

Going for a consultation?

Be prepared to provide information about your health status, medications, diets you have tried in the past and the current or expected diet. Keep track of what you generally eat (see below) and write down questions you want to ask.

A typical session

A health professional will likely help you identify your eating patterns, behaviours and goals. The assessment may include the use of 24-hour recalls – where you identify everything you ate over the past 24 hours or previous day, including nutrition information – and helping you to identify goal-setting health behaviours, and discussing possible barriers and supports in relation to achieving those goals.

See a qualified professional

Make sure you ask the potential consultant questions. In some areas, the term 'nutritionist' can only be used by a trained, qualified professional, but in other places the term can be used by anyone! The term 'registered dietitian' is usually more closely regulated for use by trained health professionals. But do not take anything for granted – ask about the consultant's credentials and training.

Check these out

The Bristish Dietetic Association: www.bda.uk.com
Freelance Dietitians: www.freelancedietitians.org
Use these online directories to find a registered dietitian in the UK.

Be honest in your diet record to give the nutritionist a true picture of your eating habits. Only then will he or she be able to help you.

Recording your eating habits

To make the most of your time with a registered dietitian, keep a diet record. For three to five days prior to the visit (include at least one weekend day) write down everything you eat, how much, where you got it from (was it made at home or bought in a restaurant?). Try to include level of hunger (1 = not hungry to 4 = extremely hungry) and emotional state such as bored, happy, sad, angry. Keeping a diet record that is based on how you actually eat will allow a dietitian to make an accurate assessment. Changing your eating habits or skipping writing down some items you eat will hinder your chances of working together successfully. A sample diet record might look like this:

MEAL OR SNACK? 1pm Snack

FOOD OR DISH
• Spanish omelette
• 275 ml (10 fl oz) orange juice

INGREDIENTS
1 egg, ½ medium sliced fried potato, 110 g (4 oz) onion

LOCATION
Bought and ate at café

HUNGER LEVEL
2 A bit hungry, very thirsty

EMOTION
Upset over work issue

Nutrigenomics: What's in it for you?

The best weight-loss diet is the one that is planned especially for you!

Based on knowledge of your specific genetic risks, a dietitian/nutritionist can personalize your plan and tailor your food choices to meet your individual needs. No more one-size-fits-all diet plans.

The future is bright in that it will be possible to design health care especially for you. In five to ten years, with valid and reliable genetic testing and advancing research on functional food ingredients (foods or ingredients made for a specific purpose) to change gene expression (such as decreasing your risk for diabetes), personalized nutrition will be the new diet. What will it look like? Today, we can make general recommendations for specific diet types depending on family history and disease risk (see below). However, in the future, people will have a gene map and know what diseases their genes predict in 10, 20, 30 or 40-plus years and what foods can affect the expression of those genes by turning them on or off to reduce risk.

> The future is fast approaching and the diets of that future will be informed by genetic information about each patient.
>
> Catherine Christie, Associate Dean and Professor, University of North Florida

This will require a lot of research to identify the disease risk genes (this is already happening), identify the food ingredients that can modify the expression of those genes (this will take longer) and then determine the right time to eat those foods, as there are critical periods for changing gene expression. Here is an example of a critical period: preliminary evidence indicates that foods containing soya eaten during puberty may reduce the risk of breast cancer in later life but have no positive effect if started after menopause. Another example may be that some people will lose weight on a higher-carbohydrate low-protein diet, while others may respond better to a low-carbohydrate high-protein diet.

Examples of personalized eating strategies

You can't change your parents, but you can change your behaviours

You cannot alter your genetic predisposition – the likelihood of getting a disease based on your genetic makeup, or what you inherited from your ancestors (such as potential for type 2 diabetes) – but you can decrease the potential of getting that disease by avoiding related risk factors.

Kidney disease risk
If kidney disease runs in your family, keeping blood pressure under control is critical. Avoid high-sodium and processed foods as much as possible and keep weight under control.

Heart disease risk
If heart disease runs in your family, avoid smoking or other tobacco products. Eating a heart-healthy calorie-balanced diet with predominantly monounsaturated and polyunsaturated fat sources makes sense. Limit saturated fat and avoid becoming overweight. Learn to like foods and their natural flavour – without added salt – and monitor blood pressure regularly. Learn to handle stress and stay physically active most days of the week.

143

Have a session in a Bod Pod

Have a qualified professional measure your body composition in a Bod Pod, if you have access. You sit inside the large egg-shaped piece of equipment for a few seconds and a qualified health professional will then interpret the results. It's an accurate and efficient way to assess your body composition – how much fat and muscle you have and your resting metabolic rate.

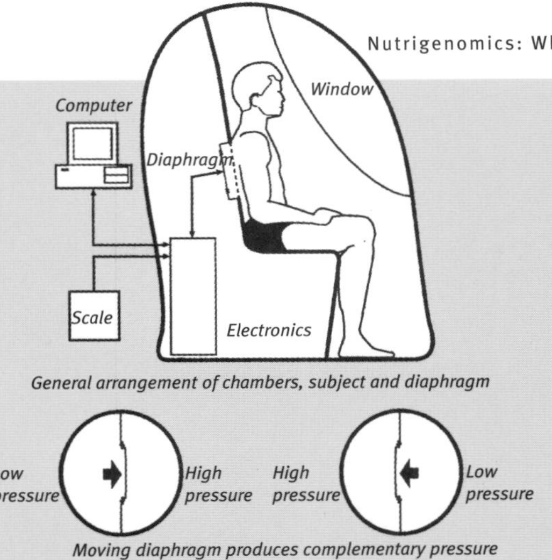

General arrangement of chambers, subject and diaphragm

Moving diaphragm produces complementary pressure changes in the chambers

Not as scary as it looks, or sounds!
A test in a Bod Pod calculates body composition (including fat percentage and amount) by measuring pressure changes between the front and back chambers of the Pod caused by oscillations of the central diaphragm system. All you need to do is sit in your bathing suit and breathe normally!

Access and ethics
Genetic testing is currently available in some parts of the world over the counter and direct to consumers without medical professional interpretation or involvement. This has raised red flags because of lab-testing inconsistencies and the recommendations of supplements for sale by the same companies who provide the test. Privacy concerns have also been raised in that employers or insurance companies might request predictive genetic information and deny employment or coverage based on future risk.

In the meantime, as we wait for these ethical and other issues to be solved, diets should be personalized as much as possible using what we currently know about family history and disease risk.

Accuracy in predicting what is best for each patient based on his or her genes will increase drastically. Skill in helping patients to change their eating and exercise behaviours will depend on our understanding of the behaviour-change process and the development and provision of the ideal foods and ingredients for each genotype.

Popular resources

American Heart Association: www.heart.org
Packed with information on specific conditions, general health and lifestyle, and current scientific research.

www.geneticseducation.nhs.uk/nutritional-genomics
Fact sheets and further information.

National Heart, Lung, and Blood Institute: www.nhlbi.nih.gov
Includes guide to lowering blood pressure.

Breast cancer risk
If breast cancer runs in your family, consider working to prevent excess weight gain with age. Limit alcohol intake and tobacco use and focus on a diet high in vegetables, fruits, poultry, fish and low-fat dairy products. If skin cancer runs in your family, keep skin protected and always use sunscreen. For other cancers, follow the same rules as for breast cancer until more specific recommendations emerge from the research.

Diabetes risk
If diabetes runs in your family, keeping extra weight off in childhood, early adulthood and middle adulthood is a smart strategy. Emphasizing aerobic exercise for calorie burning and restricting high-calorie foods and drinks makes sense. Limiting non-nutrient-dense foods such as desserts, sweetened drinks and crisps and snack foods may also be prudent. It would also be important to know precisely how many calories you burn in a day so intake can be adjusted. This can be done using a Bod Pod (see above) or underwater weighing.

Do this...

✓ Talk with your family members about their health conditions and discuss them with your doctor and dietitian.

...Not this

✘ Spend your money on a mail-order 'saliva test' that claims to show if you are at risk of diseases and health conditions. The method has not yet been fully demonstrated to be effective or standardized for valid results.

Detox diets

Detox diets are very short-term options that may have some benefits, but only if done in the right way, if you are healthy and if you can manage them.

It is important to consult your doctor before starting a detox diet, to make sure that certain foods are not harmful to you.

The need for detoxification diets comes from the idea that the tissues of your body store up pollutants and toxins from the environment, poor diets and medications. By fasting for a set period of time from the typical Western diet and choosing mostly plant-based foods, it is thought that the body's natural detoxification system can be accelerated or enhanced.

Your body, however, is equipped to naturally detoxify every day. The liver's main function is to filter the blood (to remove waste), detoxify chemicals and break down drugs. This is a crucial role that supports overall health. In extreme cases, when the liver is not healthy or able to detoxify properly, by-products of metabolism, alcohol or drugs can build up in the blood, causing illness and perhaps even leading to death.

Helping your liver to help itself

An overall healthy diet is the key to keeping your liver running on all cylinders. A wide variety and ample intake of fruits and vegetables is the first and most important component of a detoxification diet. Specifically, produce that contains sulphur compounds – such as onions, garlic, broccoli, cabbage, kale, cauliflower and Brussels sprouts – is particularly well equipped to provide nutrients to power the liver. These foods should be enjoyed daily in both raw and cooked forms.

Spices like turmeric and cinnamon have also been found to support the liver's function and should be used for flavouring instead of salt or added fat. Fruits like apples and pineapples contain important enzymes and nutrients that aid in breaking down food and eliminating waste.

Steering clear

There are a few things that should be avoided while following a detox diet. Having to metabolize alcohol and foods high in fat such as fried foods diverts the liver from performing its other important functions. It is also recommended to avoid caffeine and instead drink water and hot decaffeinated green tea.

EVERYDAY TIPS

1 Eat a fruit or vegetable at every meal. This will help support your body's natural detoxification system.

2 Foods that contain certain phytonutrients support the liver's process for detoxifying at the cellular level.

3 Keep caffeinated drinks to one a day or less and drink lots of water and green tea instead.

4 Drink alcohol only on occasion (one to two times a week or less) to support a healthy liver.

5 Prefer spices and herbs daily over salt and extra fat.

Pros	Cons
Mentally, following a 'detox' diet plan for a short period of time can help to jump-start health and better decision-making, through eating more fruit and vegetables.	Although the science is not strong, preliminary research suggests that detox diets are not a good way to lose weight and keep it off.
Although it may seem contradictory, 'detoxing' is something that can be achieved every day by eating, not avoiding, healthy foods.	There are a host of supplements and food replacements sold as part of a 'detox' regimen that are best avoided. Most are laxatives, and many could be unsafe or harmful.
Following a detox plan can heighten your awareness of the keys to feeling great and having a healthy liver for life.	Strict plans carried out over long periods of time or that rely on supplements are generally considered unsafe, and there's no proof that they offer benefits.

sample menu

DETOX PLAN

~

BREAKFAST

Whole-food smoothie made of fresh orange, apple, kale, carrots, ginger and turmeric

Hot green tea

~

LUNCH

Cooked quinoa or brown rice with chopped tomatoes, lettuce, avocado and broccoli

~

SNACK

Fresh berries sprinkled with cinnamon

~

DINNER

Brussels sprouts roasted with garlic
Miso soup

Top 9 foods
TO SUPPORT DETOXIFICATION

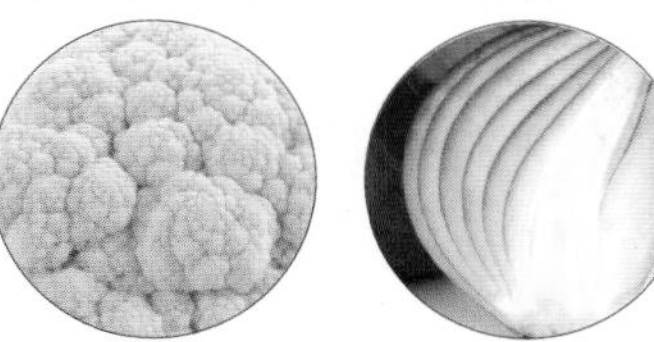
Cauliflower

Onions

Apples

Green tea

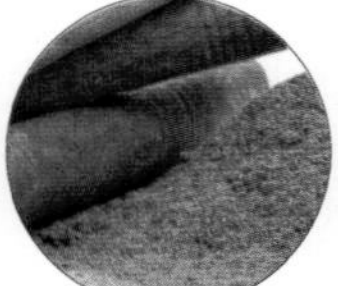
Cinnamon

Beetroot

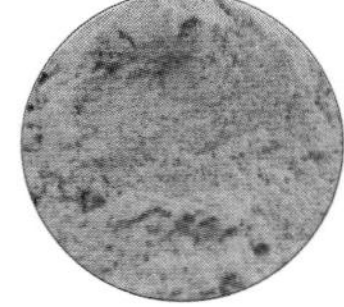
Turmeric

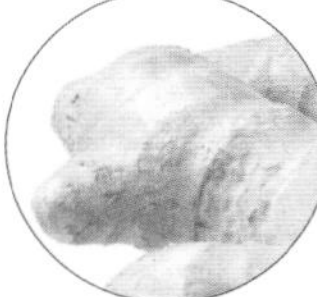
Fresh ginger

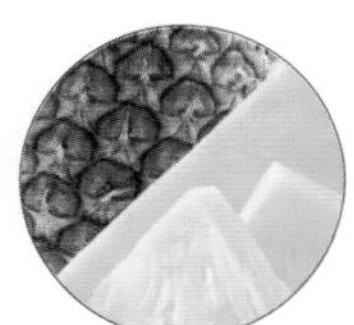
Pineapple

Detox smoothie

serves 1

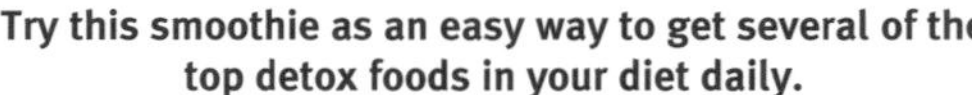

Try this smoothie as an easy way to get several of the top detox foods in your diet daily.

Ingredients

110 ml (4 fl oz) carrot juice

110 ml (4 fl oz) water

50 g (2 oz) fresh kale

1 medium apple, cut into chunks

40 g (1½ oz) fresh or frozen pineapple chunks

2.5-cm (1-in) piece of fresh root ginger

1 tablespoon turmeric

Directions

Put all ingredients in a blender and process until smooth. Add more water if necessary to achieve your preferred consistency.

176 calories, 2 g total fat, 0 g saturated fat, 0 g trans fat, 0 mg cholesterol, 93 mg sodium, 41 g total carbohydrates, 7 g dietary fibre, 17 g sugar, 4 g protein, 257% vitamin A, 187% vitamin C, 15% calcium, 27% iron

> Think of the top detoxification foods like scrub brushes for your body. They go through your blood, tissues and organs 'scrubbing out' the harmful stuff, allowing your body to work at peak performance.
>
> Jenna Braddock, Consultant and Sports Dietitian, University of North Florida

See your doctor
Anyone considering going on a fast should consult a physician before embarking on this extreme diet. Prolonged fasting is dangerous and not advised.

Pros

A quick way of shedding pounds – fat and muscle are used up and water lost.

You don't need to fast for long – it should never exceed a period of two days.

Cons

Once food is re-introduced, the body will gain weight quickly as it replenishes.

Causes some physical discomfort – a complete lack of food will cause you to feel weak and so restrict your activity levels.

Generally not recommended by any dietitians.

After a period of deprivation, the dieter runs the risk of either eating uncontrollably or overeating.

Patients with a heart condition or other illnesses should be very careful or avoid it altogether.

Fasting

The oldest and most radical of diets, fasting is the practice of refraining from eating food alongside the sole consumption of water or juice.

The rationale behind a fast is that the total avoidance of food provides a quick weight-loss method. In some cultures, this practice serves as a form of penitence for overindulgence and has religious overtones.

How it works

Without food, blood sugar levels go down as no essential fuel in the form of energy is entering the body. This dip is registered and a neurochemical message is sent to the brain, causing hunger pangs to kick in. During a fast, feelings of hunger come and go as the body is reminding you that you will need to eat at some point. During the first few hours of the fast, the body will obtain energy or glucose either from the glycogen stored in the muscles (only for use by the muscles) or the liver (for use by the rest of the body). This energy reserve lasts for several hours, generally about half a day, or two to three skipped meals. Once used up, and if food does not enter the body, protein from muscle and fat will be broken down and turned to glucose as energy.

Proceed with much caution, if at all

With prolonged fasting, a physical state known as ketosis kicks in. Fasting causes water loss and large amounts of muscle breakdown because it is largely composed of protein. As muscle is broken down, nitrogen is eliminated from the body. Important minerals such as sodium, potassium and calcium are depleted and this has harmful effects on the body. Low potassium levels, for example, negatively affect the state of the heart and can even be a cause of death during fasting.

The importance of glucose in a healthy functioning body cannot be overstated. The brain consumes the largest amount of glucose, so when blood sugar levels drop, the brain is unable to function properly. As a result, the person may feel confused, dizzy, lightheaded and have difficulty concentrating. The dieter may feel weak because the muscles are lacking in fuel and the blood is not pumping enough energy to the muscles and the cells. To make up for this decrease in energy, the metabolic rate slows down.

Consider a more relaxed approach

In an attempt to moderate the physical consequences resulting from muscle loss, some variations on the fasting method are more of a partial fast and include the consumption of juices. See pages 96–97 for detox diet methods.

Popular diets

Daniel fast
A partial fast that includes fruits, vegetables and water.

Juice fast diet
Includes raw vegetable and fruit juices and water.

The 5:2 diet
Intermittent fasting diet in which you eat for five days and then eat one quarter of your usual calories for two days.

FASTING KNOW-HOW

1 Planning a fast? First check with your doctor to make sure you are physically healthy for 'no food' for a couple of days. Once given the OK, make sure you fast during days where nothing vigorous, new or different is scheduled. Try a restful weekend.

2 Do not go on a fast if you have diabetes, heart disease or any other health condition, or are taking medication. See your doctor first for approval, and if obtained, a registered dietitian to help you plan a safe way to fast.

3 Remember: You should never fast for longer than two days.

Sample menu

149 FASTING PLAN

~

You can build up to fasting gradually, over the course of a week. Start by eating a healthy, full three meals a day, then in the final three days:

~

Day 5

BREAKFAST

Cold cereal, milk, banana; wholewheat toast and jam; tea

LUNCH

Vegetable stir-fry with tofu, pak choi, peppers and brown rice; tea

DINNER

Beef barley soup; green salad; fruit salad; tea

~

DAY 6

BREAKFAST

Vanilla yogurt; honeydew melon; tea

LUNCH

Vegetable soup; green salad; tea

DINNER

Miso soup; crackers; green tea

~

DAY 7

Tea and water throughout the day

150 Drink water, and plenty of it

During a fast, the kidneys have to work hard to get rid of the excess waste products with significant water loss. It is vital to drink lots of water during a total fast to avoid toxins accumulating in the blood and promote their elimination through urine. Fasting may give the intestinal tract a rest but the kidneys are overworked and other organs will suffer breakdown for use as energy.

Do this...

✓ Watch for signs such as thirst, dizziness, shakiness, weakness, chills, lethargy, incoherence or other physical effects that indicate potential danger.

...Not this

✗ Ignore physical signs of stress and risk a health crisis.

151 Other drinks

Most fasts do not allow consumption of drinks other than water. Try adding a slice of fruit or a berry for flavour – just don't eat it! Some fasts, however, may allow teas, in which case mint and chamomile are sound choices. Coffee, juices or plant-based smoothies may be permitted in partial fasts.

The raw food diet

The raw food diet is a type of diet in which people eat food that is not cooked or processed.

Raw foodists do not eat many, if any, cooked foods because they believe that cooking destroys living plant enzymes that help with digestion and that it reduces vitamins and minerals in food. Common reasons for following this diet include beliefs that it can prevent or cure disease, improve health and energy and result in weight loss.

What can you eat?

Raw foodists eat at least 70–75% of foods (by weight) raw. Allowed foods include raw fruits, vegetables, nuts, seeds, beans, grains, seaweed and sprouts. Avoided foods include cooked foods, alcohol, caffeine and refined sugars. Some people do not eat cereal grains. Many raw foodists are vegetarian or vegan. Some eat unpasteurized dairy foods and raw meats or fish. Strict followers only eat one type of food at a time.

You can heat food to 33–48°C (92–118°F) and the food is still considered raw. Over this temperature, raw foodists believe food changes from living to dead as heat destroys enzymes and vitamins. Instead of cooking, raw foodists use dehydrators, blenders, juicers, soaking and sprouting to process their foods.

The cooking debate

Our bodies have all the enzymes needed to get nutrition from food. In fact, the plant enzymes in uncooked foods do not even make it through the stomach since they are made up of proteins, which cannot survive stomach acid. Cooking does change the nutrition of some foods and can reduce or improve nutrition. For example, vitamin C can be lost when you cook vegetables in water and B vitamins are lost when manufacturers refine grains. However, your body can more easily absorb lycopene in tomatoes and proteins in eggs when they're cooked. Heat also destroys bacteria and toxins that can cause food-borne illness.

Many testimonials for this diet are from people who previously ate processed 'junk' foods. Replacing high-calorie, nutrition-poor processed foods with low-calorie nutrition-rich whole foods could be the reason for the improvements. Testimonials do not provide sufficient valid evidence for the health and safety of a diet.

Pros		Cons	
High in vitamins, minerals, and fibre; low in saturated/trans fats, cholesterol and added sugars.	Appears to reduce symptoms of rheumatoid arthritis and fibromyalgia.	Not recommended for growing children.	May increase some cardiovascular risk factors, such as lowering HDL (good) cholesterol and increasing homocysteine levels.
May decrease some cardiovascular risk factors, such as reducing blood pressure, cholesterol and triglyceride levels.	Improved immune system function.	In women, low calories can lead to excessive weight and body-fat loss and result in loss of menstruation.	Increases risk of food-borne illness from bacteria, parasites, toxins and unpasteurized foods.
Followers have a lower body mass index (BMI) than meat eaters and vegetarians (are less likely to be overweight).	Followers report improved health and better quality of life.	A large amount of misinformation and unproven claims (raw food cures cancer, cooked oils are more fattening than uncooked oils).	
Less time spent in kitchen because of minimal hands-on preparation time.		Followers report being continually hungry.	Lowers bone mass.

152 EVERYDAY TIPS

1 Interested but don't want to go totally raw? Try eating more salads and fresh, raw fruits and vegetables.

2 Munch on washed crispy sugar snap peas, carrots, celery, asparagus and mushrooms tossed with chopped herbs and pepper for savoury snacks.

3 Mash your favourite berries into a purée and spoon over chopped fruit as a healthy sweetener.

4 To make sure your body gets all the nutrition it needs, take a multivitamin/mineral and work with a registered dietitian.

RAW FOOD DIET

~

BREAKFAST

Quinoa soaked overnight in water, topped with bananas, blueberries, cinnamon and raw honey

Juiced wheatgrass and carrots

~

SNACK

Walnuts, grated dried coconut and raisins (or fruit dried in a dehydrator)

~

LUNCH

Sashimi

Seaweed salad

Herbal tea with stevia sweetner

~

SNACK

Homemade salsa (tomatoes, jalapeños, coriander, onion, lime juice, cayenne)

Raw flax crackers or plantain chips (made with a dehydrator)

~

DINNER

Courgette 'spaghetti' (cut into small strands) topped with tomato sauce (tomatoes, garlic, basil, olive oil, pine nuts, mixed using a blender) and raw-milk cheese

Spinach, strawberry, avocado salad topped with cold-pressed olive oil

~

DESSERT

Chocolate banana 'ice cream' (chop frozen bananas and place in food processor with raw cacao powder; blend on high adding water as needed)

Top 10 foods

TO EAT RAW

> There is not much scientific research on the raw diet, but there are testimonials about improved health and quality of life.

Alexia Lewis, Wellness Dietitian, University of North Florida, and Nutrition Consultant

Popular resources

The RAWvolution Continues: The Living Foods Movement in 150 Natural and Delicious Recipes
By Matt Amsden (Simon & Schuster, Inc./Atria Books, 2013)

www.webmd.com/diet/raw-foods-diet
A useful summary of the diet along with suggestions for further reading.

Living and Raw Foods: www.living-foods.com
The largest community on the Internet dedicated to educating the world about the power of living and raw foods.

The vegan diet

When following the vegan diet, people do not eat any foods that come from animal sources.

People may follow a vegan diet for their health, out of a concern for animal welfare or the environment, to reduce the cost of their food or for religious or cultural reasons.

Vegans do not eat anything that comes from an animal. This includes meat, poultry and seafood as well as derivative foods such as milk, cheese, butter, yogurt, eggs, mayonnaise and honey. Strict vegans do not use any products that have come from animals, such as leather, wool, fur, silk or pearls. There are many animal ingredients in foods that appear to be vegan. To follow a vegan diet, you will have to learn to read food packets to search for ingredients such as lecithin (from eggs), casein (from milk), gelatine (from animals) and lanolin (from sheep).

Not eating any foods that come from animals can sound like a challenge, but with planning, a vegan diet can be nutritionally complete, and for some people, can be a technique for weight loss.

Safety and suitability

A vegan diet is safe and appropriate for any stage of life from infancy through childhood, adulthood and into the elderly years. In some cases, families may choose to provide children with a lacto-ovo-vegetarian (dairy and eggs) diet to facilitate the inclusion of proteins and adequate calories in the diet. It is also safe for pregnant and nursing women. However, not all vegan foods promote health. It depends on the foods that you choose (see opposite).

You can follow a properly planned vegan diet and still have excellent nutrition and health. It is a good idea to talk to your doctor about changing your diet before doing so to determine if there is a need to monitor your levels of iron, vitamin B12 and vitamin D.

Pros		Cons	
Low in saturated fat and cholesterol; high in fibre, folate, vitamins C and E, magnesium, potassium, phytochemicals (plant compounds).	Lower BMI and weight.	Low in vitamins B12 and D, calcium, iron, zinc, omega-3 fatty acids and possibly low in iodine if not using iodized salt.	Supplementation may be needed for vitamins B12 and D.
Lower total and LDL (bad) cholesterol levels.	Lower blood pressure.	Packaged foods can be high in saturated and trans fats, sodium and sugar.	Increase in meal-planning time to ensure the diet is providing appropriate nutrition.
Lower risk of cardiovascular disease, hypertension, type 2 diabetes and certain cancers.	Improved blood sugar control in people with type 2 diabetes.	Must combine foods to get complete proteins (animal products are complete proteins because they contain all essential amino acids; plant foods do not so they must be paired over the course of the day to provide all amino acids).	

Use substitutions in oking and baking, such s ground flaxseed and ater instead of eggs.

2 To promote health, eat plenty of plant proteins, grains, fruits and vegetables.

3 Avoid foods that are fried or high in sugar and sodium, which may be vegan but do not promote health.

4 Eat fortified foods or take a multivitamin/mineral – it takes a lot of planning to get the right mix of nutrition out of your foods.

VEGAN PLAN

Sample menu

~

BREAKFAST

Toasted oat cereal topped with raisins, sliced almonds, soya milk

Coffee (soya milk and sweetener if desired)

~

SNACK

Roasted chickpeas (see page 35)

~

LUNCH

Hummus wrap (vegan tortilla, hummus, lettuce, tomato, cucumber)

Apple

~

SNACK

Sweet and salty smoothie (chop banana and pineapple, place in food processor with peanut butter and ground flaxseed, blend on high, add water/ice to achieve desired consistency)

~

DINNER

Wholewheat spaghetti with sauce made from fresh tomatoes, onions, mushrooms, garlic, marinara sauce, silken/soft tofu, basil, oregano, red pepper flakes (blend after cooking if desired)

Garden salad with oil and vinegar

~

DESSERT

Strawberry banana 'ice cream' (mash and freeze strawberries and bananas with stevia sweetner)

Popular resources

Becoming Vegan: The Complete Guide to Adopting a Healthy Plant-Based Diet
By Brenda Davis and Vesanto Melina
(Book Publishing Company, 2000)

Oldways: http://oldwayspt.org/
Go to: Oldways Resources/Heritage Pyramids/Vegetarian/Vegan Diet and Pyramid

Vegan pyramid

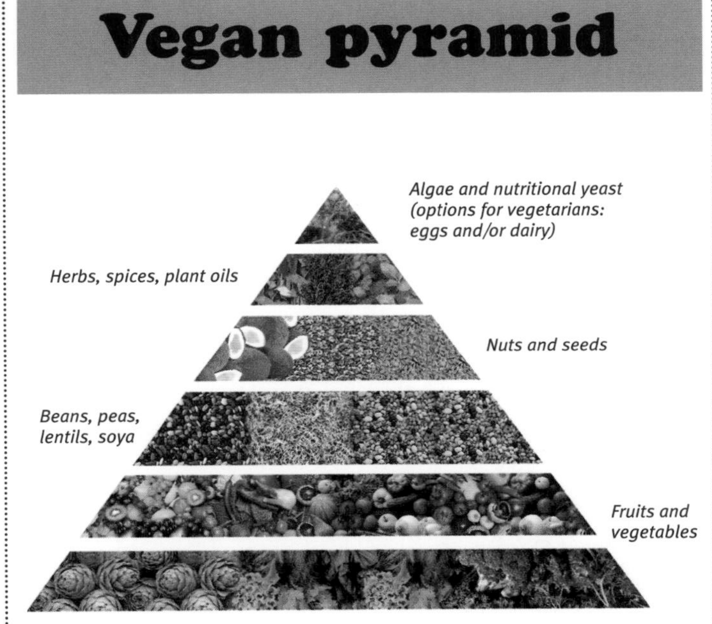

Quinoa lettuce wraps

serves 12

Ingredients

275 g (10 oz) quinoa, rinsed then cooked

1 raw courgette, diced

1 slice red onion, diced

2 carrots, diced

1 large stalk celery, diced

Handful of chopped walnuts

Handful of raisins

Red wine vinegar, to taste

Black pepper, to taste

Romaine lettuce leaves, rinsed

Directions

1. Mix all ingredients except the last three together.
2. Add red wine vinegar and black pepper in small increments until the dish has a flavour you enjoy.
3. Serve a spoonful of the quinoa mixture onto the raw romaine lettuce leaves and wrap up.

Nutrition per serving (1 wrap): 66 calories, 2 g fat, 18 mg sodium, 10 g carbohydrate, 2 g fibre, 3 g sugar, 2 g protein

The DASH diet

Dietary Approaches to Stop Hypertension (DASH) can help prevent or manage high blood pressure and provide a balanced diet appropriate for anyone.

The DASH diet increases servings of foods with nutrients that lower blood pressure. Specifically, the diet provides you with less sodium (salt), saturated fat and cholesterol, and more potassium, calcium, magnesium and fibre. The DASH diet provides specific numbers of servings from food groups (see below). It encourages you to eat 27% of your calories from fats with 6% being saturated fats, 18% of your calories from protein, and 55% from carbohydrate.

You have flexibility to choose your foods, as long as you stay within the guidelines – the diet gives you a number of servings from different food groups to eat every day.

Scientific research

Researchers used the DASH diet, previously called the combination diet, to investigate the effect of different diets on blood pressure. The initial study in 1997 recruited 412 American adults with high blood pressure. It compared the typical Western diet to the DASH diet and different levels of sodium. The researchers found the DASH diet – especially when combined with lower sodium – reduced blood pressure. Since that time, many researchers have studied the diet. They have found that is it effective in lowering blood pressure; lowering total cholesterol, LDL cholesterol and triglycerides; and increasing HDL cholesterol. It also reduces risk for cardiovascular disease and may be helpful in managing type 2 diabetes.

In addition, The National Heart, Lung and Blood Institute of the US National Institutes of Health studied diets to see if they had an effect on hypertension and found that DASH did lower blood pressure.

The DASH diet promotes good health and healthy attitudes towards food and eating. It is a great way to decrease your calorie intake. If you are concerned about your heart health and blood pressure and you are looking for a non-restrictive well-balanced diet, the DASH diet is right for you.

If you eat 2,000 calories a day, then you should eat:

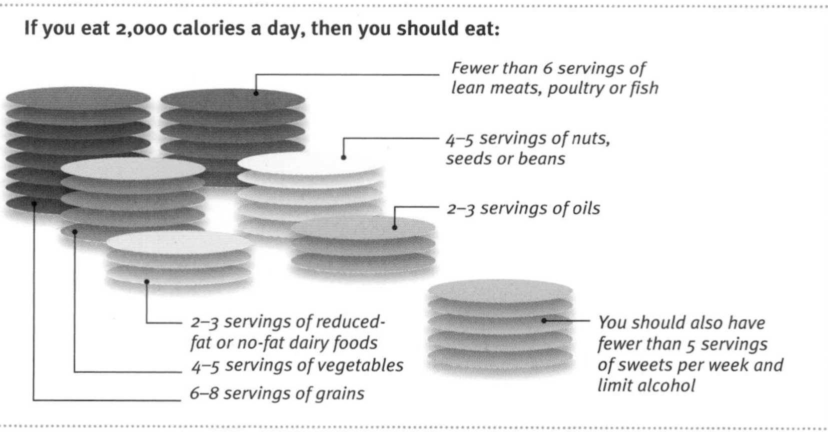

Pros		Cons	
High in fruits, vegetables, fibre; low in saturated and trans fats, sodium, added sugars.	High in potassium, calcium and vitamins D and B12.	Increase in food preparation time (not relying on packaged or convenience products).	Increase in cost (purchasing fresh fruits and vegetables).
Does not restrict or avoid any food groups.	You can modify it for special needs such as vegetarian/vegan, gluten-free, etc.	Eating in some restaurants may be difficult (typically high in sodium and fat).	Flavour may be lacking at first due to using less salt, but taste buds will adjust.
Promotes a lifestyle approach instead of a dieting approach.			

157 EVERYDAY TIPS

1 It is recommended to do 30 minutes per day of moderate exercise, alongside the diet plan.

2 Does 8–10 servings of fruits and vegetables a day seem like too much? Start slowly. Identify a meal or snack that typically does not include a fruit or vegetable and find a way to include it. Continue adding to meals and snacks over several weeks.

3 All the foods are readily available from a supermarket and/or grocery store, so shop easily but wisely – see Shopping for vegetables and Shopping for fruit on pages 48–51.

4 To avoid becoming bored with your diet, pick up a fruit or vegetable that you have never tried before.

Popular resources

The DASH Diet Eating Plan: dashdiet.org
The ultimate resource, including related articles, book lists, recipes and FAQs.

The DASH Diet Weight Loss Plan
By Marla Heller (Grand Central Life & Style, 2012)

Top 5 foods
FOR THE DASH DIET

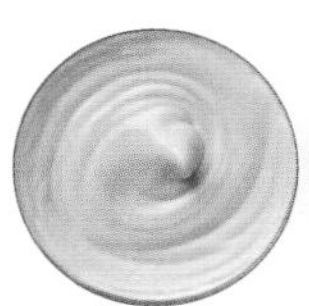
Low-fat yogurt

Apricots

Beans

Kale

Popcorn

158 CHICKEN RATATOUILLE

serves 4

Ingredients

- 1 tbsp vegetable oil
- 4 chicken breast halves, skinned, boned, fat removed and cubed
- 2 courgettes, thinly sliced
- 1 small aubergine, cubed
- 1 onion, thinly sliced
- 1 green pepper, chopped
- 225 g (8 oz) fresh mushrooms, sliced
- 1 tin whole tomatoes, cut up
- clove garlic, minced
- 1½ tsp dried basil
- 1 tbsp fresh parsley
- black pepper

Directions

1. Heat the oil in a frying pan. Add the chicken and sauté for 3 minutes, or until lightly browned.

2. Add aubergine, courgette, onion, green pepper and mushrooms. Cook for 15 minutes, stirring occasionally.

3. Add tomatoes, garlic, basil, parsley, and pepper; stir and continue cooking for 5 minutes, or until the chicken is tender.

Serving size: 350 g (8 oz)
266 calories per serving

159 DASH PLAN

sample menu

~

BREAKFAST

Egg-white omelette cooked in trans-fat-free margarine with tomatoes, broccoli and peppers

Wholemeal toast topped with mashed strawberries

Coffee or tea with skimmed milk

~

SNACK

Apple with peanut butter

~

LUNCH

Cottage cheese with walnuts, peaches and pineapple on wholemeal crackers

~

DINNER

Chicken stir-fry (courgettes, peppers, onion, etc.) cooked with rapeseed oil, served over brown rice

Edamame and corn salad

~

DESSERT

Yogurt parfait with strawberries and sliced almonds, sprinkled with cocoa powder and cinnamon

The Paleo diet

The Paleo diet is based on the idea that we should eat like our paleolithic ancestors to prevent the onset of today's chronic diseases.

Never go foraging for wild foods without adequate knowledge, skill and permission!

Eat like the cavemen ate with plenty of meat, poultry, eggs, seafood, vegetables, fruit, honey and nuts, but no grains (bread, cereal, rice, pasta, oatmeal, biscuits, cakes, pies, pastries, muffins, etc.), beans, dairy foods, refined sugars, caffeine or alcohol. There are several proclaimed health benefits to this diet, and proponents of the diet argue that our ancient ancestors were largely unaffected by 'diseases of affluence' such as heart diseases, type 2 diabetes and obesity. However, the common lifespan during that time was about 35 to 40 years, so others argue that people didn't live long enough to get these 'modern-era' chronic diseases. Also, in reality there was no one Paleo diet, because people lived in many different regions throughout the world and were limited to choices available in their environment.

The science behind the diet

The diet fits best into the category of low-carbohydrate high-protein diets. The omission of dairy products and grains may be its most controversial feature. While the diet also promotes whole foods versus processed foods, nutrients that may be limited by dairy and grain restrictions include calories, calcium, vitamin D, B vitamins, fibre, iron, magnesium and selenium. To date, there is limited to fair evidence that this diet is effective. The diet may also be associated with increased food expense, especially for those buying only grass-fed meats and organic fruits and vegetables.

Beneficial aspects of the diet when compared to current nutritional issues such as obesity and related chronic diseases include potential restriction of calories, carbohydrate, sugar and salt, and increased consumption of fruits and vegetables, seafood and nuts.

As you can see, this diet requires major changes for most people and the increased cost may be a deterrent. However, those who adopt this diet tend to be very positive about how they feel and the potential for weight control they experience. So, eating like our cave ancestors did is difficult, requires determination, and may not actually be feasible for you, but many seem to find adopting the hunter-gatherer mentality associated with the Paleo diet is certainly a conversation starter!

> The Paleo diet may be tough at first for those who have trouble controlling carbohydrate intake from grains and sweets. But, after a period of adjustment, the diet may be healthier and more helpful in weight control due to the elimination of those food categories.

Catherine Christie, Associate Dean and Professor, University of North Florida

Pros		Cons	
Proclaimed benefits include weight loss; reduction in body fat; improved muscle growth, glucose control and insulin sensitivity; and lowered risk of heart disease.	Fewer calories and carbohydrates; less sugar and salt; more fruits, vegetables, seafood, nuts.	Limited evidence that this diet is effective for weight loss and prevention of diseases of affluence.	Grocery costs and time spent shopping are likely to increase when sourcing specialist foods.
Promotes whole foods over processed foods.	Can be an interesting lifestyle choice, enabling you to learn about the diet of your ancestors.	Restriction of dairy produce can lead to deficiencies.	Requires extensive lifestyle changes and plenty of determination.

160 EVERYDAY TIPS

1 Try the diet for a short time, if it helps you kick-start your weight loss.

2 Focus on large quantities of fresh fruits and vegetables to provide fibre, which is missing due to the limitation of grains.

3 As a rule of thumb: if you can't hunt or pick it, don't eat it!

4 While following the plan, it is advisable to increase physical activity and drink lots of fresh water.

161 PALEO PLAN

Sample menu

~

BREAKFAST

Grilled cod with sliced tomato

Melon cubes

~

LUNCH

225 g (8 oz) baked free-range chicken

Salad with lettuce, carrots, cucumbers, tomatoes, walnuts and lemon juice

~

DINNER

225 g (8 oz) sirloin roast

Steamed cauliflower and broccoli

Salad with mixed greens, cabbage, tomatoes, avocado, almonds, onions and lemon juice

Mixed berries

~

SNACKS

Fresh fruit or vegetables

162 Questions to ask yourself when considering the Paleo diet:

- Do you enjoy grains? Do you like dairy products? Are you willing to give them up permanently?
- Can you think of other options, such as moderating the amounts of these foods?
- Are you at potential risk for some health conditions, and how might such a plan impact you? Do you have a family history of osteoporosis? Are you prone to anaemia or planning on getting pregnant, when iron intake is very important?
- Is it difficult for you to get some of the foods required on the Paleo plan either geographically or financially?
- Do you live alone? How might following the diet impact others?
- How easily will it fit your lifestyle, such as eating at work or eating out?

Popular resources

The Paleo Diet Revised
By Loren Cordain (Houghton Mifflin Harcourt, 2010)

Living Paleo for Dummies
By Melissa Joulwan and Kellyann Petrucci (For Dummies, 2012)

See your doctor
If you are thinking about trying a Paleo plan, see your doctor to be sure your health conditions will not be aggravated by eliminating some important food groups from your diet.

Where there's a high amount of sugar, there's usually a high amount of fats – especially saturated fats – lurking within as well. So that's two good reasons to steer clear!

Ways to overcome sugar cravings

When it comes to food-related cravings, the dreaded sugar craving is at the top of the list for most people. Fortunately, there are ways to overcome the urge to splurge.

Empty calories

First of all, let's look at how pointless eating added sugar really is. Refined white sugar (the sort used in manufactured foods) is a carbohydrate that provides energy but none of the desirable extra nutrition supplied by other carbohydrates, such as whole grains. So while sugar might not actually be 'bad' for you, it's not good for you either, and eating too much of it certainly isn't. Studies are currently being carried out to establish whether it is addictive.

Break the habit

Hard though it is to imagine as you reach for yet another biscuit, it takes only 21 days to break a habit. Easy as that? Almost! If you can discipline yourself to follow a holistic plan that includes eating plant-based foods at regular intervals, washed down with plenty of water, as well as engaging in meditation, deep breathing, and gentle exercise every day, with a good night's sleep to round it all off, you'll find that your sugar cravings will be diminished considerably. Even those infamous premenstrual give-me-chocolate-or-I'll-scream cravings, endured both by women and their long-suffering nearest and dearest, simply vanish!

Manage your sugar consumption

Once you've broken the habit, you'll still need to keep your sugar intake under control:

Never shop when you're hungry. When your blood sugar is low, your instinct is to reach for generous quantities of anything sweet.

Include plenty of healthy fats in your diet. Illogical though it might seem to include 'plenty' and 'fat' in the same sentence, fats actually inform your brain when you're full – unlike sugar, which simply encourages you to keep eating even to the point of feeling nauseous.

Learn a few savvy tricks for including things in your diet that have a sweet taste to satisfy your taste buds.

- Snack on almonds, which are naturally sweet, filling and full of nutrients.
- Add a pinch of cinnamon to porridge instead of sugar – not only is it a warm, sweet spice but it also contains traces of coumarin, a compound that stabilizes blood sugar levels.
- Learn a new way of baking, using ingredients such as sweet potatoes, beetroot and ground almonds to provide sweetness. You'll soon find that manufactured or even home-baked sugar-laden products taste far too sweet.
- Nominate one day a week as your ritual 'cheat' day (if cheating appeals to your psychology) or a 'treat' day (if treating feels better than cheating). Find a special location in which to cheat/treat – a lovely café that serves home-baked goodies in an environment that appeals to you. Perhaps take a half-hour walk first, just enough to release endorphins but not so energetic as to make you ravenous, then go and enjoy ONE special sugary treat. Afterwards, walk away and look forwards to next week!

Try baking at home with alternative healthy ingredients. Experimenting with colour can further entice your appetite for health.

Graze your way through the day

Forget about 'trying not to eat between meals'. Sensible snacking will keep your blood sugar levels stable and you will be far less likely to binge on something sweet if you eat breakfast, a mid-morning snack, lunch, a mid-afternoon snack and dinner. To maintain a stable weight, allow 500 calories for the main meals and 250 calories for each of the snacks (or increase or decrease the amount, depending on your daily calorie requirement for your gender/age/weight/activity level). Choose your snacks wisely: this is not a legitimate opportunity to eat a pastry in the morning and a chocolate bar in the afternoon! See pages 34–35 for healthy snack ideas.

Eat mindfully

This is perhaps one of the most important things you can do for your health, and certainly in terms of overcoming sugar cravings. Mindfulness is an ancient Buddhist practice that is now being applied to many aspects of life, and it is exactly what it suggests: keeping your awareness in the 'here and now' so that you are mindful of everything you do. If you usually eat on autopilot, unconscious of what's going into your mouth as you catch up on reading emails at your desk or flop in front of the TV, try instead to focus completely on what you're eating. Be mindful of every bite, and your brain will register satisfaction.

Head off stress

Sugar cravings are often triggered by stress, which causes physiological changes in the body that are exacerbated by sugar, rather than relieved by it. Arm yourself against stress by eating a diet rich in stress-busting foods, such as broccoli, fish, almonds, bananas – and chocolate. Not the cheap, mass-produced type, but a good-quality very dark chocolate rich in polyphenols, which repair damage caused by stress hormones.

5

Special health concerns

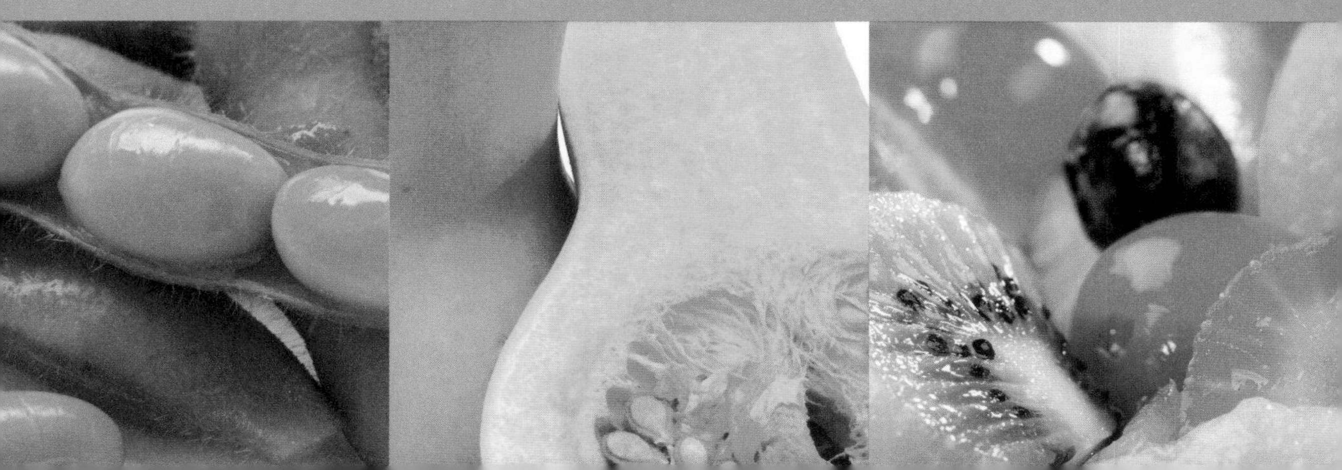

Specific dietary requirements

You can eat healthy, delicious foods even when you have special health needs. With the right knowledge, you can easily navigate your daily eating with success.

A person's diet is determined by many factors. Age, gender, health concerns and lifestyle all play a role in why you should eat a certain way. If you need a special eating plan for any reason, embrace it and know that you can enjoy a healthy and delicious diet with practice and time.

The most common reasons people need a specialized diet are:

• When the body has higher-than-usual nutrient demands, such as times of accelerated growth or related needs, as in the first year of life, during pre-teen and teen years, in pregnancy, or during sports training.

• When trying to avoid or treat a specific health condition, such as an allergy or heart disease.

• When lifestyle changes mean you require less energy, such as when you age.

Reactions to food

Food sensitivity or intolerance is another area where specialized diets are needed. Food intolerance is different from an allergy. An allergy is the result of the body's immune system reacting to a food – even a small amount has the potential to be fatal. But a food intolerance or sensitivity is usually a gastrointestinal response to a food. With a food intolerance or sensitivity, you may not require total elimination of foods that you struggle with and may be able to eat and enjoy a small amount of the food. Knowing exactly what is going on with your body will help you make the best diet decisions.

Many of today's major causes of death are lifestyle-related. If you have a risk of heart disease, diabetes, high blood pressure or kidney disease in your family history, eating in a certain way can help significantly to reduce that risk. In fact, a healthy diet has been shown to help reverse certain diseases or, even better, prevent them altogether. Even though it is difficult to make some changes, you can be certain that they will make a big difference to your long-term health.

> Look after your lifestyle – it will look after your health.
>
> Dr Joy Dauncey, Senior Scientist and Adviser in Nutritional and Biomedical Sciences, University of Cambridge

Do this...

✓ Get antioxidants from foods, such as resveratrol (which may lower risk of heart disease) from red and purple foods such as grapes or pomegranates. That way you will get many other antioxidants at the same time.

...Not this

✗ Get the same antioxidant from a pill or think that you can only get it from red wine.

163

Easy preventive measures

Evaluate why and if you really need a special diet. Often people are mostly influenced by dieting trends instead of considering what will truly benefit their health.

Add flavour to your meat, fish or poultry without calories or salt by 'reducing' flavoured vinegar and using that instead of gravy or sauce (for example, heat balsamic vinegar in a pan until some water evaporates, or produces a 'reduction').

Increase your folic acid intake by making your smoothies with orange juice instead of water.

Increase your iron intake by cooking in cast-iron pans.

Eat to prevent cancer by emphasizing cruciferous vegetables. Want an easy way to find them? Look for veggies that have leaves that 'cross or overlap' each other (members of the cabbage family, such as cabbage, cauliflower, broccoli, Brussels sprouts, pak choi, etc.).

164

Your place in the life cycle

Understanding where you or your loved ones are in your life cycle and health needs will enable you to make the best diet choices for long-term health and vitality. You should always take into account your personal needs and concerns before deciding to jump on the latest eating trend. A simple awareness of growth patterns and physiology can help you make the best choices for your optimal health. For example:

- Babies approximately triple in weight and double in height in the first year of life, and this is why they need to be fed so often during the day.
- Girls need to increase their iron intake when they begin menstruation.
- Pregnant women ideally need to consume adequate amounts of folic acid before they get pregnant.
- Men need lycopene, which is found in tomato and tomato products and may help prevent prostate cancer.
- As you age you need fewer calories but the same amount, or more, of some nutrients, which means your diet has to be more 'nutrient-dense'.
- Some athletes think they need a lot more protein and fewer carbohydrates than they actually do.

Have to resort to a frozen dinner?

Using a food journal, check for protein (10–20 g), sodium (500–700 mg) and calories (400–600) per serving.

Diabetes

Living with diabetes can be a challenge – you have to learn to balance your meals and make the healthiest food choices possible.

Living with diabetes may leave you constantly asking yourself, 'What *can* I eat?' There is not a universal nutrition approach for people with diabetes; however, it is possible to give a few basic tips to help you make positive choices.

When you find out you have diabetes, you may feel that knowing what to eat is confusing. Once you become comfortable with making appropriate choices throughout the day, you will realize that you can incorporate a variety of foods into your meal plan, manage your blood sugar and enjoy a healthy life.

A steady and correct amount of healthy carbohydrates throughout the day will help stabilize blood sugar levels.

What can you drink?

Don't forget that the calorie-containing beverages you drink also raise your blood glucose levels and may cause weight gain if they contribute to excess calories. Drink zero-calorie or very low calorie beverages such as:

- Water
- Unsweetened teas and coffee
- Diet cola
- No-calorie drink mixes

Avoid sugary drinks that raise blood glucose levels and can provide hundreds of calories in one serving. For example:

- One 350 ml (12 fl oz) can of cola: about 150 calories and 40 g of carbohydrate (or 10 teaspoons of sugar)
- One 240 ml (8 fl oz) glass of fruit punch or other sugary fruit drinks: about 100 calories (or more) and 30 g of carbohydrate (or 7–8 teaspoons of sugar).

Alcoholic drinks are generally not recommended if you have diabetes, unless approved by your doctor.

Quick guide to carbs

One serving of carbohydrate equals 15 g. Examples include:

- 1 slice white or whole-wheat bread
- 75 g (3 oz) unsweetened dry cereal
- 110 g (4 oz) cooked beans or corn
- 110 g (4 oz) cooked pasta or rice
- 1/8 of 30 cm (12 in) thin pizza (crust)

Remember that 15 g is one carbohydrate serving and about 4–5 g of sugar are one teaspoon of sugar. If the label says 15 g of carbohydrate and 10 g of sugar, two thirds of those carbohydrates per serving are sugar!

Check this out

Diabetes UK: www.diabetes.org.uk
Information on food and fitness for diabetics.

168

Eating for diabetes

1 Emphasize whole grains and avoid the processed white flour-based products, especially the ones with added sugars. Look at the Nutrition Facts label and try to select cereals and grains with at least 3 g of fibre per serving – not all whole-grain items are high in fibre.

2 It is important to choose grains that are rich in vitamins – especially B vitamins – and contain minerals, fibre and phytochemicals. Look for quantities on the Nutrition Facts label.

3 Protein foods are an important part of a balanced diabetes meal plan. Plan a meal with balance and moderation, which means about 50–150 g (2–5 oz) of meat, poultry or fish.

4 Avoid sugary drinks, saturated fats and trans fats. Steer clear of processed snack foods.

169

Fats and carbs in protein

Meat, poultry and fish do not contain carbohydrates but do contain protein and fat, which can help with satiety (the feeling of fullness) and do not raise blood glucose levels. But one area to watch for in meat and poultry is the amount of saturated and total fats. For meat substitutes, check whether the product contains carbohydrates. This will be important for you to know so you can include that amount into your carbohydrate meal plan and your total intake. This is important for managing your blood sugar levels.

170

Plating up the protein

Make one quarter of your plate high-protein foods, such as a small chicken breast or 75–110 g (3–4 oz) of lean beef or pork loin, one quarter from whole grains and the other half from vegetables and fruits. When you have a mixed dish or casserole that includes a starch and meat (such as lasagne or a shepherd's pie), that equates to about half the plate. The other half of your plate should be made up of non-starchy vegetables.

171

Remember dairy

Dairy products provide you with good-quality protein and are also an easy way to get calcium in your diet. Among the better choices in dairy products are:

- Fat-free or low-fat milk (1%)
- Plain non-fat regular/light or Greek yogurt
- Low or non-fat cheeses

Low-fat Greek yogurt

Top 5 foods in main groups

Whole grains (rich in vitamins, minerals, fibre and phytochemicals)

Brown rice

Whole oats/ oatmeal

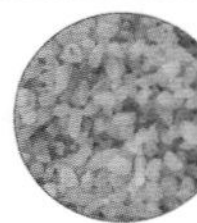
Buckwheat

Millet

Quinoa

Starchy vegetables (great sources of vitamins, minerals, and fibre)

Butternut squash

Corn

Green peas

Parsnips

Plantain

Protein foods (lowest in saturated fats)

White fish

Skinless chicken or turkey breast

Pork loin

Egg whites

Dried beans, lentils, peas, legumes

Fish (high in omega-3)

Tuna

Salmon

Herring

Mackerel

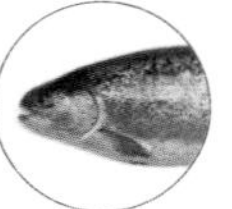
Rainbow trout

Shellfish (high in omega-3)

Clams

Crab

Lobster

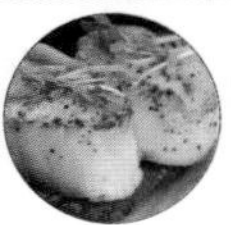
Scallops

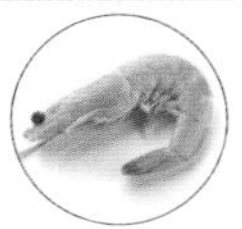
Prawns

Monounsaturated fats (can help lower cholesterol)

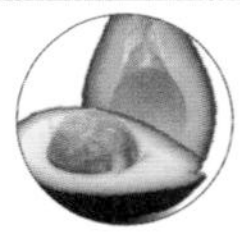
Avocados

Nuts

Olives

Peanut butter

Sesame seeds

Do this...

✓ Estimate how much of the carbohydrates in each meal are appropriate for you.

✓ Get plenty of fibre from beans, fruits, vegetables, nuts, seeds and grains, such as brown rice or whole-wheat breads.

...Not this

✗ Get most of the carbohydrates in your meal from breads, crackers or pasta made from refined white flour.

✗ Have a diet that is primarily refined carbohydrates or concentrated sweets, such as white bread or cakes.

High blood pressure

You can still eat delicious foods when you have high blood pressure – low in salt does not mean low in flavour.

Blood pressure is the force or pressure of blood against artery walls and is recorded as two numbers. The systolic pressure number is the pressure when the heart beats and the diastolic pressure is when the heart relaxes between beats. Did you automatically assume that a diagnosis of high blood pressure meant a life of bland, boring food? Well, the good news is that when you cut back on sodium or salt, you actually learn to enjoy the wide range of flavours of foods, instead of adding flavour with salt.

A low-salt diet means limiting the amount of table salt (sodium chloride) added to your food, whereas a low-sodium diet means limiting table salt and the sodium found in other forms (for example, monosodium glutamate). Remember that fresh foods will offer the least amount of salt compared to the same foods that are tinned and processed, such as high-salt tinned vegetables. Look to buy fresh produce and frozen alternatives.

Ready-made, restaurant-cooked, homemade

Food labels list foods as low-, lower-, reduced- or no-salt-added versions. At home, you have more control over the amount of salt you add to food, so salt can be reduced or not included at all in homemade dishes. Also, when eating out, ask how the meals are prepared. For example, a potato could be rolled in salt before it is cooked, so ask questions about how items are prepared and cooked, and ask for a salt-free version of your dish if necessary.

Lifestyle changes

Not only is watching your salt and sodium intake important, but there are other ways you can manage high blood pressure like losing weight, adopting the Dietary Approaches to Stop Hypertension (DASH) eating plan (see pages 104–105), regular aerobic exercise (see pages 36–41) and moderating alcohol consumption (see pages 86–87).

Food ingredient label red flags: salt, sodium chloride, sodium, monosodium glutamate (MSG), sodium nitrate, sodium alginate and sodium bicarbonate

Better to make it fresh!

> It is important to learn to read labels, taking special care to look for and read sodium levels.
>
> Corinne Labyak, Assistant Professor, University of North Florida

You can still enjoy your favourite foods with just a few slight twists. Put down the salt shaker and read the labels for sodium content. You will find your taste buds might take a few weeks to adjust but it's worth it in the end.

Effects of alcohol

Although a small amount of alcohol such as wine may help lower blood pressure, if you don't drink, don't start just with the intent of lowering blood pressure (losing weight or lowering sodium intake are better ways to do this). Alcoholic drinks in large amounts may worsen (increase) your blood pressure. This may occur with two, three or more drinks consumed at one event. Alcoholic drinks also contain calories, which may contribute to weight gain. If you are taking medications for high blood pressure, it is important to ask your doctor if alcohol interferes with your medicine's effectiveness or increases its side-effects.

173 Five ways to reduce your salt intake and lower your blood pressure

1 Avoid foods that are listed as pickled, cured, smoked or stock.

2 Check the label and select the low-, reduced-sodium or no-salt-added versions of foods.

3 Choose fresh or frozen fruits and vegetables.

4 Identify high-sodium foods within your diet and read labels to find lower-sodium replacements.

5 Have unsalted versions of your favourite nuts as a snack.

Tempt the taste buds	
Like savoury? Instead of salt:	**Like spicy or hot? Instead of salt:**
Add coriander with tomatoes	Add cayenne pepper to popcorn
Add balsamic vinegar to grilled vegetables	Add jalapeños on top of a baked potato or to your homemade chilli
Add dill weed or rosemary to rice	Add a dash of Tabasco (pepper) sauce to your soups or stews

175

Easy meal

Marinate chicken in lemon juice and dried parsley that contains no sodium. Grill it for 6–8 minutes on each side and serve with a baked potato with 1 tablespoon of unsalted butter and a side salad with your favourite oil and vinegar.

Cooking with a grill or ridged griddle pan not only creates attractive, tasty lines on meat – it also prevents the meat from sitting in grease while it cooks.

174

Four ways to manage stress

Whether stress causes long-term high blood pressure is uncertain, but there is no doubt that behaviours linked to stress (overeating, smoking, drinking, insomnia) contribute to the condition; in the short-term, stress causes your blood pressure to peak, which over time can culminate in a high blood pressure condition. Try these ways for combatting the stress in your life.

1 Avoid situations, people, topics or things that upset you. Walk away from the stressful situation.

2 Alter the way you respond. Instead of yelling, try a 10-minute 'cooling off' period before explaining what upset you.

3 Adapt to situations you cannot control. Determine how you can manage the issue and find a positive aspect to the situation.

4 Accept things that cannot be controlled or changed, forgive and let go of grudges, old anger, disappointment or hostility.

Do this...

- ✓ Make your own soups to keep sodium content to a minimum.
- ✓ Add fresh seasonings to your meals. Consider growing your own in window boxes or in your garden.
- ✓ Keep stress at bay with a soothing herbal tea such as chamomile.

...Not this

- ✗ Buy commercial soups. Read the label – most are high in salt or sodium.
- ✗ Add salt substitutes or commercial seasonings. Some contain potassium chloride and need to be avoided by people with kidney disease or certain medications for your kidneys, heart or liver.
- ✗ Reach for caffeine-fuelled tea or coffee when you are feeling under pressure.

Top salt-busters

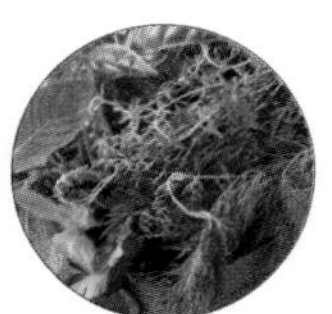

Fresh herbs

Vinegars

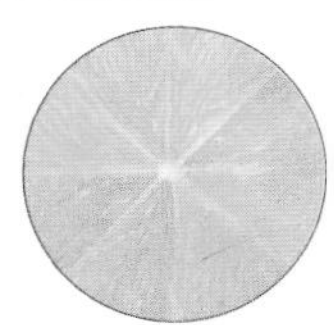

Lemon

Spices

Heart disease

Eating certain foods can reduce your risk of coronary heart disease or help you manage existing heart disease.

Heart disease is a health concern worldwide. According to the American Heart Association and the European Heart Network, the number of people dying from heart disease is decreasing, but it is still the leading cause of death. Heart disease may be a result of damage to blood vessels from a build-up of plaque (coronary heart disease), from bacteria (rheumatic heart disease) or from being born with congenital heart disease.

The good news is that you can eat in a way that keeps your heart more healthy. Nutrition also affects conditions that increase risk of heart disease (high blood pressure, high cholesterol, diabetes and overweight/obesity). Manage your total caloric intake to avoid the excessive calories that lead to overweight/obesity. Limit your intake of saturated fats which are found in meats, coconut, whole-fat milk or cheese, and cholesterol, which is found in animal sources such as meat or egg yolks.

Recovering from surgery

If you have had heart bypass surgery manage your recovery to help decrease the possibilities of complications. Make sure you take the prescribed medications, monitor symptoms and eat a heart-smart diet. This includes at least five servings of fresh fruits and vegetables, and low-salt, low-saturated-fat and low-cholesterol foods.

People recover in different ways from heart bypass surgery so don't compare your recovery to anyone else's recovery in terms of length of time or abilities.

Get jumping to get that heart pumping. Don't forget to exercise today.

176

Eat the right fats

Trans fats are in packaged foods and bakery items, and can appear in foods as 'partially hydrogenated' oils. To replace saturated fats with unsaturated fats, choose liquid over solid oils. Add foods like avocado, almonds and rapeseed oil, which are high in unsaturated fats. Include more meatless meals; many meats are high in saturated fat and cholesterol.

177

Follow these guidelines for a heart-healthy diet

1 Enjoy at least 4–5 servings of whole fruits and vegetables a day. These are full of fibre and heart-healthy vitamins and minerals such as potassium and magnesium. They are low in calories, which means they fill you up without increasing your weight.

2 Eat at least two servings of fish (75–110 g/3–4 oz) a week. Fish is heart-healthy because it includes omega-3 unsaturated fat. Choose fatty fish like salmon, mackerel or herring. If you don't eat fish, eat other sources of omega-3 fats such as walnuts, rapeseed oil or ground flaxseed. Fish is also a lower-calorie, lower-fat protein than meat.

3 Focus on fibre-rich foods. Women should eat 21–25 g and men 30–38 g of fibre a day. Choose foods that have at least 3 g (ideally over 5 g) of fibre per serving. Eat plenty of whole-grain foods and don't just limit yourself to wholewheat bread and pasta – try brown rice, popcorn, quinoa and millet.

COUNTDOWN COUNTER

GRAINS AND LEGUMES | FIBRE

Split peas | **16.3 g** per serving

Lentils | **15.6 g** per serving

Black beans | **15 g** per serving

Bulgur wheat | **8 g** per serving

Bran flakes | **7 g** per serving

Whole-wheat pasta | **6.3 g** per serving

Chia seeds | **5.5 g** per tablespoon

Almonds | **2 g** per serving

Flaxseed meal | **3.8 g** per 2 tablespoons

Brown rice | **3.5 g** per serving

Raspberries are low in fat and have high levels of polyphenols, which help reduce heart disease risk.

178

Cholesterol watch

A fatty substance produced naturally by the liver, cholesterol only becomes a problem for the body when the levels are too high. Eating the wrong types of foods can cause levels to reach potentially harmful levels, clogging arteries and putting you at risk of major heart disease. Try to minimize foods that are high in saturated fat, such as eggs, meats and dairy products with fat, butter or lard.

Food	Cholesterol
1 egg	185 mg
75 g (3 oz) minced beef, 80% lean	77 mg
1 glass whole milk	24 mg
1 tsp butter	10 mg
1 glass skimmed milk	5 mg
25 g (1 oz) grated coconut	0 mg

Top 10 foods
FOR HEART HEALTH

Dark chocolate

Ground flaxseed

Salmon and other fatty fish

Olive and rapeseed oil

Nuts

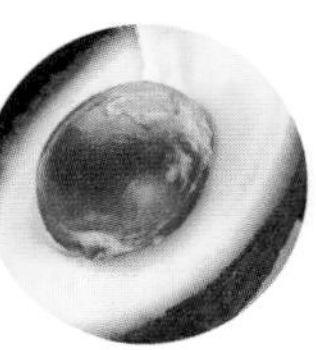

Avocado

Red grapes

Blueberries

Green tea

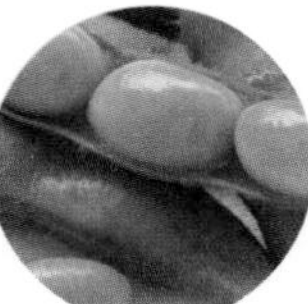

Beans

COUNTDOWN COUNTER

FRUIT AND VEGETABLES | FIBRE

Artichoke, cooked | **10.3 g**

Green peas, cooked | **8.8 g** per serving

Raspberries | **8 g** per serving

Avocado, half | **6.7 g**

Pear | **5.5 g**

Broccoli | **5.1 g** per serving

Turnip greens | **5 g** per serving

Sweet potato | **4.8 g**

Apple | **4 g**

Corn, cooked | **4 g** per serving

Raisins | **1.5 g** per serving

4 To reduce blood pressure, choose fresh foods instead of packaged or tinned foods. If you use tinned foods, rinse to reduce sodium. Season your dishes with spices, herbs or lemon juice.

5 Limit sugar-sweetened drinks to less than 500 calories a week. Added sugars are associated with increased heart disease risk, possibly because they increase weight and triglycerides. Make soft drinks, sweets, desserts and sugar-sweetened foods a treat instead of a daily part of your diet.

6 Avoid trans fats, replace saturated fats with unsaturated fats and limit dietary cholesterol to 300 mg a day.

Crisps and the alternatives

Crisps tantalize your taste buds and test your willpower. The combination of carbs, fat and salt is irresistible – let's face it, once you've started, it's virtually impossible to stop.

The percentages of the recommended daily value shown below are typical for a 25-g (1-oz) – tiny! – serving of sea-salt flavour natural potato crisps, the least processed type of crisp. Frightening, isn't it?

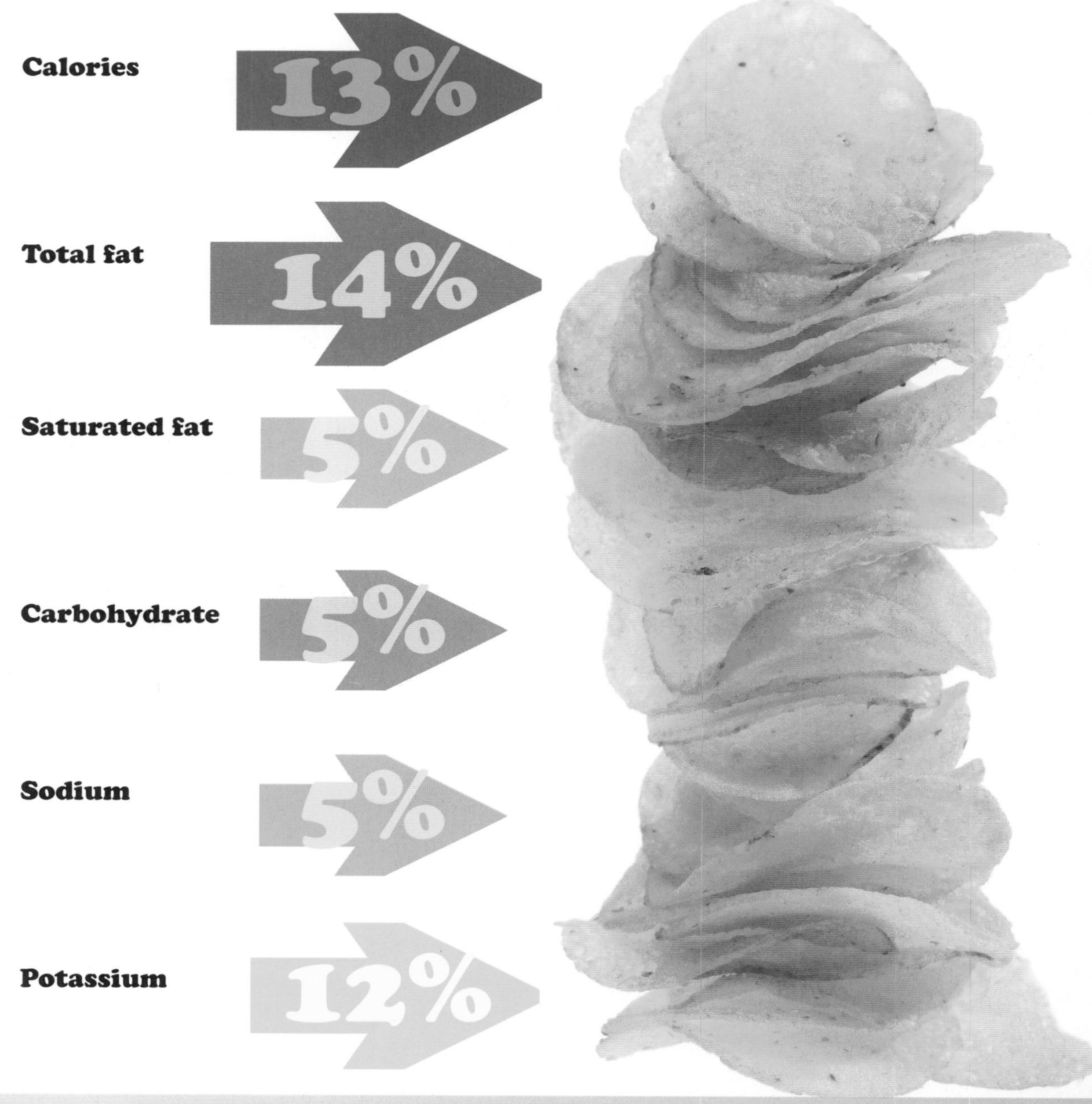

Crisp cravings tend to fall into two categories: a little something to nibble on while you relax with a glass of wine or lager, or a snack while watching a game or a movie on TV. A substitute therefore has to be satisfying as well as healthy. Any manufactured snack product is likely to be as bad as crisps, if not worse, so plan ahead and make your own.

5 Healthy alternatives

Become an olive connoisseur and enjoy the variety on offer.

1 Green olives

The ultimate 'snack in a pack', green olives have a firm, crisp texture and a delicious, slightly astringent flavour that goes really well with chilled white wine. Choose a variety preserved in olive oil rather than brine and check the Ingredients List for 'hidden' additives (see pages 64–65) such as MSG. A typical 25 g (1 oz) drained weight serving provides less than a third of the calories in crisps, less than half the total fat, and only negligible saturated fat, carbohydrates and sodium.

Nibble seeds one by one so they take longer to eat – ideal for munching through films.

2 Kale crisps

Low fat, low salt, low calorie and so easy to make! Strip kale leaves from the tough stem, rinse and dry thoroughly and rip pieces into a bowl. Spritz with olive oil and toss well, then scatter over a baking sheet. Sprinkle lightly with unrefined sea salt and freshly ground black pepper, and bake in a preheated oven (180°C/350°F) until crisp (about 12 minutes), turning carefully once.

3 Tamari roasted seeds

Tamari is a more concentrated, less salty and wheat-free version of soy sauce, with a rich, intensely savoury taste. Toss pumpkin and sunflower seeds in a little tamari and roast on a baking sheet in a preheated oven (150°C/300°F) for about 20 minutes, until crunchy. More filling than crisps, and fiddly to eat, which effectively stops you being too greedy.

4 Dips

Part of the joy of eating crisps is dunking them in a dip. Manufactured dips tend to be very salty, so whiz up your own in a blender, or even mash the ingredients together with a potato masher. Instead of crisps, cut raw celery into sticks for dunking – it has a naturally salty flavour. Try:

- Hummus
- Guacamole
- Bean – fava, black, your favourite!

5 Tapas potatoes

Tapas potatoes will satisfy your flavour cravings. The potatoes are cut into chunks rather than thin slices, so there's far less surface area to absorb oil, and they're oven-baked rather than deep-fried. Mix a little unsalted tomato paste with a sprinkling of smoked paprika, a pinch of unrefined sea salt and a splash of olive oil, and toss 2.5-cm (1-in) chunks of waxy potato in the mixture. Bake in a hot oven (200°C/400°F) until crisp and delicious. Enjoy!

Ageing well

Visit your dentist routinely. Adjust your dentures if they do not fit.

Ageing is a natural and irreversible process. However, a healthy lifestyle, including being physically active and following a healthy diet, will help you enjoy your later years to the full.

As you age, you may notice changes in your body shape, be less active or be less interested in food. As we get older, we lose muscle – also called lean body mass – and get more fat mass. As a result, we need fewer calories. This has a negative impact on heart function and increases the risk of chronic diseases including heart disease (see pages 118–119), high blood pressure (see pages 116–117) and diabetes (see pages 114–115). Fat tends to concentrate in the trunk and it may increase the risk of hyperlipidemia (high levels of fat in your blood). During the ageing process, we lose bone density for various reasons, including menopause in women. This can lead to osteoporosis or bone fractures.

Ageing may also increase your needs for some nutrients. Iron and calcium intake sometimes are low. Moreover, vitamin B12 deficiency, which can result in pernicious anaemia, is more common in the elderly. You may become more sensitive to dehydration because you may lose some of your sense of thirst and therefore not drink enough fluids.

Take heart, however, as it can be easy to adopt a few techniques and additions to your diet that will help you combat the main stresses and strains of the ageing process.

> Eat an optimal diet and keep as active as you can – it's never too late to help your physical and mental health.
>
> Dr Joy Dauncey, Senior Scientist and Adviser in Nutritional and Biomedical Sciences, University of Cambridge

Key food groups and how to attain them

	Benefits	Sources
Lutein and zinc	Can support hearing and vision during ageing.	Lutein: Kale, turnip greens and dandelion. Zinc: Sesame seeds, beans and almonds.
Vitamin E	Antioxidant that can protect against the forming of free radicals in the body, which are dangerous to health.	Corn oil, soya oil, margarine and dressings.
Magnesium	Plays a role in preventing both stroke and heart attack. Increasing intake may decrease the risk of diabetes, asthma and osteoporosis.	Spinach, fish and beans.
Vitamin B12	Very important in blood synthesis; inadequate intake may cause anaemia.	Low-fat dairy, fish and lean red meat.
Vitamin B9/ Folate	Important vitamin for making blood.	Beans, spinach, asparagus and lentils.
Calcium and Vitamin D	Support bone health and help prevent osteoporosis.	Calcium: Dairy, especially low-fat milk, and artichokes. Vitamin D: Sun exposure, fish, fortified cereals and dairy products.

Top 5 foods
HIGH IN VITAMIN B12

Seafood

Liver

Dairy

Fortified cereals

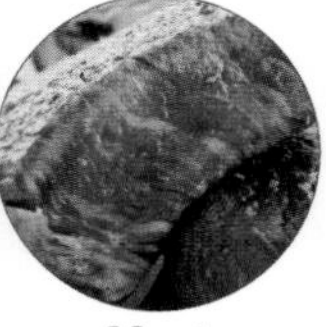
Meat

179

Seven easy ways to increase calcium intake

1 Have two to four servings of dairy products every day – skimmed milk with cereal, yogurt as a midday snack, cheese sandwich at lunchtime and chocolate milk in the evening.

2 To make sure you have some calcium at lunch, use low-fat cheese spread on your sandwich.

3 Sprinkle hard cheeses such as Parmesan on salads, meats, pasta, potatoes, cooked vegetables, eggs and toast.

4 Use undiluted low-fat evaporated milk for soups or mashed potatoes instead of cream or butter.

5 Add powdered dry skimmed milk to your liquid skimmed milk for an additional boost of calcium and protein.

6 Make your porridge or hot cereal with low-fat milk instead of water.

7 If you are lactose-intolerant, try lactose-free milk or calcium-fortified soya milk.

Do this...

✓ Eat enough calories, even when eating alone.

✓ Keep your body fuelled for the afternoon with a variety of wholemeal breads, lean protein and fibre.

✓ Chop meats or hard foods so they are easier to chew.

...Not this

✗ Have an 'easy' dinner of tea and toast that will not provide enough calories or nutrients.

✗ Skip meals: This causes your metabolism to slow down, which leads to you feeling sluggish and possibly making poorer choices later in the day.

✗ Avoid important food groups because the foods are too hard to chew.

180

Food preparation

To make your food tender and easier to chew, cut it up, or chop, grind or grate it, then steam or stew it. Unlike extensive boiling, this helps minimize loss of nutritional value. Soak dry beans before cooking, discard the soaking water and place in fresh water to cook.

181

Check these out

Age UK: www.ageuk.org.uk/health-wellbeing
Nidirect government services:
www.www.nidirect.gov.uk/healthy-eating-for-over-50s
Advice on healthy eating and general wellbeing.

182

Seven easy ways to make sure you are drinking enough fluids

1 Drink plenty of water, milk, juice and other fluids regularly to avoid dehydration, constipation and kidney dysfunction. Drink at least five to eight glasses of fluids every day.

2 Take a tea 'break' at least once per day.

3 Eat hearty vegetable soups for lunch.

4 Have cereal with low-fat milk for a snack instead of crisps or sweets.

5 Drink fluids with each meal and snack and throughout the day.

6 Put 2 L (4 pints) of water in your refrigerator every day and make it a goal to drink it. Drink more if the weather is hot.

7 Keep a bottle of water at the front of the refrigerator shelf or an empty glass by the tap. Have a glass of water every time you wash your hands.

Nutrition for women

Just as your outlook on life changes over the years, so do your nutritional needs. Each life stage of womanhood brings new health challenges and opportunities.

Check out these facts to energize your body and stay healthy throughout the life cycle.

The teenage years

With the transition through puberty comes an increased need for dietary iron. This is to offset the amount lost via monthly menstruation. In fact, the daily requirement for iron jumps from 8 to 15 milligrams (mg) at 14 years of age to meet the demand. See Top 5 sources of iron, below. Young women should build strong bones to help ward off osteoporosis later in life. Did you know that over 90% of adult bone mass has been formed by age 18? Three nutrients – calcium, phosphorus and protein – make up most of the skeleton's weight: be sure to get enough of them throughout life.

Calcium: See 10 stellar sources, opposite.
Phosphorus: Fish, milk, yogurt, meat, cereal, nuts and eggs.
Protein: Beans, meat, fish, milk, yogurt, soya milk and nuts.

Pregnancy

Pregnancy presents many nutritional challenges as your body meets the baby's growth and nutritional demands.
Energy (calories): 300 additional calories each day.
Protein: 25 grams of extra protein per day, to total 71 grams a day.
Folate: Beans, orange juice, leafy green vegetables, black beans, fortified breakfast cereal and grains.
Omega-3 fats: Salmon, tuna, mackerel, sardines, flaxseed oil, walnuts.
Choline: Eggs, milk, chicken, beef, pork, nuts.
Vitamin A: Liver, fish, milk, eggs, sweet potato, kale, broccoli, carrots.
Vitamin D: Salmon, sardines, mackerel, milk, fortified breakfast cereals.
Calcium: See 10 stellar sources, opposite.
Iron: See five top sources, below.
Fibre: 30 grams per day.

Motherhood and beyond

The years spent raising children and/or building a career are rewarding yet often stressful as well. Get in the habit of practising excellent self-care: Caring for yourself first means you can better care for others.

- Eat meals and snacks that are regularly spaced throughout the day.
- Drink adequate fluid, particularly water, about 8 cups a day.
- Get plenty of sleep, typically 7–9 hours a night.
- Exercise daily, even if it's just a few five-minute walks.
- Reach out to others for emotional support.
- Look within by meditating for 10 minutes each day.

Top 5 sources of fibre, in grams per serving	
Haricot beans, cooked	9.5 g
Ready-to-eat bran cereal	8.8 g
Kidney beans, tinned	8.2 g
Split peas, cooked	8.1 g
Lentils, cooked	7.8 g

Top 5 sources of iron	
Breakfast cereal, iron-fortified, 1 serving	8 mg
Prune juice, 110 ml (4 fl oz)	4.5 mg
Round steak, 85 g (3 oz)	3 mg
Baked beans, 110 g (4 oz)	3 mg
Spinach, cooked, 110 g (4 oz)	2.3 mg

Top 5 sources of protein	
Milk, yogurt, 150 ml (5 fl oz)	8 g
Fish, 25 g (1 oz)	7 g
Meat, 25 g (1 oz)	7 g
Egg	7 g
Beans, 90 g (3½ oz)	6.5 g

Hormonal imbalances

any of the health issues women face are tied to unbalanced hormone levels. Learn more about these common conditions and you could soon feel good again.

ondition	Symptoms	Action
erimenopause he gradual progression ›wards menopause. Many 'omen start to notice hanges in their forties, ut it could happen earlier r later.	• Mood changes • Menstrual irregularity • Hot flushes, night sweats, sleep problems • Vaginal and bladder problems • Decreased oestrogen levels – may contribute to unhealthy changes in cholesterol levels and to a loss of bone mass • Weight gain	• See your doctor if symptoms interfere with your wellbeing • Well-balanced, high-fibre diet, with emphasis on plant-based food for the natural phytoestrogens • Aerobic exercise and weight-bearing activities for strong bones • Adequate dietary calcium, vitamins D and K and magnesium to protect bone health
olycystic ovary syndrome PCOS) ffects 5–10% of women of eproductive age; tends to un in families with history f infertility, menstrual roblems, type 2 diabetes r obesity.	• Menstrual irregularities • Overweightness or obesity • Abnormal facial and body hair • Insulin resistance • High testosterone levels • Infertility	• Weight loss of 5–10% of initial body weight • Individualized eating and exercise plan: whole grains, fruits and vegetables high in antioxidants and fibre; regularly spaced meals; non-fat dairy products; marine sources of omega-3 fatty acids; carbohydrates with a low glycemic index • Medication
ashimoto's disease ommon cause of ypothyroidism, or low hyroid function; immune ystem attacks the thyroid land, resulting in nflammation.	• Weight gain and fatigue • Constipation • Dry skin and puffy face • Increased sensitivity to cold • Muscle weakness and stiffness in joints	• Work with a registered dietitian to manage calories and weight; increase fruits, vegetables and grains; limit saturated fats, if LDL levels (cholesterol) are too high • Supplemental thyroid hormone

183

Easy ways to treat your body to the nutrients it needs

By adding a little here and a little there, you can soon make sure your diet is maximizing on nutrients.

Sprinkle wheatgerm – a source of fibre and folic acid – on hot or dry cereal.

Make stews and soups in an iron pan to increase the iron content of foods.

Eat porridge for gut health and give yourself a facial with a paste of oatmeal, honey and unflavoured yogurt.

Make your own high-calcium and folic acid smoothie: Blend ice, milk and orange juice or concentrate.

Use prune purée instead of sugar when making brownies or chocolate cakes, for added iron.

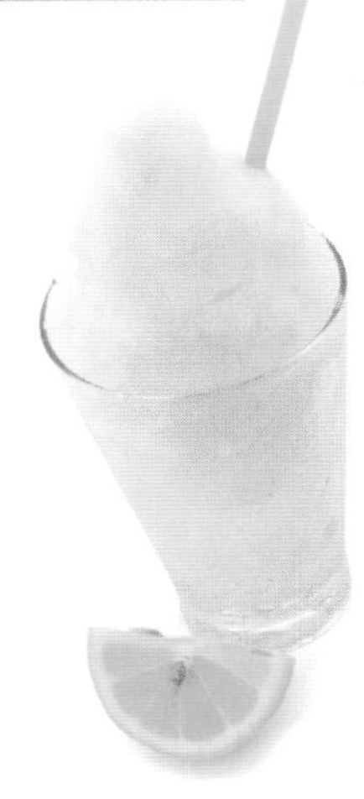

COUNTDOWN COUNTER

10 STELLAR SOURCES OF CALCIUM | MILLIGRAMS (MG) CALORIES

Beans, cooked, 90 g (3 ½ oz) | **60 mg**

Cottage cheese, low fat, 110 g (4 oz) | **69 mg**

Greens, cooked, 90 g (3 ½ oz) | **179 mg**

Pudding, milk-based, 110 g (4 oz) | **185 mg**

Tofu, processed with calcium sulfate, 110 g (4 oz) | **200–420 mg**

Cheddar cheese, 25 g (1 oz) | **204 mg**

Romano cheese, 25 g (1 oz) | **300 mg**

Skimmed milk, 240 ml (8 fl oz) | **301 mg**

Orange juice, with calcium, 240 ml (8 fl oz) | **350 mg**

Yogurt, low fat, 225 g (8 oz) | **413 mg**

Nutrition for men

To be a healthy man is to achieve balance: a diet that provides enough, not excessive, calories; a lifestyle that allows for relaxation and exercise amid the stresses and strains of family and work demands.

Generally, men need more calories than women because they are typically bigger and have more muscle. The calorie needs for a man with a moderate physical activity is between 2,000 and 2,800 calories, but this depends on weight and height. However, men should be cautious about extra calories because abdominal fat has a direct correlation with the risk of heart disease – one of the major health risks for men, along with prostate cancer.

Drinking excessively may increase the risk of certain cancers – of the mouth, throat, oesophagus, liver and colon. High alcohol consumption may also interfere with testicular function and male hormone production, causing incapability and infertility. Excessive alcohol consumption may also contribute to abdominal obesity, which is a risk factor for diabetes mellitus, hypertension and coronary heart disease.

But there is much you can do to remain in good health and shape.

Food groups for lifestyle

In men older than 30 years, being overweight, having a sedentary lifestyle and an unhealthy diet are considered major causes of disease and death.

Men are typically meat eaters. Meat contains protein, iron, magnesium, zinc, vitamin E and B vitamins, but may be high in saturated fat. Too much meat consumption may have a negative impact on heart health because of its fat content. For less fat, go with lean cuts.

Protein is necessary for exercise and building or rebuilding tissue but you can get it from many sources, not just meats. Protein foods include: lean meats, seafood, poultry, eggs, beans and peas, nuts, seeds, soya products, dairy products and grains.

Have a healthy lifestyle:

- Eat and drink healthily
- Be physically active
- Have regular checkups
- Get vaccinated
- Be smoke-free
- Prevent injuries
- Sleep well
- Manage stress

> Message for men planning to become dads: keeping fit and slim is great for you, and the physical and mental health of your future baby.

Dr Joy Dauncey, Senior Scientist and Adviser in Nutritional and Biomedical Sciences, University of Cambridge

Packing in the nutrition

1 Make vegetables your main dish by topping a salad with your choice of a protein food.

2 Roast a whole chicken. When cooled, remove the skin, bones and fat. Serve the meat as is, or use in a recipe.

3 Switch up your protein! Trade in your ham sandwich for one made with peanut butter, tuna or tinned salmon.

4 Vary your veggies munching on cucumb broccoli or red and green peppers instea of crisps when you ha a sandwich at lunch.

5 Enjoy eggs as your protein food choice – up to one a day, on average, doesn't raise blood cholesterol levels. Top your salad with a hardboiled egg to add protein and other nutrients.

6 Pack a peanut butter and banana sandwich with a bag of homemade trail mix for lunch.

185

Use whole grains instead of refined grains

Whole grains are important sources of dietary fibre, B vitamins (thiamin, riboflavin, niacin and folate), and minerals (iron, magnesium and selenium). Consuming whole grains may reduce the risk of heart diseases and also some types of cancer.

186

Fishing for protein

Fish is a good source of protein, with low saturated fatty acids, and should be eaten two to three times per week. Some types of fish like salmon and herrings are good sources of omega-3 fatty acids that reduce the triglyceride level in the blood and also have an anti-inflammatory effect.

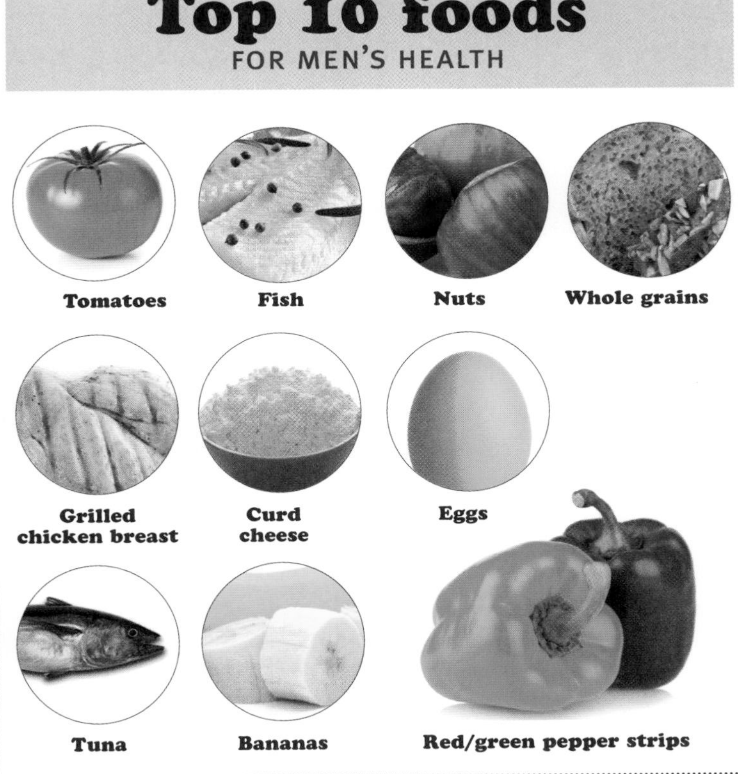

187 Apple pie protein shake

serves 1

This recipe contains a large serving of high-quality protein, important for repairing or building body tissues.

Ingredients

1 scoop vanilla whey protein

1 apple

225 g (8 oz) vanilla Greek yogurt

Cinnamon

Water/Ice

Directions

Blend all ingredients together to the desired consistency.

245 calories, 30 g protein

188 Cobb salad

serves 1

This recipe contains high-quality protein and vitamin B12 (turkey, egg) in addition to monounsaturated fats (avocado). The leafy greens provide some fibre, iron, niacin and zinc.

Ingredients

50 g (2 oz) turkey, cubed

50 g (2 oz) avocado, cubed

1 egg, hardboiled and chopped

40 g (1½ oz) fresh spinach

Directions

Toss all the ingredients together and sprinkle with lemon juice or vinegar.

245 calories, 21 g protein

Do this...

✓ Be the best grill cook! When grilling or barbecuing, choose healthy options like veggie kebabs, grilled fish steaks and low-calorie grilled chicken.

...Not this

✗ Fill your grill with hot dogs or fatty sausages and burgers.

189

Tomatoes for prostate

Eat tomatoes/tomato products at least once a week. Tomatoes are a good source of lycopene, which is an antioxidant that helps maintain a healthy prostate.

190

Stay in shape with fibre

Try to have at least 38 g of fibre every day and 30 g if you are 50 years or older. Consuming fibre may reduce the risk of heart diseases and constipation. When looking for the best sources of fibre, check the Nutrition Facts label.

Excellent = 5 g or higher of fibre per serving

Good = 3 g or higher of fibre per serving

Nutrition for children

Habits are learned at a young age, so modelling healthy behaviours for children is important from the outset. However, as your child grows, so should their ability to make their own healthy decisions.

0–18 months

Infants: Breastfeeding
A baby will triple in weight and double in size in the first year. Breast milk is filled with important carbohydrates, proteins, fats, vitamins and minerals. Certain amino acids (building blocks of proteins) and fats, like DHA, are high in breast milk and are an integral part of proper brain growth. The vitamins and minerals found in breast milk are more bioavailable (better absorbed and used by the body) than those in formulas. The first few weeks of nursing can be difficult for mum and baby, but if you are successful, it is the best nutrition you can offer your child.

18 months–4 years

Pre-schoolers: Playing and snacking
By throwing, spilling and maybe eating their food, toddlers are learning about textures, amounts, distance, depth. How can you teach social and healthy eating habits at this age? With patience, a plan and flexibility. A few of the important nutrients needed are calcium and vitamin D. After age two, offer low-fat cheeses and skimmed-to-low-fat milk as snack choices. Providing regularly timed, healthy snacks for pre-schoolers is important, enabling them to eat in short periods of time that are aligned with their appetite and attention span.

4–10 years

School age: Off to a good start
Breakfast is the most important meal of the day, especially for children. This will provide the necessary nutrients to help them power through their school day. Make a breakfast with a high-quality protein like eggs and add a piece of wholemeal bread toasted with just a dab of jam. Also, provide nutritious after-school snacks that will get them through until dinner, such as digestive biscuits with peanut butter. Help your school-age child to make healthier choices by being physically active. After all the homework is done, encourage sports with friends and active play.

11–13 years

Tweens: Convenience for on the go
Tweens are likely grabbing the most convenient choices that are high in calories. Pack a low-fat yogurt for their day. Encourage them to drink low-fat or skimmed milk or water. They are always on the go, but don't let your tween stand while eating. Encourage dinnertime to be a time when the family sits together and talks about their day.

14–18 years

Teens: Responsible power snacking
These individuals want to make their own decisions, so talk to your teen about healthy choices and physical activity. Popular sugary, caffeinated drinks are empty calories so encourage power snacks and drinks like low-fat milk and homemade fruit smoothies. Watch for disordered eating at this age. If you think your child is not eating enough, skipping meals or whole food groups, then talk with him or her and, if warranted, contact a health professional.

Five things you may be doing to sabotage your kids' eating habits

1 Making a face when you see certain foods (vegetables or fruits) put on your own plate.

2 Ordering a sweet fizzy drink instead of water in front of your kids.

3 Eating while standing up at the kitchen table.

4 Encouraging your child to finish their plate. Forcing a child to eat when not hungry or once full predisposes the child to overeating.

5 Creating a sweets-based reward system and unhealthy food chain by encouraging your child to eat a good dinner so that they can have dessert.

192 Get moving

Increasing physical activity and reducing sedentary behaviour are just as important as proper nutrition for a growing child. Get up off the couch and try out some of these ideas with your children:

- Put on some fun music and dance around the house.
- Go for a long bike ride and talk about your day and the beautiful surroundings at dinnertime.
- Go window-shopping with your teenage daughter for a good walk.

193 Picky eater strategies

Involve your child in the food prep and give them options.

Praise all attempts at trying new foods.

Let them dip fun finger foods such as carrot sticks in low-fat dressing or homemade hummus.

Add some diced or blended veggies into their favourite dish.

Never offer a sweet or unhealthy treat as a reward for good behaviour or for doing chores. Offer praise and your time and attention instead.

Do this...

- ✓ Enjoy physical activity with your kids.
- ✓ Talk about the good things your kids did that day during the family meal.
- ✓ Have a range of healthy meal enders such as fruit salad or herbal tea.
- ✓ Have a favourite healthy food day per family member, such as Dad's Friday, Mum's Monday, Toddler Tom's Tuesday, Tween Kimberly's Thursday.
- ✓ Try a different preparation method for a food if it is not liked the first time it is served.

...Not this

- ✗ Make exercise a chore or something they have to do.
- ✗ Argue with or reprimand your children at the dinner table.
- ✗ Always have a cake or sweet after a meal.
- ✗ Make all meals based on just one family member's preferences.
- ✗ Give up and never try serving the food again. Sometimes you just have to find a preparation method that is liked!

Five easy snacks

1 Fresh fruit

2 Homemade trail mix (nuts, dried fruit, whole-wheat cereal)

3 Peanut butter spread on celery

4 Leftovers

5 Whole-grain cereal with milk

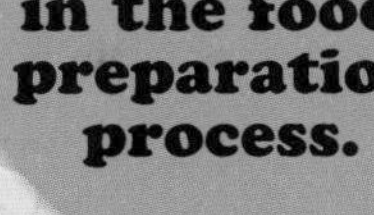

Involve your child in the food-preparation process.

194 Follow these guidelines for a heart-healthy diet

1 Have them select the dinner vegetable. Give parameters such as 'a green one', etc.

2 Have them select where the family will eat out. Give parameters such as 'price range, must include salad options', etc.

3 Make sure the television is off and the whole family is sitting down for dinner.

4 Have them take one bite of their food and tell the family what their favourite part of the food is, whether it's flavour, texture, taste, etc.

5 Make a healthy dessert together like low-fat frozen yogurt with a small dab of their favourite topping.

Fuelling the athlete

The diets of highly active people require more fluid and energy, and are a crucial component of athletic success.

For the average exerciser (someone who participates in moderate intensity fitness for 60 minutes or less, one to five days a week), specific nutrition strategies are not really necessary to ensure optimal performance. However, if you typically train for a minimum of 60 minutes, five to seven days a week, your nutrition (and rest) is just as important as your training sessions.

Before training or competition

In order to perform your best, your body needs fuel in your system. Consuming a meal or snack and adequate fluids between 60 minutes and 4 hours prior to training is ideal for providing this necessary fuel. Choose foods that are familiar to you, high in carbohydrate content, moderate in protein and low in fat. The quantity of food should decrease the closer you are eating to the start time of your training session. Experiment with different meal and snack options until you find one that digests easily and makes you feel energized.

During training or competition

Carbohydrate intake during training or competition has been shown to effectively extend athletic performance. In endurance sports (distance running, cycling, swimming or the like) as well as prolonged practices lasting at least 60 minutes, taking in at least 60–90 g of carbohydrate per hour is recommended. It is best to spread this intake out over the training period, ingesting about 30 g of carbohydrate every 15–20 minutes from the start.

After training or competition

The need for a post-training meal is dependent on the intensity and duration of the workout, as well as when the next high-intensity workout will occur. Intense workouts lasting longer than 90 minutes should be followed by a carbohydrate-rich meal containing high-glycemic-index foods to help replenish muscle glycogen stores. This is especially important if you plan to have more than one workout a day or have strenuous workouts on back-to-back days. Adding about 20–25 g of protein to your post-training meal has been found to support muscle repair and building, and is important for both strength and endurance athletes.

Hydration

Athletes require more fluid due to greater sweat loss. To prepare for training or competition, athletes should drink about 250–750 ml (9–26 fl oz), depending on body size, in the 4 hours prior to the event. During training, drink water, about 2–4 sips every 15 minutes, and use sports drinks to provide energy and replenish electrolytes if you are working for more than an hour. It is especially important if you are a heavy or salty sweater to closely monitor sweat loss and be diligent about replacing lost fluids. To do this, weigh yourself before and after training or competition. For each pound of body weight lost, drink 475–700 ml (16–24 fl oz) of fluid in the time immediately following the completion of training.

"Pay attention to combinations of power foods that work particularly well for helping you feel fuelled and energized for your workouts. These are unique to each person and may be something off the beaten path of your regular food choices."

Jenna Braddock, Consultant and Sports Dietitian, University of North Florida

- **Fuel early and often for optimal performance during endurance sports.**
- **Nutrition, hydration and rest are just as important as training.**
- **Carbs are fuel for your body. Protein is the building blocks. Both are important.**

Do this...

- ✓ To perform at your best, always have some sort of fuel in your system before working out.
- ✓ Choose moderate-protein pre-workout foods like granola bars, a lean-meat sandwich, peanut butter sandwich or low-fat yogurt.
- ✓ Practise different food options before, during and after exercise to find the combination that works for your body, and have a plan for training and competition.

...Not this

- ✗ Fast or eat a heavy-fat meal in the hours prior to an event.
- ✗ Have extremely high-protein shakes (more than 40 g protein).
- ✗ Try something new or rely on event planners for your nutrition before an event.

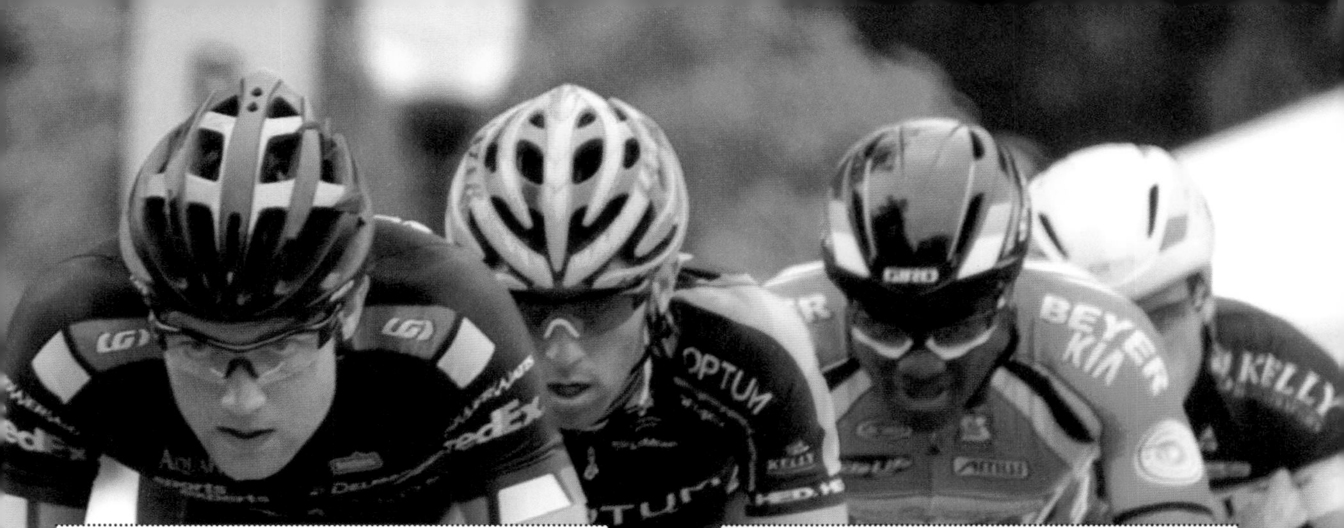

195

PRE-EVENT NUTRITION

Eat a full meal including high carbohydrate, moderate protein and low fat
Example: Sandwich on wholewheat bread with turkey, cheese and vegetables and a piece of fruit.
+ 250–750 ml (9–26 fl oz) of water, depending on body size, in the 4 hours prior to the event.

Eat a large snack consisting mostly of carbohydrate
Example: Low-fat yogurt and banana.

Eat a small snack that you are familiar with and is almost completely simple carbohydrate
Example: Energy gel or bar; piece of fruit.

196

EVENT NUTRITION

Consume foods with 15 g of carbohydrate every 15–20 minutes during exercise or competition lasting longer than 1 hour:

- 240 ml (8 fl oz) of a sports drink
- 15 jelly beans
- 1 small peppermint sweet
- About 3–4 orange slices
- One small banana
- ½ sachet of energy gel
- ¼ energy bar (varies by brand)

+ 2–4 sips of water every 15 minutes

197

POST-EVENT NUTRITION

Replenish with a carbohydrate-rich meal containing high-glycemic-index foods, such as:

- Large baked sweet potato
- Corn and black bean salad
- Large roll

Add a grilled chicken breast for protein.

+ For each pound of body weight lost, drink 475–700 ml (16–24 fl oz) of water immediately following the completion of training.

Food and mood

Do the foods you eat affect your mood and productivity? Research says they do, and you can change how you feel by following a few simple steps.

Are you alert and invigorated in the morning, grouchy before lunch or cranky mid-afternoon, or does your mood improve as the day goes on? Some of us are naturally morning people and others come to life in the afternoon or evening. If you want to change your mood, what should you change about your food?

Brain science

The neurochemicals in the brain most associated with mood are serotonin, dopamine, norepinephrine and melatonin. While certain nutrients are needed for the production of these brain chemicals, their regulation may be more a function of particular foods than individual nutrients unless you have a deficiency.

While individual nutrients do not correct mental health problems, if you are low in them, adding more can make a difference to how you feel. You want your brain to be at optimal performance for maximum cognitive ability, so eating well is important.

The bottom line is that what you eat and drink can influence your brain chemistry, which then affects your mood. Awareness of your particular patterns of intake and mood changes can be gained by keeping a food and mood record for a week or so. Writing down everything you eat and drink for that length of time will give you clues about the particular relationship between food eaten regularly or sporadically, and associated changes in mood.

Eat breakfast!

Avoid the midmorning slump.

A cup of coffee may give a morning boost, but too much will give you jitters. Check your tolerance levels.

199

Check your caffeine intake

Caffeine has been shown to increase alertness, productivity and even athletic performance – but it has also been linked to irritability, anxiety and mood swings. Different people have different tolerance levels: some cannot sleep at night if they consume caffeine in the afternoon; others enjoy an espresso before bed. Get to know your own reactions to the stimulant and assess whether your intake suits them. If you decide to reduce or eliminate caffeine consumption, do so gradually, to prevent the withdrawal symptoms of headaches and body aches. Be aware, too, that energy drinks and other soft drinks can be loaded with caffeine.

198 Mood-enhancing guidelines

1 Eat Mediterranean style. In a recent study, foods typical of the Mediterranean style of eating were associated with positive effects (good mood) while Western diet foods were associated with low positive effects and negative emotions in women. Mediterranean foods in the study were fresh vegetables, fresh fruits, milk, cheese, olive oil, nuts, fish and legumes. Western foods in the study were red meat, processed meats, fast food, sweets and desserts and soft drinks or cola.

2 Have a snack, especially if you only ate a light meal. Snacking has been associated with improved mood. See pages 34–35 for some healthy snack ideas.

3 Combine protein and a carbohydrate for increased alertness. Eating a carbohydrate alone as a snack can cause a blood sugar increase followed by a decrease that can negatively influence concentration and mood. Protein contributes to satiety, making you feel more satisfied.

For some, cookies are a snack comfort food. If you must indulge, make it a small, single cookie and favour one with oatmeal or nuts.

Do this...

✓ Use mealtimes to talk about positive events of the day or good news. This will create positive associations with food.

...Not this

✗ Quarrel, reprimand or discuss bad news. Avoid associating food with negative feelings.

200

Comfort eating

Tempted to overeat when you are angry or sad? Plan and avoid the associated weight gain by eating low-calorie foods (avoid sweets and high-salt and fat foods) and increasing physical activity to boost energy and mood. If you are feeling grouchy, reflect and determine if maybe you are just hungry. If so, pick up a yogurt, a piece of low-fat cheese and fruit, a glass of milk and a few nuts.

201

The chocolate debate

Some recent studies have pointed toward cognitive enhancement following ingestion of chocolate; other studies have not. In most cases, alterations in brain activation patterns following chocolate consumption have been determined. However, it is unclear whether the effects of chocolate on the brain are due to the sensory effects of eating chocolate or pharmacological actions of the chocolate constituents like cocoa flavanols or methylxanthines. More research is needed; in the meantime, a little of what you fancy may well do you some good.

The science of whether, physiologically, chocolate affects mood is still unclear – but enjoying a small piece of dark chocolate will surely make you smile!

Food allergies

Food allergies can be serious, even life-threatening, conditions. By learning more about the diagnosis and treatment of an allergy, you'll be on your way to vibrant health.

> Prevalence of food allergy has almost doubled during the past 20 years.
>
> Jackie Shank, Didactic Program in Dietetics Director and Nutrition Instructor, University of North Florida

Have you experienced bloating, flatulence, hives, nasal congestion, diarrhoea or an itchy dermatitis after eating a particular food? Could a food allergy be the cause of your symptoms? It's possible. If you have one, however, you don't have to face a lifetime of tummy troubles and bland eating. Armed with an accurate diagnosis and a hefty dose of nutrition education, you can learn to manage your food allergy and will soon feel good again.

Diagnosis

Over 90% of all food allergies are due to eight foods: wheat, milk, eggs, soya, peanuts, tree nuts, fish and shellfish. Whatever the offending food, it's critical that an accurate diagnosis is obtained. Technically, a food allergy – also called food hypersensitivity – occurs when the immune system reacts to a food protein that the body mistakenly identifies as harmful. The reaction can occur almost instantly or within 2 hours of ingesting, inhaling or coming into contact with the food. In contrast, intolerance is an adverse reaction to a food caused by other means. For instance, the following can cause symptoms in susceptible people:

- **Phenylethylamine** A substance in aged cheese, chocolate and red wine
- **Sulphites** In dried fruits and vegetables, wine and beer
- **Tartrazine** A yellow food dye in many orange- and yellow-coloured processed foods

An accurate clinical history will help your doctor make the correct diagnosis, so be prepared to answer a lot of questions about your symptoms and the suspected foods. Additional diagnostic tools include:

- Keeping a detailed food and symptom diary
- A physical examination to look for skin abnormalities and signs of poor nutrition
- Laboratory tests such as the skin prick test (or SPT – a common, simple, safe and fast allergy test in which a minute amount of allergen is 'pricked' into the skin to check for a small localized response such as a bump or redness) and two blood tests: the radioallergosorbent test (RAST), and the enzyme-linked immunosorbent assay (ELISA)
- An elimination diet

Easy substitutions	
Instead of...	**...Try this**
Ready-made trail mix	Homemade sulphite-free trail mix
Wheat flour	Rice, millet, quinoa, corn, lentils
Cows' milk	Rice milk
Egg (in baking)	1 tablespoon ground flaxseed mixed with 3 tablespoons lukewarm water

Do this...

✓ See a qualified medical professional for an accurate diagnosis if you suspect that you or your child may have one or more food allergies. This same professional can guide you through an elimination diet and food challenge (see below).

...Not this

✗ Try to diagnose yourself and start omitting food groups from your diet.

Elimination diet

You'll eliminate all forms of the possible offending foods (for example, wheat, eggs, milk, nuts, fish, shellfish and soya). Then you add each one back slowly, over time, while carefully noting your symptoms. You may have to repeat the test to confirm the allergy. Nutritional supplements might be needed if multiple foods are removed from the diet for longer than 14 days.

After your symptoms have completely resolved and you're feeling much better, a food challenge is conducted, during which you'll be checked for the recurrence of symptoms after consumption of the suspected food allergen. This should only be done in a medical setting to ensure your safety.

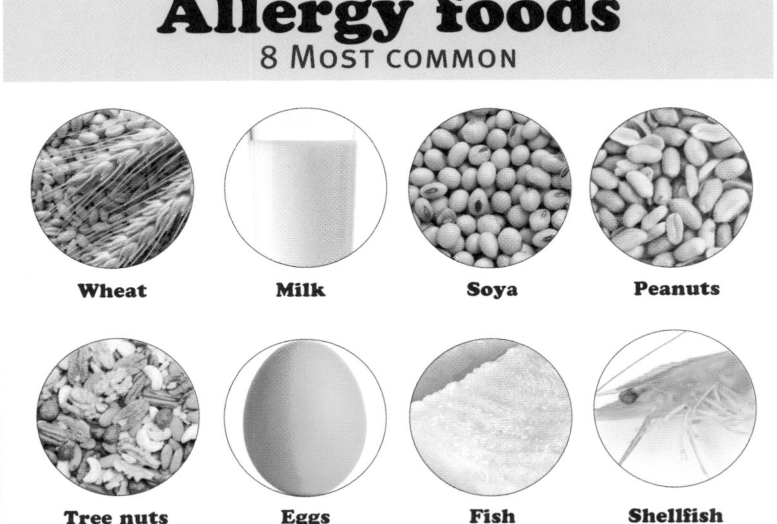

202

Eating away from home

If you're unsure about the establishment, why take a chance? Bring safe food with you. Ask detailed questions about menu items and their preparation. If you use medicine, be sure to carry it with you at all times.

203

Label reading and grocery shopping

Food manufacturers are continually updating their products so be sure to check nutrition labels often. Both the UK and the US have regulations that require the disclosure of the most common food allergens in the product's ingredient list. You can often find additional information on company websites or by emailing a customer service representative.

204

Check these out

Food Allergy Research and Education (FARE): www.foodallergy.org
Extensive information about allergies; tools and resources for managing them in all aspects of life.

Asthma UK: www.asthma.org.uk
National charity that raises awareness of asthma and provides information and resources for sufferers.

Gluten sensitivity

It is important to establish if you have coeliac disease or a sensitivity to gluten, so if you suspect one or the other, make sure you get tested by a qualified health professional so you do not subject yourself to unnecessary food restrictions.

Coeliac disease is an immune reaction to foods containing gluten that results in breakdown of the intestines. Many people who think they have coeliac disease may actually have sensitivity to gluten – a less-severe reaction to foods containing gluten that does not damage the intestines – and it may be more common than coeliac disease.

Gluten is a protein in wheat, barley and rye. People with gluten sensitivity may have the same type of reaction when they eat foods with gluten as people with coeliac disease, such as diarrhoea, abdominal pain and bloating. Symptoms of gluten sensitivity may also include headache, joint pain, and a numb feeling in the arms, legs or fingers.

There is no diagnostic test that can tell you if you have gluten sensitivity. If you have symptoms after eating foods containing gluten, see a doctor to test for coeliac disease. If negative, your physician may recommend you stop eating foods with gluten. If your symptoms go away, you may have gluten sensitivity.

Adapting to the diagnosis

If you are diagnosed with gluten sensitivity, you should be able to reduce or eliminate your symptoms with a gluten-free diet (see below).

Living gluten free takes time, as you learn how to change your diet. Once you work through the changes, it will become much easier. You will find that it is well worth the effort when you are free from the symptoms of gluten sensitivity.

Liven up your gluten-free meal by trying:

- Amaranth bread
- Buckwheat pancakes
- Polenta
- Millet muffins
- Oatmeal bread
- Potato (baked or boiled)
- Quinoa and beans
- Brown rice pilaf
- Sweet potato (baked or boiled)
- Wild rice casserole

Gluten-free and with high nutritional value, sweet potatoes are a healthy option, despite containing more sugar than white potatoes.

Gluten-free pasta substitutes include:

- Barley
- Rice (including wild rice)
- Potatoes
- Ethnic root vegetables: water chestnuts, green plantains, cassava

Gluten-free diet

1 A gluten-free diet can be high in calories and low in fibre, iron, calcium, vitamins A, D, E, K and the B vitamins.

2 Focus your meals on fruit, vegetables, protein, dairy foods and gluten-free grains. You can use flours made from beans, peas or seeds to replace wheat flour.

3 Distillation removes gluten, so choose distilled alcohol or wine instead of beer or drinks with mixers. You can also use distilled vinegars.

4 There are gluten-free products available; just be sure to choose foods that fit in with your overall diet goals and are not high in extra calories or sugar.

Foods to avoid

To eat gluten-free, avoid foods that naturally contain gluten, such as wheat, barley and rye as well as bran, bulgur, couscous, durum/semolina flour (pasta), orzo, whole-wheatberries, spelt, farina, buckwheat, beer and matzoh.

Other foods may also have gluten from processing or additives. You must read Ingredients Lists on food packets for hidden sources of gluten. These foods include oats, luncheon meats, energy bars, candy, baked beans, nuts, ice cream, soups, salad dressings, soy sauce, vinegars, marinades, flavourings, seasonings, some alcohol, vitamins and supplements.

Check these out

www.celiaccentral.org/non-celiac-gluten-sensitivity
Basic information about non-coeliac gluten sensitivity.

www.ext.colostate.edu/pubs/foodnut/09375.html
Gluten-free diet guide for people newly diagnosed with coeliac disease, including lists of foods to include/avoid and a long list of resources.

www.ext.colostate.edu/pubs/foodnut/09376.html
Gluten-free baking guide including flour substitutions for types of baked goods.

www.celiaccentral.org/gluten-free-recipes
Easy gluten-free recipes from the National Foundation for Celiac Awareness.

Raspberry ice

This gluten-free sweet dish provides antioxidants, fibre, vitamins and minerals while increasing your fruit intake.

Ingredients

225 g (8 oz) frozen raspberries

Syrup (60 ml water with 2 tbsp sugar)

Directions

Purée frozen raspberries with a small amount of syrup to the desired consistency and sweetness. Serve immediately or store in the freezer and allow to thaw slightly before serving.

162 calories

Do this...

✓ Make some healthy whole-grain side dishes that provide carbohydrates to help you with satiety and a feeling of fullness.

...Not this

✗ Make a lot of fried potatoes or other fried foods to help you feel full. They are loaded with calories and fat.

Glossary

Aerobic fitness An individual's ability to exercise for a long period of time without getting out of breath. Also referred to as *cardiovascular fitness*. Both terms refer to how efficiently an individual transports oxygen that is breathed into the body, through the cardiovascular system into the exercising muscle cells, where it can help to make energy, allowing physical movement to continue.

Alcohol (Also known as *ethanol* or *grain alcohol*) An intoxicating drink made from fermented sugars. Drinks such as wine, beer, whiskey, gin and vodka contain alcohol, which provides 7 calories per gram.

Blanch Immerse in boiling water for a very short period of time. This helps with vegetable or fruit skin removal, and to slow ripening and enzymatic action. Often done prior to other preparation or freezing.

Calorie The measure of energy a certain food provides. In scientific terms, a calorie is the amount of energy needed to raise the temperature of one gram of water by one degree Celsius. When referring to food, the measure is a *kilocalorie*, which is the energy needed to raise the temperature of one kilogram of water by one degree Celsius. This measure (*kcalories*) is used to measure the energy in foods, but in other parts of the world the measure used may be the *joule*.

Calorie-dense Foods that are high in calories and low in nutrients, commonly called *junk* or *empty-calorie foods*. (See *nutrient-dense*.)

Carbohydrate Compounds made of single (simple) sugars or multiple (complex) compounds that may be in the form of digestible starches or nondigestible fibres such as celluloses. Digestible carbohydrates such as starches and sugars provide 4 calories per gram.

Chronic disease Thought to be mostly caused by lifestyle and environmental causes, chronic diseases take time, even decades, to develop, and often do not have initial symptoms. Examples include heart disease, stroke, obesity and some types of cancers.

Electrolytes Electrically charged ions that dissolve in water and are important in the body's fluid balance both within and outside the cells.

Energy The capacity to do work. Energy from food is measured in and referred to as calories, and is absorbed during digestion.

Fats Consist of a large group of compounds, known as *lipids* that are either solid (fats) or liquid (oils) at room temperature. Fats play a role in body temperature regulation, cell function and organ insulation. Eating too many solid fats can lead to cardiovascular disease, while eating liquid oils has protective qualities. Recommended intake is approximately 30 percent of total calories, based on adequate caloric intake for healthy weight maintenance.

Fibre, dietary The non-starchy parts of plant foods that are not digested. There are two types important for colon health – soluble and non-soluble. Soluble fibre dissolves in water and is associated with lowering cholesterol; non-soluble does not dissolve and helps promote regularity of bowel movements.

Flexibility The extent to which an individual is able to move body joints through complete range of motion. Can be improved by engaging in specific forms of exercise such as stretching and yoga.

Food exchange system Diet-planning tools that group foods according to their nutrient content and/or calories. Ensures that the same calories or grams of carbohydrates are being consumed.

Glucose A carbohydrate that is a simple sugar; the body's main source of energy, used in metabolism. Glucose is essential, and the only form of energy used by the nervous system and red blood cells.

Glycemic Index (GI) Ranks foods with carbohydrates on a scale from 0 to 100 according to how much they raise blood sugar levels after eating compared to a reference amount of sugar or white bread.

Glycogen Glucose stored in the liver and muscles, used when blood glucose levels are low or during exercise.

Grazing Eating several (five or more) small meals or snacks throughout the day.

High blood pressure The force of blood pushing against the walls of the arteries as the heart pumps blood. Consistently high blood pressure may damage important organs of the body such as the heart and/or kidneys.

High-density lipoprotein (HDL) Found in blood and a component of total cholesterol. Considered the 'good cholesterol', levels of about 60 mg/dL or higher have been shown to be protective against heart disease.

Hydrogenation In relation to food, the process of adding hydrogen to a liquid fat to make it solid. The trans fats created as part of this process are associated with increased risk of heart disease.

Insulin resistance Cellular resistance to the sugar-regulating hormone insulin; results in an undesirable increase of blood glucose levels.

Lactose Naturally found sugar in milk; digested with the help of the enzyme lactase, which breaks down lactose into two simple sugars called glucose and galactose. If a person does not produce enough or any lactase, he or she may have difficulty digesting unfermented milk products. Among the symptoms are bloating and gas, and mild to severe nausea, cramps and diarrhoea.

Symptom severity depends on the amount of lactose tolerated, digestion rate, meal combination, etc. Lactose intolerance is sometimes confused with milk allergy, which is an immune-system reaction to the proteins, not the sugars, in milk.

Low-density lipoprotein (LDL) Component of total cholesterol. Considered the 'bad cholesterol', levels of above 100 mg/dL have been shown to be a major risk factor for developing heart disease.

Metabolic syndrome A combination of insulin resistance or high fasting blood sugar, abdominal obesity, high blood pressure, low HDL cholesterol and high blood triglycerides that increase a person's risk of cardiovascular disease.

Mindful eating An awareness and focused emphasis on experiencing the present moment and activity, in order to make more appropriate self-care and food choices.

Minerals Inorganic non-calorie (energy) elements found in varying amounts and forms in human bodies and in the earth. Minerals required in human nutrition have a specific role or function in the body. In nutrition, the major minerals include calcium, phosphorus, sodium, potassium, magnesium, chloride and sulphate.

Monounsaturated fats Have one unsaturated fatty acid in their chemical compound; from plant sources and are liquid at room temperature. This type of fat may help raise the 'good' HDL cholesterol and is considered an ideal source of dietary fat.

Muscular endurance The ability to do repeated muscular work or contractions against some kind of resistance over an extended time period.

Muscular strength The maximum amount of force that a muscle group can exert while working against some kind of resistance or object of some sort, such as a weight.

Nutrient-dense or nutrient-rich Food that is high in one or more nutrients in relation to the amount of calories it contains; that is, the ratio of nutrients to the total energy (calorie) content is high. Nutrient-dense foods provide a large amount of vitamins and minerals with few calories. (See *calorie-dense*.)

Nutrigenomics Integration of genetics and other sciences to human nutrition. A new discipline that is expected to affect future nutrition care because differences in genotype should impact the relationship between diet and health at individual levels.

Omega-3 and omega-6 fats Polyunsaturated fats (PUFAs) with a variety of functions in the human body. Plant sources such as soya beans and sunflower seeds are sources of vegetable oils that contain omega-6 fats. Certain nuts (almonds and walnuts) and seafood, especially fatty fish (tuna and salmon), are good sources of omega-3 fats, which are known for contributing to heart and brain health and for reducing inflammation.

Phytonutrients or phytochemicals Compounds or chemicals found in plants that are not required in a diet, but have been found to be beneficial to health.

Plant stanols or sterols Similar to cholesterol but found in plants. Help remove 'bad' cholesterol from the body.

Polyunsaturated fats Derive their name from their chemical structure, because there is more than one site of unsaturated fatty acids. These fats are liquid at room temperature and may help reduce total cholesterol.

Portion The amount of food selected to be eaten at a meal or snack by an individual. Not to be confused with a *serving size* (see below). Portions chosen by the general population have increased over time, such that 'larger' sizes have become the norm. This is known as *portion distortion*.

Protein Compounds made up of multiple arrangements of amino acids. Some amino acids are not made by the body and must be obtained through foods (essential amino acids). Proteins provide 4 calories per gram.

Safe foods Prepared hygienically and sourced responsibly; not from a food safety recall or illness outbreak. For persons who have food allergies, a safe food is free from ingredients that may provoke a reaction.

Serving size The recommended amount of food to be served. This differs from a *portion* (see above).

Sugar alcohols Types of sweetener, which do not actually contain alcohol, but do include erythritol, glycerol, isomalt, lactitol, maltitol, mannitol, sorbitol and xylitol. While considered safe, some people may experience stomach trouble as a result of consuming too much at one time.

Trans fats Mostly occur as a result of creating a solid fat from liquid oil through the process of partial or full hydrogenation of plant oils. Also occur naturally in some meat and dairy products but in small quantities. Consumption of trans fats, which are most common in foods processed with hydrogenated fats, has been associated with increased risk of heart disease.

Vitamins Non-caloric compounds of nutrients that are required in very small amounts and are essential for metabolism. Deficiency of these compounds may be harmful. Vitamins are divided into two groups: fat-soluble and water-soluble. Fat-soluble vitamins include A, D, E and K; water-soluble vitamins include B and C.

Resources

At home

- www.styleathome.com
- www.stilltasty.com
- www.thekitchn.com

Calorie information

- http://caloriecount.about.com
- www.fatsecret.com
- www.fitday.com/webfit/nutrition
- www.livestrong.com
- http://ndb.nal.usda.gov/ndb
- http://nutritiondata.self.com
- www.sparkpeople.com

Cooking

- American Association of Family and Consumer Sciences. 2001. *Food: A Handbook of Terminology, Purchasing, & Preparation.* American Association of Family and Consumer Sciences
- Bennion, M., Scheule, B. 2000. *Introductory Foods.* Prentice Hall
- Herbst ST, Herbst R. (2007) *The New Food Lover's Companion.* Barron's Educational Series
- www.bhg.com/recipes
- www.cdkitchen.com
- www.cookinglight.com
- www.ehow.com
- http://everydaylife.globalpost.com/blanch-red-potatoes-peeling-31680.html
- www.finecooking.com/recipes
- www.gardenersnet.com/recipes
- www.healwithfood.org/chart/vegetable-steaming-times.php
- www.livestrong.com
- http://recipes.howstuffworks.com
- http://thaifood.about.com
- www.vegancoach.com

Cultural foods

- Kittler, PG, Sucher, KP. (2008) *Food and Culture.* Thomson Wadsworth
- Zibat, E. (2010) *The Ethnic Food Lover's Companion: A Sourcebook for Understanding the Cuisines of the World.* Menasha Ridge Press
- www.delish.com/recipes/cooking-recipes/healthy-soul-food-opr0910
- www.eatingwell.com/recipes_menus/recipe_slideshows/soul_food_recipes
- www.foodbycountry.com/Spain-to-Zimbabwe-Cumulative-Index/Spain.html
- www.jnto.go.jp/eng/attractions/dining/food/jfood_01.html
- www.nrdc.org/health/effects/mercury/sushi.asp
- www.pbs.org/independentlens/soul-food-junkies/recipes.html
- www.rd.com/health/healthy-eating/healthy-eating-best-bets-for-chinese-takeout
- www.webmd.com/diet/features/diets-of-world-japanese-diet

Diets

- Agatston, A. (2011) *The South Beach Diet.* Rodale
- American Dietetic Association. (2009) Position of the American Dietetic Association: Vegetarian Diets. *Journal of the American Dietetic Association.* 109(107): 1266–1282
- Amsden, M. (2013) *The RAWvolution Continues: The Living Foods Movement in 150 Natural and Delicious Recipes.* Simon & Schuster, Inc., Atria Books
- Bolduan, J. (2011) *Green Smoothie Detox Diet.* WP Enterprise, Inc.
- Carmody, RN, Wrangham, RW (2009) The Energetic Significance of Cooking. *Journal of Human Evolution.* 57:379–291
- Cordain, L. (2010) *The Paleo Diet.* Houghton Mifflin Harcourt
- Craig, W.J. (2010) Nutrition Concerns and Health Effects of Vegetarian Diets. *Nutrition in Clinical Practice.* 25:613
- Cruise, J. (2006) *The 3-Hour Diet.* HarperCollins Publishers
- D'Adamo, P, Whitney, C. (1997) *Eat Right for Your Type.* Putnam
- Diamond, H., Diamond, M. (2010) *Fit for Life.* Grand Central Life & Style
- Dukan, P. (2011) *Dukan Diet.* Crown Publishing Group Random House
- Ellerbeck, Susan. (2014) *The Raw Food Diet for Beginners.* CreateSpace Independent Publishing Platform
- Guiliano, Mireille. (2013) *French Women Don't Get Fat.* William Morrow
- Link, LB, Jacobson, JS (2008) Factors Affecting Adherence to a Raw Vegan Diet. *Complementary Therapies in Clinical Practice.* 14:53-59
- Marcus, E. *The Ultimate Vegan Guide: Compassionate Living without Sacrifice.* 2011
- Mitchell, S, Christie, C. *Fat is Not Your Fate: Outsmart Your Genes and Lose the Weight Forever.* Simon & Schuster. 2005
- Mullin, GE (2010) Popular Diets Prescribed by Alternative Practitioners – Part 2. *Nutrition in Clinical Practice.* 25:308
- Niemerow, A. (2012). *Super Cleanse.* William Morrow
- Perricone, N. (2010) *Forever Young.* Simon & Schuster, Inc., Atria Books
- Harrison, K. (2013) *5-2 Diet.* Ulysses Press
- Rodriguez, JC. (Ed.). (2007) *The Diet Selector.* Running Press
- Rolls, B. (2011) *Volumetrics.* Harper Collins
- Tribole, E, Resch, E. (2012) *Intuitive Eating.* St. Martin's Griffin
- Westman, Eric C, Phinney, Stephen D. and Volek, Jeff S. (2010) *The New Atkins for a New You: The Ultimate Diet for Shedding Weight and Feeling Great.* Fireside
- www.bing.com/videos/search?q=Ted+Paleo+diet
- www.nwcr.ws/Research

- http://weirdworldofhumans.wordpress.com/2009/06
- http://ybefit.byu.edu/Portals/88/Documents/How%20Does%20The%20BOD%20POD%20Work.pdf

General health and nutrition

- Larson Duyff, R. (2012) *American Dietetic Association Complete Food and Nutrition Guide*. Houghton Mifflin Harcourt
- http://dietsindetails.com/article_fat.html
- www.bda.uk.com
- www.caloriesecrets.net
- www.dietitians.ca
- www.eatright.org
- www.freelancedietitians.org
- www.fruitsandveggiesmorematters.org
- http://healthylivingforlife.com
- www.helpguide.org
- http://m.ibosocial.com/Shipe/pressrelease.aspx?prid=250421
- www.mayoclinic.org
- www.mikesweightlossstory.com/Whole_Grain_Foods.html
- www.nutritionblognetwork.com
- http://nutritiondata.self.com
- www.safefruitsandveggies.com
- www.whfoods.com
- http://wholegrainscouncil.org

Meals and snacks

- American Dietetic Association. (2009) Position of the American Dietetic Association: Weight Management. *Journal of the American Dietetic Association*. 109(2):330–346
- Miller, R., Benelam, B. Stanner, S.A., Buttriss J.L. (2013) Is Snacking Good or Bad for Health: An Overview. *British Nutrition Foundations Bulletin*. 38, 302–322
- http://frac.org/wp-content/uploads/2009/09/breakfastforlearning.pdf
- www.cookinglight.com/food/quick-healthy
- www.eatingwell.com
- www.rd.com/health
- www.realsimple.com
- www.schoolnutritionandfitness.com
- www.southernliving.com/food/whats-for-supper
- www.webmd.com

Parties

- www.cookinglight.com/entertaining
- www.dummies.com/how-to/content/cooking-for-crowds-for-dummies-cheat-sheet.html
- www.pinterest.com/juzt4j/recipes-to-feed-a-crowd

Physical activity

- http://eatingforperformance.com
- www.fitclick.com
- www.fitwatch.com
- www.glycemicindex.com
- www.healthstatus.com
- www.hsph.harvard.edu/nutritionsource
- www.jissn.com
- www.mayoclinic.org
- www.myfitnesspal.com
- www.nutristrategy.com/activitylist.htm
- www.scandpg.org/sports-nutrition
- www.sparkpeople.com/resource/fitness.asp
- www.webmd.com

Recipes

- http://allrecipes.com
- www.bbcgoodfood.com/recipes
- www.cookinglight.com/entertaining
- www.eatingwell.com
- www.epicurious.com
- www.food.com/recipes
- www.foodnetwork.com
- www.realsimple.com/food-recipes

Shopping

- www.fda.gov/Food/IngredientsPackagingLabeling
- www.fruttarefruitbars.com
- www.healthcastle.com/healthy_kitchen_staple.shtml
- http://salestores.com/
- www.webmd.com/food-recipes/features/healthy-ingredients
- www.yasso.com/products

Special health concerns

- Brown, J. (2011) *Nutrition Through the Life Cycle*. Wadsworth, Cengage Learning
- Christie, C. (Ed.). (2013) *Manual of Medical Nutrition Therapy*. Florida Academy of Nutrition and Dietetics
- Eckel RH, et al. *AHA/ACC guideline on lifestyle management to reduce cardiovascular risk: A report of the American College of Cardiology American/Heart Association Task Force on Practice Guidelines*. Circulation. 2013
- Go AS, et al. *Heart disease and stroke statistics—2014 update: A report from the American Heart Association*. Circulation. 2014
- Lewis, A. (2013) *Celiac Disease: Basics & Beyond*. Professional Development Resources. www.pdresources.org/course/index/1/1148/Celiac-Disease-Basics-Beyond
- Lichtenberg, M. (2006) *The Open Heart Companion: Preparation and Guidance for Open-Heart Surgery Recovery*. Open Heart Publishing
- McDonald, L. (2014) *Quick Check Food Guide for Heart Health*. Barron's Educational Series
- National Heart, Lung, and Blood Institute. (2006) *Your Guide to Lowering your Blood Pressure with DASH*. U.S. Department of Health and Human Services
- www.nhlbi.nih.gov/health/public/heart/hbp/dash/new_dash.pdf

Continued on next page

Resources
(continued)

Special health concerns

- University of Chicago Celiac Disease Center. (2013) *Jump Start your Gluten-Free Diet: Living with Celiac Coeliac Disease & Gluten Intolerance.* Gluten Free Passport
- USDHHS. (2006) *Lowering your Blood Pressure with DASH.* U.S. Department of Health and Human Services
- www.aaaai.org/home.aspx
- www.camplejeuneglobe.com/sports/article_659da148-1b09-11e3-8c44-001a4bcf887a.html
- www.cancer.org/healthy/eathealthygetactive
- www.celiaccentral.org
- www.cureceliacdisease.org/living-with-celiac/resources
- www.diabetes.org/food-and-fitness
- www.eatright.org
- www.ext.colostate.edu/pubs/foodnut
- http://fnic.nal.usda.gov/lifecycle-nutrition
- www.foodallergy.org
- www.heart.org
- www.how-to-lower-cholesterol.com
- www.mayoclinic.org
- http://mylifecheck.heart.org
- www.nhlbi.nih.gov/health/public
- www.nia.nih.gov/health/publication
- www.nlm.nih.gov
- www.nutrition.gov/life-stages/seniors
- www.wpbs.org/parents/food-and-fitness/eat-smart/stay-on-track-with-healthy-snacks
- www.sharecare.com/health/diabetes/how-dairy-diabetes-meal-plan
- www.thatsfit.com/2009/12/03/healthy-kids-snacks
- www.womenshealth.gov/publications/our-publications/fact-sheet/hashimoto-disease.html

Index

Credits

Books are a labour of love – and in this case teamwork, too. Many thanks to all the contributors, as well as Katie LeGros, who helped with preliminary edits, Pam Chally, the Dean for the Department of Nutrition and Dietetics at the University of North Florida (and the department's number one fan), and my husband, George, who forwent his loved days at the beach on weekends to stay home with me while I wrote. Thank you also to Kate Kirby and Katie Crous at Quarto.

With special thanks to Jenni Davis for writing the following articles:
- Superfoods, pages 52–55
- Unmasking marketing, pages 66–67
- 5 Ways to overcome sugar cravings, pages 108–109
- Crisps and the alternatives, pages 120–121

Quarto would like to thank the following agencies and manufacturers for supplying images for inclusion in this book:

a9photo, Shutterstock.com, p.59cbl • Afanasieva, Olha, Shutterstock.com, pp.21b, 48bl • Africa Studio, Shutterstock.com, p.118b • All ingredients images on pp.31, 61, 81, 86b, 87b, 97t, 101t, 105t, 107, 115, 117bl, 119, 123, 127, 133b, 134b, 137t Shutterstock.com • amenic181, Shutterstock.com, p.132t • AN NGUYEN, Shutterstock.com, p.47br • Andrey_Kuzmin, Shutterstock.com, p.123br • antpkr, Shutterstock.com, p.114t • Ariwasabi, Shutterstock.com, p.37 • B. and E. Dudzinscy, Shutterstock.com, p.15 • Baibaz, Shutterstock.com, p.55b • Bain, Kitch, Shutterstock.com, p.59t • Banner, Shutterstock.com, p.54tl • Barbone, Marilyn, Shutterstock.com, p.84t • Bergfeldt, Barbro, Shutterstock.com, p.137b • Beth Galton, Inc., StockFood, p.28t • Bozhikov, Aleksandar, Shutterstock.com, p.5tl • brulove, Shutterstock.com, p.117t • Cobraphotography, Shutterstock.com, p.77 • Cooke, Colin, StockFood, p.75b • dannylim, Shutterstock.com, p.126br • Drfelice, Shutterstock.com, p.59ctl • Duncan, James, StockFood, p.73bl • Eising Studio—Food Photo &Video, StockFood, pp.2bc, 34, 121b • Elisseeva, Elena, Shutterstock.com, p.28bl • Elovich, Shutterstock.com, p.2tr • EM Arts, Shutterstock.com, p.108 • Foodfolio, StockFood, p.59b • FoodPhotogr. Eising, StockFood UK, p.85b • friis-larsen, Liv, Shutterstock.com, p.83c • Gayvoronskaya_Yana, Shutterstock.com, p.99t • Gerber, Gregory, Shutterstock.com, p.4tc • Getty Images, pp.18, 24, 45, 71, 81, 91 • goldnetz, Shutterstock.com, p.115bl • Gray, Michael C., Shutterstock.com, p.73t • Guyler, David, Shutterstock.com, p.133t • Hera, Jiri, Shutterstock.com, p.56b • Hong Vo, Shutterstock.com, p.136b • HONGYAN, JIANG, Shutterstock.com, p.17cl • Image courtesy of www.cosmed.com, p.95t • In Green, Shutterstock.com, p.129 • ISTL, StockFood, p.20 • Istochnik, Shutterstock.com, pp.134–135t • iStockphoto.com, pp.2tl, 14, 52tc, 66c • Jackiso, Shutterstock.com, p.2c • Jasmine_K, Shutterstock.com, p.32c • JOAT, Shutterstock.com, p.49bl • Karandaev, Evgeny, p.27br • Karandaev, Evgeny, Shutterstock.com, p.13 • Kentoh, Shutterstock.com, pp.72b, 75tr • Kesu, Shutterstock.com, p.73br • Kovac, Juraj, Shutterstock.com, p.76 • Kristensen, Lasse, Shutterstock.com, p.2cbl • Kucherova, Anna, Shutterstock.com, p.50c • Leonori, Shutterstock.com, p.2tc • M. Unal Ozmen, Shutterstock.com, p.17br • Mackenzie, Robyn, Shutterstock.com, p.84b • Maria, Lapina, Shutterstock.com, p.32bl • Melica, Shutterstock.com, p.120 • MJ Prototype, Shutterstock.com, p.125b • Molin, Kati, Shutterstock.com, p.26bl • Mycteria, Shutterstock.com, p.2br • Narodenko, Maks, Shutterstock.com, pp.52tl/tr, 126br • Nattika, Shutterstock.com, p.126bl • Olson, Tyler, Shutterstock.com, p.65 • Omelchenko, Anna, Shutterstock.com, p.2bl • OPOLJA, Shutterstock.com, p.99b • Papp, Ildi, Shutterstock.com, p.5tr • Photo Cuisine, pp.2ctl, 3tl/bl, 5tc, 46t, 49, 51, 53, 60bl, 78, 82bl/tr, 85t, 87, 121t • Pierre Javelle, StockFood, p.54 • Piyato, Shutterstock.com, p.79b • Popova, Olga, Shutterstock.com, p.47c • pr2is, Shutterstock.com, p.97b • Razumova, Valentina, Shutterstock.com, p.3bc • Resnick, Joshua, Shutterstock.com, p.92 • Restyler, Shutterstock.com, p.23br • Sarsmis, Shutterstock.com, pp.3tc, 105b, 113 • Schild, Rena, Shutterstock.com, p.131 • Shaiith, Shutterstock.com, p.3br • Sheridan Stancliff, StockFood, p.74b • SOMMAI, Shutterstock.com, p.103br • Spaxiax, Shutterstock.com, 19br • Staroseltsev, Alex, p.3tr • stockcreations, Shutterstock.com, p.117b • tarog, Shutterstock.com, p.119t • Tepsuttinun, Winai, Shutterstock.com, p.28br • Tkacenko, Andris, Shutterstock.com, p.133cr • Topseller, Shutterstock.com, p.4tr • Viktor1, Shutterstock.com, p.17t • Vincek, Dani, Shutterstock.com, p.16b • Volkov, Valentyn, Shutterstock.com, p.59b • Volosina, Shutterstock.com, p.46b • Vostok, Dan, Shutterstock.com, p.67 • wheatley, Shutterstock.com, p.124t • Wierink, Ivonne, Shutterstock.com, p.109b • Wiktory, Shutterstock.com, p.57